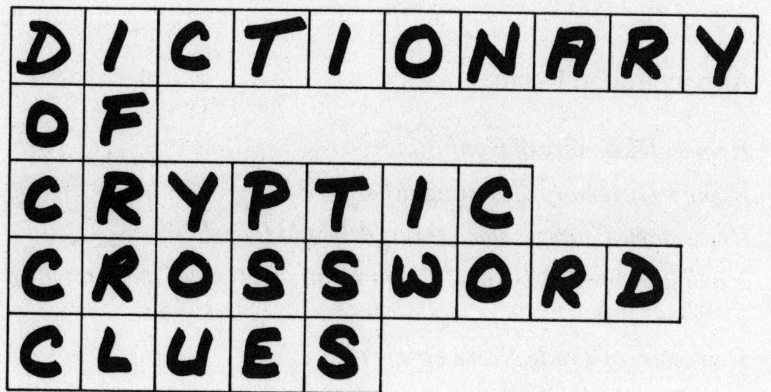
DICTIONARY
OF
CRYPTIC
CROSSWORD
CLUES

Also by Adrian Room

Room's Dictionary of Confusibles

Room's Dictionary of Distinguishables

Place-name Changes since 1900: A World Gazetteer

Naming Names: A Book of Pseudonyms and Name Changes with a 'Who's Who'

Dictionary of Trade Name Origins

Room's Classical Dictionary: the Origins of the Names of Characters in Classical Mythology

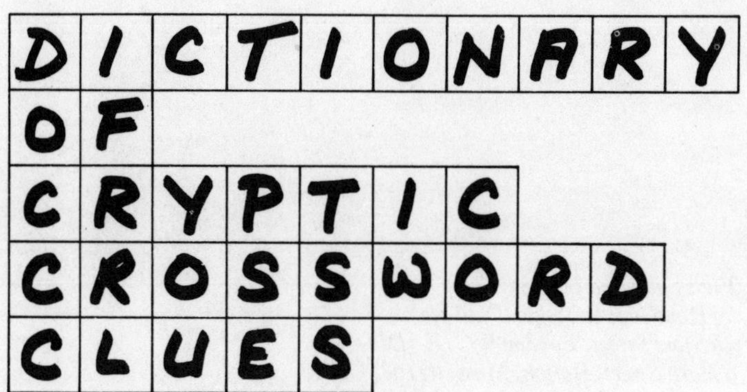

Routledge & Kegan Paul
London, Boston, Melbourne and Henley

First published in 1983
by Routledge & Kegan Paul plc
39 Store Street, London WC1E 7DD,
9 Park Street, Boston, Mass. 02108, USA,
296 Beaconsfield Parade, Middle Park,
Melbourne, 3206, Australia, and
Broadway House, Newtown Road,
Henley-on-Thames, Oxon RG9 1EN
Set in Plantin by
Rowland Phototypesetting Ltd, Bury St Edmunds, Suffolk
and printed in Great Britain by
St Edmundsbury Press, Bury St Edmunds, Suffolk

Library of Congress Cataloging in Publication Data

Room, Adrian.

Dictionary of cryptic crossword clues.
Bibliography: p.
1. Cryptograms – Glossaries, vocabularies, etc.
I. Title.
GV1507.C8R66 1982 793.73 82-18057

ISBN 0-7100-9415-9

Contents

Acknowledgments

The majority of the cryptic clues in this Dictionary were devised by myself, but some came from 'professional' crosswords, as published in newspapers, magazines and books, and I should like to thank the following for permission to reproduce such clues: Cavenham Communications Ltd, for clues from issues of *Now!* Magazine; Fontana Paperbacks, for clues from the *Fourteenth Fontana Book of Crosswords*; the *Guardian*, for clues from *The Penguin Book of Guardian Crosswords*; The Observer Ltd for clues from the 'Everyman' crosswords in the *Observer*; Times Newspapers Ltd for clues from both *The Times* and the *Sunday Times*, and Colin Parsons for clues from his crosswords in the *Sunday Telegraph*.

As mentioned in the Introduction, I am very grateful to Colin Parsons for reading the Dictionary at proof stage and giving his professional verdict on my own clues. In the light of his comments I altered some clues, simplified others and withdrew one altogether. Where I did not follow his recommendations, however, I alone must bear the responsibility and take the consequences, and if crossword solvers reading the Dictionary feel that a few infelicities or ambiguities still remain, I should be glad to hear from them. They have merely to contact me c/o the publisher, whose address will be found on the reverse of the title page. I know that professional crossword compilers receive their fair share of comments regarding the wording of their clues, and I do not wish to dodge my own obligations, even though this is not a conventional crossword book.

Finally, I should like to express my sincere thanks to Jackie Holford, who typed a lengthy and 'fiddly' manuscript, full of capital and small letters, signs and symbols, with great care and patience.

'I need not mean what I say, but I must say what I mean'

(summary of a clue-writer's duty as expressed by the veteran crossword compiler Afrit, otherwise Alistair Ferguson Ritchie, who died in 1954)

Introduction

Achieving the correct complete solution of a crossword is one of the most curiously rewarding mental activities undertaken by man, and most crossword devotees, in their thousands, tend to remain loyal to one of two distinct types of puzzle.

First, there is the 'definition' type crossword, whose more or less straightforward clues lead to a fairly predictable answer. An example might be 'Eminent musical composer' (7). Depending on any letters already available in the answer, this can lead to BRITTEN, PURCELL or VIVALDI, say, or perhaps to MAESTRO. Such clues are a good test of a solver's general knowledge and cultural awareness, and the crosswords themselves are eminently suitable for a train journey, coffee or lunch break, or the odd half hour in the evening between TV programmes. They also serve as an acceptable nightcap to some solvers, who may even, alas, drop off some considerable time before 24 down ('Undirected train of thoughts in meditation' (7), R–V–R–E) has been reached.

But then there is another kind of crossword. This is the one with so called 'cryptic' clues, where a definition of the answer may well be given, but where also an allusive, punning or downright disconcerting collection of words appears, words that on the face of it mean one thing, but – with the solver specifically in mind – actually mean another. Such a cryptic clue might be 'Belly-ache after half the buns in the country' (7). What is one to make of this apparently gargantuan feat and its hardly surprising consequence? What is 'real' here, and what is false? What does it *mean*?

The aim of this Dictionary is to help solvers of such clues 'crack the cryptic code' and assist them to interpret crosswordese. Over 1800 cryptic terms are thus listed in this book, in alphabetical order, and one or more interpretations are given for each.

Broadly speaking, cryptic terms can be divided into two categories. First, there are those words and phrases that have traditionally come to acquire a standard 'translation' familiar to experienced solvers. This 'translation' is usually simply a small group of letters, even a single letter, rather than a whole word, so that 'bachelor' for example, translates as the letters BA, and 'highway' oftens turns out to be ST. Both these letter groups, and many more, are in fact perfectly regular abbreviations (in this case, of 'Bachelor of Arts' and 'Street'), and the important role played by abbreviations in cryptic crosswords is a subject we shall be resuming a little later.

The other type of cryptic term is what might be called the 'indicator'. This is virtually a direct instruction to the solver to manipulate a word or letter group in some way, and treat it as an anagram, for example, or a 'burial'. (We shall be examining such manipulations shortly.) In the clue about the belly-ache quoted above, for instance, the word 'half' is an indicator that a word in the clue needs to be cut in half, and thus have half its letters used in the answer to the clue.

Once the solver can 'read' such cryptic terms confidently, the deduction of the required answer to the clue becomes a much more manageable operation, and a much speedier one, and what at first seemed an irrelevant and even surrealist sentence takes on a much more significant and obvious sense.

In this present Dictionary, both types of cryptic term, the 'translation' and the 'indicator', are intermingled, the idea being that the solver can look up actual words in the clue and find, in their respective entries, the required interpretation or explanation. He can thus look up 'bachelor' and find BA, and 'half' and be told to 'halve' a word. In the case of 'indicators', he will almost always be given an actual example of the indicator at work, together with a brief analysis of the word once it has been duly manipulated.

Definition of terms

But before proceeding any further, we should perhaps define our terms more precisely. The solving of cryptic crosswords is something of a linguistic science – or at least an art – and as such demands its own technical jargon. I have endeavoured to keep such jargon to a minimum in the book, but certain terms are unavoidable, and their meaning and usage must be explained here.

All crosswords, both cryptic and non-cryptic, involve a duel of minds, with the person who devises the puzzle matched against the person who attempts to solve it. What are we to call these antagonists? The deviser of a crossword is usually called a compiler, composer or setter. I have chosen the first of those words since it is generally the most popular and the most readily understood. Although 'compiling' sounds rather a mechanical process, the term is nevertheless a valid one for the activity undertaken by the person who arranges the pattern of the crossword (its words 'across' and 'down' and all the blocks or bars at the end of them), selects the words for the puzzle, and finally devises the clues for them. This is a cumulative process, which 'compiling' seems to signify more accurately than simply 'composing'.

For our purposes, however, it is not the compiler who will need this book – he will presumably be already versed in his art and experienced in it – but the layman who tackles the cryptic crossword. What are we to call him? (Or her, of course, since although there appear to be few lady compilers, the number of feminine crossword 'doers' is by no means small, and may even be greater than the number of men.) I have already used the word 'solver', and this, it seems to me, is the best word to use, since after all the aim of a crossword 'doer' is to solve it, that is, to complete it correctly. So let us have a solver rather than a dilettante-sounding 'puzzler' or a snobbish-sounding 'cruciverbalist'. (The term 'crossworder' or even 'crosswordist' is too imprecise, since this could mean either a compiler or a solver.)

We have already said something about 'clues' and 'solutions'. Here I must make my own usage clear, which may deviate a little from that of the experts. By a 'clue' I mean either the whole written part of the text that gives the information needed for the answer (for example, 'Belly-ache after half the buns in the country' is a complete 'clue'), or else the cryptic section of a complete 'clue' that needs to be treated as an individual unit, apart from the definition. In the complete 'clue' just quoted, thus, the cryptic 'clue' is actually 'Belly-ache after half the buns' (and 'in the country' is the definition). There are thus 'clues' within 'clues'. Then, when you have solved a complete clue, you fill in the answer to it in your crossword. So, having worked out that 'belly-ache' is COLIC, and that 'half the buns' means 'half the word BUNS', you put COLIC 'after' BU, getting BUCOLIC (defined as 'in the country'), and write this word in the seven squares. Such an individual result to a clue I call the 'answer' to it, keeping the word 'solution' for the total 'answers' to a crossword that mean you have successfully completed it.

So much for clues, answers and solutions.

Analysing a clue

When it comes to analysing the answer to a clue, we can talk in terms of 'letters', 'elements' and 'words'. The complete answer (as BUCOLIC here) will almost always be a word, so there is little problem here. However, a single word, especially a longish one, can be cryptically clued in terms of shorter words which happen to comprise it. PORTABLE, for example, can be broken down into the two words PORT and ABLE, and LOGISTICS can be displayed as the three little words LOG, IS and TICS. We thus have words as a complete answer to a clue, and 'words within words' on occasions when we dissect it. Indeed, in BUCOLIC we have the smaller word COLIC (clued as 'belly-ache'). But the initial BU is not a word, however, it is what I shall be calling in this book an 'element', that is, an individually cluable part of a word. To give another example, an answer BASIN can be analysed as the element BA and the word SIN, with BA clued by a 'bachelor' (probably) and SIN clued in terms of a synonym, perhaps, such as 'evil'. Any other, smaller part of a word will usually be just a 'letter' or possibly group of 'letters'. An example might be GENERAL, where we have a word (GEN) plus another word (ERA) plus a letter (L), or PITTANCE, where we have a word (PIT), another word (TAN) and the letters CE to clue somehow, either together or separately.

There is in fact no great complexity here, since everyone knows what a letter and a word is! All we need to define specially is the 'element', which as mentioned is a group of letters that can be clued as an individual unit.

Cryptic devices

At this point we must take a closer look at the various cryptic treatments of words that the solver will encounter. These are the 'manipulations' referred to earlier that each have their individual indicators.

Without any doubt, the most common cryptic treatment of a word is the *anagram*, where the letters of a word or words are rearranged to make another word (or words). Anagrams have become a particularly popular form of word play over the years, so much so that they are by no means confined to crosswords. Some have become classics of their kind, such as the name of FLORENCE NIGHTINGALE which has been anagrammatised to FLIT ON, CHEERING ANGEL, and HENRY WADSWORTH LONGFELLOW, who WON HALF THE NEW WORLD'S GLORY. Such delicate aptness, and indeed such lengthiness, is not likely to be encountered in crossword anagrams. Even so, the solver may well be advised by his 'indicator' to turn a SHE-GOAT into a HOSTAGE, to transform a LEMON into a MELON, to convert NICE LOVE into VIOLENCE (or the other way round), or to recognise that FOUR VOICES can become VOCIFEROUS.

Anagram indicators are so many and varied that it would be impossible to include anything like a comprehensive coverage of them in the Dictionary. Instead, a sizeable selection of them – over 500 – is given separately as Appendix I, page 264. It will be seen that almost any word can serve as an anagram indicator, so long as it denotes an alteration or adjustment of some kind, ranging from the apparently innocuous 'with' to the more obvious 'haphazard'.

A special sort of anagram is a *reversal*, where a word is read from back to front, so that LIVE becomes EVIL, STAR turns into RATS, and LAGER may well be REGAL. Indicators for reversals often talk in terms of 'returning' or of going 'east to west' (in an across clue) or 'south to north' (in a down one).

In its turn, a special sort of reversal is a *palindrome*, which is a word that reads exactly the same both forwards and backwards, such as TOT, NOON, KAYAK or REVIVER. (Some of these have become classics in their own right as well, like the celebrated A MAN, A PLAN, A CANAL – PANAMA!) Palindrome indicators are usually on the lines of 'backwards and forwards' or 'whichever way you look at it', and are usually more readily recognisable than the hundreds of anagram indicators.

A more contrived device is what I have called the '*burial*', also known as the hidden word. This is when a word lies concealed – either inside a longer word or running from one word to one or more others. For example, the word 'lengthiness' has 'thin' concealed inside it, and in the phrase 'minor matters' the word 'norm' lies hidden. In a sense, of course, such a cryptic expedient is very much to the solver's advantage, since his desired answer is already there, spelled out in front of him, and he only has to spot it and transcribe it.

The virtual opposite to the 'burial' is what I am calling the '*straddle*'. This is found when a word or group of letters surrounds or 'straddles' another, thus making a different word. For example, if TIME is split round EAT, thus 'straddling' it, the result is TEA-TIME and if SING surrounds TALL the outcome is STALLING. In fact the 'burial' and the 'straddle' are closely inter-related, since although SING 'straddles' TALL, at the same time TALL can be said to be a 'burial' in SING. The respective indicators for these two devices will therefore be either active, to denote a 'straddle', or passive, to denote a 'burial'. To take a particular example: suppose we wish to produce the answer WHEELING. We can either talk of a HEEL being 'held' by a WING in some way, or of a WING 'holding' a HEEL. The first of these involves a 'burial' (HEEL in WING), the second involves a 'straddle' (WING round HEEL). The same indicator (the verb 'to hold') is used for both, except that for the 'burial' it is passive ('held') and for the 'straddle' it is active ('holding'). The verb 'to hold' is of course only one of a number of possible verbs that can be used for the 'burial' or 'straddle', and it should be borne in mind that for any verb listed in the Dictionary as indicating a 'burial', a 'straddle' will also be possible, and that a verb said to indicate a 'straddle' can also be used to denote a 'burial'.

To these five devices – anagram, reversal, palindrome, 'burial' and 'straddle' – can be added a sixth. This I am calling the *homophone*, choosing this term (as distinct from the more popular 'homonym') for a word that has the exact sound of another, such as 'board' and 'bored' or 'Rome' and 'roam'. Clearly, these offer good scope for puns, and are usually indicated by a reference to 'sound' or to 'hearing', or of course to their actual pronunciation. ('I hear' or 'we hear' are popular homophone indicators.)

All six such treatments will be found fairly fully represented in their different guises as indicators, and wherever one appears in an entry in the Dictionary, it will always be accompanied by an example of its use (except, as mentioned, when it is an anagram, since these are too numerous – and too familiar anyway – to be illustrated).

What must specifically be borne in mind in the case of all six is that the appropriate indicator may apply not only to the answer but to the clue itself, that is, the 'burial' may already exist in the clue, and not need to be arranged by the solver, and the homophone (say) may need to be provided by the solver and not be already present in the clue. In fact, 'burials' are usually more common in clues, and most of the other five devices more common in the answers. But this is only a general guide, and the precise wording of the indicator will show which is meant.

In case all this technical talk sounds more than daunting to a would-be solver of cryptic crosswords, let it be said here and now that almost every clue that contains a cryptic element will also contain a relatively 'straight' definition to boost one's confidence and see that one is on the right path after all. For example, in the clue 'Priestly race – sad lot somehow' (10), the 'somehow' is clearly an anagram indicator (for the ten letters of RACE SAD LOT), but the 'priestly' is a straightforward definition of the answer required. This turns out to be SACERDOTAL, so that the anagram is thus nicely supported by the definition, since 'sacerdotal' means 'priestly', as any dictionary will attest. Similarly, 'Repetition in the choir' (4) has the definition 'repetition' to back up the 'burial' (indicated simply by 'in') that lies in 'th*e cho*ir'. The solver can thus quickly and confidently enter ECHO in his four blank squares.

Abbreviations

When mentioning earlier the standard cryptic definitions found in cryptic crosswords (so that 'sailor' almost always means TAR or AB, and 'enclosure' usually works out as PEN), we said that abbreviations have an important part to play. This is perhaps something of an under-statement, since for short elements or letter-groups, and certainly for single letters, abbreviations are the crossword compiler's prime resource. If he needs to clue MO, for example, he will very likely turn first to some standard abbreviation represented by these letters rather than, say, devising an 'endless mob' or a 'half-moon' (although these possibilities must not be ruled out!). So he will offer the solver a 'medical officer' or a 'doctor' or a 'physician' or even a 'short month' or 'Missouri'. The solver must thus be very abbreviation-conscious, especially when building up a word by means of cryptic elements. The high frequency of abbreviations as cryptic clues can be seen by glancing through Appendix II, page 270 ('Clues for single letters') and, perhaps even more, in Appendix III, page 272 ('Cryptic clues for two-letter groups'). Indeed, almost every vowel-plus-consonant group in the English language has its abbreviation (AB as 'sailor', AC as 'account', AD as 'advertisement', AF as 'Admiral of the Fleet', AG as 'silver', and so on), and these soon become firmly established in the solver's crosswordese vocabulary. Where a less well known abbreviation is used as a cryptic clue it may well have some kind of indicator, such as the accompanying word 'little' or 'short' (as in the 'short month' above). Another sign of an abbreviation is a phrase whose words begin with capital letters, such as 'Public

Address' (to produce PA) or 'Transport Officer' (to lead to TO). Abbreviations also, of course, include shortenings of words, as well as initial letters. Common examples are ED for 'editor', REP for 'representative', BRO for 'brother' and GEN for 'general information'.

Arrangement of the dictionary

The Dictionary is arranged in two parts.

The first part (pages 23 to 118) contains the 1800-plus cryptic clues in alphabetical order, each clue having its own entry. The entries deal, as appropriate, with the 'translation' of the clues and with clues that are 'indicators'. The translations are always given first, and are listed in alphabetical order. The indicator clues follow any translations, and one or more examples of their use will be given and explained. The examples of translations given for any one clue cannot, of course, be fully comprehensive. For instance, there are likely to be many more translations of 'churchman' than the three given (DEAN, FR and REV). Yet if none of these is the actual translation needed by a solver for a particular clue, then at least he will have been pointed in the right direction, and can extend the chain of thought or interpretation as necessary. Here, for example, he can also consider RR ('Right Reverend') and VEN ('Venerable').

Following the clue information in each entry, a 'trial' clue will be given for the solver to attempt. This will be given in standard crossword form, complete with the number of letters in the answer. Where there are more than one interpretation (as for the 'churchman' just mentioned), then the clue will be based on one of these translations, without any actual specification being given as to which. Of course, unlike a real crossword, there can never be any crossing letters already present in the answer to help, and the solver will thus have to deal with each clue 'from scratch'. At the same time, however, he will have a very good idea regarding one part of the answer, since this will have been told him in the entry. Thus the solver attempting the clue that accompanies the 'churchman' entry will know that somewhere in his answer one of the three elements DEAN, FR or REV will feature. And in those entries where just one single interpretation is given (for example 'expert', which is translated as ACE), his clue answer is off to a very good start, since it must contain these three letters!

The second half of the book (pages 119 to 263) is a kind of mirror image of the first. Here the same 1800-plus cryptic clues will be found in the same alphabetical order, together with a repeat of the clue that was given in the first half. But here in the second half the *answer* is given to the clue, together with an explanation of how it was arrived at. This explanation is in effect a mini-commentary on the clue and an analysis of the answer, together with any additional relevant information and often with a cross-reference to another clue or to an identical answer that had been clued differently.

These two halves of the Dictionary – the 'clue' half and the 'answer' half – are thus complementary to each other but are not necessarily dependent on each other. Thus the first half will, it is hoped, be of practical help to the solver when he is working on his favourite cryptic crossword, whether in a book of crosswords or in a daily or weekly newspaper or magazine. The second half can be read or browsed through by the solver who is interested in the anatomy of cryptic clues – and the devious workings of a compiler's mind! He can see what a typical cryptic clue looks like, what its answer is, and learn *why* this is its answer. (Some answers are undoubtedly rather more – or rather less – effective than others, and in such cases I have dared to say so. There is nothing more satisfying than a good, neat clue, and nothing more frustrating than an imprecise or sloppy one. I think it is fair to say, however, that on the whole crossword compilers are masters of their art, and that there are far more good clues than bad ones.)

The Dictionary is, however, rather more than just a plain reference work, and I would like to think that many readers (or solvers) will like to work through some or all of the first half, solving the clues as they go. There is indeed nothing to stop them jotting down the cryptic clues, which are mostly hardly more than a few words, and writing their answers next to them. These clues can then be checked in the second half and the answers duly noted. Two readers, in fact, each with his or her own copy of the book (for ease of use), can run their own 'cryptic crossword quiz': one works through the entries in the first half, solving the clues as he goes, and the other checks his progress in the second half, even perhaps gleefully timing the 'solver's' rate for the correct handling of a given number of clues. The roles can – or certainly should – be then reversed, with the checker turning solver.

It should be noted, incidentally, that in the examples given to illustrate indicators in the first half of the book, a full clue will not always be given. Frequently just a part of a clue will be quoted, this being the section needed to show the indicator at work. Such part-clues, not being complete sentences, start with a small letter rather than a capital (unless, of course, the first word happens to be a proper name). Part-clues are often given where an example of a 'burial' is quoted.

Anagram indicators, as already mentioned, have their own Appendix (page 264), so do not have their own separate entries in the first part of the book. Where, however, an anagram indicator can also act as another kind of cryptic clue, it *will* appear in its appropriate entry. An example is the word 'like'. This may serve as an anagram indicator, but it may equally well be translated as AS. The 'like' entry, giving this translation, will also include the clue's use as an anagram indicator.

The reader or user of this Dictionary will doubtless like to know where all the clue elements and their translations or interpretations came from. Some of the clues were suggested by books on crosswords, in particular the 'how to solve it' ones listed in the Bibliography (page 291). The vast majority, however, come from my own first-hand working of several hundred crosswords, both in periodicals and books of crosswords. Dissecting a crossword while simultaneously solving it proved at times a somewhat laborious task, and truth to tell often blunted the keen sense of satisfaction derived from solving a particular clue. Who, after all, stops a piece of taped music every few bars in order to analyse each melodic line? But I felt that such 'fieldwork' was essential to capture each cryptic clue in action as well as to ensure the genuineness of the crosswords themselves. These were not 'model' crosswords, specially devised for academic or instructional purposes, but real, everyday ones, as printed, week in week out, in the various publications. As the main grist to this cruciverbal mill I worked through the crosswords of four weekly publications for approximately eight months from September 1980 to April 1981 and backed these up with crosswords from published selections. Full particulars of these are given in the Acknowledgments, but the reader may like to know at this stage that the four publications were the *Sunday Times*, the *Sunday Telegraph*, the *Observer* ('Everyman' Crossword) and *Now!* magazine (whose last crossword, alas, appeared in the periodical's final issue of 24 April 1981). The crosswords from these four were supplemented by ones from *The Times* of mostly more recent date and those from the *Guardian* published in book form by Penguin Books, as well as crosswords from one of the many Fontana Books of Crosswords.

Actual full-length clues from all of these sources are occasionally used as specimens in the entries here in the Dictionary, and in every case where this happens the name of the source is given (in abbreviated form) and, where appropriate, the date of publication. Such professional clues are, however, in the minority, and most of the clues in the book were devised, for better or worse, by myself, and readers who wish to challenge a clue for any reason are welcome to write to me, care of the publishers, stating the 'nature of their complaint'. I very much hope, in fact, that most of the clues will pass muster, since I have taken considerable pains to provide cryptic challenges that as far as possible match up to those of the experts. In this respect, I would like to express my sincere thanks to Colin Parsons, compiler of crosswords for the *Sunday Telegraph*, who checked all my home-brewed clues at proof stage and advised on their suitability or otherwise. I am much indebted to him for his ready and generous professional advice.

Most of the cryptic clues I devised are fairly standard in their format, but occasionally I yielded to temptation and produced a clue in the form of a rhyming couplet. This is not simply in order to introduce a little variety: solvers who move on to higher things in the world of cryptic crosswords may encounter such eccentricities, and I felt a little gentle preparation for such deviation from the norm might not come amiss. Solvers who graduate to the crosswords of the *Listener*, for example, will know that there are much more devious and tortuous things in Cryptic Crossword Land than innocent rhyming couplets!

Mention has already been made of some of the five Appendices, and these, each with its own introduction, will be found beginning on page 264.

Tackling a cryptic clue

Much of the success and reward gained by a solver in the working of cryptic crossword clues lies in his (or her) mental approach to the task, as well as his 'logistics' or technical back-up. What difficulties lie before him? What is to be expected of him? How long does solving a crossword take? How can he be sure he has the correct answer to a clue? These are some of the questions that face a solver every time he tackles a puzzle.

I would like to venture a few 'clues to the clues', a few

suggestions for the solver to bear in mind as he works on a crossword and its clues.

The first thing to remember is that in any cryptic crossword, of whatever degree of complexity, *all the clues are solvable*. The compiler will put up a good fight, but if he does his job properly and is scrupulously fair and precise, as he must always aim to be, he will always lose in the end – and the solver will always win! This sounds like a statement of the obvious, yet how many solvers 'give up' on the grounds that 'it's too hard', 'he's too obscure' or 'I just can't think of it'? The solver *must* win by completing the crossword: indeed, an honest compiler will freely admit that he actually wants the solver to win. A compiler whose crosswords are too difficult or obscure is a poor compiler, and deserves to lose the support of the crossword-solving public. So remember: you, the solver, may stand four-square against the compiler at the start of the contest, but ultimately you can be certain that you will win and he will lose. The triumph and satisfaction of victory is therefore fore-decreed, and you can smile confidently as you tackle 1 across.

As you work through the clues, remember that all you need are an average general knowledge of things and a good awareness of the structural possibilities of the English language. Since an experienced compiler will *always* say what he means – even though he may not mean what he says at first sight – the information you need is there, somewhere, before you. For this reason it is always important to read a clue carefully – and not be afraid to re-read it. Your attitude should be: 'This is what he says – but what does he really mean?' Some clues are so effective or neat that they can bemuse you if you will let them. This often happens with short clues. For example, 'Equal rank' (4), you read. 'So what', you say – 'equal rank'? Read it again, one word at a time. 'Equal', 'rank'. Can you think of a four-letter word meaning 'equal'? No? Perhaps 'just'? But that doesn't fit in with 'rank'. 'Even', then? But that doesn't fit in, either. But perhaps it's a noun you need, not an adjective? Let's think: 'an equal', 'he's my equal', 'he's my . . .' what? PEER, that's it! An 'equal' is a PEER, and a PEER is a 'rank' of the nobility. So in goes PEER, and you can now move on to the next clue. With every clue like this the solver must always be prepared to consider all possibilities. If he reaches a dead-end one way, he must try another tack. And if that fails he must try another. And so on. If necessary, he can move on to other clues if really 'stuck', and come back to it with fresh eyes. And if after an hour or more, say, you are still left with an incomplete crossword, put it aside and come back to it later – the next day, if necessary. It's surprising how the most intractable clue will prove solvable in this way. Before, you couldn't see the wood for the trees; now all is instantly crystal clear. But whatever you do, you *must* return to the final battle. Don't be content to 'leave it at that' or 'call it quits'. Abandoning a crossword for good can be as depressing as completing one can be exhilarating.

A cryptic crossword should thus be taken reasonably seriously, as a challenge to be reckoned with, and to this end the solver should select physical surroundings that are as conducive to his task as possible. He will need to think, consider, and above all, concentrate, and therefore a quiet and relatively undisturbed environment is desirable. At best this will be an evening or Sunday morning armchair ('morning' since for most people the brain is fresher then), at worst it will be a seat on a train or a lunch-hour office desk. At very worst it will be a seat in a pub, café or restaurant. Most important of all, perhaps, is the time factor. The solver does not work well when time is limited. He should feel that he has a reasonable amount of undisturbed time at his disposal – up to an hour, if necessary. In short, the crossword solver needs the kind of environment that the schoolchild ideally needs for his homework: no noise, no interruption, and no undue time constraint.

He also needs patience, perseverance and persistence – what might be called the three P's of the crossword solver! He needs to be patient, since not all clues will yield their answers easily. He needs to persevere, since 'where there's a will there's a way' and all the clues are known to be solvable. And he needs to persist, since the compiler has thrown down the gauntlet and he, the solver, has accepted the challenge. To withdraw or retire is to lose face! (True, the compiler will never know, but such defeats can rankle, and a half-hearted solver is no true solver at all.)

So now, given the fighting spirit and the best available physical environment, we come to the tools of the trade. What, apart from his brain, does the solver need to tackle his cryptic clues?

Aids for the solver

Starting with the least of his requirements, he needs a *pen* and a *pencil*. It is always wise, especially when embarking on a career as a cryptic clue solver, to fill in the answers in pencil, so that any errors subsequently discovered can be easily erased before the final answers are filled in in ink. (Of course, a pen writing in erasable ink will do just as well.) Fairly soon, after a little experience, a solver can progress to filling in his or her answers directly in ink without the intermediate 'erasable' stage. In a way, this will make him more cautious and therefore more thoughtful about the words he enters, which is no bad thing. And if an error is made, he can in fact resort either to a razor blade, to scrape the mistake gently out, or to correction fluid or paper as used for typing errors. Of course, he may not wish to bother with such niceties, but simply over-write the mistake in darker ink. If the crossword is a prize one, however, and is to be submitted as a correct solution, all traces of errors must be eliminated as cleanly as possible.

Then he should have one or two scrap pieces of *paper*. Any available writing area will do, such as the margins of the newspaper or magazine in which the crossword is printed. This can be used, among other things, for transcribing incomplete answers so as to obtain a good visual impression of what is required. It may well also be helpful for anagrams, which some veteran solvers recommend writing in a circle for ease of 'spotting'.

And then we come to the aids proper, the chief of which will almost certainly be a *dictionary*. The question is – which? Does it matter? Will any dictionary do?

Of course, any dictionary is better than none, but most solvers (and compilers) will particularly recommend *Chambers Twentieth Century Dictionary,* whose own Preface in fact talks of the book being 'the crossword addict's favourite tool'. (Some crossword compilers, especially those offering prize puzzles, specifically recommend *Chambers* to their solvers.)

How should the solver best use his dictionary, and why is *Chambers* regarded as being particularly helpful?

For the solver of cryptic crosswords, a dictionary has three main uses.

The first of these is for *checking* the sense of an answer, in particular where a clue leads to a word with which the solver is unfamiliar or about whose precise meanings he is uncertain. This is not an infrequent occurrence in solving a crossword, that both the cryptic section of a clue and the definition lead to a particular word, which in turn 'fits in' with existing letters from other words, and yet the solver does not quite follow how exactly the answer was obtained. To take a concrete example: the clue 'Salmon-spears – jockey's carrying one' (8) appears to lead to

LEISTERS, since you already have L–I–T–R–, and the 'jockey' must be LESTER (Piggott) who is 'carrying one' or 'straddling' the letter I, with the answer obviously plural ('salmon-spear*s*' and 'jockey'*s*') and so ending in S. But is this answer correct? The dictionary will confirm, and sure enough in *Chambers*, on looking up 'leister', we find 'a salmon-spear' (even with the hyphen, as exactly in the clue). Or take the clue, 'Well-founded rumour' (5). This turns out to be SOUND, and you can see that this can mean 'well-founded'. But 'rumour'? Can a SOUND be a rumour? The dictionary will help again. On looking up 'sound' in *Chambers* we find fourteen meanings given of the word as an adjective (with 'well-founded' as the tenth), but 'rumour' is obviously not among them since it is a noun. So we look under 'sound' the noun – and there, as the fifth of six meanings given, we find 'report, rumour', thus confirming the correctness of our answer (and incidentally, as with the salmon-spear, enlarging our own vocabulary).

A dictionary can thus help to check rare words (like 'leister') and words with several meanings (like 'sound'). And it is precisely in these two fields that *Chambers* excels, since its coverage of rare words and of multiple meanings is particularly extensive. It claims, for example, to include all the words in the Bible and in Shakespeare, and, being a Scottish-based dictionary (it is printed and published in Edinburgh), it includes a number of Scottish words – some of which are regularly used in crosswords.

The second main use of a dictionary is for *word-searching*. This is perhaps something of a desperate measure, employed when you have the maximum number of letters in an answer available from other clues, but cannot actually reach the answer by the normal route, i.e. that of the clue. For example, you have failed to solve the clue, 'It is a comfort the sun has one' (6), and as it stands your answer, with letters from other clues, reads: –O–A–E. In frustration you turn to your dictionary, and work through the alphabet to find a word that will be six letters long, contain these three vowels, and of course answer the clue. So you start with AO- words (very few of these), then move on to BO- words, CO-, DO-, and so on. Eventually you come to SO- words and find the answer you require: SOLACE! Of course, if you have the first letter of your answer, the search will be that much easier, since you can concentrate on this single letter of the alphabet. (And if you already had the *consonants* of this particular answer, as S–L–C–, you would almost certainly not have needed to search through the dictionary anyway. A careful compiler will see to it, however, that most cross-checking letters are vowels, not consonants!)

The third use of a dictionary is for *sense-searching*. This is almost a 'cheating' method of arriving at an answer, since it involves actually looking up a word in the clue to get the required definition for your answer. In a dictionary like *Chambers*, this method can in fact pay dividends, since the many different senses of a word, particularly a common one, are clearly and distinctly listed. The theory behind this method of clue-solving is that if A can be defined in terms of B, then B can be defined in terms of A. In other words (to quote the clue we used earlier), if a 'sound' is a 'rumour', cannot a 'rumour' be a 'sound'? Let us apply the 'sense-search' method to this particular clue, which was 'Well-founded rumour' (5). Looking for the definition in the clue, rather than the cryptic section, we first choose 'rumour' and look it up in *Chambers*. We find five senses listed: 'clamour', 'general talk, repute', 'hearsay', 'flying report', and 'a current story'. Although 'story' has five letters, it hardly seems to be the answer, and cannot be backed up by the other half of the clue, 'well-founded'. So we have drawn a blank here. We therefore look up 'well-founded'. Here we find two senses: 'built on secure foundations' and 'based on solid evidence or sound reasoning'. And there, of course, in the second definition, is our answer, SOUND.

This particular method works best with common words, that are likely to be defined in terms of each other, rather than rarer or more specialised words, where the definition (as with the salmon-spear) will be a one-way one. On the whole, however, dictionary consultation is a time-consuming business, and it is obviously quicker and more satisfactory (and more satisfying, too) to reach the answer via one's own brain-power rather than through the secondary medium of a dictionary.

Even so, the use of reference books in solving crosswords is perfectly respectable and legitimate, even though some hardened (or masochistic) solvers despise them and maintain that if brain-power alone cannot produce the answers, then a solver is not worthy of the name!

Reference books

Apart from traditional encyclopedias and handbooks, there are two further books that can be of assistance to a crossword solver, and we can add them to *Chambers* to form a kind of 'table-top trio'.

The first of these is a good thesaurus of some kind. This will clearly be helpful in the last operation just described, the 'sense-search'. Any thesaurus or book of synonyms will be useful here, but perhaps the well-tried favourite is *Roget's Thesaurus of English Words and Phrases* in one of its editions (the Longman one is very dependable). Instead of ploughing through the alphabet to find SOLACE just now, for example, we could have looked up 'comfort' in *Roget* and fairly quickly found this precise answer (in the section headed 'Relief').

The second crossword aid which a solver should have in addition to *Chambers* is a book of classified or categorised lists of specialised words, arranged by subjects. In other words, if one needs a breed of dog in six letters starting with T, it is obviously helpful to have a book that can readily provide this information. There are in fact a number of such books, specifically designed to assist the crossword solver, with perhaps the most comprehensive and satisfactory being *The Hamlyn Crossword Dictionary*.

This book arranges several thousand words, almost all of them nouns, in classified sections ranging from narrow and precise categories such as 'jockeys' and 'rocks' to more general groups such as 'food' and 'people'. In each section, words are arranged alphabetically by number of letters, so that in the 'dogs' section, for example, there are 12 breeds of three and four letters, 15 of five letters, 25 of six letters (including our 'talbot' that we were after), and so on. The book is particularly strong on names, which, of course, feature in many crosswords, and there are accordingly lists of boys' and girls' names as well as an almost unnecessarily comprehensive section on 'characters in literature' (with most of the characters, major and minor, in Shakespeare's plays, for example). *Hamlyn* is useful for such clues as 'See bird wave cylinder' (6) where you need a six-letter bird beginning with R quickly: a few seconds' reference is enough to advise you that ROLLER is what you are after in this clue.

It is always worth remembering, of course, that the crossword compilers themselves use all three books in this triple group, and that definitions, for example, will frequently be given exactly as they are found in *Chambers*. The solver cannot do better than match the enemy's fire-power with his own armament!

If *Chambers, Roget* and *Hamlyn* are essential back-up material for the crossword solver, there are two further books that may also prove helpful on occasions.

The first of these is a specialised dictionary which can be of assistance in checking word endings alphabetically, just as *Chambers* is useful for checking word beginnings. This is Martin Lehnert's *Reverse Dictionary of Present-Day English*, published in Leipzig, East Germany. The dictionary contains no definitions, but several thousand words listed alphabetically *starting with their final letters*. This does not mean that the words are printed backwards, but that the alphabetical order runs from the end of the word to the front, rather than from the front to the end, as is usual. For example, the next word after 'bass' in the dictionary is 'carcass', since 'c' (the middle letter of 'carcass') follows the 'b' of 'bass'. Similarly, 'class' will be followed by 'glass', since 'g' comes after 'c'. This arrangement means that words are grouped by endings, so that all words ending in -DEN, for example, will be together, or all words ending in -LAR. This can be of great help to the solver when he has an answer outlined as --O–I–H or as --P–A. For the first of these he can run down the columns of words ending in -IGH, -ISH, -ITH, and so on, and for the second look for words ending in -PEA, -PHA, -PIA, and so on. (The two actual answers here are intended to be NEOLITH and SEPIA.)

Finally, although most crossword compilers will restrict themselves to abbreviations listed in *Chambers*, it may well be helpful to the solver to have available a copy of *Everyman's Dictionary of Abbreviations*. In this work he will discover, for example, that the single-letter abbreviation 'g' means not only 'gram' and 'gravity', as shown in *Chambers*, but can also stand for 'garage', 'gauge', 'gelding', 'gender', 'general', 'genitive', 'gilt', 'goal', 'gold', 'good', and many others!

What makes a good crossword?

What constitutes a good crossword? Most solvers (and compilers) would probably agree that range and balance are what chiefly matter.

The range of answers should be within the 'word-power' of the solver, or at any rate should not include unfamiliar words that cannot be deduced by means of the clue (and checked, as necessary, in a dictionary). Here, for example, are the complete answers to a *Guardian* crossword:

Across: CARAFE, ARMADA, PRIG, ELECTORATE, RIOTED, TEAM GAME, BENCH-MARK, STOT, BEAR, INTENDANT, ADVANCES, DOTAGE, CONTROLLER, NEAT, KERNEL, RECORD. *Down:* CARMINE, RIGHT, FREEDOM, RATTAN, ABROGATED, ATTEMPT, BETTER ONESELF, CHARACTER, BEDROCK, ENDORSE, NIGGARD, OCHONE, TANGO.

Of these twenty-nine answers, probably only two words (STOT and OCHONE) will be 'remote' to most solvers, with perhaps CARMINE and RATTAN (and possibly ABROGATED) being regarded as 'difficult'. Yet the clue for STOT is 'Children retreating from young ox' (i.e. a reversal of TOTS, the standard translation of 'children'), and OCHONE is clued as 'Round church one finds lamentation' (i.e. O as 'round' plus CH as 'church' plus ONE). Both words can then be checked in *Chambers*, of course, where 'stot' is (what else?) 'a young ox' and 'ochone' is (predictably) 'interjection of lamentation'. And this is to say nothing of the cross-checking letters that the solver would have in these words, with STOT already shown as –T–T and OCHONE appearing from letters of across words as –C–O–E. The other three 'difficult' words can be similarly arrived at with confidence. And when all is said and done, who – and particularly a crossword solver – is not the better for increasing his vocabulary?

The balance of a crossword is a more subtle matter. It involves not only a satisfactory 'grid' or lay-out of squares and blanks (whether blocks or bars), but also a good but not extravagant mixture of common words and rarer ones, short words and long words, 'dictionary' words and common names, even topical ones. (We recall Lester Piggott who featured earlier in connection with the salmon-spears.)

It also, to my mind, involves even an aesthetic balance, a satisfactory and enjoyable complement of clue and answer. We expect the answers to a crossword to be 'reasonable', and the solver also has a right to be offered 'reasonable' clues. This means that any clue that seems unduly artificial, contrived, or just plain impossible (in rational terms) is probably a poor clue. 'Round church one finds lamentation', for example, is a good clue, whatever its answer, since its image rings true. On the other hand, 'See bird wave cylinder' makes undue demands on the imagination – even if one allows that the 'bird' is a girl. The solver can identify with a lamentation round a church, or children retreating from an ox, but not really with a 'bird' waving a cylinder! Although they are solvable, I must confess to a feeling of nonfulfilment when tackling a clue such as 'Monster makes Eleanor so upset in the Bull' (12). The fact that I arrive at BRONTOSAURUS does not mean that I feel at home with this alien Eleanor and the Bull (presumably a pub) where she is 'so upset'. However, this is a personal reaction, and as a solver I accept the fact that many compilers use the names of personalities (in this case Eleanor Bron) as cryptic elements for their clues. They therefore find their place in this Dictionary – including the very Miss Bron who figures here.

There is also the balance between the cryptic part of a clue and its definition, and this indeed is one of the prime things the solver should aim to establish on reading through a clue for the first time. In the clue above, for example, 'monster' is the definition, and the rest of the clue the cryptic section. Similarly, in the two previously quoted clues, 'young ox' and 'lamentation' were the definitions. This does not mean that every cryptic clue will consist of a definition balanced by a cryptic section. Two-word clues such as 'Well-founded rumour' are also fairly common, and here there is no actual cryptic element as such, but two disparate definitions. Even so, the balance is there, and the clue is thus a success.

Last of all, there is the unwritten balance that comes from the 'trial of strength' between compiler and solver. We considered this earlier, and said that ultimately it is the solver who wins – who *must* win. Yet even when he has won, the balance has not really been upset, since the compiler devised a complete crossword on the one hand, and the solver has produced a complete solution on the other. Each, therefore, has created a fully rounded work, and one that is all the more satisfactory since although complete in itself it is also complementary to its other half: without the compiler's crossword there could be no solution, and without the solver's solution, no crossword can ever be complete.

Adrian Room
Petersfield, Hampshire

Abbreviations

The following abbreviations are used for crossword sources in the Dictionary:

Font.	*Fourteenth Fontana Book of Crosswords* by Christopher Patterson
Guard.	*The Penguin Book of Guardian Crosswords*
Obs.	the *Observer*
S.T.	the *Sunday Times*
S. Tel.	the *Sunday Telegraph*

a
1 A 2 I 3 ONE
Awkward name given to a flower (7)

abandon
1 RAT 2 indicates removal of letter(s) from word, e.g. 'medical man abandons limb' – LI (i.e. LIMB abandons MB); 3 = anagram
Cat abandons ship, going to Northchurch for a drink (5)

(is) **able**
CAN
This clergyman is able to get on (5)

aboard
indicates word or letters to be inserted in S . . . S, e.g. 'tearful aboard' – SWEEPERS
Equal value aboard for the masts and yards (5)

about
1 C 2 CA 3 RE 4 = reversal, in across clue, e.g. 'man about' – NAM 5 = 'straddle', e.g. 'doctor about a . . .' – DAR 6 = anagram
Puzzle about the bus (5)

above
indicates that letter, element or word comes before another, in down clue, e.g. 'church above Rome' – CHROME
Painter studies above board (9)

abroad
1 OUT 2 indicates foreign word (usually French), e.g. 'cat abroad' – CHAT
Good place to spend the night abroad if camp fire is started (3)

absorb
= 'straddle', e.g. 'book absorbs monarch' – BROOK
Scotsman absorbs oxygen, lights up at night (4)

abstainer, abstinent
TT
Abstinent in commercial success? That's the lowest of the low! (6)

Academy, academician
RA
Second-class academician in first-class centre of learning! (5)

Academy chief
PRA (i.e. President of the Royal Academy)
Academy chief is oriental dignitary, which is commendable (12)

accent see **foreign** (sort of) **accent**

acceptable
1 OK 2 U
House has acceptable angled shape (4)

accommodate
usually = 'burial', e.g. 'we accommodate silver' – WAGE
Very poor eastern editor accommodated in New York (5)

accomplished
DID
Accomplished turn is round head of class – that's good teaching! (9)

account
1 AC 2 STORY 3 TALE
Account I should write quickly and send casually is bitter sweet (4, 4)

accountant
CA (i.e. Chartered Accountant)
Accountant comes back to tea, that's something done! (3)

acknowledgments of indebtedness
IOUS
Stimulus gets acknowledgments of indebtedness, but they're not genuine (8)

across the Channel
indicates French word, e.g. 'bridge across the Channel' – PONT
Life across the Channel (in the north) should provide plenty of drink (4)

act [see also next entry]
DO
Act very loudly and really take off! (4)

act(ion)
DEED (especially 'in action' meaning 'in DE . . . ED')
Was flat out in action, so got held up (7)

acting
ON
Sam's acting the tough guy (6)

actor
EXTRA
Actor caught short in passage (7)

actors
CAST
Outspoken actors on the air (9)

address
O(H)
Address the people and you will get a sign (4)

admiral (Admiral)
ADM
Crazy admiral really *is* crazy (3)

admit
OWN
A number admit the truth, which is plain-spoken! (9)

(he) **admits**
IM
He admits he's fit but in fact he's just the opposite (8)

advertisement
AD
See advertisement and charge (4)

affirm
AVER
Revolutionary leader to affirm he's a crazy person (5)

afloat
indicates word or letters to be inserted in S . . . S, e.g. 'old boy afloat' – SOBS
Pat's afloat – I can see his gaiters! (5)

after
indicates (usually) that answer is word added to one given, these forming a new word, e.g. 'After flu she gets a part in *Henry V*' – ELLEN (i.e. ELLEN after FLU, which gives FLUELLEN, the Shakespeare character)
After do, this servile dependent achieves mastery (6) (*Obs.*, 25.1.81)

afternoon
1 PM 2 indicates letter, element or word after N (i.e. noon), e.g. 'in afternoon' – NIN
'An Old Etonian in the afternoon . . .' That could be the first line of one! (4)

afterthought
PS
Painter has an afterthought that strikes him (4)

again
RE (with element or word clued, almost always a verb, e.g. 'go wrong again' – RESIN)
Unite again, trash! (6)

against
1 ANTI 2 CON 3 V
Clergyman and I against the Queen – that's stimulating! (7)

agent
1 REP 2 SPY
Unusual agent on ship, maybe one of a gang to force men to enlist (5)

agreement
YES
Eastern agreement or eastern hideosity? (7)

air
1 MIEN 2 TUNE 3 indicates reference to *song*, e.g. 'German air' – LIED
Race in the air – then put this on to keep warm (6)

airline
1 BEA 2 BOAC 3 TWA (and obviously others, although these are the most common)
Airline goes to the north, love, isn't it fun! (5)

airman
ACE
Trainee airman is worthy of tears (9)

alack (!)
indicates word minus A, e.g. 'Disturbed weasel, alack, found on west coast' – WALES (i.e. anagram of WEASEL minus A)
Married outside Israel, alack! – being improperly attached (10) (*Guard.*)

Albert
AL
Albert did not tell the truth – he was in league (6)

alcohol
1 GIN 2 RUM 3 TOT
Alcohol comes to Albert, and that's the lot! (5)

Alexander
AL
Alexander to prepare for war? That's a dangerous sign! (5)

all but
indicates element or word minus one letter, usually the last, e.g. 'all but ready' – READ
Wanting all but few evicted – that's nasty (9) (*Obs.*, 12.7.81)

allow(ed)
LET
Journey allowed for one of three? (7)

all right
OK
Hey, all right – I'll catch it! (4)

all up (!)
indicates (in down clue) solution clued as reversal, as well as normally, e.g. 'Shoots to end, it's all up' – POTS (i.e. POTS – shoots, STOP – to end)
Ridicules love, in store, getting ring – it's all up! (4–5) (*Times*, 4.7.81)

almost
indicates incomplete element, or word, usually minus last letter, e.g. 'to begin almost' – OPE, 'almost any' – AL
It's almost time, I would say, and I am not very brave (5)

also
AND
The second letter, also the second to last – that's crooked! (5)

alternative
1 OR 2 OTHER
Special constable, 1st class, in alternative movie award (5)

always
E(V)ER
God embraces love, church poets always get comfort from it (4, 5)

amateur
1 HAM 2 L
Talk to amateur in Kent (7)

ambassador
HE (i.e. His Excellency)
Ambassador goes to Cuba, mother of Paris is there (6)

America(n)
1 STATES 2 US 3 indicates American term, word or spelling, e.g. 'parlour in America' – PARLOR
Stigmatic padre, an American, very holy, too (5)

American city
1 LA (i.e. Los Angeles) 2 NY
Merriment comes to American city, that's laughable (5)

American soldier
GI
Scotsman embraces American soldier – wonderful! (5)

American uncle
SAM
Black American uncle thrown from ship (6)

amid
IN
Amid loud labourers little children see (7)

amidships
indicates element or word to be inserted in S . . . S, e.g. 'spring amidships' – SWELLS
High sail amidships stays put (5)

among
= 'burial', e.g. 'One against one among the Seven Sleepers' – EVENS (in *Seven S*leepers)
For look and see – the barefoot walker goes
Among the frozen fields and Alpine snows (6)

amputate
indicates letter(s) removed from beginning or end of word, e.g. 'amputated leg' – LE or EG
Amputated thumb at pit-head, a real blow (5)

ancient
indicates old word or spelling, e.g. 'your ancient' – THY
Hesitantly put on my ancient fur (6)

ancient city
UR
Endless fluid runs to oriental and ancient city – it's alcoholic! (7)

ancient Roman see **Roman**

ancient times
BC
Twisted irony in ancient times, poetically cynical (7)

and
AND
A member of the House of Commons, and the Queen, and a state leader, and . . . and . . . (9)

and not
NOR
A marsh, and not a resort (6)

and so on
ETC
Half skip, and so on, to top of hill – that's a brief outline (6)

anger
IRE
The Poles contain their anger, thanks to this fascinating woman (5)

Anglo-Saxon
AS
Anglo-Saxon granted agreement (6)

angry
1 HOT 2 = anagram
Angry at the Spanish inn (5)

animal
among the most common 3-letter ones are APE, ASS, CAT, CUR, DOG, PIG, PUG, PUP, RAT, RAM, SOW, TEG; often more specific indications will be given, e.g. 'little dog' – PUP
Confused animal goes to church to get fruit (5)

answer
ANS
Hard answer for German boy (4)

antique
OLD
Note antique coat of arms, you can see the bird (9)

apparently
1 = 'burial', e.g. 'Pagan from the Athenian district, apparently' – HEATHEN ('t*he Athen*ian') 2 = homophone, e.g. 'Servant girl did it, apparently' – MAID 3 = homograph (one or more words of identical spelling but different meaning), often a single word split into two parts, as PAST/ORAL or PAN/TRY, e.g. 'Metal conduct' – LEAD, 'Tree family barrel, apparently' – FIRKIN (i.e. FIR/KIN)
Didn't make contact in the fog apparently (6) (*S.T.*, 8.2.81)

appearing (in)
1 = 'burial', e.g. 'Man appearing in last omnibus' – TOM (i.e. in 'las*t om*nibus') 2 = anagram
Girl appearing in violin dance (5)

apprentice
L
Apprentice gets pigment for furniture (6)

approach
ADIT (a rare word but a handy one!)
Return approach by learner is regulated by sea currents (5)

approval
1 OK 2 PAT
Proprietor giving approval to Ronald (6)

arbitrator
REF
Arbitrator at home with editor, made it more cultured (7)

archbishop
EBOR (official title of Archbishop of York, being abbreviation of Latin *Eboracensis*, 'of York')
Archbishop returns to the five hundred, fully dressed (5)

archdeacon
VEN (i.e. Venerable)
Archdeacon goes to tea, we hear, for escape (4)

archeological work
DIG
In archeological work northern worker is angry (9)

arena
RING
First rate arena is drying out and warming up (6)

aright
AR (i.e. 'a' and 'right')
Listen to him aright (4)

aristocratic
U
Aristocratic and knowledgeable man provides treatment (5)

'ark
EAR (i.e. 'hear' minus 'h')
'Ark, the bird's 'ome – that's serious! (7)

around
1 C (Latin *circa*) 2 = anagram 3 = 'straddle', e.g. 'Heath around river' – HEARTH 4 = 'burial', e.g. 'Hut she dances around' – SHED ('*she d*ances)
To rouse the guest, I ran around (4)

arrive
AR(R)
Arrive on burst tyre at main channel of communication (6)

article
1 A 2 AN 3 THE (i.e. grammatical indefinite and definite article)
Biting article of Scottish origin (6)

artillery
RA (Royal Artillery)
Artillery I'd attack (4)

artist
RA (Royal Academy member, or Royal Academician)
Instruct artist in metal (5)

art master(s)
MA
A long coat for the art master? Aren't they the limit! (6)

arts supporter
EASEL
Arts supporter follows Welsh, furtive fellow! (6)

as before
1 DO (i.e. 'ditto') 2 indicates old word or meaning, but usually quite well known, e.g. 'bag as before' – SCRIP
The Spanish road in chaos, as before – yet this is the land of the Spanish conquerors! (8)

ascend(ing), in the ascendant
= reversal (in down clue), e.g. 'ascending crow' – WORC
School's reputation in the ascendant (4)

as it were
indicates indirect or non-literal or punning sense; as Robins put it: 'definition not to be taken at face value', e.g. 'Worker in detail, as it were' – DOCKER (i.e. DOCKER as worker and as one who 'docks' or de-tails) (*Guard.*)
Sequence of words given in docking procedure, as it were (8)

aspiration
H (the letter that is an 'aspirate')
Mother's aspiration is rather a muddle (4)

assembly
1 BALL 2 = anagram
Base assembly needed for this game (8)

assistance
AID
A number get assistance from this servant (4)

assistant
AIDE
Assistant in Rolls is robber (6)

astern
AFT
Handle is hard astern (4)

as they say
indicates (usually) pun of some kind, e.g. 'Bird to show sign of fear, as they say' – QUAIL
Floor is something worth writing about, as they say (6)

as well as
AND
Mountains along west coast of South America, as well as east and south (5)

at
TO
At piano I'm the best (3) (*Now!*, 6.3.81)

'at
AT
Soft 'at is sign of approval (3)

at home
IN
Senior officer at home getting money (4)

at last
indicates final letter(s) of word, e.g. 'a dog's life at last' – CURSE (i.e. CUR'S and last letter of 'life')
Tom home at last, as the great book tells (4)

at rest
indicates element or word to be insert in BED or COT (usually as B . . . ED and CO . . . T), e.g. 'Royal retinue of ancient city at rest' – COURT (i.e. UR in COT)
Shed blood of many at rest (4)

attempt
TRY
Friend has an attempt but it's insignificant (6)

attention
EAR
Attention in off-stage area is tiring (7)

Attila
HUN
Attila's in the way, let's move him over (5)

attorney
DA (i.e. District Attorney)
Attorney and politican are 'wet' (4)

audience
EARS
Noisy audience is scared (5)

auditor
EAR
Auditor is after a penny as it's expensive (4)

automation pioneers
RUR (i.e. the automatons in Karel Čapek's *R.U.R.*, i.e. *Rossum's Universal Robots*)
Automation pioneers, and a number from the country (5)

autumn
FALL
Autumn, with its own endless untilled land (6)

available
IN
Beer available in physical training (4)

avenue
AV(E)
Quit avenue in sheltered side (5)

average
1 AV 2 PAR
Average college lecturer gives remission of punishment (6)

award
probably most common are OBE and OM, but also used are: CH, DSO, MBE, VC
Prince gets award for investigatory work (5)

away
1 OUT 2 indicates letter(s), element or word to be removed, e.g. 'drive right away' – DIVE (i.e. DRIVE minus R)

Sick fitter remains, but pines away – so end it all! (9) (*S. Tel.*, 12.4.81)

B

bachelor
1 B (i.e. as component of such abbreviations as BA, BS) 2 BA
Fruit for the bachelor goes straight down (5)

back and forth
= palindrome, e.g. 'Bird flies back and forth' – TIT
Holy woman goes back and forth (3)

back from
= reversed 'burial', e.g. 'Back from the car for a run' – RACE ('the *car*' reversed)
Back from America, is Eli sojourning in Europe? (7) (*Guard.*)

back in see **back from**

back(ing)
1 BET 2 = reversal (in across or, less often, down clue), e.g. 'back-room' – MOOR, 'paperback' – GAR
An Italian lute contains this backbone (4)

backslide
= reversal, usually in across clue, e.g. 'Meg, backsliding,' – GEM
Tim's backsliding before hard worker (5)

back(ward), from the back
1 HIND 2 = reversal (in across or down clue), e.g. 'cat from the back' – TAC
Backward kid goes east to the ditch (4)

backwards or forwards, backwards and forwards
= paiindrome, e.g. 'Type of carriage that goes backwards or forwards' – GIG
This instrument goes round and round as well as backwards and forwards (5)

bad
1 ILL 2 = anagram
Bad head – a symptom of this? (7)

bad grade
F (i.e. bottom grade in US schools)
Bad grade in first half of German – it's a pointer (6)

ball
O
Drunkard has ball in street (3)

base
1 LOW 2 indicates last letter of element (in down clue), e.g. 'base of table' – E
Frame to relieve spinal base (5)

base metal
ORE
Soft base metal here – a whole flood of it! (4)

battalion
BN
A senior officer in the battalion can be usually found at breakfast (5)

batting
IN
Father batting? That hurts! (4)

battleship
HMS
A battleship wrecked – what a bungle (4)

beam
RAY
Beam reflected to Pole – quite a story! (4)

bearing
1 E 2 MIEN 3 N 4 S 5 W
Chicken loses bearings but finds her baby (5)

beast(ly)
indicates (usually) reference to *animal*, real or fictional, e.g. 'Occupant of the old maze was rather beastly' – MINOTAUR
Little beasts do break up the organisation of crime (7) (*Font.*)

beat
1 LICK 2 TAN 3 = anagram
Tandem song, having no beat, is out of fashion (6) (*Obs.*, 18.1.81)

beauty
BELLE
Beauty queen has love and endless phone calls for brave Greek (11)

become
1 BE 2 = anagram
Become good man – or even more than that! (4)

bed
1 COT 2 CRIB
As bed, very fashionable (5)

bee
B
Bee is on edge of glass – upper edge (4)

beer
1 ALE 2 LAGER
Knock back a beer for a royal treat (5)

before
ERE
Caught before a beginner – that's corny! (6)

before noon
1 AM 2 indicates element followed by N, e.g. 'bar before noon' – BARN
A wee tipple for GP before noon (4)

beginner
1 L (i.e. 'learner'); 2 indicates first letter of word, e.g. 'young beginner' – Y
Mixed team is joined by rustic beginner, which makes it less exciting (5)

beginning
indicates first letter of word or element, e.g. 'the beginning' – T
Naturally beginning to clear up causes deep depression (5) (*Guard.*)

behead
indicates first letter of element or word to be removed, e.g. 'king beheaded' – ING (but see next entry!)
Cad beheaded a river creature (5) (*Font.*)

beheaded king
CHAS (i.e. Charles I)
First the beheaded king, then his small sister – and then the gun carriage (7)

behind
indicates that answer, or part of it, follows after element clued, e.g. 'Animals reveals this other animal behind pole' – CAT (i.e. CAT behind POLE, so that first 'animal' of clue is POLECAT)
Game bird has this narrow crest in behind part (5) (*S.T.*, 28.6.81)

behold
LO
Behold the feathers of the bird,
And then the noise of cows is heard (6)

bend
1 U 2 = anagram
Bend over upside-down tin to get one (4)

beneath
indicates one word or element comes under another in down clue, e.g. 'bottomless valley beneath me' – MEDAL (i.e. DALE minus E beneath ME)
Beneath the rug a lock you'll see
And there's the bed for you and me! (8)

Benedictine
DOM (i.e. title of Benedictine monk, from Latin *dominus*, 'lord')
Benedictine in charge of French island – he lives there! (8)

be painful
AIL
Question is painful; answer is 'flinches' (6)

be quiet
SH
Mother, be quiet, give us the potato! (4)

beset
= 'straddle', e.g. 'Men beset by outsize portents' – OMENS (i.e. MEN beset by OS)
I'm beset by the French fruit (5)

beside
AT
Beside the Spanish mountain range (5)

besiege
= 'burial', e.g. 'Soldiers besiege prime minister to get transport for infantry!' – PRAM (i.e. RA besiege PM)

Teetotallers besiege tree trunk to get drink container! (6)

betting
SP (i.e. starting price)
Betting on a champion chaser to get real glitter! (7)

biblical town
(usually) UR
Holy man has gone to biblical town – gone over to get fish (8)

big bell
TOM
The big bell loudly rings for Law Society beginners – they're so silly! (8)

big timekeeper
BEN
Big timekeeper has little time for criminal (4)

bill (Bill)
AC(C)
Bill Stringer makes an agreement (6)

bind
TIE
Big vessel binds baby ones (7)

bird
1 among the most common 3-letter ones are: EMU, HEN, MOA, OWL, ROC, TIT; among the most common 4-letter ones are: DOVE, ERNE, MINA, TEAL, TERN 2 indicates reference to woman or girl, e.g. 'bird of paradise' – HOURI
A boy and a bird – and another bird (6)

bird home
NEST
Me with a bird home? That's the lowest of the low! (7)

bishop
1 ODO (i.e. the Anglo-Norman prelate who was the half-brother of William the Conqueror) 2 RR (i.e. Right Reverend)
Bishop goes to Bible city to get the sweet smell of sanctity (5)

bit
ION
The French bit is painful (6)

(a) **bit of**
1 indicates one or more letters, usually the first, of the following word or element e.g. 'a bit of cake' – C or CA 2 = 'burial', e.g. 'A bit of Roman enterprise, this horsehair' – MANE ('R*oman e*nterprise')
A bit of novelty indoors for these contributors (6)

(a) **bit off,** (a) **bit short**
1 indicates word or element minus one letter, usually the last, e.g. 'page is a bit short' – PAG 2 (bit off) = anagram
Rafter not in actual use, being a bit short (4) (*Obs.*, 18.1.81)

black
1 B 2 JET
Black Jack goes back for a kid who deserves a smack! (4)

bloomer
indicates reference to *flower* or *plant*, e.g. 'American poet, confused, went to New York – what a bloomer!' – PEONY (i.e. anagram of POE+NY)
A rude stare is a bloomer! (5)

blow
RAP
Blow true, false delight (7)

blue
TORY
Man's blue tale (7)

bluff (Bluff)
1 indicates reference to cape or headland, e.g. 'Bluff William to get the bird' – HORNBILL (i.e. Cape HORN+BILL) 2 = HAL when preceded by 'king', 'monarch', etc. (i.e. reference to 'Bluff King Hal', otherwise Henry VIII)
Tough and bluff, showing obduracy (8)

blushing
RED
Poor Vera, blushing, swore it was true (7)

board
1 SIGN 2 TABLE 3 'burial', e.g. 'I boarded van, being conceited' – VAIN (i.e. I boarded VAN) 4 indicates reference to *ship*

(compare **aboard**), e.g. 'fifty boarded boat' – BLOAT
Pennon showing king has boarded ship (8) (*Guard.*)

Bob
S (i.e. shilling)
Bob made his mark and went ahead fast (8)

bodyguard
SS
The fool has a bodyguard in the south as they're all murderers (9)

bolshie (Bolshie)
RED
Bolshie player helps to make paint (3, 4)

bolt
BAR
Taff to bolt back with bit of cheese on toast (5, 6)

book(s)
1 NT (i.e. New Testament) 2 OT
First poem in book with bit of a choice (6)

boozer
1 BAR 2 PUB
Boozer has 51 to 100 at the counter – in this part, anyway! (6, 3)

border
1 EDGE 2 HEM 3 RIM
Border in a town and port in northern Italy (6)

born
1 B 2 NEE
Was she born in sin, taken aback? (6)

boss
1 HEAD 2 STUD
Mixed-up boss comes to Queen for special flag (6)

bother
ADO
It's ripped – bother! And this will only cause more damage! (7)

both ways
= palindrome, e.g. 'bad both ways' – DUD
Miss Derek to look both ways. She's a forgetful girl (2, 4)

bottom
1 BED 2 indicates last letter of word or element, in down clue, e.g. 'bottom of bag' – G
Mother sits on bottom of bed – is she angry? (3)

bounder
CAD
Bounder gets points over Civil Engineer, that's his downfall! (7)

bowled
B
Bowled and not exactly youthful – was he blindfolded? (8)

box
SPAR
'Box, brown' – that's the old military way! (7)

boy
1 LAD 2 SON 3 indicates a boy's name, among the most popular 3-lettered ones being: ABE, BEN, BOB, DAN, DES, DON, HAL, IAN, KEN, LES, NAT, NED, PAT, RAY, REG, SAM, SID, TIM, TOM, VAL, VIC; note also the commonly used 2-letter names AL and ED
James the scholar boy (5)

(the) **branches**
TREE
Southern branches lead to sort of square on this highway (6)

break
1 = 'burial', e.g. 'beginner breaks training' – PLE (i.e. L breaks PE) 2 = anagram
Ball breaks cup – that's a blow (4)

breather
LUNG
Breather in middle of exercises, then a dive (6)

brief(ly)
indicates shortened or abbreviated word or element, e.g. 'export brief' – EXP, 'into brief . . .' – TO, 'brief account' – AC
Brief moment on the French spot (4)

bring back
= reversal, e.g. 'bring back the cat' – TAC
Bring back the employer to me, then we can continue (6)

bring in
= 'straddle', e.g. 'Boy bringing in poles is healthy and handsome' – BONNY (i.e. BOY bringing in NN)
Here are the bears, now bring in the horse – what rogues they all are! (7)

British
1 B 2 BR
British, i.e. French cheese (4)

British island
IOM (i.e. Isle of Man)
British island reverts to holy man, it's quite damp (5)

British Museum
BM
A pupil goes into the British Museum to find some peace (4)

broach
= 'burial', e.g. 'king broaches tub' – TRUB
Reversed nail broaches vat – that's courageous (7)

brother
BRO
Brother NCOs are quite wild (7)

brown (Brown)
1 TAN 2 TOM (i.e. Tom Brown of *Tom Brown's Schooldays*)
Brown turned, 'I've an African man here' (6)

brushworker
RA (i.e. member of Royal Academy)
Quick getaway for brushworker in Britain (4)

brute
indicates reference to **animal** (which see)
Up and away! There's a brute in there! (5)

Buddhist priest
LAMA
Buddhist priest introduces religious scholar, getting Greek letter (6)

burn
SINGE
Burn fifty in one (6)

(for) **Burns**
indicates Scottish word or name (i.e. as used by Scottish poet Robert Burns), e.g. 'Burns potato' – TATTIE
Baby for Burns (5)

bury
1 INTER 2 = 'straddle', e.g. 'we buried the silver' – WAGE (i.e. WE buried AG)
King buried in tomb with one brass instrument (8)

bust-up
1 BRA 2 = anagram
Bust-up in nerve centre (5)

busybody
1 ANT 2 BEE
Bring in the busybody, it's urgent (9)

butter
1 RAM 2 GOAT
After tea is announced, the butter runs along the rails (4)

by the sound ot it
= homophone, e.g. 'Animal has bad throat, by the sound ot it' – HORSE (sounding like HOARSE)
Being there with gifts, by the sound of it (8)

Caesar
indicates Latin word, e.g. 'Caesar's day' – DIES
Caesar's force in unusually poor condition (7) (*Times*, 29.8.81)

California
CAL
California goes French on endless draught of liqueur! (8)

Cambridge town
ELY
Fifty-four come to Cambridge Town – they're a rowdy lot! (6)

can
1 ABLE 2 TIN 3 (can be) = anagram
Little Viola can, she's capable of anything (6)

cancel
indicates letter(s) to be omitted, e.g. 'Fred cancelled loudly' – RED (i.e. F cancelled)
Track had first train cancelled producing extreme anxiety (4)

Canonbury district
NI (i.e. London district of N1)
Drove car round Canonbury district, checked on broadcasts (9) (*Times*, 23.5.81)

cap
indicates that one word or element, in down clue, comes before another, so that it 'caps' it, e.g. 'she caps two pupils' – SHELL (i.e. SHE caps LL)
Baron caps us, and we all go home in this (3)

capital
1 AI 2 CAP 3 indicates first letter of following or preceding word(s), usually a geographical name, e.g. 'capital of France' – F, 'German capital' – G 4 indicates name of capital city, among most common being: BONN, PARIS, ROME
Shuns every small Cossack hamlet except Western Siberian capitals (7) (*S. Tel.*, 1.3.81)

captive
1 POW 2 = 'burial', e.g. 'captive king in bow' – BROW (i.e. R captive in BOW)
Trace captive queen in row of houses (7)

card
1 ACE 2 TEN
Threaten the fellows with a card (6)

care of
CO
'Care of North Street' can get you a policeman (9)

caricaturist
SPY (i.e. the pseudonym of Sir Leslie Ward, the caricaturist)
West African caricaturist is spiteful (5)

carry
1 = 'straddle', e.g. 'we carried Henry' – WHALE (i.e. WE carried HAL) 2 indicates that word or element, in down clue, follows or 'carries' another above it, e.g. 'men carry nothing' – OMEN (i.e. MEN carry O)
Scotsman carries little Sarah to get the fish (6)

case
= 'straddle', e.g. 'confused sailor with brown case' – TARTAN (i.e. confused ART with TAN case, otherwise TAR with TAN 'straddling' it)
Where to sort out vegetable case (7) (*Guard.*)

cash
TIN
File has top-class cash for Russian monk (8)

cat
1 MOG 2 OUNCE 3 PUSS 4 TOM
Low noise of cat grabbing ball at home (6) (*Now!*, 10.4.81)

catch (see also **caught**)
1 GET 2 NET 3 = 'straddle', e.g. 'cat catches nail' – MOPING (i.e. MOG catches PIN)
Drunkard catches cold living north of the border (4)

cathedral city
ELY
Half London went to cathedral city, maybe they felt in need of company? (6)

caught
1 C (abbreviation used in cricket) 2 CT 3 GOT 4 = 'burial', i.e. opposite of **catch** (which see), e.g. 'ball caught by cat' – COAT (i.e. O caught by CAT)
Caught, and, I'd say, quite fair (6)

celebration
DO
A celebration about love (5)

censor
CATO (the Roman censor, 234–149 BC)
He comes to censor with doctor for a large number of victims (8)

central heating
CH
Shed has central heating as it is a home for pets (5)

centre
indicates exact centre of word or element, possibly acting as a 'burial', e.g. 'centre of industry' – US or DUST, 'cream centre' – E, 'centre of town guide' – G (middle letter of 'town guide')
Exact centre of map – it has significant meaning (4) (*Guard.*)

centre of gravity [compare **centre**]
1 CG 2 V (centre of GRAVITY)
Centre of gravity holds zero reading and it stops the wheel (3)

century
C
A double century – and mixed post as indication of approval? (7)

(a) **certain amount** (of)
= 'burial', often within a single word, e.g. 'a certain amount of acclamation' – CLAM
A certain amount of duplicity is allowable (5) (*Guard.*)

certainly
YES
Most shy, certainly, in bed (6)

champion
ACE
Forbidding champions make ugly faces (8)

(Mr) **Chaney**
LON (i.e. Lon Chaney, the American film star)
Mr Chaney comes to scholar in capital city (6)

Channel Isles
CI
Disturbances in Channel Isles with signs of impact by blunt instrument (9)

chap
MAN
A chap gets a notice back for a girl with a lovely name (6)

chaps
MEN
Chaps go down these hills (6)

chapter
1 C 2 CH
Dean and chapter meet in some confusion at the ball (5)

character(s)
1 indicates letter(s), often in an anagram, e.g. 'old characters' – DOL, 'Greek character' – PI, 'last character' – R (i.e. last letter of 'character') 2 = anagram
Nude characters pursued by Communist bore (7) (*Guard.*)

cheat
DO
Cheat the railway – here's a small boat (4)

chemist
MPS (i.e. Member of the Pharmaceutical Society)
Caught a chemist in the service stations (5)

chief
1 ARCH 2 indicates first letter of word or element, e.g. 'chief of state' – S
Chief, I've a document here (7)

child
1 IMP 2 IT 3 SON 4 TOT
Completely childless colleague (4) (*Guard.*)

children
1 LITTER 2 SEED
Noisy children run quickly about (7)

children's nurse
NANA
Bachelor and children's nurses together – that's crazy! (7)

chimney
LUM
Chimney, surrounded by lead, is quite vertical (5)

(a) **choice word**
OR
Prepare a choice word – 'entrance' (4)

choose
PICK
Choose the French onions in brine (7)

Christian dispensation
NT (i.e. New Testament)
A Christian dispensation for this worker (3)

Christmas
1 DEC 2 NOEL
Christmas is all wrong when you're on your own (4)

Christopher
1 KIT 2 SLY (in Shakespeare)
Christopher's central heating is very vulgar aesthetically (6)

chuck
indicates letter(s), element or word to be removed, e.g. 'chuck ball from goal' – GAL (i.e. chuck O from GOAL)
Charity chucks it, being cautious (5)

church
1 CE (i.e. Church of England) 2 CH 3 RC
Scholar comes to church and we see his sign of authority (4)

church dignitary
VEN (i.e. Venerable, title of an archdeacon)
Address the church dignitary – 'What's cooking?' (4)

churchman
1 FR (i.e. Father) 2 DEAN 3 REV
Churchman is also editor, so examined and corrected (7)

church service
MASS
Is 'collect' a church service? (4)

cigarette
FAG
Cigarette sent back to returning umpire – he's the foreman! (6)

circle
1 O 2 RING
Get the black circle (5)

circuit
O
This animal ran about two hundred circuits (7)

city (City) (district) (of London)
EC
Tea-time delicacy in city hide-out (6)

Civil Defence
CD
Painter is back in Civil Defence – he's a real joker! (4)

Civil Service
CS
There's work in the Civil Service for the police (4)

clamour
1 DIN 2 ROW
Clamour in oil well is continuing (6)

Clara
BUTT (i.e. Clara Butt, the English singer)
Clara comes to the Queen for a tea-time spread (6)

clasp
= 'straddle', e.g. 'cat clasps pole' – CAST (i.e. CAT clasps S)
A Pole clasps me – so be it! (4)

classy
U (i.e. *u*pper-class)
Sit in classy costume (4)

cleaner
CHAR
Cleaner brings two notes for the cost (6)

clergyman
1 DD 2 FR 3 REV
Clergyman, in love with the German Queen, is all of a tremble (8)

climbing
1 = reversal, in down clue, e.g. 'climbing creature' – LAMINA 2 may be reference to *climbing plant, animal*, etc., e.g. CLEMATIS, VINE
Climbing cat goes on the tile, moving by touch (7)

clique
SET
The 'Back Rodney' clique is in Wessex (6)

close, closing
indicates final letter of word or element, e.g. 'close of play' – Y
Constituent at close of day may be Conservative or Labour (5)

clothing
1 GEAR 2 = 'straddle', e.g. 'coat clothing skinhead' – COAST (i.e. COAT clothing 'head' or first letter of 'skin')
Rumpled clothing makes me lose my temper (4)

club
1 BAT 2 IRON (i.e. golf club)
Old soldier has small coin to join upper-class mixed club (9)

(the) **C.O.**
CO
The C.O. comes up to a recruit, and is very hot-tempered (4)

coach
BUS
Coach comes to a headland – that's its job (8)

Cockney (says)
1 indicates word minus initial H, e.g. 'Cockney hand' – AND 2 indicates substitution of Y or IE for AY in word such as 'play', e.g. 'Cockney play' – PLY or PLIE (to represent Cockney pronunciation of 'ay')
Primitive weapon is of the Cockney school (5)

code
MORSE
Trainee follows the code for a bit (6)

coin
1 BOB 2 D 3 P 4 S 5 indicates a common foreign coin, e.g. ANNA, CENT, ECU, LIRA, MARK, REAL, SOU
Coin-op favourite, a darling girl (6)

cold
1 BRR 2 C
Cold sailor gets a taxi (3)

college
ETON
Famous college is back with quite a large number (5)

colonel
COL
Colonel brings back the rope – that's terrific! (8)

colour(ed)
(usually) RED
Scholar coloured, being undressed (5)

coloured fluid
INK
Coloured fluid in ship's basins (5) (*Obs.*, 12.7.81)

come back (to)
= reversal (usually in across clue), e.g. 'Tom comes back to her' – MOTHER (i.e. reversal of TOM followed by HER)
Mr Runyon makes a comeback – he's always on the move (5)

come round, come around
1 = reversal (as for **come back**) 2 = 'straddle', e.g. 'she comes round before noon' – SHAME (i.e. SHE round AM)
He comes round fish, being in place of concealment (4)

come to
indicates that one word or element joins another, e.g. 'cat comes to the Queen' – CATER (i.e. CAT comes to ER)
Holy man comes to a king – and it was this that led him (4)

come up
= reversal, in down clue, e.g. 'clergyman comes up' – VER
There's a prohibition order on young Roger coming up to North Wales town (6)

commanding officer
CO
Commanding officer at home to get some money (4)

commercial
AD
With commercial backing, engineers are bold (4)

Commie
RED
Commie and German worker dismissed from work! (9)

commit(ted)
PUT
I'm committed to the editor, so charged (7)

common(ly)
indicates slang or popular form of a word (including one minus initial H), e.g. 'common business' – BIZ, 'common prison' – NICK, 'common food' – EATS, 'common hat' – AT
The common fool – he'd put a coat on! (7)

Common Market
EEC
Gravity about rioting Common Market country (6)

common sense
NOUS
He and I have common sense – is that so terribly wicked? (7)

Communist
RED
Tedium for Communist in capitalist commercial activity (7)

companion
CH (i.e. Companion of Honour)
Shrewd painter comes back to companion (4)

company
CO
Prison company work (4)

comparatively
indicates comparative of word or element clued, e.g. 'comparatively reckless' – RASHER, 'comparatively dull stuff' – MATTER
British possessor, yet has comparatively dark skin (7)

competition
RACE
Weight competition has easy elegance (5)

complaint
ILL
Doctor's complaint is pneumatic (5)

component(s)
indicates letter(s) in word(s) or element(s) clued or in answer, e.g. 'car components' – CAR
Five engine components found scattered at end of the day (7)

compound
PEN
London prison compound moves to northern town in France (11)

comprise
= 'straddle', e.g. 'Kit comprises northern contract' – KNIT (i.e. KIT comprising N to mean 'to contract')
Set comprises mined elements, mixed, which form a deposit (8)

conceal(ing) [but compare next entry]
= 'burial', e.g. 'Joseph, I allege, is concealing a bottle' – PHIAL (i.e. 'Jose*ph*, *I al*lege' conceals PHIAL)
George, the rascal, conceals anaesthetic liquid (5)

concealed [but see also previous entry]
HID
Mythical monster concealed rare flower (6)

concerned with, concerning
1 ON 2 OVER 3 RE (as in 're your letter')
Retirement is concerned with an agreeable excursion or a party (7)

concert
PROM
Concert exercises are performed at once (6)

conclusion
indicates final letter of word or element, e.g. 'conclusion of meeting' – G, 'concert's conclusion' – T
For the record, retaliatory attack has speedy conclusion (5)

condition
IF
Tom's back condition is a recurring subject (5)

conducted
LED
Greek character conducted, made a heap (5)

(in the) **confine(s) of**
= 'burial', e.g. 'senior officer in the confines of the street' – SCOT (i.e. CO confined in ST)
Tax collection for five in the confines of the field (4)

confused type
PIE (i.e. printing type that has become muddled)
Confused type of church musical composition (5)

consequence
END
Add 504 to 499 and the consequence is a pay-off (8)

Conservative
1 C 2 CON 3 TORY
5+99 = Conservative gain (7)

conspirator
CASCA (who was one of the conspirators in Shakespeare's *Julius Caesar*)
Conspirator, an artist, the cause of many a purge (7) (*Obs.*, 12.7.81)

constituent of
= 'burial', e.g. 'constituent of Chipping Ongar' – GONG (i.e. part of 'Chipping *Ong*ar')
Seize the constituent of Newton Abbot (3)

consumed
ATE
Patrol leader consumed dish (5)

contains, container, content
1 indicates with letter(s) inserted, otherwise 'straddle', e.g. 'Pot contains right kind of wine' – PORT (i.e. POT contains R) 2 = 'burial', e.g. 'content of irregular chest' – LARCH or ARCH (i.e. 'irregu*lar ch*est') 3 indicates reference to *container, vessel,* e.g. URN, POT, etc. (see **vessel**)
Fear not, the river is content (4) (*Guard.*)

continental (Continental)
indicates foreign word, usually French, e.g. 'some continental' – DES
First class – the continental beer (3)

continue to
indicates word ending in ON, e.g. 'continue to play' – BATON, 'continue to wave' – FLAGON
Continue to carry box (6)

contribute (to)
= 'burial', e.g. 'Office seeker contributes to refreshments' – ICES (i.e. 'off*ice s*eeker')
New agent contributes payment (4)

cooler
FAN
Soldiers in cooler attempt (8)

copied
APED
Medical man copied and assumed a casual pose (6)

copper
1 CU (Latin *cuprum*) 2 D (i.e. penny) 3 P (new penny) 4 PC (i.e. police constable or 'copper')
Copper Street sounds like Milky Way! (4)

coppers
PENCE
Coppers in Southern Region find a woman's under-garment (7)

copy
1 APE 2 CRIB
Typed top copy is found on recording instrument (4)

core
indicates centre letter(s) or word or element, e.g. 'apple-core' – P (or PPL)
Tap core of the earth in pitfall (4)

(this) **corner**
1 NE 2 NW 3 SE 4 SW (i.e. the four corners of the compass, but can also refer to

location in corner of puzzle, e.g. NE = top right corner, etc.)
Corner street provides cosy home (4)

Cornwall and Devon
SW (i.e. south-west England)
Urge to come to Cornwall and Devon for a change (6)

(that's) **correct**
1 SIC (Latin – 'so', the word being used to show that a quoted original is correct) 2 = anagram
Acid for President of the United States? That's correct (7)

corroded
ATE
Silver corroded, Ruby? (5)

costly fiddle
STRAD (i.e. rare violin by Stradivarius)
Costly fiddle led astray, shooting beyond and short of the target (8)

councillor
CR
A councillor, on my return, gives a word like Ernie (7)

count
TELL
Conservatives count leaderless nation – but they can't count all the stars here! (13)

counter
BAR
Counterweight in the farmyard (6)

country
1 LAND 2 often turns out to be US but can also be, among others: GB, UK, WALES
Uninteresting, second-rate country (5)

county
1 CO 2 usually indicates an abbreviated name, e.g. MON (Monmouthshire), SOM (Somerset), with counties no longer existing (since boundaries were redrawn in 1974) perhaps being referred to as 'old' or 'former'
County cricketer takes in pupil, thus getting a special blue (6)

couple
indicates repeated letter(s) or elements, e.g. 'couple of times' – TT, 'couple of bills' – ACAC
A couple of hundred points will give you admittance (6)

court
WOO
Court quite a number among the trees (4)

cover
1 LID 2 = 'straddle', e.g. 'exercise to cover the bill' – PACT (i.e. PT covers AC)
Five per cover fulfilling the necessary conditions (5)

crack pilot
ACE
Crack pilot sets off from South Pole into cosmos (5)

crash into
1 = 'burial', e.g. 'leader of heat crashed into tree' – THREE (i.e. 'leader of *h*eat' crashed into TREE) 2 = anagram
Albert crashes into house, and wins this aura of sanctity! (4)

creature
(often) EFT, but can be any **animal** (which see)
Sinister creature went off (4)

credit
CR
Credit for us? Hard in this dense mass of people (5)

crew
EIGHT
Means to see the crew about agreement (8) (*S.T.*, 5.7.81)

cross
1 X 2 = anagram
Did she make Socrates cross, diffusing the pain round philosopher's head? (9) (*Now!*, 20.2.81)

crowd
1 MASS 2 MOB 3 PRESS 4 high

Roman number such as C, D or M
Crowd I'll say is able to move (6)

cunning
SLY
Former president is cunning – deliberately! (9)

Cupid
EROS
Tender Cupid flies back (4)

currency
usually indicates a *foreign coin*, such as CENT, ECU, LIRA, MARK, SOU, YEN (see also **coin**)
Same currency for the dean (5)

current
1 AC 2 DC 3 indicates name of **river** (which see)
Current account is first class return for those who live in this traditional suburban avenue (6)

current fashion
GO
Current fashion points to a soft kind of talk (6)

curtailed
indicates word or element minus last letter, e.g. 'curtailed story' – STOR, 'curtailed cat' – CA
Curtailed dog or where he comes in (4)

custom
USE
Examine each custom (6)

cut (out)
indicates letter(s) to be removed, e.g. 'cut out page of "Post"' – OST (i.e. remove P from POST)
Cut out article from Indiana for this country (5)

Dad(dy)
1 PA(PA) 2 POP
Dad has six lions in the tents (9)

daily
CHAR
Daily mass has special influence (5)

dandy
1 BEAU 2 FOP
Dandy returns with mangled fish – is that why he looks so solemn? (2-5)

Daniel
DAN
Daniel follows us up to this Middle East Country (5)

darling
PET
Darling pupil comes in – so hide! (4)

day
D
Day One is over (4)

(the) **day before**
EVE
It's common the day before Railway Day (8)

day of victory
VE (i.e. *V*ictory in *E*urope, end of the Second World War in 1945)
Day of Victory – right, I go,
Turning makes my head spin so (7)

dead
1 D 2 LATE
Dead – with a mask of fine linen (6)

deadly
FELL
Deadly gin doctored, making him collapse (7)

death
END
Death in the arena is heart-breaking (7)

debtor
OWER
Dead debtor has an endowment (5)

debt(s)
1 IOU(S) 2 RED
Endless vice and debts make him ill-tempered (7)

decapitate
indicates first letter of word or element to be removed, e.g. 'decapitated cat' – AT
Looks after the meeting and still lives even when decapitated! (8) (*S.T.*, 21.6.81)

December
DEC
December – note Roman confusion of the ten-day tales (9)

declare
AVER
Mick goes over to declare he's a non-conformist (8)

decoration
most common are OBE and OM; also used frequently are CH, DSO, GM, MBE, VC
Decoration on the king is anti-metathetical and pro-theistic (9)

deep
indicates reference to *sea* or *ocean*; compare **main**
Deep freezer (7)

defeat
ROUT
Defeat after tea, so hurry off quickly (4, 3)

deflated
indicates word or element minus letters AIR, e.g. 'deflated fairy' – FY
Marriage god found among deflated hairy men (5)

degree
1 BA 2 D(EG) 3 MA
Girl gets a degree (1) with her study (6)

deity
GOD
Deity holds love, is kindly (4)

delayed
Pass a special law, for member is delayed (9)

deliver
RID
Eddie comes back to deliver mixed gin – is he making fun of us? (8)

demon
IMP
Demon donkey goes east, there's no way out of it (7)

demonstrate
= 'burial', e.g. 'Homeland demonstrates impetuosity' – ELAN (i.e. 'hom*eland*')
Young Alastair demonstrates the festivities (5)

depart
indicates removal of letter(s), e.g. 'Irritable model departs from store' – SORE (i.e. T departs from STORE giving SORE – 'Irritable')
Inspire novice to depart when I'm melancholy (5) (*S.T.*, 31.5.81)

department
DEPT
The Department for First Defence is in East London (8)

depend
indicates reference to *hanging*, e.g. 'Garment depends on place where game is watched' – COATSTAND (i.e. COAT depends on (hangs from) STAND)
China depends on prize secured by pirate (3-4) (*S.T.*, 19.4.81)

depression, depressed
DENT(ED)
Mad life in France leads to depression, that's obvious (7)

Descartes
RENE (i.e. René Descartes, the seventeenth-century French philosopher)
Descartes got married and began a fresh lease of life (7)

desert(er)
RAT (i.e. in the sense 'to change sides')
Deserter – one on a fixed allowance (6)

despatched
SENT
Agreement as despatched (6)

detailed
indicates word or element minus final letter,

i.e. 'de-tailed', e.g. 'Anthony detailed to get £100' – TON (i.e. TONY detailed)
Girl detailed to go across (6)

detective
1 DICK 2 TEC
Detective has drink, getting something to do with building (8)

detectives
CID
Drink for detectives of the Queen (5)

devil
1 DEMON 2 IMP 3 SATAN
The devil has a tune, but this will make it worse! (6)

devotee
FAN
Devotee has exciting stay – in imagination only (7)

devour
= 'straddle', e.g. 'Bob devours egg – that's a mistake!' – BOOB (i.e. BOB devours O)
Chum sees me devour 'at (4)

dial?
LAID UP (i.e. DIAL reversed in down clue)
Unable to move dial? (4, 2)

diamond(s)
D
Diamonds smuggled in this old Sussex port to reach this Isle of Wight one (4)

Diana('s)
DI(S)
Diana's flower is a calamity (8)

(old) **dictator**
IDI (i.e. Idi Amin, dictator of Uganda, ousted in 1979)
Old dictator rang round when making his assault (7)

died
1 D 2 OB (i.e. *obiit*, Latin = 'died')
Mr Chaney died on the 'Capital' (6)

diminutive
indicates (usually) short name or standard abbreviation, e.g. 'diminutive lieutenant' – LT, 'diminutive head of state' – PRES (i.e. President)
Diminutive person has first-class return to ancient middle east country (6)

dine
EAT
Hundreds dine, eating this (4)

dined
ATE
The good man dined in Mississippi or Missouri (5)

diocese
SEE
Jolly jaunt for priest in diocese (5)

diplomatic letters
CD (i.e. French *Corps Diplomatique*)
Used for securing, or in diplomatic letters (4)

direction
1 E 2 N 3 S 4 W
Information from all directions (4)

director
DIR
Director to get curtailed funeral hymn (5)

dirty
MESS
Reports tell of dirty times (8)

dirty dog
CUR
Dirty dog is with veterinary surgeon and gives a jump (6)

disagreement
1 NO 2 = anagram
Churchman has the power to comprehend disagreement (5)

disc
1 EP 2 LP 3 O
Employees break pole with disc (6)

discover
1 = 'burial', e.g. 'In Africa I nearly discover the murderer' – CAIN (i.e. in 'Afri*ca I n*ear-

ly', Cain being the biblical murderer of his brother Abel) 2 = anagram
In Parma, I zealously discover a cereal (5) (*Font.*)

disease
often TB
Disease weeded out in this unhealthy place of growth (6)

disfigure
1 MAR 2 = anagram
Disfigure lines of vegetables (7)

disheartened
indicates word or element minus centre letter(s), e.g. 'disheartened flier' – FLER (i.e. FLIER minus centre letter I)
Disheartened day amid misfortunes, leading to happy episodes (6) (*Obs.*, 10.5.81)

dismissed
OUT
King dismissed! Riot ensues! (4)

disorientated
1 indicates word or element minus E (i.e. 'dis-orient-ated'), e.g. 'disorientated snipe' – SNIP 2 = anagram
Queen, disorientated, comes to church after a gin cocktail, slaking her thirst (9)

dispense with
indicates omission of letter(s), e.g. 'Postman dispenses with old Bob and becomes a beer dispenser!' – POTMAN (i.e. POSTMAN dispenses with S)
Player dispenses with pupil, being the one who has to find the fee (5)

display
= 'burial', e.g. 'Lady Neal displays force' – DYNE (i.e. 'La*dy Ne*al')
Lord Erpingham displays his system (5)

dispute
1 ROW 2 = anagram
Bird box dispute! (7)

dissipated fellow
RAKE
Arouse once more terrible awe in a dissipated fellow (7) (*Obs.*, 12.7.81)

district
usually a London postal district, e.g. EC, NE, NW, SE, SW
District to take up weapons for this mass of flying insects (5)

district attorney
DA
District attorney meets British politician – a 'wet' (4)

ditched
indicates omission of letter(s) or element, e.g. 'top quietly ditched' – TO
Flier ditched noisily, and as a result he's now flat on his back (4)

ditto
DO
Launched in sea exercises – mountain exercises ditto (7)

divide
= 'burial', e.g. 'we divided set' – SWEET
He divides conservative thinking (6) (*Guard.*)

divine
DD (i.e. Doctor of Divinity)
O divine son, thou hast a better chance (4-2)

divinity
GOD
Divinity protects ancient city and is represented in bottle-like fruit (5)

do
1 ACT 2 DO
Do in for business agent (6)

doctor
1 DD 2 DR 3 GP 4 MB 5 MD 6 MO 7 = anagram
Doctor has endless quarrel – it's his constant theme! (5)

dog
1 CUR 2 among popular three-letter dogs are: POM, PUG, PUP
Dog has tail cut short (7)

dog-end
1 G (i.e. end letter of DOG) 2 TAIL
Sold dog-end in grass! (8)

do it yourself
DIY
Abstainer is into do-it-yourself with a merry tune (5)

dollar
S
New dollar hits the headlines (4)

(it's) (what's) **done**
U (i.e. '*u*pper-class')
Places regularly visited – the done thing in Hants (6)

don't, doesn't [see also next three entries]
NT
PLA doesn't do this with bombs or trees (5)

don't fail (to)
DO
Don't fail to use a heavy blow (5)

don't know
DUNNO
Don't know half of Alick's birds (8)

don't make changes
STET (i.e. Latin = 'let it stand', written by a deletion in a text to show that the matter should not be deleted after all)
Don't make changes, kid, put this on your head (7)

Dorothy
DOT
Dorothy and the youth leaders are quite crazy! (5)

double
indicates repeated letter or element, e.g. 'double century' – CC
Do double time? Editor put a stop to it! (6)

double bend
S
Double bend on river will give you a ducking (5)

doughboy
GI
Scoffed at doughboy going to bed (5)

draft
MS (i.e. 'manuscript')
Fail to notice draft is in (4)

dram
TOT
Mix the dram reluctantly for this slippery customer! (5)

dress
1 ROBE 2 = anagram
Dress right, going with a girl (7) (*Obs.*, 12.7.81)

dressed
1 CLAD 2 ROBED
She came in dressed – and we arrived at the same moment (7)

drink
usually either a kind of drink or a measure of drink, among the most popular being: ALE, GIN, JAR, NIP, PORT, SUP, TOT, TOAST
Hard drink healthy? Sounds like hard water! (4)

drive(n) from
indicates omission of letter(s) or element, e.g. 'He is driven from the house to the junction – one way to expel a person' – OUST (i.e. HE is driven from HOUSE, so that OUS adds T)
Truck is driven from Vancouver and you lose the lid (5)

driver
often reference to type of golf club, especially IRON
Dead body means car has shaken driver (7)

driving place
TEE
Long seat is fixed driving place (6)

drop (off) (a bit)
indicates omission of letter(s) or element, e.g. 'Submitted ref dropping off wasn't right' (*Obs.*, 8.2.81) – ERRED (i.e. REFERRED dropping REF)
Name-dropping car salesman out to get villains (7) (*S. Tel.*, 3.5.81)

drop aitch(es)
indicates element or word minus H(H), e.g. 'Heather drops her aitches when consuming this kind of apple' – EATER (i.e. HEATHER minus two H's)
Insinuator, that chap, dropping aitches in the meantime (7) (*Obs.*, 8.2.81)

drove (car)
MOTORED
Mum, in this state, drove crazily and very hard, having nothing in! (10)

drum
EAR
Soft, a drum, a big brown beast will come! (4)

drunk(ard)
1 SOT 2 = anagram
Drunk and in love – looks black! (4)

dry grass
TED (a rare word but a handy one for this common verb ending)
Noticed no dry grass (5)

duck
O (i.e. zero score in cricket indicating no runs, originally called a 'duck's egg'; compare **egg**)
Duck on Scottish river, right in it, too, is another sort of bird! (6)

dug
TEAT
Dug right into a real feast! (5)

dull
MAT
Marriage in dull church (5)

(in) **duplicate**
indicates repetition of letter(s) or element, e.g. 'duplicate notes' – GG
It's crazy to duplicate the General Assembly (4)

duplicating machine
RONEO
Sure upset about duplicating machine going wrong (9) (*Times*, 18.4.81)

during
= 'burial', e.g. 'east during the war' – WEAR
Proper scare for king during fight (6)

dusky damsel, dusky maiden
EVE
Dusky damsel doesn't feature in sports programme (5)

Dutchman, Dutch boy
HANS
Dutch boy takes tea in south of England (5)

E

'e
E
'E 'as 'is 'at, so will 'e do this to it if 'e's wrong? (3)

each
1 EA 2 PER
Authority given for each young lady with one on (10)

ear
LUG
With ear pinned back, pupils see these sea birds (5)

earlier
EX
Not quite right in earlier performance (7)

early
AM
Doctor gets in early, having a brolly (4)

early evening
VI (i.e. 6 o'clock)
Called in the early evening, having lots of angry things to say (6)

earth
DIRT
Earth round this district is level (6)

east(ern)
E
To the east there's a peninsula (3)

eaten
FED
United force, having eaten special food supply, enters note (10)

eat(ing)
1 SUP 2 = 'straddle', e.g. 'Sing eating pie, and getting going' – STARTING (i.e. SING eating TART)
Holy man eats very little pudding (5) (*Obs.*, 8.3.81)

ebb(ing)
= reversal, e.g. 'ebbing river' – EED
'Ebb Tide' or 'I Go to the Italian Leader' (9)

echo
= homophone, e.g. 'Soft echo is incomplete' – LACKS (i.e. echo of LAX)
Waterfall echo makes horse stop (4)

'e'd
ED
Reverse of coin 'e'd shadowed (6)

Eddy, Edward [which also see]
ED
Eddy points to paradise (4)

edge
1 HEM 2 RIM
The top, where the water is – note the edge (4)

edgily, edging
indicates first and last letters of word, often qualified with such a word as 'away', e.g. 'race edgily away from that pint' – HATPIN (i.e. take away TT from '*t*hat pin*t*')
Screen with red centre and unusual rose edging (7)

editor
ED
William comes to editor, having sent his account (6)

Edward
1 ED 2 NED 3 TED
Edward has acknowledgments of debts – how boring (7)

effort
TRY
Country workers produce peas – with an effort (9)

egg
O
I egg on boss in photo workshop (6)

Egyptian goddess
ISIS
When crown is placed on Egyptian goddess, that's the turning point (6)

eject
indicates letter(s) or element to be removed, e.g. 'eject coin from spinner' – SINNER
The EEC engine stops, and sots are ejected – oddly, for not much British money! (8, 5) (*S. Tel.*, 14.6.81)

Eleanor
BRON (i.e. Eleanor Bron, the British TV revue actress)
He met Eleanor by the river where Abraham dwelt (6)

elected
IN
Jack and Paul elected to supply the waterproof cloth (9)

electroplated
EP
Electroplated? Och, it's no a wee while! (5)

elevated
= reversal, in down clue, e.g. 'I'm elevated' – MI
Albert is elevated by the French boy's voice (6)

eleven(th)
1 II 2 SIDE 3 TEAM 4 XI 5 reference to *county cricket team*, usually in the form of abbreviated county name, e.g. SOM (see **county**)
Poisonous to the eleventh century (5) (*Guard.*)

Eliot
TS (i.e. T. S. Eliot, the American poet)
About Eliot . . . these are his practical ones! (4)

elite army group
SAS (i.e. Special Air Service Regiment)
Elite army group go to Kent after German, yet find Englishman! (9)

Elizabeth
BESS
Jack goes to Elizabeth, the religious leader (6)

'em
EM
I rid 'em, stop 'em all rushing about in the afternoon! (4, 8)

embarrassed
1 RED 2 = anagram
Confused country girl got embarrassed, looked angry (6)

embrace
= 'straddle', e.g. 'At what place did we embrace her?' – WHERE (i.e. WE embraced HER)
Man embraces girl to get the stone (9)

eminence
indicates reference to *mountain*, so usually = TOR, HILL, MT, etc.
His Eminence is in charge – it's quite an important event (8)

employ(ment)
USE
Mother has employment in Kent, being a sort of contact healer! (8)

empty
1 indicates word or element minus centre letter(s), e.g. 'empty house' – HOSE 2 indicates word or element in which O (= nothing) has been inserted, e.g. 'empty bar' – BOAR
Tailless cat goes on empty road – he's quite a character! (4)

encage
= 'straddle', e.g. 'She encages cat, getting an injury' – SCATHE (i.e. SHE encages CAT)
Judge returns and encages bird – but he also hunts down birds of another kind! (6)

encircle
= 'straddle', e.g. 'Communists encircle eastern marsh plants' – REEDS (i.e. REDS encircle E)
Men encircle little Lolita to get fruit (5)

enclose
= 'straddle', e.g. 'Sam encloses bottom of pole in crack' – SEAM (SAM encloses E)
Father enclosed right leg (4)

enclosure
1 PEN 2 = 'burial' (see **enclose**)
Has tumbledown enclosure to put into shape (6)

encountered
MET
Military commander encountered a heavenly body! (5)

(at the) **end** (of)
indicates last letter(s) of word, e.g. 'end of play' – Y, 'Mile End' – E, 'at the end' – T
Young bird has no end of elegance (4)

endless(ly)
indicates word or element minus last letter, 'endless talk' – TAL, 'try endlessly' – TR
He protests about endless belt (5)

energy
PEP
Energy in love with the French race (6)

enfold
= 'straddle', e.g. 'arms enfold the French' – ALARMS (i.e. ARMS enfold LA)
Torn sheet enfolds apprentice coming to king, giving some protection (7)

engage (in)
= 'burial', e.g. 'Bob engaged apprentice' – BLOB
Bill engages redhead and a worker – splendid! (9)

engineer(s)
1 CE (i.e. Civil Engineers) 2 RE (i.e. Royal Engineers)
Went underground in the Engineers – but was given the job (5)

English, England
1 E 2 ENG
English ogre raving to feed on blood! (7)

Englishman's castle
HOME
First meal in Englishman's castle for Frenchman (5)

engulfed (by)
= 'burial' (in), e.g. 'bottom of boat engulfed by sand' – STAND (i.e. T engulfed by SAND)
Cricketer engulfed by river – we had a serious discussion about it (6)

enmesh
= 'straddle', e.g. 'Saracen's head enmeshed in net' – NEST (i.e. S enmeshed in NET)
Songstress enmeshed in Kremlin network (6)

ensconce
= 'straddle', e.g. 'Young animal ensconced in local farm' – CALF (i.e. ensconced in 'lo*cal f*arm')
Bird ensconced in a better nest (4) (*S.T.*, 19.4.81)

enter (in), **entertain**
1 = 'burial', e.g. 'Father entertained by holy man's gaiters' – SPATS (i.e. PA entertained by STS)
Priest entertained by Roman Catholic memorial (5) (*Guard.*)

entrance
GATE
Tailless arrow flies to entrance – I claim it as mine (8)

envelop
= 'straddle', e.g. 'Mist envelops top of oak, making it damp' – MOIST (i.e. MIST envelops O)
Fog envelops royal leader – is this what he turns into? (4)

epoch
1 AGE 2 ERA
Fine feathers for a fine epoch (7)

equal (to), **equality**
PAR
Head of state, equal to king, is a bright, lively fellow (5)

equipment
KIT
Equipment, at end of game, is sent up (4)

'er
ER
Send 'er a wall-chart (6)

erect(ion)
= reversal, in down clue, e.g. 'erection of War Office' – OW
Pole erected at end of passage, giving escape (5)

'e's
1 ES 2 indicates letter E+preceding element or word, e.g. 'cutlet 'e's cooked' – LETTUCE (i.e. anagram of CUTLET+E)
Pot 'e's smashed – how 'e drinks! (5)

essay
TRY
Harshly criticise essay – there's food for thought! (6)

(the) **establishment**
CE (i.e. Church of England, the established church of Britain)
Power for the establishment (5)

etc.
often indicates part of anagram, e.g. 'Raised wild deer etc.' – ERECTED (*S.T.*, 29.3.81)
Working well if fine, etc. (9) (*Font.*)

European
indicates reference to European *nationality*, in particular DANE, FINN or POLE
European tailless mice are controversial (7)

even
EEN
Unable even to find a place to eat (7)

every
EACH
Soft – every fruit (5)

everyone, everything
ALL
Quiet, everyone – I *will*! (5)

evidence of liability, evidence of debts [etc.]
IOUS
Irreverent rascal has evidence of debts (7)

evil
1 BASE 2 ILL 3 SIN 4 VICE
Destroy the king's evil (4)

exam(ination)
1 ORAL 2 TEST
Bad-tempered exam at the end of the day (5)

examine
CON
Examine the island – plenty of sand and gravel there! (8)

excellent
AI
Both are excellent in public relations (4)

excerpt(s) (from)
= 'burial', e.g. 'excerpt from "Albert Herring" shows a ship's quayside location' – BERTH (i.e. excerpt from 'Al*bert H*erring')
Excerpt from 'Measure for Measure' needs to be improved (6)

exclude
indicates letter(s) or element to be removed, e.g. 'Compensate amateur excluded from play' – PAY (i.e. L excluded from PLAY)
Tasty morsel can be had from two birds, excluding the tern (6)

exercise(s)
1 PE 2 PT
Approve business exercises (5)

exhibition
TATE
Mothers' Union came to exhibition to get something different (6)

exist
1 ARE 2 BE
Exist on tea for a wager (3)

exists
IS
Equality exists for the capital (5)

exotic
1 indicates foreign word, usually French, e.g. 'exotic wine' – VIN 2 = anagram
Six learner drivers go east and come to this exotic town (5)

expel
indicates letter(s) or element to be removed, e.g. 'Pupils expelled from hall' – HA
Risk of empire is having one expelled (7) (*Now!*, 27.3.81)

expert
ACE
Mike's the first expert, he carries the mark of authority, too (4)

explosive
1 HE 2 TNT 3 = anagram
Explosive at high temperature (4)

expose
= 'straddle', e.g. 'First, Petty Officer exposed the edge' – PRIMO (i.e. PO exposed RIM)
Sid exposed article – or so he maintained (4)

extra large
OS
Award for extra large vehicle (5)

extreme(ly), extremists
1 EW (or WE) 2 NS (or SN) 3 indicates first and last letters of word or element, e.g. 'extremes of exercise' – EE, 'extremely brave' – BE, 'extremists in Kremlin' – KN 4 indicates superlative of adjective or adverb, ending in -EST, e.g. 'extremely nice' – NICEST, 'extremely good' – BEST
Extremely modest way to return to university and do no work! (6) (*Now!*, 24.4.81)

extremity
1 FOOT 2 HAND 3 TOE
A thousand in extremity – well, a good volume, anyway! (4)

eyesore
STYE
Nasty environment – real eyesore there (4)

F

fabulous bird
ROC
Fabulous bird, a department head in bed – dressed in silk, too! (8)

face
DIAL
Note it has round face, this watch, although no hands (7)

fair
FINE
Limit study on fair (7)

fair bit of
indicates word or element minus one or two letters, usually the last, e.g. 'fair bit of hugging' – EMBRA
Fair bit of noise among workers, so pours oil on (7)

fairy
PERI ('a Persian fairy', according to *Chambers*)
Takeover threat by the Chinese? The cowardly fairy left (3, 6, 5) (*Obs.*, 12.7.81)

fall sideways
= reversal (in across clue), e.g. 'horse falls sideways' – GAN (i.e. reversal of NAG)
Cat falls sideways, having itches. What are its plans? (7)

famous person
NAME
Famous person returned, getting date mixed up, and then sallied forth (8)

farewell
TATA
Turkish warrior gives farewell to the king (5)

Fascist leader
1 DUCE 2 F (i.e. 'leader' of *F*ascist)
Down-graded Communist receives Fascist leader (7)

(-) **fashion**
ALA (i.e. à la = 'in the manner of')
Marine-fashion call to arms (5)

fashionable, the fashion
IN
Fashionable bird points to prisoner (8)

fast
LENT
Fast time nothing! It's slow! (5)

father
1 DAD 2 FR 3 PA 4 POP
Father swallowing bird's bone (5) (*Times*, 11.7.81)

favourite
PET
I'm the favourite to go to America, and I have a real incentive! (7)

FBI types
GMEN
Among Atlantic Treaty leaders top-class FBI types require increase (7) (*Times*, 18.4.81)

feature (of) (**feature in**)
= 'burial', e.g. 'Dodgson girl features in special ice-show' – ALICE (i.e. features in 'spec*ial ice*-show', Dodgson being real name of Lewis Carroll)
Concise – a feature of better sermons (5) (*Obs.*, 1.3.81)

federal agents
GMEN
Federal agents are in a fit – it's just a fabrication! (7)

(the) **fellow**
1 CHAP 2 DON 3 F (i.e. as in abbreviation FRA) 4 HE 5 MAN 6 indicates man's name (see **boy** for most popular names)
Fellow has two articles, one inside the other – but he's uncivilised! (7)

fellows
MEN (or plural of **fellow**, which see)
Notice passes round fellows, to get more fellows to come to tea for a change! (9)

female
1 HEN 2 HER 3 SHE 4 reference to some *female animal*, with most popular being

COW, DAM, DOE, EWE, ROE, SOW
Female and French – and fit to go to bed (5)

feminine
1 F 2 HER 3 SHE
A feminine or backswept frizzy hairstyle (4)

festivities
GALA
Festivities, with count in charge – it's out of this world! (8)

(a) **few**
indicates low Roman numeral, especially V or X or a compound such as IV, XI
A few of the Irish are reluctant (6)

fifty (50)
L
Fifty-one go to head of queue on French back street to get Benedictine (7)

final
1 END 2 indicates end of word or element, e.g. 'final match' – H
I'm going to cup final – aren't I naughty! (3)

find [but compare next entry]
simply an indicator to location of letter, element, etc. needed for answer, e.g. 'I find' indicates I, 'find it' – IT
Find green plant on Greek mountain for Greek girl (8)

find in [but compare previous entry]
= 'burial', e.g. 'Mineral found in Regent's Park' – SPAR (i.e. found in 'Regent'*s Par*k')
Find money in Omar Khayyam (4)

fine
OK
See fine appearance! (4)

finish
1 END 2 indicates last letter of word or element, e.g. 'finish supper' – R
Like an infant not finishing cold food (8) (*Guard.*)

finished
1 ENDED 2 OVER
Started at Land's End, finished in Kent port (5)

firm
CO
Firm has fifty bonds for its associates (10)

(at) **first,** (in the) **first** (place), **firstly**
1 indicates first letter of word or element, e.g. 'Ferdinand the First' – F, 'first of January' – J 2 indicates the element or word that must come first in the answer, e.g. 'Fish caught first. Stick close!' – CLING (i.e. C comes first, before LING, the fish)
Firstly, Satan's prime responsibility is to encourage some little devils (7) (*S. Tel.*, 21.6.81)

first-class
1 A 2 AI
First-class railway is nice and open, too (4)

first lady (First Lady)
1 EVE 2 L (i.e. first letter of *L*ady)
First Lady surrounded by students, all equal (5)

first piece
OPI (i.e. Op. 1)
First piece in long aerobatics display (7)

first rate
AI
It's first rate in the Royal Navy, but you get wet! (4)

(the) **first woman**
EVE
The first woman – right? – to put on weight for a football club (7)

fish
fish are a good source of unusual letter combinations, among the most useful being the following: BASS, CARP, CHAR, COD, DAB, EEL, HAKE, ID(E), LING, RAY, SOLE
Fish rises at slight twitch of a beginner – that's efficient! (9)

fitting
APT
Advertisement fitting skill – and the power to vary one's skills, too (12)

five (5)
V
A 'five' at end of revue for French nude in Champs-Élysées (6)

five hundred (500)
D
Ban the Five Hundred, they're a real gang! (4)

five hundred and one (501)
DI
501 trucks for the couches (6)

five hundred pounds (£500)
DL
Beast took in £500 – it's a real fraud (7)

flag
IRIS
Note flag on hospital, it's quite attractive (7)

Fleet Street area, Fleet Street district
EC
During the day, the Fleet Street area looks pretty rotten (5)

flier
1 ACE 2 indicates reference to *bird*, usually in literal sense (see **bird**)
The 'Seafoam Flier' skims over it (7)

(getting) **floored**
KO
Lout holds note, floored, and prevents us getting in (7)

flower
1 indicates reference to *flower*, among the most popular being: ASTER, CLOVER, ERICA, FLAG, IRIS, LUPIN, MAY, PINK, ROSE, VIOLA 2 indicates reference to *river*, including RIVER itself, i.e. 'flow-er', with most popular being, among others: CAM, DEE, DON, EXE, NILE, OUSE, PO, SEINE, STOUR, TEES, TEST, URE, WEY 3 = anagram
Flower power? (7)

fluorine
F
Fluorine, released from lift, started a fire (3)

fluter
PHIL (i.e. from popular song 'Phil the Fluter's Ball')
Fluter making sweet music in orchestra (12)

flutter
1 BET 2 = anagram
First letter provides flutter – and there are 25 more to complete it! (8)

flying saucer
UFO
Flying saucer goes round Pole to land, remove article, and give display (6)

fold
LAP
Applaud a hundredfold! (4)

follow(ing)
1 DOG 2 F 3 indicates that letter(s) or element comes after what has been clued or given, not before it, e.g. 'prince followed by train' – PRY (i.e. P followed by RY)
Irishman followed by Ronald as a sponsor (6)

fool
ASS
Fools, two of them, and a land of murder (13)

foot
FT
One foot behind (3)

football body
FA
United Nations football body has a right – but this is not right! (6)

footnote
PS
'Abscinds' (see footnote) (4)

for
1 FOR 2 usually indicates that first half of clue (often descriptive) will lead to answer via second half (often indirect or punning), e.g. 'Metal for a pack-animal to run into' – WOLFRAM (i.e. 'Metal', descriptive word, provides answer, *for* which solver must combine 'pack-animal' and 'to run into') 3 = anagram
Medicine for weight (99) (5)

forbid
BAN
Article to forbid university man to give up (7)

force
G (i.e. 'gravity')
A force to imitate with wide-open mouth? (5)

for each
PER
For each change there is variation on a theme (11)

foreign (sort of) **accent**
indicates name of written accent, such as ACUTE, GRAVE or (less often) TREMA
Very sharp salesman turned up, with a foreign sort of accent (8) (*Obs.*, 12.7.81)

foreign(er)
indicates foreign word, usually French, e.g. 'foreign agreement' – SI, 'thanks to foreigners' – MERCI, 'foreign nobleman' – DUC
Foreign word I've put means 'reason' (6)

Foreign Office
FO
Foreign Office to the right and – er – that's the Market Place (5)

for example
1 EG 2 indicates that example of answer required is given in clue, e.g. 'That half-warmed fish, for example' – SPOONERISM (i.e. 'half-warmed fish' is an example of a spoonerism)
Poor people are Grade Two, for example, having an assortment of rags (7)

for instance
1 EG 2 indicates that example of answer required is given in clue (compare **for example**)
Dog guide, for instance (7)

former(ly)
1 EX 2 PAST 3 indicates a former or 'historic' sense, as clued, e.g. 'former king' – GR, 'president formerly' – CARTER
Former operation was accurate (5)

fortissimo
1 DIN 2 FF 3 ROW
Sally by a fortissimo fighter and talismanic character (7)

fortune
LOT
Where Arthur stopped and came to a fortune (7)

forty (40)
XL
One in forty in ease, I hear, in banishment (5)

forty-nine (49, '49)
IL
Dossier for the 49 in Further Education (4)

found
MET
George found a railway using this mathematical system (8)

four (4)
IV
Act Four, I feel, should be rewritten, to give something that's far from boring (6, 4) (*Guard.*)

frame
= 'straddle', e.g. 'we framed her' – WHERE
Lees framed the Poles using these pieces of photographic equipment (6)

(of) **France (in France)**
indicates French word, e.g. 'land of France' – TERRE, 'street of France' – RUE
Calm swim, backstroke, in lake in France (6)

free
1 RID 2 = anagram
Horseman to free the Queen (5)

French
1 FR 2 indicates French word, and particularly the following, which are commonly used: 'of French' – DE, 'of the French' – DU or DES, 'the French' – LE, LA, LES, 'a French' – UN or UNE, 'this French' – CE, e.g. 'Instruction for the French boy' – LESSON (i.e. for 'the French' – LES+'boy' – SON)
Abject misery of the French couple (7)

French girl
MLLE (for 'Mademoiselle')
I got involved with French girl on centre of gliding ground (6)

Frenchman
M (for 'Monsieur')
Frenchman is mixed-up idle fellow. That's something new! (6)

Frenchwoman
MME (for 'Madame')
Confused girl embraces Frenchwoman in the candle-light (7)

French writer
usually turns out to be GIDE, but also occasionally DUMAS or SAGAN
Turgid essay reveals the French writer (4)

Friday
FRI
Friday goes on for ever, and I'm alone in the world (10)

friend
1 ALLY 2 MATE 3 PAL
Friend in Rome holding diamond could be Anna, for example (10)

from
1 indicates removal of letter(s) or element, e.g. 'remove pupil from class' – CASS (i.e. remove L from CLASS) 2 often indicates 'burial', e.g. 'Provided letters from a poet' – OVID (*Guard.*) (i.e. from 'provided') 3 = anagram
To get the bird, extract redhead from cattle-herd (4)

from east to west
= reversal (in across clue), e.g. 'Boat travels from east to west strait' – GUT (i.e. reversal of TUG)
Star goes from east to west? Rubbish! (4)

from either end
= palindrome, e.g. 'Equal from either end' – LEVEL
Erected from either end (3, 2) (*Guard.*)

from the sound of it
= homophone, e.g. 'heavy, from the sound of it' – WAIT
End of European race, from the sound of it (6)

front (of)
indicates first letter of element or word, e.g. 'front of house' – H, 'front tooth' – T
Front beds are quite empty (4)

frost (Frost)
RIME
Violation of law about frost (5)

fruit
among popular ones are: CLOVE, DATE, LIME, NUT, PEAR
Source of rejected mixed fruit (5)

funny
1 RUM 2 = anagram
Note funny soft bit (5)

fuss
ADO
Fuss for the navy men, the first overall dressing (9)

G

gallery
TATE
Condition of south gallery (5)

Gallic see **French**

game
often turns out to be CHESS
Pane broken during game – a sign of how little it cost (9)

game body
FA (i.e. Football Association)
Game body of learners on double bend collapses (5)

(a) **garden**
EDEN
Prior article found by detective next to garden before tea (10)

gather (round)
1 = 'straddle', e.g. 'we gather round Henry'

– WHALE (i.e. WE gather round HAL) 2 = anagram
Bands gather round it – they're robbers, too! (7)

gee
G
Gee, I'm allowed to have half a glass of gin and lime! (6)

general
1 GEN 2 LEE (i.e. American General Robert E. Lee)
Mixture of snow and rain is general, in a way (5)

George (the writer)
1 GEO 2 usually turns out to be SAND (i.e. George Sand, the French writer whose real name was Amandine Dudevant)
Quick, George, it's treacherous (4)

Georgia
GA
Yacht race is exciting treat in Georgia (7)

German
indicates German word, especially one of the following: 'the German' – DER, DIE or DAS, 'a German' – EIN or EINE, also common words and names such as: 'German boy' – HANS, 'German gent' – HERR, 'German' – OTTO
Young people gather round the German pals (7)

get
1 usually indicates that letter(s), element or word join another, i.e. 'get' it, e.g. 'We get Eddie, a worthless fellow' – WEED (i.e. WE get ED) 2 = anagram
I'm getting it to eat, funnily – you do the same (7)

get in
= 'burial', e.g. 'Scarcely able to get in street' – SCANT (i.e. CAN get in ST)
Church singer somehow not getting in car (6)

get round
= 'straddle', e.g. 'Mechanical monster gets round ill-gotten gain' – ORGANIC (i.e. ORC gets round GANI which is 'ill-gotten' GAIN, with one meaning of ORGANIC being 'mechanical')
Rodney gets round middleman – and gets his way! (4)

giant
TITAN
Giant is muddled – he is the first person saying there are no gods (10)

gin
1 TRAP 2 when preceded by 'mixed', 'spilt', etc., or followed by 'sling', 'cocktail', etc., equals ING, e.g. 'Whistling, Pip has mixed gin' – PIPING (i.e. PIP has mixed GIN)
Sir Robert's back with gin cocktail, and he's oblivious to the world! (8)

ginger (Ginger)
RED
Was anxious about Ginger (5)

gipsy (fellow)
1 CHI (Romany word for 'person', actually feminine) 2 NOMAD
Gipsy points to ravine (5)

girl
1 BELLE 2 CHIT 3 GAL 4 HER 5 LASS 6 MISS 7 SHE 8 indicates a girl's name, among the most popular being: ADA, AMY, ANN, ANNA, BET, CON, DEB, DI, DORA, DOT, ENA, EVA, ETTA, FAY, FLO, IDA, IRA, IRIS, ISA, KIM, MAY, MEG, NAN, PAT, PEG, RITA, SAL, SARA, UNA, VAL, VIV
Master takes girl pupil in marriage (7) (*Guard.*)

give (him, etc.)
1 indicates element or word to be added to another, e.g. 'give Russian a hoe' – IVANHOE 2 = anagram
Give artist a basin for the plant (6)

give(n) permission
LET
I came in to give permission for the dressing (6)

give over
= reversal, e.g. 'Jug we give over to eastern

king' – EWER (i.e. WE give over to E+R)
Give over, lad – 'e's a part of t'scenery in t'North! (5)

Glasgow see **Scottish**

glasses
OO
Lord Provost in glasses on his circuit (4)

globe
O
Cricketer goes round the globe – presumably on this? (4)

glove
MITT
Sent back glove packed in grass (8)

go (to)
indicates letter(s), element or word to join another, or 'go' to it, e.g. 'Student goes to vessel to get bird' – LARK (i.e. L goes to ARK)
Father goes to tent to get certificate (6)

god (God)
1 BAAL 2 LAR 3 PAN 4 THOR
Theft of 'God and the Church of England' (New York) (7)

go(ing) north
= reversal (in down clue), e.g. 'Sid goes north with a map, getting dismissal' – DISCARD (i.e. reversal of SID+CARD)
Mat's going north for the day to this Lincolnshire town (8)

go into
1 = burial, e.g. 'Old boy goes into house – he's a tramp' – HOBO (i.e. OB goes into HO) 2 = anagram
Ball goes into road – maybe this drunk was responsible? (3)

gold
1 AU (Latin *aurum*) 2 OR (heraldic term, as well as French for 'gold')
Gold piece goes round (5)

good
PI
A small number after a good instrument (5) (*S.T.*, 5.4.81)

Goodfellow (good fellow)
ST
Be a good fellow: give the utmost (4)

good man, good person
ST
The good man, a boy at heart, quietly comes to a halt (4)

good queen
BESS (i.e. Good Queen Bess, the nickname of Queen Elizabeth I)
Good queen has a horse, excellent to back, in the old country (10)

go outside
= 'straddle', e.g. 'Holy man goes outside hut with hesitation – to put this up?' – SHUTTER (i.e. ST goes outside HUT with ER)
Men go outside to help a girl (6)

go round
1 = 'straddle' (same as **go outside**, which see) 2 = reversal, e.g. 'May go round to get fruit' – YAM
Mr Crosby goes round the end, bowing (7)

go up
= reversal, in down clue, e.g. 'Tam goes up to get rug' – MAT
Roy goes up to the king in northern city (4)

governor
often indicates name of *leader*, such as head of state, president, prime minister, etc., e.g. CARTER, HEATH, SADAT
Governor returns with a table that can be drawn up towards the body (11)

go west
1 = reversal (in across clue), e.g. 'Sal goes west, therefore, to get a rope for the horses' – LASSO (i.e. SAL goes west SO) 2 = anagram
Boy goes west to meet girl who lost a dollar in this Texan town (6)

grab
= 'straddle', e.g. 'He grabs fish in place of concealment' – HIDE (i.e. HE grabs ID)
Happy Jo's grabbing you! (6)

graduate
1 BA 2 MA
Graduate has a wry grin, coming to the edge (6)

grand
G (i.e. 'grand' in sense of 'a thousand dollars')
Grand lad is bright and cheerful (4)

grasp
= 'straddle', e.g. 'I'm grasping Lawrence, for one thing' – ITEM (i.e. IM grasping TE)
Cricketer grasps the ball – that's a smack! (4)

grass
REED
Girl in grass given a feast (7)

grass land
1 LAY 2 LEA 3 LEY
Ban on grass land for this crop (6)

gratitude
TA
Welshman expresses gratitude very loudly at end of play (5)

grave inscription
RIP
Grave inscription on N. Yorks town (5)

gravity
G
Single person displays longer lack of gravity (5)

great
GT
Great run-in causes low throaty noise (5)

great man
HERO
Great man in bed produces cigar! (7)

Great North Road
AI
Great North Road leads to noted Yorkshire valley – could be a real bitch! (8)

great number
indicates high Roman number, e.g. C, D, L or M
A great number found love and then separated (5)

Greek letter, Greek character
most popular are the short names of letters of the Greek alphabet, especially ETA, MU, NU, PI, PHI and CHI
In the past, this Greek character was a supporter of the pope (6)

green (Green)
VERT (not so much the French word as the heraldic colour)
For all to see, making love on green (5)

grip
= 'straddle', e.g. 'He grips disc implement' – HOE (i.e. HE grips O)
Friendly kid grips pole (4)

g-string
GUT
Novice in g-string – that's rather too much of a good thing! (4)

gun
GAT (i.e. the Gatling machine-gun)
Game beauty, holding a gun (9) (*Times*, 4.7.81)

gunner(s)
RA
Fanatic gunners make an offer (5)

Gwynne
NELL
Prudence and Gwynne with a strong fabric (8)

gypsy see **gipsy**

hail
1 AHOY 2 AVE 3 HI
Hail! The king is coming here! (6)

half (of) **(half a)**
indicates exactly half a word or element, e.g. 'half London' – LON, 'in half' – N, 'half each' – EA, 'better half' – BET or TER
No half-term report! (4)

half a dozen
VI
Half a dozen cars close to the church (6)

half-day
indicates half the name of a day of the week, e.g. SUN, MON or FRI
A half-day can be continental (7)

half (a) **score**
1 TEN 2 X
Occupies half a score workers (7)

Hampshire town (Hants town)
LISS
Bachelor goes to Hants town – it's like paradise! (5)

harbour
= 'straddle', e.g. 'we harbour nothing' – WOE (i.e. WE harbour O)
Soldier harbours boy on a hill – Roman soldier, that is (9)

hard
1 H 2 = anagram
Guard hard edge (5)

Hardy heroine
TESS (i.e. the heroine of Thomas Hardy's *Tess of the d'Urbervilles*)
Hardy heroine stands astride almost empty river – perhaps she will bring it to the Test? (9)

harker (Harker)
EAR
Reginald Harker is to put in harness again (6)

Harry
TATE (i.e. Harry Tate, the English music-hall comedian, whose real name was Ronald Hutchinson)
Wave the silver one, Harry! (7)

has
1 indicates that letter, element or word joins another, i.e. 'has' another, e.g. 'Jack has donkey' – JACKASS 2 = 'burial', e.g. 'Mrs Whitehouse has a winner' – HIT ('W*hit*ehouse')
Victor has debts – that's bad (7)

hat
1 LID 2 TILE
So, hat is quite strong (5)

have
1 indicates that letters, element or word join another, i.e. 'have' another 2 = 'burial' (for examples of both these, see **has**)
Writers have one on old age benefit (7)

he
1 MAN 2 indicates boy's name (see **boy**)
He is in Red House, where bad boys stay (6, 4)

H.E.
TNT
Shelter for H.E. round bottom of mine (4)

head
1 C (i.e. 'capital C') 2 NESS 3 TOP 4 indicates title of head person of some kind, e.g. MASTER 5 indicates first letter of word or element, e.g. 'university head' – U, 'head girl' – G, 'egghead' – E, 'Hindhead' – H 6 indicates that letter, element or word precedes another, i.e. 'heads' it, e.g. 'we headed large number' – WED (i.e. WE headed D)
E is for Intellectual! (7) (*Times*, 18.7.81)

head away
indicates word or element with first letter missing, e.g. 'head away nomads' – OVERS (i.e. ROVERS with R missing)
Pickets head away cyclists (7) [word not in most dictionaries but easily deducible]

head chopped off
indicates word or element with first letter missing, as for **head away** (which see)
Head chopped off flower further down (5)

headless
indicates word or element with first letter missing, as for **head away** (which see)
Headless corpse is battered – it's a real mystery (5)

head of
indicates first letter of word or element, e.g. 'head of department' – D

Sam goes to head of police with the French specimen (6)

head office
HO
Head office uses these buildings (6)

head over heels
= reversal, in down clue, e.g. 'Delia was unwell, having fallen head over heels' – AILED
Tom tumbled head over heels and went to her – after all, she *is* a boy's best friend! (6)

head to tail
indicates that first letter of word or element is placed at end, e.g. 'cat turns head to tail' – ATC
Bud and I head to tail in beer, as good speakers should be (7) (*Obs.*, 15.2.81)

hear(d), (from what one) **hears**
= homophone, e.g. 'Direct channel, I hear' – STRAIGHT (homophone of STRAIT)
Mangle heard in the belfry (7) (*Guard.*)

hearing aid
EAR
Be wary of loud hearing aid! (4)

heart
indicates centre of element or word, e.g. 'Heart of Midlothian' – OT, 'heart of the matter' – TT, 'boy at heart' – O, 'heart of Texas' – X
Cop in heart of Florida has a big haul (4)

hearten
indicates that letter(s) should follow centre of word or element, e.g. 'Country boy heartened by first nest' – LAND (i.e. LAD heartened by first letter of NEST)
Black man, heartened with tea, has plenty of drive (5)

heartless
indicates that centre letter(s) of word or element must be removed, e.g. 'heartless foe' – FE
Editor, the heartless guy, is irritable (4)

Heath
TED (rather the prime minister Edward Heath than the band leader Ted Heath!)
Point Heath noticed (7)

heath(er) (Heather)
1 ERICA 2 LING
Stick close about Heather (5)

heat source (source of) **heat**
SUN
Avoid heat source in hospital (4)

heavyweight
TON
Heavyweight forces needed for this gripping and lifting instrument (5)

height
H(T)
Glide-round at height gives great pleasure (7)

held (in)
= 'burial', e.g. 'Article held in bed is a little ball' – BEAD (i.e. A held in BED)
Examination held by me to get sense of discipline (6)

Helen
NELL
On the stroke of a bell, the king came to Helen (5)

hell(ish)
DIS (a name for Pluto, and thus the Underworld, in classical mythology)
Hellish company in this music and dance club (5)

help
AID
Amateur help is applied (4)

help(s) to make
= 'burial', e.g. 'Girl helps to make lapis lazuli' – ISLA (i.e. 'lap*is la*zuli)
Dancing girl's performance helps to make astronaut cheerful (6) (*Guard.*)

Henry
HAL
A fish for Henry I, on the other hand (7)

her see **girl, she**

Herbert
1 APH (i.e. A. P. Herbert, the English journalist and writer) 2 LOM (i.e. Herbert Lom, the Czech film actor)
Record it, Herbert – the words will remind us of him (7)

here
often indicates 'burial', e.g. 'Sat in a glen here, what a thrill!' – TINGLE ('sa*t in gle*n')
Found all a senator's letters here in Texas (6)

Hertfordshire town (Herts town)
1 TRING 2 WARE
Note sent to South Herts town – it covers the bare essentials! (1-6)

(with) **hesitation, hesitantly**
1 ER 2 UM
From the starting point, child hesitantly goes to the top! (8)

he would
HED
Eat up, he would, when pressed (6)

hide, hidden
= 'straddle' or 'burial', e.g. 'abstainer hides a king' – TART (i.e. TT hides AR) or 'a king hidden by abstainer' – TART (i.e. AR hidden by TT)
Celebrity hides in Latin America (4)

(good) **hiding**
TAN
Charles loses points, and gets a good hiding, being a false pretender (9)

high class
U (see **classy**)
Artist got in high-class, highly seasoned stew (6)

high explosive
HE
The proposal is: put high explosive in hill, then bring me back (7)

high priest
ELI (i.e. in the Bible, the high priest who brought up the prophet Samuel)
High priest surrounded by strong smell – it must be gas! (6)

high tension
HT
Set up high tension? Correct! (5)

highway
1 RD 2 ST
To live on the highway is most satisfactory! (4)

hill
TOR
The tale of a hill in Surrey (5)

hill dweller
ANT
From half-plot hill dweller to full-root earth dweller! (5)

him see **he**

hint
1 CUE 2 TIP
Hairdresser almost gets hint that there is to be an outdoor party (8)

(on) **hire, hired**
LET
Amateur actor hired for village (6)

His Excellency
1 BATES (i.e. H. E. Bates, the English author) 2 HE
His Excellency is in a pet – it's a fraud! (5)

hit
1 LAM 2 RAP 3 SLAP
Officer hit in half an hour – what an outcry! (7)

hold
= 'burial', e.g. 'Song holds key for woman' – LADY (i.e. LAY holds D)
Men hold a fish for the girl (6)

hold up
= reversed 'burial', in down clue, e.g. 'Railway holds up beer' – RELAY (i.e. RY holds ALE reversed)
Beam of light holds up the French race (5)

hole
O
Hole in bat? Better than hole in this! (4)

holy man
ST
It's a strain, having a holy man about the ship (6) (*Obs.*, 19.7.81)

Holy Writ
1 NT 2 OT
Humbug about Holy Writ (4)

home
1 IN 2 PAD
Team member sends thanks home to team leader (7)

Home Guard
HG
Home Guard, surrounding article, are undecided (4)

honour
indicates **decoration** (which see, for most popular)
Honour your leader, and do this, too! (4)

horrific
H (referring to former 'H' category of horror films)
Horrific change in the hanging rope (6)

horse
1 COB 2 GEE 3 GG 4 NAG
Horsecloth – although not for horses, even when produced by spinners! (6)

horseplay
RAG
Horseplay over a TV horse (of a sort) – a disreputable fellow (10)

hospital
H
Negative terminal at hospital, in disguised form (7) (*Obs.*, 19.7.81)

hot
H
Is this where hot love comes to me? (4)

hot and cold
HC
Team game is hot and cold – nothing between them – on this scale (6)

hotel
INN
Third-class hotel has a bar – you can get a mineral there, too (8)

hour
1 H 2 HR
Hour One: 'Sharp on Smooth' (4)

house
HO
House in London district covers a good number of feet (4)

howler
usually a reference to a dog or to something that *howls*, e.g. wolf or a baby
Sat between Alfred and Ian – what a howler! (8)

huff
PET
Learner in huff having to speed (4)

hug
= 'straddle', e.g. 'Chet hugs fabulous bird – that's a real knit!' – CROCHET (i.e. CHET hugs ROC)
Where one girl hugs another (6) (*S.T.*, 28.6.81)

huge
OS
Bird has huge victim (6)

humble
BASE
Humble rank at the end of the court (4, 4)

humorist
WIT
Humorist and her decline (6)

humour
WIT
Holy man has humour in his northern, twisted way:
'My power's in my reins', he quipped, 'for more than just one day!' (7)

(a) **hundred (100)**
1 C 2 TON
A hundred at the Pole – sound like 'chin chillers'! (4)

hungry
indicates word or element containing O (i.e. nothing), e.g. 'Hungry man has cause to do this' – MOAN (i.e. MAN containing O)
Hungry cat could need a thicker one (4)

huntress
DI (i.e. Diana, the famous huntress in classical mythology)
Can huntress have a boy-friend? She is prepared to have a try! (9)

Hunts
MEETS
Navy man after his ship in Hunts. Could he be wearing one of these? (4, 7)

hurried
RAN
Arthur hurried to get some (7)

hurry
HIE
After tea, hurry to get fellows' leader – he's a burglar! (5)

husband
1 MAN 2 MATE 3 SAVE
Warrant officer with her husband – only she can have one! (5)

hush
SH
'Hush! Out!' is the cry (5)

hydrant
H
Hydrant in Wales can send up columns of water! (6)

hydrogen
H
Much obliged for hydrogen in containers (6)

hypocrisy, hypocritical stuff
CANT
Noisy, hypocritical stuff about strike (7) (*Obs.*, 19.7.81)

I

I
1 I 2 ONE 3 points to the word(s) forming the answer, this often being the completion of a well-known saying or proverb, e.g. 'I took turns with Box' – COX
I am in a love part, being a bird (6) (*S.T.*, 19.7.81)

I am
IM
Meaning I am left with? (6)

Ian
1 IAN 2 indicates Scots word or name, e.g. 'Ian, man . . .' – MON
Schoolboy sends note back to Ian (7)

I'd
ID
While waiting, I'd got in Mr Crosby (6)

if (with)
1 AN (the old word for 'if' found, for example, in Shakespeare) 2 = if indicated letter, element or word is added, a different (longer) word is formed, e.g. 'If guy gets gal, we have a charge' – MAN (i.e. if MAN gets DATE we have MANDATE)
Wild fear, if one's taken in by copper (5)

if not
OR
Circling, if not gripping with the teeth (8)

I had
ID
Objectives I had with jumble sale (6)

I have
IVE
The others I have are impatient (7)

Illinois
ILL
Illinois in Surrey? That's stupid! (5)

I'll say
ISLE
Doctor came round, I'll say, and made inaccurate diagnosis (6)

illuminated
LIT
Illuminated some part of the prayer book (6)

I'm
IM (but see also **I**)
I'm ashen-faced having to put body on stake (6)

imitate
APE
'Page to imitate the king' – headline in this? (5)

impertinence
LIP
Such loud impertinence is over-smart (4)

imprison
= 'straddle', e.g. 'Sees ten imprisoned men and women' – SEXES (i.e. SEES X imprisoned)
Judge imprisons evil leader with reluctance – maybe possession of this caused the sentence? (6)

impudent talk
LIP
Obliterate censored word of second-rate impudent talk (4)

in(to)
1 IN 2 = 'burial', e.g. 'A spell in the French army' – CHARM (i.e. in 'Fren*ch army*') 3 = anagram
Backward in composition, and in severe trouble (5) (*Obs.*, 19.7.81)

in addition
AND
Set down learner driver, in addition (4)

in advance
ON
Allowance made in advance in Devon (8)

in a vessel
indicates letters, element or word to be inserted in S . . . S, e.g. 'These birds are pale in a vessel' – SWANS (i.e. are WAN in S . . . S)
Found on the shore and in a vessel (5)

in a way
1 indicates letter(s), element or word to be inserted in S . . . T, e.g. 'Scarcely sufficient tin, in a way' – SCANT (i.e. CAN in S . . . T) 2 often indicates outrageous pun, with clue frequently ending in exclamation mark, e.g. 'Vessel of delight, in a way!' – PLEASURE BOAT 3 = anagram
In the forefront of domestic heating recession, in a way! (5) (*S. Tel.*, 26.4.81)

in both directions
= palindrome, e.g. 'Little dog runs in both directions' – PUP
The language of Malabar is written in both directions (9)

in charge
IC
Man in charge is afflicted by mental illness (5)

include
= 'straddle' or 'burial', depending how clue is worded, e.g. 'Holy man includes company' – SCOT (i.e. ST includes CO) or 'Scot includes company' – CO (i.e. 'S*co*t' includes CO)
Scouts' camp invariably includes a dish of sea-food (6) (*Obs.*, 2.8.81)

in connection with
RE
Come round again in connection with dog (5)

incorporated
1 INC 2 = 'burial', e.g. 'Snake incorporated in Christmas party' – ASP
Royal consort incorporated in press (8)

indeed
includes letter(s), element or word to be inserted in DE . . . ED
Committed indeed to be sent as an agent (7) (*S.T.*, 22.3.81)

(an) **indefinite number**
N
Aborigines – an indefinite number at four points (7)

indisposed
ILL
Doctor indisposed after mixed gin? That's boring! (8)

in favour (of)
PRO
In favour of the test (5)

infiltrate
= 'burial', e.g. 'Great number infiltrated pits, perhaps they were the ancient Scots' – PICTS (i.e. C infiltrated PITS)
Engineers infiltrate river – they're the very best (5)

information
1 GEN 2 INF(O) 3 NEWS
Get information in at . . . But he will know! (5)

in France see **French**

in Germany see **German**

in good condition
FIT
Suit of clothes abroad and in good condition (6)

ingredient (of)
1 = 'burial', e.g. 'Egg is ingredient of tart – could mean a fortune' – TAROT (i.e. O is ingredient of TART) 2 (ingredients) = anagram
One third of an eclair is ingredient of pie. Like a bit? (5)

in grip of
= 'burial', e.g. 'King in grip of band – that's a mark of infamy' – BRAND (i.e. R in grip of BAND)
In charge of learner in grip of ice – cool and to the point! (6)

in Italy see **Italian**

initial(ly)
indicates first letter(s) of word(s), e.g. 'the initial' – T, 'Song used in *La Traviata* initially used by cowboys' (*Guard.*) – LARIAT (i.e. ARIA in initials of *La Traviata*)
Evangelical Alliance initially came to Kent to give freedom from pain and rest from work (4)

inlaid
= 'burial', e.g. 'red and inlaid with silver' – RAGED (i.e. RED inlaid with AG)
Sets of armour inlaid with gold for wooers! (7)

inn
PUB
Silence in the inn, everyone – here's a game for you! (8)

in operation
ON
Uprush of liquid in operation for man in operation! (7)

in order
1 OK 2 = anagram
Corner on reversing in order (4)

in part
= 'burial', e.g. 'Mountain range in part of Nubian Desert' – ANDES (i.e. in part of 'Nubi*an Des*ert')
On the seashore in part of Hants and Sussex (5)

in respect of
BY
Sailor to return in respect of infant (4)

in Rome see **Roman**

insect
among the most common are: ANT, BEE, BUG, FLEA, GNAT, MOTH, NIT, TICK
Scottish insect not commonly found (5)

in short
indicates an abbreviation, usually a standard one, e.g. '"Treasure Island's" author, in short' – RLS
Port authority, in short, doesn't get equipment (5)

inside
= 'burial', e.g. 'Nothing inside flat for carnival vehicle' – FLOAT (i.e. O inside FLAT)
Left inside with no clothes on? Roar! (5)

insolence
LIP
Cold insolence deserves this over the ear (4)

in Spain see **Spanish**

intelligence
NOUS
Uri, when bending, has intelligence, but the result is disastrous! (7)

intelligence department
MIV
Intelligence department get their strength back! (3)

intend to
AIM
150 intend to make a demand (5)

interior
indicates centre of word, usually whole word minus first and last letters, e.g. 'interior of casket' – ASKE, 'house interior' – OUS
Repair French mill's interior with an eastern shrub (9)

international organisation, international agency
UN(O)
Part of speech that needs no international organisation! (4)

interrupt
= 'burial', e.g. 'we interrupt set' – SWEET
Sid, embarrassed, interrupts meal – a wrong way to set about things! (7)

in the main see **main**

in the morning
indicates letter(s), element or word in A . . . M, e.g. 'in the morning, student . . .' – ALM
In the morning, lawyer comes to worker, and he's insistent (7)

in the place of
FOR
Former head of country in the place of department head (4)

in the way of
ALA
Page in the way of the establishment at royal residence! (6)

in this place
HERE
Stick advertisement in this place (6)

in this way
SO
In this way clergyman comes to quarters – wet through! (6)

into a mess, into a muddle [etc.]
indicates anagram of -ATION, e.g. 'Set street into a mess' – STATION
The Spanish get into a muddle, resulting in high spirits! (7)

introduce
= 'burial', e.g. 'Introduce Mr Jolson to me, man!' – MALE (i.e. AL introduced to ME)
Introduce First Lady to James the Fair (5)

introduction (to)
indicates first letter(s) of element(s) or word(s), e.g. 'Scholar has introduction to Rudyard Kipling, getting "The Cry of the Wolf"' – BARK (i.e. BA has introduction to RK)
Tom has introduction to Eric, the bookmaker (4)

intrusion
= 'burial', e.g. 'With an intrusion, be a cause of evil' – BANE (i.e. intrusion of AN in BE)
With her intrusion, small creatures become little angels (7) (*S.T.*, 7.12.80)

invert, inversion
= reversal, in down clue, e.g. 'Invert top, put on can – now it's drinkable!' – POTABLE
One gent has inverted hat on – how industrious! (8)

involved (in)
1 = 'burial', e.g. 'he's involved in Social Democratic alliance' – SHED (i.e. HE is involved in SD) 2 = anagram
Apprentice involved in fight – this was the best way to escape! (6)

Ireland
1 EIRE 2 ERIN
Supporter in Ireland giving sidelong look (7)

Irish
1 ERSE 2 indicates Irish word or name, e.g. 'Irish boy' – PAT (or BROTH)
Clergyman, Irish – that's back to front! (7)

Irish hill
TARA (a hill in County Meath, the ancient religious, political and cultural capital of Ireland)
Befuddled Nat, 'twixt Irish hills,
A trumpet hears – a sound that thrills! (11)

Irishman
PAT
Irishman in a film (6)

iron
FE (Latin *ferrum*)
Iron discipline – and a cane to enforce it! (6)

is
IS
'The South' is the subject of my dissertation (6)

I shall
ILL
I shall enter this side of the stage, if agreeable (7)

island, isle
some short popular ones are: ARAN, DOGS, ELY, IONA, MAN, RUM
An island and a rocky boat – what a place to be in! (8)

island retreat
ABLE (i.e. reversal of ELBA)
Way island retreat is established (6)

issue
1 CHILD 2 SON
Justification concerning one issue (6)

it
IT
Please bring us back to it! (4)

Italian
1 I 2 = Italian word or name; among common clue elements are: 'the Italian' – IL, 'Italian flower' – PO, 'Italian leader' – DUCE
The Italian boy's first – that's easy (4)

Italian chief = **Italian leader** (see **Italian**)

item
LOT
Item No. 1 is back – it's a liquid preparation for the skin (6)

it seems see **apparently**

it's said
1 usually indicates a reference to key word or phrase in a proverb, e.g. 'They die many times before their deaths, it's said' – COWARDS 2 = homophone, e.g. 'Jerry at tiller, so it's said' (*Guard.*) – THE HUN (i.e. 'at tiller' is said as 'Attila')
Stronger than nature, it's said (7)

I've
IVE
I've got in the doctor for him – he's often very low! (5)

I will
ILL
The odds are on I will have a fall! (5)

I would
ID
Arena I would enter for cycling (6)

J

Jack
reference to naval word or term, especially AB and TAR
To one side of Jack is a piece of timber (5)

Japan (perhaps)
E (i.e. 'east')
Ban in Japan for this vegetable? (4)

jay (Jay)
J
Jay is sick when kept in these places of captivity (5)

jerk
1 TIC 2 = anagram
Account of half roll, half back jerks, makes impressive gymnastic display (10)

jet
MIG
Jet speeds and goes overseas (8)

jockey
LESTER (i.e. the English jockey, Lester Piggott)
Medical man comes to jockey, a trouble-maker (8)

jog
TROT
Jog by a revolutionary riot along the French pavement (8)

John
BULL
John, why is he such a cruel person? (5)

join [see also next entry]
ADD
Fish join in the drink! (7)

join(ing) [see also previous entry]
indicates combination of two words or elements to form the answer, e.g. 'Tom joins a bird – what a killer!' – TOMAHAWK
Cup-bearers have the cheek to join the Royal Society (7)

jolly good
AI
Terrier is jolly good about the valley (8)

Jolson
AL (i.e. Al Jolson, the American singer and film actor)
Bring a drink to Mr Jolson in the main entrance! (6)

Jonson
BEN (i.e. Ben Jonson, the English poet)
Jonson has one son, a real source of joy (7)

Josephine
JO
Reply about Josephine and the At Home (6)

journal
MAG
Fancy, a journal in Japan! (7)

journalist
ED
Not the journalist that wrote the report (5)

jug
EWER
Holy jug or wholly pot! (6)

junction
T
Junction needs oil to work (4)

junior
1 JR 2 SON
Junior has one in a pot (3)

K

Kay
K
Kay in her family circle (3)

keep
often indicates a short verb to which ON is added, e.g. 'keep pestering' – NAGON, 'keep eating' – EATON, 'keep pulling' – DRAGON
Keep moving, stupid! (4)

keep quiet
SH
Over-hasty gunners keep quiet (4)

Kent
SE
Drive off car in Kent (5)

key see **note**

kill
END
Modishly original in attempt to kill (6)

killer
GUN
Killer comes to king, result is a sticky end! (4)

king
1 E (i.e. Edward) 2 G (i.e. George) 3 K 4 LEAR 5 R

King Edward is a man who favours sweeping changes (3)

King George
GR
Seize King George and the snake (5)

Kingsley
AMIS (i.e. Kingsley Amis, the English novelist)
Kingsley South? That's wrong! (5)

King's Square (king's square)
KI (i.e. K1, the chess notation for the King's square)
Poles in King's Square presumably have a white one? (4)

kiss
X
Love and a kiss for Diana cut short by this university scholar! (9)

knight (Knight)
1 KT 2 SIR
Very much wanted to be a knight. Indeed! (7) (*S. Tel.*, 19.7.81)

knock back
= reversal, e.g. 'Knock back a beer, Ted – that'll make you feel exhilarated!' – ELATED (i.e. ALE knocked back + TED)
Knock back two rums and you could have the symptom of a dicky heart (6)

knockout
KO
This drink is a knockout back in the establishment! (4)

L

label
1 TAB 2 TAG
Label on the French picture (5)

laboratory
LAB
Docket shows that laboratory is L-shaped (5)

lack(ing)
indicates letter(s), element or word removed, usually from previous word group, e.g. 'not rich, lacking love' – POR (i.e. POOR lacking O), 'A bad mark for the errant magistrate lacking a rebuke' – STIGMA (i.e. anagram of MAGISTRATE minus RATE)
Rail for back door lacking nothing (3)

ladder
RUN
To harden, I get a ladder up the top of Everest (5) (*Obs.*, 9.8.81)

lady
1 HER 2 SHE 3 MIS+homophone indicator, such as 'I'd say', 'we hear', e.g. 'Bit of a blow for Lady Luck, we'd say' (*Times*, 4.7.81)– MISCHANCE 4 indicates a girl's name (see **girl** for the most popular)
The lady's a goddess (4)

lake
L
Softly circle round the lake,
You will thus still water make! (4)

Lancashire town (Lancs town)
1 BURY 2 LEIGH 3 WIGAN
Ride to Lancs town, then to Kent one (10)

large
OS
The Queen turns round twice before the multitude on the large screen (7)

largely
indicates that element or word is (usually) minus its last letter, e.g. 'core largely contains soft . . .' – COPR (i.e. COR contains P)
Sweet largely takes soft range (5)

large number
indicates high Roman number, usually one of C, D, L or M
Points to a large number of monkeys (5)

last
usually indicates that letter(s), element or word come last, e.g. 'at last' – word ending in -AT, 'last one' – word ending in -ONE
Split U.N. atom in last large quantity (8)

last letter
Z
Last letter sent to the Queen 'with love' means nothing (4)

last letters
RIP
Note the last letters – they really hold your attention (4)

last word
AMEN
Foretell the last word in this condition (11)

late
1 D 2 EX
Disinter the late cardinal (6)

late monarch
ANNE (a reference to the expression 'Queen Anne's dead', meaning 'That is old news')
Late monarch buried in the lines when this military flag flies (6)

lawful
LICIT
The child is lawful, that's understood (8)

lawgiver
SOLON (i.e. the Athenian lawgiver, one of the so called Seven Wise Men of Greece)
Lawgiver gets note. It says 'Goodbye for now' (2, 4)

Lawrence
1 DH (i.e. D. H. Lawrence, the English novelist and short story writer) 2 TE (i.e. 'Lawrence of Arabia', the British archeologist, soldier and writer)
Lawrence is into jazz – it's really hot! (7)

lawsuit
CASE
Run after head of house in lawsuit (5)

lawyer
DA
Lady lawyer visits me (4)

layer
HEN
Rock layer, for example, goes back to this famous megalithic complex (10)

lead
PB (Latin *plumbum*)
Herbert in first-class lead, having self-possession (6)

leader
1 CO 2 KING 3 PM 4 indicates first letter of word (or element), e.g. 'class leader' – C, 'UN leader' – U, 'ringleader' – R, 'the leader' – T
'Famous orchestra leader disappears', the notes declare (6)

leaderless
indicates loss of first letter of word (or element), e.g. 'leaderless men' – EN
Leaderless crowd come to end of rally – they're very noisy (5)

leading light
STAR
Leading light approaches king,
And so you see a naked thing (5)

leaf
P (i.e. page)
Leaf on tree and French fringe (6)

learned person
1 BA 2 MA
Learned person and apprentice boy get together in a song (6)

learner
L
Striking weakness about a learner (8) (*S.T.*, 19.7.81)

learning
1 LORE 2 SC (i.e. 'Science', as in BSc)
Learning about Busoni variation – it's slower than Mach one (8)

leave [see also next entry]
1 GO 2 QUIT 3 = 'burial', with answer 'leaving' the clue, e.g. 'Bird leaves the nest and flies to an upside-down shrub yielding red pigment' – HENNA (i.e. HEN leaves '*the n*est' and flies to AN upside-down) 4 indicates that letter(s) or an element are to 'leave' a word, e.g. 'Had left the best knight for a festive occasion' (*Font.*) – GALA (i.e. HAD left GALAHAD)

One I leave in New York is responsible for crime (8) (*S.T.*, 18.1.81)

leave out [see also previous entry]
= **leave** 4, i.e. letter(s) or element to 'leave' a word or phrase
Friend leaves out the king, the devil! (5)

left [see also **leave** and **leave out**]
1 L 2 PORT (often clued as 'left on board' or 'left at sea')
Left at it, so due for allowance (8)

left and right
= palindrome, e.g. 'River runs left and right' – EXE
Turn for information, left and right (5)

left hand
LH
Left hand as in the flick (4)

leftist
RED
Trained second-grade leftist (4)

leg
PIN
Leg on top of the table? Could be after two or three of these! (4)

legislator
MP
The French legislator is a source of illumination (4)

Leonard
LEN
Leonard comes to tea in fast time (4)

less
indicates that letter(s) or element should be removed, e.g. 'score, nothing less' – SCRE (i.e. SCORE less O), 'petrol a pound less' – PETRO (i.e. PETROL less L)
Loveless Romeo, in confusion, gets what Oliver wanted (4)

let it stand, let it remain
STET (see **don't make changes**)
The French let it remain in ruins – yet it's the most recent! (6)

letter
1 ALLOWER 2 indicates a word or syllable pronounced like a letter of the alphabet, among the most common being: BEE, CEE, DEE, JAY, KAY, EL, EM, EN, ESS, TEE, YOU, EX, WHY
Swordsman, as it were, points to letter (9)

lettuce
COS
Lettuce planted by journalist – he made a fuss of it (8)

liberal
1 L(IB) 2 = anagram
Liberal standard to balance (7)

lid
indicates first letter of word or element, in down clue
Circle or lid of box (3)

lie in
= 'burial', e.g. 'Very pretty model lies in sun at noon with mixed gin' – STUNNING (i.e. T lies in SUN at N with mixed GIN = ING)
American Veteran leaders lie in state and all the officers and men are there (4)

lieutenant
LT
Graduate lieutenant in charge – of ship in this fleet? (6)

light
1 BEAM 2 RAY
Street light is out of place (5)

like
1 AS 2 = anagram
Rise, like money (6)

limb
LEG
For horse-flies, put top part of cream over limbs (5)

limit
END
Despatch to south limit (4)

Lincoln
ABE (i.e. Abraham Lincoln, 16th president of the USA)
Students in Lincoln make a record (5)

line
1 RAIL 2 RY
French 'iron line' is in fact a cross-channel service (5)

lines
1 BR 2 RY
Lines on last letter are copper in colour (7)

linesman
1 POET 2 can indicate name of famous writer, among the most popular being: AMIS, GIDE, POE, SAND and TWAIN
Linesman has sort of square – and there's another! (4)

liquid
1 OIL 2 indicates *drink* of some kind, with the most popular being, among others: ALE, GIN, PORT, RUM, TEA
Sulphur liquid from the earth (4)

liquor
= **liquid** 2, i.e. *drink*
Penny on liquor – can you beat it! (4)

list
1 LEAN 2 ROTA 3 TABLE 4 TILT
No list is worth considering (7)

listen (to) see **we hear**

listener, listening device
1 EAR 2 indicates a reference to ear, e.g. 'Some of the listeners often get a ring' (*S. Tel.*, 22.2.81) – LOBES
Approaches northern listeners (5)

little
1 BIT 2 WEE 3 indicates abbreviation, e.g. 'little time' – MO, 'little sister' – SIS, 'a little publicity' – AD, 'great little' – GT, 'little girl' – (e.g.) SAL 4 indicates a *diminutive* or small version of something, as a child or the young of animals, e.g. 'little child' – TOT, 'little flower' – STREAMLET, 'little beast' – CUB 5 = 'burial', e.g. 'little bit of Christmas pudding' – ASP (i.e. little bit of 'Christm*as p*udding')
Go round the hospital a little way – that's the spirit! (5)

little fellow, little demon, little devil [etc.]
IMP
Little fellow to go on the stage – that's a blow (6)

little woman
JO (i.e. one of the four young heroines of Louisa M. Alcott's book *Little Women*)
Little woman not half keen – that's funny! (4)

live
1 BE 2 (for 'lives') IS 3 RESIDE
A gentleman in love lives as a god (6) (*S.T.*, 19.7.81)

local
PUB
Local student is her announcer (9)

loch
NESS
Seaman's leader in vessel on loch's huge expanse (8) (*Obs.*, 19.7.81)

lock (of hair)
TRESS
Diana's lock of hair is in a sorry state (8)

locker
KEY
Donald has got on top of the locker, silly ass! (6)

lodgings
DIGS
Hurry along to lodgings for the lively celebrations! (8)

London area
the complete list of London postal districts is as follows, but usually the two-letter ones are preferred: E, EC, N, NW, SE, SW, W, WC
London area tea service (3)

(a) **long time**
1 AGE 2 EON 3 ERA
Officer at home a long time – is this something he's made up? (7)

look
1 LEER 2 LO 3 SEE 4 = 'burial', e.g.

'Father off the dog-lead, look, getting amorous!' – OGLE (i.e. look in '*dog-lead*')
Lingering look in different directions (4)

looking glasses
OO
It's forbidden to fasten a loop onto the looking glasses (5)

look out
1 WARE 2 indicates that a word clued as **look** (which see) must be omitted, e.g. 'look out in balloon' – BALON (i.e. BALLOON with LO out)
He keeps a look out in Donhead North (6)

loop
O
Measure loop for size of page (6)

lop
indicates word or element minus final letter(s), e.g. 'lop elm' – EL, 'beech lopped' – BEE or BEEC
Lop tree, lop more – what a thrill! (6)

lord
1 LD 2 LUD
Proceed, Lord Rich! (4)

Los Angeles
LA
Direct fix in Los Angeles (5)

lose
indicates removal of letter(s), element or word, e.g. 'Poet who has lost his head goes crazy' – RAVES (i.e. GRAVES who has lost G); 'Choir lost one on meadow in Lancashire' (*Guard.*) – CHORLEY (i.e. CHOIR lost I on LEY)
The Hidalgo's lost love has turned up. That'll please him! (7) (*S. Tel.*, 18.1.81)

lose (your, his, its [etc.]) **head**
indicates removal of first letter or word or element, e.g. 'Bill lost his head being unwell' – ILL (i.e. BILL lost B); see also **lose**
Noblemen make precious things lose their head (5) (*S.T.*, 19.7.81)

lose heart
indicates removal of centre letter(s), e.g. 'Colin loses heart but gets money' – COIN (i.e. COLIN loses L)
Diver loses heart, gets all tangled – it's dreadful (4)

(a) **lot** (of)
indicates (usually) word or element minus final letter, e.g. 'a lot of blood' – GOR (GORE minus E)
Bind a lot of corn with copper (4)

loud
F
Kind of musical instrument, a loud lute (5)

love
1 O 2 NIL
Bob in love – that's a mistake! (4)

loveless
indicates word or element minus O (see **love**), e.g. 'loveless one' – NE
Loveless hero gets confusing clues – and he's such a strong man! (8)

lover (before)
EX
A special message for lover before journalists (7)

low
MOO
Low ridge-top is broad heathland (4)

low-down
GEN
Class has low-down on America (5)

lower
COW
Lower undergarment is primrose (7)

L(-shaped)
EL
Man visits L-shaped church (6)

lubricate
OIL
About to lubricate ring (4)

lurk (in)
= 'burial', e.g. 'redhead lurks in taxi' – CRAB (i.e. R lurks in CAB)
Doctor lurks in study, the devil (5)

M

MacTavish
indicates reference to *Scotsman* or to *Scottish word*, name or pronunciation, e.g. 'Ken MacTavish would say . . .' – KNOW (i.e. Scottish 'ken'), 'MacTavish child' – BAIRN
Cried like MacTavish: 'nice to see you!' (7) (*S. Tel.*, 14.6.81)

made a meal
ATE
Jack made a meal and people came to tea, the result being less all round (9)

made a mistake
ERRED
Umpire made a mistake, did this to rules (8)

magazine
MAG
Picture that is in magazine (5)

magistrate
DOGE
Magistrate a Communist? Well, looking rather shabby, anyway (3-5)

main(ly)
1 reference to *sea* or *ocean* in some way, e.g. 'main song' – SHANTY, 'main weapon' – TORPEDO, 'main force' – RN 2 indicates that answer can be found in most of letters of clued word or phrase, e.g. 'Fish is found mainly in ditch' – TENCH (i.e. found in most of TRENCH)
Volume is mainly in stream (4)

make a meal
EAT
Make a meal on half a tray? What a feast! (5)

make a mistake
ERR
Make a mistake and you get sent on this! (6)

make hay
TED (an example of a rareish word often used as a handy device, especially for a verb ending)
Scholars make hay – get properly thrashed (6)

make notes
SING
The fathers make notes when going by (7)

male
1 GENT 2 HE 3 HIM 4 MAN
A male detective (5)

man
1 a man's name (see **boy** 3) 2 GENT 3 HE 4 HIM 5 MALE 6 MAN 7 OM
Man in charge in mischievous mood (6)

managed
1 RAN 2 = anagram
Although confused, Marti managed to get the boat (8)

manipulate
RIG
Robbers to manipulate in bands! (8)

man of account
CA (i.e. Chartered Accountant)
Man of account has his way – he can be a joker at times! (4)

man of art
RA
Can man of art enter the series? (5)

man of no spirit
TT
A man of no spirit – tipsy Scot to achieve it! (6)

man of the cloth
1 DD (i.e. Doctor of Divinity) 2 REV
A man of the cloth in charge of the tea – or is he hooked on the stronger stuff? (6)

(the) **man's**
HIS
Man's conservative account (7)

manuscript
MS
Main manuscript by Lock found in a sewer (10)

Manx
indicates word or element minus last letter, that is, 'detailed' like a Manx cat, e.g. 'Manx

cat' – CA, 'Manx name' – NAM, 'Manx race' – RAC
Manxman joins East-West emergency inflation measure! (3, 4)

Manx race
TT (i.e. the *T*ourist *T*rophy motor-cycle race held on the Isle of Man; but see also **Manx**)
Forecaster includes the Manx race, the dog! (6)

many
1 C 2 D 3 L 4 M (i.e. the higher Roman numbers)
Many a mile for mother (3)

March
MAR
March to a gold flower (8)

mariner
1 AB 2 JACK 3 TAR
Mariner achieves results (7)

Marines
RM
Tea is given to the Marines in Gateshead – very nice! (8)

married
1 *M* 2 MATED 3 WED
Walk delicately when married in church! (5)

marry
1 MATE 2 WED
Marry a redhead – or her mother! (5)

marsh, marshy ground, marshy place [etc.]
BOG
Paddy Marshfoot (3-7)

martyr
1 S 2 ST
Public martyr consumed (5)

Marxist
RED
Colour of Marxist study (6)

mass (Mass)
M (i.e. as mathematical abbreviation)
A mass in church is the ultimate perfection (4)

massage
RUB
Rub hard, namely, massage (5)

master
1 ACE 2 *MA*
Physical education master gets a respite (5)

material
1 indicates a type of fabric, often turning out to be REP 2 = anagram
Material increase means renewed spell of action (7)

mathematical symbol
usually PI
Mathematical symbol's next to 'ton' to indicate type of engine (6)

mature
AGE
Look closely at mature members of the nobility (7)

Mauretanian
MOOR
Mauretanian soil is largely uncultivated (8)

me
1 I 2 *ME* 3 indicates main answer or singles out particular element or word, e.g. 'Bottomless trousers for a fool and a pantomime character, that's me!' – PANTALOON (i.e. bottomless PANTS for A LOON)
Bring the silver back to me, sport! (4)

meadow
1 LEA 2 LEY
Tom returns to the meadow with his team – a mixed bunch (6, 4)

meal
usually TEA
Rushing the meal on the cooker (7)

measure
among the most common are: CC, DRAM, ELL, EM, EN, ERG, IN, *M*, MM, TON
U.S. Navy officer to measure the mark (6)

medal(ist) see **decoration**

medic(al man), medical officer see **doctor**

Mediterranean
MED
River flowed to the Mediterranean – as I thought (6)

meet
indicates that one letter, element or word joins ('meets') another, e.g. 'Father meets Nick, I hear – what a fright!' – PANIC (i.e. PA meets NIC)
Boy meets girl – but what an affected way to talk! (2-2-2)

member
1 ARM 2 LEG 3 LIMB 4 MP
If backing genuine member, it's a danger-signal (4-5) (*S. Tel.*, 19.7.81)

member of the order
BRO
Member of the order is given an order – and this will help him to keep things in order! (5)

members of
1 = 'burial', e.g. 'Student charity procession organised by members of opera group' – RAG (i.e. by members of 'ope*ra g*roup') 2 = anagram
Regard as members of fraternity (4)

men
MEN
One to greet the men in harmony (9)

meritorious order
OM (i.e. Order of Merit)
Concerning meritorious order in capital (4)

merry
GAY
Recognise the merry bunch (7)

metal
1 ORE 2 indicates symbol of metal, among most common being AG (silver), AU (gold), FE (iron), HG (mercury), PB (lead) and SN (tin)
Metal on metal forms a hidden obstacle (4)

meteorological
MET
Officer in charge of the Meteorological Body found in space (5)

middle (of)
1 MID 2 indicates middle letter(s) of element or word, e.g. 'middle of night' – G, 'middleman' – A
Acted dumbly with me in the middle (5) (*Obs.*, 1.2.81)

Middle East
ME
Tried to get aid in the Middle East (5)

middling character
indicates middle letter of element or word (see **middle**)
Biblical personage took middling character from the chosen people (5) (*S. Tel.*, 7.12.80)

mile
M
Mile in the circuit, but also travelling light! (4)

military (man)
1 GI 2 RA 3 RE
Transported for military exercises (4) (*Guard.*)

military commander
CO
Desirable residence offered for military commander, teetotaller, mature (7)

Military Police
MP
Obtain information from someone by backing up the Military Police (4)

mimic
APE
Northern mimic talks through this, as it were (4)

mincemeat
indicates anagram of MEAT, thus obtaining ATEM, TEMA, TEAM, MATE, etc.
In this country festivities include really high-class mincemeat (9) (*S.T.*, 3.5.81)

mine
PIT
A bit of embroidery the company put in a mine (5) (*Obs.*, 19.7.81)

mineral
1 ORE 2 TIN
Mineral the German used to get a light (6)

mining engineer
MIME (i.e. Member of the Institute of Mining Engineers)
Get the vessel to the mining engineer – what a performance! (9)

minister
TEND
It's hell to minister to swell (7) (*S. Tel.*, 26.4.81)

ministry
usually MOD
Money earned in the ministry can cause trouble (9)

minor
indicates shortened form of word or abbreviation, e.g. 'minor road' – RD
Minor church to imitate leader's first place of worship (6)

minor highway
BROAD (i.e. B-ROAD)
A minor highway in another country (6)

minus
1 LESS 2 indicates word minus final letter(s), e.g. 'room minus many . . .' – ROO
Public vehicle is broken – minus junction (3)

mirror
= reversal, e.g. 'new mirror' – WEN
Hands swap mirror (4)

mischief-maker, mischievous kid [etc.]
IMP
Where ringleader brings in mischievous kid, a real cry-baby! (9)

misfortune
ILL
'Misfortune in Bed' scheduled (6)

miss(ing)
1 indicates letter(s), element or word missing, e.g. 'found missing ring' – FUND (i.e. FOUND missing O), 'Hurt and upset missing you, apparently – and everyone's in subjection!' (*S.T.*, 15.2.81) – THRALL (i.e. 'upset' HURT missing U+ALL = THRALL) 2 indicates name of well-known person who can legitimately be called 'Miss', with answer being her (usually short) first name or initials, e.g. 'Miss Gardner' – AVA (i.e. Ava Gardner, the American film actress)
He arranges for opera singer to miss gym workout (9)

Mississippi
MI
The Queen in Mississippi is the equivalent of a ruler in North Africa (4)

Missouri
MO
Missouri bird is native of America (6) (*Times*, 1.8.81)

mistake
1 ERR 2 = anagram
Mistake among misguided Conservatives getting to govern by fear (9)

Mister [in full]
MR
The painter, Mister Halfgood, is a strict disciplinarian (6)

model
1 POSER 2 T (i.e. the early type of Ford car called the Model T)
Kleenex for model kids! (7)

modern (style)
1 AD 2 MOD
Location of building where modern-style clothes can be found (7)

Mohammad [sometimes also given, incorrectly, as Mohammed]
ALI (i.e. Mohammad ALI, the famous boxer)
The African country where Monsieur Mohammad comes from? (4)

moment
1 MO 2 SEC
Energetic person has a moment in study (5)

monarch
1 ER 2 R
Monarch, having power, grows old – and rushes about wildly (8)

Monday
MON
Shakespeare character gets it coming back on Monday (5)

money
among the most common are: ANNA, C, CENT, COIN, D, DIME, L, LIRA, MARK, P, S, TIN, YEN
Good man brings in the money – it's just a day's work! (5)

money owing
IOUS
Edward has money owing – what a bore! (7)

monkey
1 APE 2 IMP
Monkey wandered around and recovered (8)

Monsieur
M
Monsieur to come back to his family saying 'Je reviens', for example (5)

monster
ORC
Monster stayed concealed in rare flower (6)

monster's home
NESS (i.e. Loch Ness, home of the 'Loch Ness Monster')
London river monster's home showing rapidity of motion (9)

month
could be full or abbreviated name of any month, but most common are: DEC, MAR, MAY, OCT
Almost a full month for this bird by the sea! (6)

Morecambe
ERIC (i.e. the English TV comedian Eric Morecambe)
'E's coming back to Morecambe – now ain't that hard to understand? (8)

more than half
indicates more than half the number of letters in element or word, e.g. 'more than half afraid' – AFRA, 'more than half residing' – LIVI (i.e. more than half LIVING)
More than half the Indian tribe are in town, and this is the total that can be accommodated (8)

morning [compare **in the morning**]
AM
Cried having spent the morning in writing (8) (*S.T.*, 19.7.81)

most [plus an adjective]
indicates that answer is a superlative, that is, ends in -EST, e.g. 'most orderly' – NEATEST, 'most incredible' – TALLEST
Fairest and most wonderful (6)

most (of), **mostly**
indicates word minus final letter (less often, internal letter), often for use as an anagram, e.g. 'most of the sofa' – DIVA, 'most of the . . .' – TH, 'most of the chairs got mixed up' – CHARI (i.e. anagram of CHAIR)
Mostly hard birds – all of them rapacious (7) (*Times*, 18.7.81)

mother
1 DAM 2 MA 3 MATER 4 MUM
She's a lady of quality, and twice a mother (5) (*Guard.*)

Mothers Union
MU
Holy man has Mothers Union in – it's a matter of obscene talk (4)

motorway
M(I)
Glide smoothly in two directions up the motorway (4)

mount(ain)
among most common are: ALP(S), BEN, ETNA, MT, TOR
A mountain high is torn asunder here,
And then a stream of water doth appear (7)

mountain lake
TARN
The mountain lake is half starting to lose its lustre (7)

mountain pass
COL
The official formula is in favour of getting to the mountain pass (8)

Mr
1 MISTER 2 (when with surname) indicates first name or initials of well-known person, e.g. 'Mr Lawrence' – TE, 'Mr Heath' – TED, 'Mr Grace' – WG
The gunners came to Mr Shaw with the silver – what an odd assortment! (6)

multitude
1 C 2 D 3 L 4 M 5 HOST
Multitude came to the Spanish inn (6)

mum
1 MA 2 MATER 3 MOTHER
Black mum loses her head – such perplexity! (6)

muscular twitch
TIC
Devotee has a muscular twitch – he's almost *too* enthusiastic (7)

musical group [see also **musicians**]
EMI (i.e. the record company Electric and Musical Industries)
Musical group sound great. Are they going to go abroad? (8)

musicians, musical group
BAND
Member of musical group has this on the sleeve (7)

mute
SH
Take mute out – now make a really loud noise! (5)

my goodness(!)
GEE
Second letter from Ealing misdirected. My goodness, that's casual, and as a man, I'm not sure I'm going to wear it! (8)

myself
I
Enter myself in run. That could be my undoing! (4)

N

name
N
Name or number, that's the rule (4)

namely
SC (abbreviation for Latin *scilicet*)
Beetle (namely, Egyptian) (6)

nation
RACE
The first nation to have a railway – it's quite a network (7)

national
NAT
International organisation provides national love (4)

naval personnel
RNMEN
A party for the naval personnel after tea looks very attractive (9)

navy
RN
A commanding officer joins the navy – a real Heart of Oak (5)

Nazi troops
SS
Famous revolutionary leader met Nazi troops on board – and they worked out their moves here (10)

nearly all
indicates that one or more words contain nearly all the letters of another, e.g. 'The state has nearly all the goods' – WARES (i.e. state of Delaware has nearly all WARES)
On the road to this town, said the poet, you have nearly all the shoes (7)

nearly fifty
IL (i.e. Roman figure 49)
Work to nearly fifty (4)

necessary to
= 'burial' (i.e. letters are necessary to phrase or word in which buried), e.g. 'Lion man

necessary to hunt a mermaid' – TAMER (i.e. necessary to 'hunt *a mer*maid')
Protective cover – necessary to prevent him bleeding (7) (*Guard.*)

neckwear
TIE(S)
Standard neckwear for these celebratory occasions (7)

never-never
HP (i.e. hire purchase)
Fashion leader is never-never on top of digging when installing this ornamental structure in the garden (8)

new driver
L
New driver comes to a quiet part of the racecourse (3)

news
1 GEN 2 INF(O)
It can be said of any member of the class – which is news to Eric (7)

newsman
ED
Diana and The Five meet newsman – maybe he did this to escape? (5)

newspapers
PRESS
Newspapers contain almost an inch for Lady Diana (8)

newt
EFT (a rare word but a handy one)
Roll over the newt – he's not right! (7)

New Testament
NT
Affected use of religious phrases about the New Testament (4)

New York
NY
'A Saint in New York' is unpleasant (5)

niche
DENT
Order for goods is in niche (6)

Nick
reference to *devil* or some word that means this (e.g. IMP)
Left Nick rather drooping (4)

nickel
NI (symbol)
Pinch nickel and penny! (3)

night(-)flier
1 BAT 2 MOTH
Night-flier on the staff (5)

nil
O
Two of the French get nil (3)

nine (9)
1 IX 2 NINE
He'll return by the 9.5 for the city, ruined (7) (*Obs.*, 2.8.81)

nine-nine-nine (999)
IM
999 to beat – in a single blow? (7)

ninety (90)
XC
90 in two directions followed by two double bends – that's too much! (6)

ninety-nine (99)
IC
Graduates get 99, that's the standard minimum (5)

no
1 NAY 2 NO 3 O 4 indicates word, element or letter(s) missing, e.g. 'Tardy priest with no silly salesman' – LATE (i.e. PRELATE with no PRE ('silly' REP) is tardy or LATE)
Certain enjoyment when no plea is entered (4) (*Obs.*, 22.2.81)

no good
NG
Typical Kentucky voice says airline is no good (5)

noise
DIN
A big noise in dwelling (7)

noisy, noisily
F
Resist the noisy one! (4)

non-alcoholic
1 DRY 2 TT
To tease Albert the non-alcoholic is coarse (8)

non-drinker
TT
A non-drinker in command? That's a tall story, in a way! (5)

non-flier
EMU
Medical men gather round non-flier as he hesitates (6)

nonsense
ROT
Loud nonsense, hotheaded chatter (5)

non-U
indicates element or word minus letter U, e.g. 'non-U guild' – GILD
Fat, but firm if non-U (4)

noon
N
Drinking bout – noon in bed! (4)

no one
NOI (i.e. NO+I)
No one points to the racket (5)

Norfolk town
DISS
Norfolk town nearly gets a badge, but we have to disguise that (9)

norm (Norm), normal
PAR
I'm normal, Edward, I made it known (8)

North America(n)
NA
Female North American red (5) (*Obs.*, 2.8.81)

north(ern)
N
Northern French river will provide a row (5)

Northern Ireland
NI
Combination of Northern Ireland and Church of England is delicate (4)

not
1 indicates letter(s), element or word to be removed, e.g. 'the vain girl, not thin' – EVA (i.e. 'th*e* *va*in' without 'thin') 2 indicates opposite of following word in clue, e.g. 'not in' – OUT, 'not left' – RIGHT
String not the way to make a telephone call! (4)

not altogether
indicates incomplete word, usually with one letter missing, e.g. 'Holy man not altogether over the cooker' – STOVE (i.e. ST + not altogether OVER)
Long-legged king not altogether annoyed (5)

not drinking
TT
Not drinking in time of prosperity, that's the fundamental thing (6)

note(d)
1 IOU 2 one of standard musical notes A, B, C, D, E, F or G 3 one of the corresponding musical notes in the so-called 'solmisation' system, i.e. DO or DOH, RE or RAY, MI or ME, FA or FAH, SO or SOH, LA or LAH, and TE (usually the two-letter forms are preferred) 4 indicates a reference to *music*, e.g. 'Noted example of inspired lunacy?' – MOONLIGHT SONATA
Note insect on part of shield (6)

noted orchestra
HALLE
Arranged for mixed drams to go round noted orchestra (10)

not entirely
indicates word minus final letter, e.g. 'not entirely closed' – SHU
Not entirely pleased over the three points, but that's just the way it turns out (7)

not half
indicates that half of word (usually the latter) is missing, e.g. 'not half hungry' – HUN, 'not half good' – GO

Snake makes horse rage – not half! (5)

nothing
1 NIL 2 O
Smell nothing grim (5) (*Obs.*, 2.8.81)

nothing short of
indicates word from which O is missing, and usually treated as anagram, e.g. 'nothing short of elation' – ELATIN, 'Involve nothing short of elation when cavorting' – ENTAIL (i.e. anagram of ELATIN which is O short of ELATION)
The fearless broken by nothing short of perdition (8) (*Guard.*)

notice
AD
2nd-class notice is not good (3)

not in
1 OUT 2 indicates that letter(s), element or word should be omitted, e.g. 'Corn not in right profit' – GAIN (i.e. GRAIN with R not in)
Church dignitary not in a study (3)

not long
indicates an abbreviation, e.g. 'It's hard – a week's not long for these birds' – HAWKS (i.e. H+A+WK+S)
Correct public relations officer not long through (6)

not out
1 IN 2 indicates word with NOT removed, e.g. 'Churchill not backing out, gains victory' – WINS (i.e. WINSTON with TON, otherwise 'NOT backing', out)
Growth not out to double (8)

not quite
indicates word with one letter missing, usually the final one, and often used as an anagram, e.g. 'Pension not quite arranged for foreign agent' – ESPION (i.e. PENSIO arranged)
Anger not quite nice in tending to promote peace (6) (*S.T.*, 2.8.81)

(I'm) **not sure**
1 ER 2 UM
River steamship? I'm not sure. What a brute! (6)

novel
1 NEW 2 indicates short name of famous novel, e.g. TESS, KIM 3 = anagram
Novel vessel in this town! (6)

novice
L
Novice nearly over state of passion (4)

now
1 AD 2 INST
Now the day is over, and he's home from work! (3)

number
1 NO 2 indicates a Roman number, either a single letter or a combination, the single letters being (in numerical order) I (1), V (5), X (10), L (50), C (100), D (500), M (1000) 3 indicates a number spelt out as a short word, the most common being TEN 4 indicates a reference to something that *numbs*, e.g. ice, cold, an injection, etc.
A pathetic number in dead-end occupation (9) (*Times*, 18.7.81)

numbers
NUM (this being the usual abbreviation for the Book of Numbers in the Bible)
Magazine numbers have top sales, producing these large liquid assets! (7)

object
1 AIM 2 END 3 IT
Object to me coming back? What a thing! (4)

objection
BUT
First presentation of foreign objections (6) (*S.T.*, 26.7.81)

obligations
IOUS
Kick out the obligations, they're false (8)

observe
1 CON 2 HEED
Observe it's true (though it goes out),
Explain to me what it's about! (8)

obstacle
BAR
1001 and 50, and 51 obstacles – but they're quite small, if weighty (9)

obtain
GET
Friend obtains allowances (7)

ocean
SEA
To cause sick feeling in Aunt, 'e tosses about the ocean (8) (*Obs.*, 19.7.81)

October
OCT
Devise something for a month (October) (6)

odds
SP (i.e. 'starting price', in betting)
The odds are on her going to Japan, maybe. That will be a real field of activity (6)

of course
indicates reference to some kind of *course*, e.g. golf, racing, a meal, etc.
They're animals, of course! (6) (*Font.*)

(go) **off**
1 indicates letter(s), element or word to be removed from a word or phrase, often involving an anagram, e.g. 'As Cyclops he must tee off after Hydra' – POLYPHEMUS (i.e. a hydra is a POLYP after which HE MUST has T off, giving POLYPHEMUS, the name of a well-known Cyclops in mythology) 2 = anagram
I feel a cold shiver. Lad goes off to get a sheet. That's cold, too (3-4) (*S. Tel.*, 7.6.81)

offence
SIN
Graduate offence – in the dock (5)

officer
the most popular, all abbreviations, are: CAP(T), CO, COL, GEN, LT
Officer points to ice-cream! (4)

offspring
SON
A time for the ocean to bring forth her offspring (6)

of yours
THY
Doctor of yours seems rather weary and worn (5)

old
1 EX 2 indicates obsolete term, often an abbreviation, e.g. 'old lawyer' – KC, 'old service corps' – RASC: see also **old Bob**
Demand and obtain old part of play (5)

old Bob
S (i.e. shilling)
Old Bob has a friend for his excursion (5)

old boy
OB
Watch the old boy start the game of tennis (7)

old city
UR (i.e. the biblical 'Ur of the Chaldees', now in Iraq)
Old city gentleman calling for immediate attention (6)

old convict
LAG
Old convict loves the north – and this lake by the sea (6)

old copper
D (i.e. the old penny)
Old copper craftwork for type of weapon (4)

old copper coin
AS (plural ASSES; the as was a Roman coin)
He values old copper coins? So right (8) (*Times*, 8.8.81)

old English
OE
Get hep and twist round old English bridgehead – that's where you'll find the moon goddess! (6)

(in an) **old-fashioned** (way)
indicates old or obsolete word or spelling,

e.g. 'you are old-fashioned' – ART, 'the old-fashioned way' – YE
The lady 'as, in an old-fashioned way, what's very fitting (6) (*Obs.*, 12.4.81)

old king
usually LUD (a mythical king of Britain said to have been buried at Ludgate, London)
Absurd old king in charge confounding ours (9) (*Times*, 18.7.81)

(the) **old lady**
1 MA 2 MUM
Old lady comes to son – he's a builder (5)

(the) **old man**
1 PA 2 POP
The old man's a real brick, allowing me to go abroad (8)

old money
D (i.e. the old penny)
A small cubical piece – old money, that is (3)

old pence, old penny
D
Benefactor puts old English penny on French gold (5)

old priest
ELI (the Old Testament prophet)
Old priest gives kiss to a king – could it be the kiss of eternal life? (6)

omen
SIGN
Specify like an omen (6)

on
1 ON 2 indicates letter(s), element or word on top of another in a down clue, or added to another in an across clue, e.g. 'man on palm-tree' – MANDATE (down clue), 'man on unfinished hut' – HUMAN (across clue)
A dog on the line – it makes me break out into a hot sweat (5)

on board
1 SS (i.e. 'steamship') 2 indicates letters or elements in S . . . S, e.g. 'hole on board' – SPITS
Condescends to take work on board, apparently (6)

once
1 EX 2 indicates former or obsolete word or usage, e.g. 'penny once' – D
Once having tea out, get leave of absence (5)

one
1 A 2 AN 3 ACE 3 I 5 ONE 6 UNIT
Does one member have this power? (3)

(from what) **one hears**
= homophone, e.g. 'Delightful set of rooms, one hears' – SWEET (although 'one hears' SUITE)
Students read attentively and sweat buckets, from what one hears (4)

one of the family
1 BRO 2 SIS
To help like one of the family before tea (6)

oneself
EGO
People round oneself getting it back – that's a successful manoeuvre (11)

one side of
indicates first or last letter of a word, e.g. 'one side of a field' – F or D
One side of wig is soft – there's a thin piece of hair there (4)

only
1 BUT 2 SOLE 3 may indicate LESS added to second half of word clued to form answer, e.g. 'only a don' – KEYLESS, 'only in' – FORMLESS
This mountain only a cairn? That's silly! (8)

onset
indicates first letter of word, e.g. 'onset of attack' – A, 'onset of storm' – S
Onset of cold followed by climb leads to muscular trouble (5)

on the contrary
indicates that answer is the opposite (usually punningly) to that suggested in the clue, e.g. 'Put under trade union ban? On the contrary' – WHITE
Does she go in for high society? On the contrary! (9)

open(er), opening
1 ADIT (a passage into a mine) 2 indicates first letter of word or element, e.g. 'bottle-opener' – B, 'Poetry has no opening in this tongue' – ERSE (i.e. VERSE with no opening), 'Leicestershire's openers' – LE
In the present era it provides an opening (4) (*Obs.*, 19.7.81)

opening of play
1 ACTI (i.e. Act 1) 2 P (see **open**)
Opening of play on Victoria's preparations for battle (6, 8)

operation
OP
Hush – operation in store (4)

opposite
1 indicates either standard opposite, e.g. 'down the opposite . . .' – UP, or negated opposite, e.g. 'just the opposite' – UNJUST 2 indicates sections of the clue to be reversed to obtain the answer, e.g. 'End of the day? Just the opposite!' – DOOM (i.e. 'day of the end')
Flower of the rush? No, quite the opposite! (7) (*S. Tel.*, 7.6.81)

or
OR (often used as a 'doer' suffix, e.g. 'Deed or one who goes through the motions of doing it' – ACTOR)
One of the chosen or one who chooses (7) (*Font.*)

order
1 see **decoration** 2 = anagram

organ
usually indicates part of the body, e.g. EAR, EYE, LUNG, NOSE
Beware the loud organ! (4)

orient(al)
1 E 2 EAST 3 indicates something oriental, e.g. 'oriental copper' – SEN (a Japanese coin)
Oriental beasts figure in concise saying (7)

originate (from)
can indicate initial letters of words in clue, e.g. 'Bird originates from corn rows (or wheat)' – CROW (i.e. '*C*orn *r*ows . . .')
Fox in each case originating from Eastern Nubia – note ears – colossal! (6) (*Times*, 18.4.81)

(the) **others**
REST
I'm dejected, with a hundred others captured (11)

other things
ALIA (i.e. from phrase 'inter alia' – 'among other things')
Five other things half hint at the heroic (7)

ouch
1 OH 2 OW
Salute the warrior chief . . . ouch! Is his bark worse than his bite? (3-3)

our
OUR
The sword our defence (6)

out (of)
1 EX 2 indicates letter(s), element or word to be removed, e.g. 'throw hothead out' – TROW (i.e. THROW with H out) 3 = 'straddle', i.e. lying 'outside', e.g. 'Put out mixed side – then there'll be an argument!' – DISPUTE (i.e. PUT with mixed SIDE outside it) 4 = 'burial', i.e. with answer taken 'out of' given word(s), e.g. 'Aristocrat picked out from best of fifty' – TOFF (i.e. out from 'bes*t of f*ifty') 5 = anagram
Out of play, to be precise (5) (*S. Tel.*, 31.5.81)

outfit
RIG
Outfit I'd find too severe (5)

outhouse
SHED
Pressed back up to outhouse (6)

out of bed
UP
Surrey redhead out of bed – how sweet! (5)

out of work
indicates word or element minus OP, e.g. 'out-of-work bishop' – BISH

Out-of-work policeman mislays the ends (6)

outside
= 'straddle', e.g. 'memorial outside an inn' – REPUBLIC (i.e. RELIC outside PUB)
Dump the drunk outside the house (5)

outsize
OS
Outsize tea brought to rich bird (7)

outskirts
indicates first and last letters of word, usually the name of a place, e.g. 'outskirts of London' – LN, 'outskirts of Paris' – PS
Officer comes to outskirts of Rome, then the centre (4)

over
1 ENDS 2 PAST 3 = reversal, e.g. 'put over' – TUP 4 indicates element or word over (i.e. on top of, in down clue) another, e.g. 'Hand over the French inns as part of the cycle' – HANDLEBARS (i.e. HAND over LE+BARS) 5 = anagram
Meal about over (6) (*S.T.*, 2.8.81)

overdraft
RED
Challenged lawyer with overdraft (5)

overhead railway
EL (i.e. in USA, an *el*evated railroad)
Is stylish overhead railway a real one? (5)

overlooking
indicates element or word on top of another (in a down clue), or before another (in an across clue), e.g. 'Pub overlooking meadow uses this in its beers and spirits' – BARLEY (i.e. BAR overlooking LEY)
Hill overlooking the church – there's a lamp there (5)

overture
indicates first letter of word, e.g. 'overtures of philosophy professor' – PP, '"Eroica" overture' – E
Make open, touching overtures to her – maybe she will become one ultimately? (6)

overturn
1 = reversal, e.g. 'overturn cart' – TRAC, 'vessels overturned' – STOP 2 = anagram
Lorry overturned by a gate – perhaps driver found it difficult to do this? (8)

owned
HAD
Owned waterway for fish (7)

Oxford Street
HIGH ('The High' being the nickname of the High Street in Oxford)
Oxford Street illuminations are the outstanding features (10)

oyster
NATIVE (a special term for an artificially raised British oyster)
As another possibility, change the oyster (11)

P

page
P
Page and king in church – king's son, too! (6)

painter
RA
Painter comes to Pennsylvania town, showing he has this greedy, grasping nature (8)

pair
1 PR 2 indicates repeated letter(s) or element, e.g. 'current pair' – ACAC, 'loud pair' – FF
Pair chosen to order men a drink (5) (*Times*, 11.7.81)

pale
WAN
First pale we see comes to the east,
And then we see the moon decrease (4)

papers
PRESS
Officer has lots of papers – give him this to keep him cool (8)

parapsychology
ESP (i.e. extra-sensory perception)
Parapsychology in Virginia is redirected to an emperor of Rome (9)

Parisian see **French**

parking
P
Parking is all right up to a point if you can shove in like this (4)

Parliamentarian
MP
One Parliamentarian is a bit of a devil (3)

parliament(ary)
HOC (i.e. House of Commons)
Parliament and monarch celebrate with this drink (4)

parson
REV
Is parson upset concerning the translation? (7) (*Times*, 18.7.81)

part(s) (of)
1 PT 2 = 'burial', e.g. 'Once a gleeful part of the bird' (*Font.*) – EAGLE (i.e. 'onc*e a gle*eful' part) 3 = anagram
Physician, heal thyself; result, in part! (7) (*S. Tel.*, 19.7.81)

particle
ION
Areas about gravity particles (7)

partly
= 'burial', e.g. 'Even nuisances partly produce boredom' – ENNUI (i.e. partly 'ev*en nui*sances'
Elizabethan architecture partly regarded as a promoter of lawlessness (6)

part of theatre
PIT
Part of theatre has central heating set up (5)

part of the Bible
1 NT 2 OT
He's over-zealous about a large part of the Bible (5)

party
1 C 2 CON 3 DO 4 L 5 LAB 6 LIB 7 SD(P) 8 SOC
Ron has a party, and chooses this music for it (5)

pass
1 COL 2 GO
Pass on the mark (5)

past
AGO
Struggle past New York (5)

patriarch's birthplace
UR
An excursion to patriarch's birthplace (4)

pay(ment)
FEE
Pay a penny and have something to eat (4)

peg (Peg)
TEE
Put the peg on this seat (6)

pelt
FUR
Pelt the ringleader as well! (7)

pen
STY
Pen the French way (5)

pence
P
Sixpence for a bigwig (3)

pence once
D
Pence once on carpet means unsellable article (4)

penetrating
= 'burial', e.g. 'Sun penetrating a red back separately' – ASUNDER (i.e. SUN penetrating A and RED back)
Look for pole penetrating shed (4)

penniless
indicates word minus D or P, this usually being the first letter, e.g. 'penniless rascals' – EVILS (i.e. minus D)
Brings into operation penniless specialists (6) (*Obs.*, 22.3.81)

Pennsylvania
PA

It's quite a stretch running from one pole to another in Pennsylvania (4)

penny
1 D 2 P
Penny on your first horse? (4)

people
MEN
Change for people in our time (5)

perch
1 POLE 2 ROD
Creature on perch stays quite straight and still (6)

perform
DO
Perform blue dance. Do it twice! (6)

perhaps
1 indicates that strong hint of answer is given in clue, often as an example, e.g. 'nitrogen, perhaps' – GAS, 'Japan, perhaps' – E (i.e. 'east') 2 = anagram
Mean well, perhaps, with the 'phone call (7) (*S.T.*, 2.8.81)

(a) **period**
1 AGE 2 ERA 3 HR
A period to celebrate, removing all traces of the past (7)

permit(ted)
1 LET 2 PASS
Radio operator permitted in this village (6)

per person
EACH
A penny per person for this fruit (5)

(a) **person**
1 MAN 2 ONE
Cold person has ice-cream! (4)

personality
1 EGO 2 ID
RAF man has personality that is decidedly ill-natured (4)

Philadelphia
PHIL
Stamp collection from Philadelphia at Cambridgeshire town (9)

physical education
PE
Genuine physical education included in the change of law (6) (*S.T.*, 26.7.81)

physical training
PT
Gunners' physical training has me spellbound (4)

physician see **doctor**

piano
P
Piano work is quite explosive! (3)

piece(s)
1 BIT(S) 2 indicates individual letter(s), as clued, usually in the form of an anagram, e.g. 'pieces of china' – CHAIN, 'piece of wood' – W
Attack with pieces of stone (5) (*S.T.*, 5.4.81)

piece of [see also **piece(s)**, above]
= 'burial', e.g. 'Piece of dry decay found in Isle of Wight' – RYDE (i.e. piece of 'd*ry de*cay')
Piece of metal covered in powder (4)

piece of wood [see also **piece(s)** and **piece of**, above]
LOG
Lots of pieces of wood needed for this footwear (5)

piggery
STY
Way of coming to the piggery? That's unobtrusiveness, if you like! (7)

pilot officer
PO
Bright light reveals pilot officer in the way (4)

pinch(ing)
= 'straddle', e.g. 'he pinches first and last letters' – HAZE
Robber in Italian city pinching coin (6) (*Times*, 25.7.81)

pipe
REED
Checked the pipe outside the cupboard (9) (*Times*, 23.5.81)

(the) **piper**
PAN
Piper goes to the Spanish doctors (5)

pirate
HOOK (i.e. Captain Hook, the one-armed pirate captain in J. M. Barrie's play *Peter Pan*)
Sea leader pirate trembled! (5)

(kind of) **pistol**
VERY (i.e. the signalling pistol invented by Edward Very in 1877)
Lied about pistol, resulting in discharge (8)

pitch
TAR
Rough fellow has a double pitch! (6)

place
1 PUT 2 SET
Flower place, by the sound of it, is actual pygmy place! (8)

place of flowers
BED
Place of flowers hit – place of uproar! (6)

place of retirement
BED
Dressed – or came back to place of retirement? (5)

players
1 BAND 2 SIDE 3 TEAM
Support the players in the rear! (8)

(it's a) **pleasure**
FUN
Back payment results in pleasure when in the red (6)

plot
1 BED 2 PLAN
Examined in favour of plot (6)

Pluto
DIS (i.e. the mythological god of the Underworld)
Pluto can cripple! (7)

pocket(ed)
= 'straddle,' e.g. 'we pocketed the shot – not the black, though' – WHITE (i.e. WE pocketed the HIT)
Doctor has pocketed extravagant fee, resulting in delay (5)

poem
1 ODE 2 VERSE
A poem's here, you soon will find:
To state its sense I'm disinclined (6)

poet
BARD
Poet to write back to glamorous film star (6)

point
1 DOT 2 E 3 N 4 S 5 W
The fat gives point to decorations (5) (*S.T.*, 19.7.81)

pointless
indicates element or word minus one or more of letters N, S, E, W, e.g. 'pointless wait' – AIT, 'pointless manner' – MAR
Pointless poem on 'Last Ship' ceremony (4)

pole (Pole)
1 N 2 ROD 3 S
Pole in bed, subject to tension (4)

police group
POSSE
Control police group on points (7)

police(men), police department
CID
Ran to the police rank (6)

politician
1 MP 2 TORY
The life story of his politician (7)

poor actor
HAM
Poor actor gets imitation bed (7)

popular
1 IN 2 POP
Teach popular class (6)

port
1 HAVEN 2 L
Isolated port on the east (4)

portent
SIGN
Surrenders position regarding portents (7)

posh
U (i.e. 'upper-class')
Posh top Scot is the fellow to live in ideal society! (7)

position
SITE
Hanger-on gets equal top position (8)

possessed
HAD
Chief cook possessed sort of fish (4)

post office
PO
Put forward a plan in favour of the Post Office for the south east (7)

(a) **pound (£)**
1 L 2 LB 3 PEN (i.e. an enclosure for animals)
Sweetmeat – I had a pound to be eaten, to tell the truth (8) (*Obs.*, 2.8.81)

preserve
1 CAN 2 TIN
Preserve the oriental sugar plant (4)

president
1 P 2 PRES
Entrance of president or church leaders (5)

(the) **press and TV**
MEDIA
Press and TV come to hill, and there is someone who can act as a go-between (8)

press association
PA
Press association take advantage of the interval (5)

press men
BUP (i.e. British United Press)
Press men return for drinks here (3)

(old) **priest**
1 ELI 2 FR 3 REV
Priest is on lake, appearing to be in a state of meditation (7)

primate (Primate)
APE
Primate is unknown, but this is the culminating point of his career (4)

prime part
indicates first letter of element or word, e.g. 'prime part of time' – T
Remain prime part of day by the spring (5)

prince (Prince)
P(R)
Prince Andrew gets a smack on the palm (5)

prisoner
1 LAG 2 = 'burial', e.g. 'Clara is real prisoner, and this disproves her argument' – REBUTTAL (i.e. BUTT is REAL prisoner)
Prisoner comes to Queen and gets beer (5)

problem
SUM
Problem account of subtropical tree (5)

professional
PRO
Professional money-saver almost shows signs of better future (7)

prohibit
BAN
Africans prohibit Trade Union (5)

promise to pay
IOU
Priest promises to pay, taking the place of the other person (9)

promissory note
IOU
Policeman gets promissory notes in plenty (7)

pronounced(ly)
= homophone, e.g. 'Level surface pro-

nounced smooth' – PLANE (i.e. PLANE pronounced PLAIN)
Direction is pronouncedly coarse (6)

propeller
OAR
Noisy propeller in enclosure (7)

prophet
1 AMOS 2 ELI 3 SEER
Tourists observe the prophets (10)

protect
= 'straddle', e.g. 'He protects the old man in his house' – HOME (i.e. HE protects OM)
Girl protects duck in prison (4)

provided
IF
Present provided in sports car (4)

(to) **provide with weapons**
ARM
It's a moral wrong and horrific to provide with weapons (4)

pub(lic house)
1 BAR 2 INN 3 LOCAL
Make hostile protest in pub bar (7)

publicity man
PRO (i.e. public relations officer)
Publicity man gets a penny as supporter (4)

publicity, public notice
AD
He stands by public notice, being the director (4)

public relations
PR
Gave earnest advice for public relations to every editor (8)

public transport
BUS
It was hell before public transport! (6)

pull(ed) up
= reversal in down clue, e.g. 'bus pulled up' – SUB
Pulled up bottom of ship, the 'Welsh Emblem' (4)

pupil
1 L 2 indicates a reference to *eye* (especially IRIS)
Pupil gets nothing on points, so fails (5)

purchased
BOT
South African purchased French-style shoe (5)

(some) **purpose**
USE
Right purpose of scheme? (4)

put in
= 'burial', e.g. 'Fat boy put in river' – LARD (i.e. LAD with R put in)
I'm put in the French trees (5)

put on
1 DON 2 indicates element or word to be joined to another, usually preceding it (especially in down clue), e.g. 'Get hold of cat put on top of church' – CATCH (i.e. CAT put on CH)
Fruit put on the heap in Ireland (8)

put out
1 = 'straddle', e.g. 'Fruit from another moat to put out' – TOMATO (i.e. 'another' MOAT with TO put out or 'straddling' it) 2 = anagram
For this reason fresh sauce has to be put out (7) (*Guard.*)

put together
indicates that letter(s), element or word is to join another or others to form answer, e.g. 'I'm put together with patrol leader, the rascal!' – IMP
Doctors are put together with C.O. and first wife – that's capital! (6)

Q

quarter
any of four quarters of the compass, E, N, S, W, and also combinations of these, e.g. NE, SE, SW
Three-quarters seen in outsize try in Shropshire (8)

quarterdeck
SUIT (i.e. a quarter of a deck or pack of cards)
A chase back up the starboard quarterdeck (7)

queen (Queen)
1 ER (usually Queen) 2 HM 3 R
The Queen in Ireland – how poetic (4)

question
ASK
Head teacher questions the exercises (5)

queue
Q
Leave the queue and you get over it (4)

quick
indicates abbreviation, e.g. 'quick reply' – ANS
Quick arrival in this part of London – but surely not in this? (6)

(a) **quid**
(A)L
Up-to-the-minute subject provided for a quid (7)

quiet(ly)
1 EASE 2 P 3 SH
Praised and clapped after a very quiet beginning (6) (*S.T.*, 19.7.81)

R

rabbit
BUN
Want something nice for tea? Pick a rabbit (5, 3) (*Guard.*)

raced
1 RAN 2 = anagram
Head boy raced for the cereal (4)

race(s)
TT (i.e. the Tourist Trophy races in the Isle of Man)
Old injury in the race results in a fight (6)

racket
DIN
Stanley has a racket and is prepared to play if needed (5-2)

radical
RED
Radical oriental gets in – the grass! (4)

radio-telephone
RT
Palace officer has top use of radio-telephone (5)

RAF information
GEN
RAF information has an attempt to name rank (6)

railway
1 RLY 2 RY
Wait for sailor by railway (5)

railways
1 BR 2 LINES
Railways are all right going east – but don't travel if in this state! (5)

raise
= reversal in down clue, e.g. 'mother raised' – MAD, 'raised part' – TRAP
In which one drives with raised whip (4) (*Times*, 1.8.81)

ramble
1 ROVE 2 = anagram
Be fond of a ramble after tea – especially if it leads to this! (8, 5)

range
1 RUN 2 indicates range of mountains, among most common beings ALPS and URAL
Examine the range for a trial drive (4, 3)

rate
MPH
Girl has the superior rate in the first game, really bounding along! (10)

read
1 CON 2 PORE 3 SCAN
Short read before tea (5)

rear admiral
RA
Fancy headwear – a rear admiral puts it on upside-down! (5) (*Guard.*)

rebound
= palindrome, e.g. 'joke rebounds' – GAG
Blunder that can rebound without effect (4) (*Now!*, 24.4.81)

receiver
EAR
It would seem to be a very quiet receiver (6)

recipe
R
Curry and fish recipe? (6) (*Guard.*)

record
1 DISC 2 EP 3 LP
A record: the scholar, although confused, has all the letters! (8)

record player
DJ
A record player is brought to us on a table. It's easily positioned (10)

recover(y)
RALLY
Doctor is close to recovery, to all intents and purposes (7)

reduce [see also next entry]
indicates one letter of element or word, not necessarily the first, to be removed, e.g. 'time reduced' – TIM, 'reduced price' – RICE or PRIC
Reduce weight by dropping a point if you want to get to holiday isle (5)

reduced [see also previous entry]
LOW
First fireman reduced the stream of water (4)

referee
REF
Referee has employment but is rejected as worthless (6)

reflect
= reversal, e.g. 'reflect ray' – YAR
Stops to reflect: maybe they mean he's caught a disease? (5)

refusal
1 NO 2 NOT
Refusal made to Hill with his debts – he's got a bad reputation (9)

refuse
1 BRAN 2 NO 3 NOT 4 ROT
It's commonsense to refuse us (4)

regiment
RE (i.e. Royal Engineers)
I think highly of the announcement that I'm returning to the regiment (6)

regulation
LAW
First fire regulation has an error (4)

reject
= reversal (usually in across clue), e.g. 'bid rejected' – DIB
Girl rejected love on this romantic lake! (6)

relative
among the most common are: BRO, DAD, MA, MUM, PA, POP, SIS
Canon is a relative eccentric (7)

relatives, relations
KIN
Relatives in jog? You must be pulling my leg! (6)

religious
PI
Religious novice is unyielding and he travels to the holy place (7)

religious books
1 NT 2 OT
Translate the religious books – using this, no doubt, in America! (4)

reluctantly
1 ER 2 UM
Reluctantly comes to love top secretary – thanks to him? (4)

remainder
REST
Forcibly twists the remainder in two directions (6)

remains
ASH
Crushed remains in the Mediterranean (6)

remove (from)
indicates remove letter(s), element or word, e.g. 'remove it from orbit' – ORB
Remove her from the boat, it's not in the right direction (3)

rent
TORN
Rent trouble creates storm (7) (*Obs.*, 2.8.81)

repeat
indicates repeated letter(s), element or word, e.g. 'repeat performance' – DODO
Turn repeated by this disco dancer, maybe (4)

representative
1 MP 2 REP
Not so wild about rising representative, one who meddles (8) (*Obs.*, 19.7.81)

Republicans
IRA
Officer half admits Republicans to be prime lawbreakers (7)

resort
1 SPA 2 indicates short name of popular (usually seaside) resort, e.g. BUDE, HOVE, RYDE 3 = anagram (i.e. 're-sort')
Resort has church and plenty of room (5)

resting
indicates letter(s) or word to be inserted in BED or COT (usually as B . . . ED or CO . . . T), e.g. 'Heavenly body? That's me resting!' – COMET (i.e. ME in COT)
Ann resting, being refused permission to take part (6)

rest in peace
RIP
Holy man to rest in peace in this long piece of land (5)

restrict
= 'straddle', e.g. 'Bob restricts the beginner' – BLOB
Shame restricts the king, so putting him under stress (6)

retire
= reversal, e.g. 'Dave retires to the east to escape' – EVADE
Star retires and quits for unworthy motives (4)

retreat
1 DEN 2 = reversal (see **retire**)
Oriental retreat is garden of paradise (4)

(in) **retrospect**
= reversal, or even reversed 'burial', e.g. 'Crazy person is in Soviet Union, in retrospect' – NUT (i.e. reversal of 'burial' in 'Sovie*t Un*ion')
Criminal organisation in America, if a misnomer, in retrospect (5) (*Obs.*, 22.3.81)

return
1 = reversal, e.g. 'to return' – OT, 'in return' – NI 2 ER, i.e. 'RE-turn'
Went astray but returned to Communist (5)

reveal
1 = 'burial', e.g. 'evil revealed in Basingstoke' – SIN 2 indicates that answer, if analysed or divided into elements, will reveal main part of clue, e.g. 'Vegetable to reveal damage line?' – MARROW (i.e. MAR+ROW)
Permission to reveal the total advance? (8) (*Guard.*)

reverse
1 =reversal, e.g. 'reverse the car' – RAC 2 indicates transposition of elements or words clued to form answer, e.g. 'benign fellow reversed' – MANKIND (i.e. KIND MAN reversed) 3 indicates opposite of word clued, e.g. 'keep in reverse' – RELEASE 4 indicates words in clue should be reversed to get correct clue to answer, e.g. 'How one got a stone of metal? No, the reverse' (*S. Tel.*, 21.6.81) – SMELTED (i.e. got not a stone of metal, but a metal of stone)
Is Mr Rees a man of vision? No, the reverse (4)

revert
= reversal, e.g. 'Deb reverts to it when tired?' – BED
Field reverts to soft gold colour (6)

revolution(ary), revolver
1 CHE (i.e. Che Guevara) 2 = reversal, usually in across clue, e.g. 'the French revolution' – EL or AL or SEL 3 = anagram or palindrome, e.g. 'Distributor is armed with this revolver' – ROTOR
Pain for a revolutionary (4) (*Guard.*)

revolutionary leader
Usually CHE as in previous entry
Revolutionary leader and leaders of Kazakh Army were once the secret police (5)

revolver
1 see **revolution(ary)** 2 reference to something that *revolves*, e.g. wheel, turnstile, turntable, planet, etc.
Revolver not affected with recoil (5) (*Now!*, 16.4.81)

Rex
1 K 2 R 3 reference to a *king* (of any kind), e.g. 'Rex Wiseman' – SOLOMON
A shout of approval for Rex taking a paddle (4)

Rhode Island
RI
Annoyed Edward in Rhode Island (5)

right
1 LIEN 2 R 3 RT
Regular journey right out east (5)

right hand
RH
Star almost caught in right hand – that's tough! (6)

right-winger
TORY
Gesture by a right-winger indicates he's made his mark (9)

ring
1 BAND 2 HOOP 3 O
Silver ring gone (3)

rise
= reversal, in down clue, e.g. 'get up' – TEG
Discharge young lady rising – wrong hour for it (7) (*Times*, 4.7.81)

river
1 R 2 indicates short name of river; for a selection, see **flower** 2
River circles Maidenhead – it covers quite an area (4)

road
1 MI 2 RD 3 ST
Calls off road works (5)

rock
ORE
Drill through soft rock (4)

rodent
RAT
Bring rodent to her? Why, of course! (6)

Rolls Royce
RR
A Rolls Royce like a tapestry! (5)

(of) **Rome, Roman**
indicates Roman or Latin word or symbol, especially a Roman numeral (I, V, X, L, C, D, M), e.g. 'five Roman . . .' – V, 'Roman greeting' – AVE, 'Father of the Roman Empire' – PATER, 'Roman country' – RUS
Do your best in Rome at forty, say? (5)

roof
indicates first letter of word, usually in down clue, e.g. 'slate roof' – S
Cosily plain under a tin roof (6) (*Obs.*, 21.6.81)

Roosevelt
FDR
Cricket stroke of Roosevelt I've followed (3-5)

(a) **rose-red city**
PETRA ('A rose-red city – "half as old as Time"!' – the only well-known quotation from the poem 'Petra' by the Rev. John William Burgon (1813–88); Petra is actually in Jordan)

A poet's composition concerns a rose-red city and a king's honour (8)

rotter
CAD
Rotter, for example, comes back to beg (5)

round
1 O 2 = 'straddle', e.g. 'pant round the lake' – PLANT (i.e. PANT round L) 3 = anagram
Clear round the swan (4)

row
1 DIN 2 LINE 3 OAR 4 TIER
Soft row to Duncansby Head for somewhere to stay and eat (5)

rowers
EIGHT
French rowers had this on board (7)

Roy
possibly HUDD (i.e. Roy Hudd, the English comedian)
Roy went first – and we all crowded together (7)

Royal Artillery
RA
Gold box for Royal Artillery band (9) (*Guard.*)

Royal Engineers
RE
Concern about the Royal Engineers (4)

Royal Society
RS
Tea at the Royal Society was a sad display (5)

rubbish
ROT
Object to having to step awkwardly round rubbish (7)

Rugby (Union)
RU
Rugby Union: Poles v. Scots. But these other players weren't involved! (8)

ruler
1 ER 2 K 3 R
Religious ruler going out to sea (4) (*Guard.*)

runner
1 HORSE 2 reference to *river* (see **flower** 2, **river**)
Runner cut off north (7) (*Obs.*, 22.2.81)

run over
= palindrome, e.g. 'Little dog run over' – PUP
Run over joke (3)

Russian
1 RED 2 SERGE
Russian army engineers come to Poles to put things right (7)

Russian city
GRAD (i.e. the element of many Russian cities such as Lenin*grad*, Volgo*grad*, that actually means 'city')
Russian city in the north is very imposing (5)

Russian fighter, Russian jet
MIG
Russian jet went east. I was inside and got a bad headache! (8)

S

's
1 S 2 = 'burial', e.g. 'Humankind's relations' – KIN (i.e. of 'human*kind*') 3 indicates 'is the answer', that is, words in clue that follow, e.g. 'It's a story!' – PARABLE
King Arthur's garden (5) (*Obs.*, 7.12.80)

Sabbath
S
Place of retirement for head of cathedral to linger around the Sabbath (8)

(it's) **said**
= homophone, e.g. 'It's said maid did it' – MADE (i.e. MADE is said MAID)
When everything's said, they're boring instruments (4) (*Guard.*)

sailor
1 AB 2 RATING 3 SALT 4 TAR
Sailor to get first taste of pie (4)

sailors
RN
Rushed to the sailors (4)

saint
1 S 2 ST 3 indicates common name of *saint*, e.g. MARK, PETER, PAUL
Bird fabled to bring babies for saint or king (5)

salesman
REP
Salesman gets a hat – he's inclined to creep! (7)

(the) **same** (again)
DO (i.e. ditto)
Deal out the same again to the French (4)

(the) **same whichever way you look at it**
= palindrome, e.g. 'The mistake is the same whichever way you look at it' – BOOB
The affair is the same whichever way you look at it (4)

sanctimonious
PI
Flier is a sanctimonious character! (5)

sapper(s)
RE (i.e. Royal Engineers)
Sappers' previous meal (6)

Sarah
SAL
Almost worship Sarah? This is a real setback! (8)

sat
POSED
Rendered favourable – where wounded pride's sat (11)

Saturday
SAT
Fine silk to be worn on Saturday at home? (5)

say
1 indicates an example of answer required, e.g. 'the 8.15, say' – TRAIN 2 indicates a definition, often a homophone, e.g. 'hit against, say' – BUTTON (i.e. BUTT ON) 3 = homophone, e.g. 'Rum? I'll say!' (*Guard.*) – ISLE (i.e. isle of RUM, with homophones I'LL and ISLE)
Czech writer's record, say? (11)

scan
1 CON 2 READ
To scan the seat, say, is a rather far-fetched idea (7)

scholar
1 BA 2 MA
Scholar gets blue in error – it's just childish nonsense! (6)

schoolwork
PREP
Rewarded in advance for schoolwork assistance (7)

science
SC
Science, chemistry and history heads give zero (0) to pupil here (6)

scoop out
indicates that middle letter(s) of word are missing, e.g. 'egg scooped out' – EG, 'soup scooped out' – SP
Slimy creatures have scooped out shell and ears with the top cut off (5)

score
XX
Not sure, love, about score – shall we see the copy? (5)

(in) **Scotland**
indicates Scots word or name, e.g. 'not in Scotland' – NA, 'only in Scotland' – AIN (see also following entries)
Gloomy lake in Scotland reveals its secret nature (8)

Scot(sman), (the) **'Scotsman'**
1 IAN 2 MAC 3 MON
Like Scotsmen from the East? (6) (*S.T.*, 2.8.81)

Scot's own
AIN (i.e. Scots word for 'own')
First great Scot's own victory (4)

Scottish chimney
LUM
Scottish chimney in some quarters was associated with the Gorbals (5)

Scottish eye
EE
To an upper-class quiet Scottish eye it's a top cover-up! (6)

scoundrel
CUR
The scoundrel's on the railway – this'll make it hot for him! (5)

script
MS
Lawyer and his script puts an obstacle in the way (4)

sea
1 C 2 DEEP 3 MAIN 4 MED
Soldiers by the sea are left behind (6)

sea-monster
ORC
'Sea-monster in West: Queen to supply cathedral city!' (9)

(a) **second**
1 B 2 MO 3 S 4 SEC
Make fun of the second to finish? (4, 2) (*Times*, 18.7.81)

second class
B
Second-class or fifth-class – it's all a wearisome matter (4)

secretary
1 CIS (i.e. member of the Chartered Institute of Secretaries) 2 SEC
Encourage secretary on the day (6)

see
1 C 2 LO 3 indicates name of cathedral city, which has an episcopal *see*; most common is ELY 4 = 'burial', e.g. 'See a gambling game in the Robin Goodfellow' – BINGO (i.e. see BINGO in 'Ro*bin Go*odfellow')
See order appear, but not distinctly (4)

seer
EYE (compare **listener**)
Porter half converts seer before the king (8)

seize
= 'straddle', e.g. 'Soldiers seize silver in anger' – RAGE (i.e. RE seize AG)
Men seize a middle position (4)

self
1 EGO 2 ID
Help oneself! (3)

self-help
DIY
Jack's a learner getting involved in self-help slowly! (7) (*Now!*, 3.4.81)

semi(-)
indicates half a word or element, e.g. 'semicircle' – CIR, 'semi-detached' – DETA
Experienced semi-nude up river (9) (*Obs.*, 9.8.81)

send round, send back
= reversal, in across clue, e.g. 'tin's sent back' – SNIT
It's sent back twice to an Italian artist (6)

sergeant-major
SM
Well turned-out sergeant-major has skill (5)

servant
MAN
Servant thanks Ray (5)

service
1 MASS 2 RAF 3 RN
State service (4)

service charge
FEE
Initial calculation of service charge for drink (6)

serviceman
GI
Serviceman on foot is present (4)

set
indicates that letter, element or word is to be written or 'set' next to another (or where

stated), e.g. 'Set foot on the "Ra", a water-borne vessel made of logs' – RAFT (i.e. FT on RA)
Huge soldier set on worker (5)

setback
= reversal, e.g. 'sad setback' – DAS
Minor setback is a drag (4)

settled
LIT
Settled on hill next to the Italian coastal district (8)

seven (7)
VII
Begs attendance of seven sent hither and thither . . . (7) (*Times*, 23.5.81)

several
indicates high Roman numeral, usually L, C, D or M
Several advertisements for the boys (4)

sex appeal
IT
Former lover had sex appeal – that's a departure! (4)

shade see **colour(ed)**

she
1 GAL 2 HER 3 LASS 4 indicates short girl's name (see **girl** 8 for common examples)
She comes to tea and has a drink (6)

sheep
1 EWE 2 RAM 3 TEG 4 TUP
Man-made port for sheep? Yes, back that! (6)

shelter
1 LEE 2 = 'straddle', e.g. 'She shelters men over end of garage, although showing signs of being disabled' – LAMENESS (i.e. LASS shelters MEN over end of garag*e*)
Shelter for old coppers by northern town (5)

(the) **sheriff's men**
POSSE
Sheriff's men brought ship to Eddie – what got into them? (9)

shilling
1 BOB 2 S
Cut off with a shilling on the summit? (4)

ship
among most popular are: ARK, BRIG, SS, SUB, TUG
A ship is the first to come to aid (6)

shivery
1 BRR 2 = anagram
Remus's buddy is shivery in the east with this poor player (4, 6)

short, shorten, shortly
1 indicates abbreviation, e.g. 'I had shortened' – ID, 'a short time' – MIN 2 indicates standard element or word minus one or more letters, e.g. 'went short' – WEN, 'spoke shortly' – SPOK
Stop short by first Woolworth's store (4)

short week-end
1 SAT 2 WE
A short week-end for Eddie, the contemptible fellow! (4)

show
= 'burial', e.g. 'Oscar Edwards shows a concern' – CARE (i.e. 'Os*car E*dwards' shows CARE)
Get at steward going North to show pomp (5)

shut in
PENT
Shut in since noon in American armed forces HQ (8)

shut up(!)
SH
Twaddle until shut up (4) (*Obs.*, 9.8.81)

shy
COY
Creature is shy and backs up (5)

sick(ly)
1 AIL 2 ILL 3 = anagram
Puny beginner is sick, so takes one of these (4)

Sid
often used in clues of the type 'if Sid turns up . . .' to produce DIS
If Sid turns up with an accusation he'll get this and be out of a job (9)

side
1 TEAM 2 XI (i.e. a cricket or other 'eleven')
Side is in and French go out (4)

side of the stage
OP (i.e. 'opposite prompt', otherwise the actor's right on a stage)
Jump from a height on the side of the stage (3)

Sidney [compare **Sid**]
SID
At home, Sidney has several debts. How underhand! (9)

sign
indicates (usually) one of signs of Zodiac, among most likely being ARIES (Ram) and LIBRA (Balance)
Sign on the line for a collection of books (7)

sign of nerves
TIC
The graduate with sign of nerves concerning a thesis (8) (*S.T.*, 9.8.81)

silence
1 MUM 2 SH
Silence for the organ – cut! (5)

silver
AG (Latin *argentum*)
Attacker got silver and gold out of work unit returning to ship (9) (*Times*, 25.7.81)

since
AS
Agreement since despatched (6)

sing
HUM
Sing softly for despondency! (4)

(a) **single**
1 ONE 2 SOLE
A hundred singles deserves some ice-creams! (5)

(a) **single performance**
GIG
Single performance is a real caper – it's great! (8)

singular(ly)
indicates plural word minus final S, e.g. 'singular times' – HOUR
Scoundrels singularly are poison! (6) (*S.T.*, 14.6.81)

sit
POSE
About to sit and have a rest (6)

sited in
= 'burial', e.g. 'metal sited in West Indies' – TIN (i.e. sited in 'Wes*t In*dies')
Tree sited in Whitechapel mews (3)

six (6)
VI
Six small stations offer good views (6)

sleep
1 KIP 2 NAP 3 NOD 4 ZZ
Lively bird has sleep in (5)

slice (of)
= 'burial', e.g. 'Slice of white meat is just one of many' – ITEM (i.e. slice of 'wh*ite me*at')
Slice of plum pudding is just a piece of stodge (4)

sloth
AI (the name of the three-toed sloth, apparently derived from its cry)
Sloth in the navy is regarded as very wet! (4)

small
1 WEE 2 indicates abbreviation or shortened word, e.g. 'small river' – R, 'small volume' – CC, 'small man' – GENT, 'small sea' – MED, 'small thanks' – TA
Small soft cry (4) (*S.T.*, 2.8.81)

small girl
CHIT
Tunic that small girl has on? (6)

smell
BO
Boy goes back to smell – he's such a lout! (5)

snake
ASP
Snake in the arena making a grating sound (7)

snare
NET
Line nearly snares birds (7)

snooker ball
RED
Gets down snooker ball, then miscues (7) (*S. Tel.*, 19.7.81)

soar
= reversal, in down clue, e.g. 'bird soars' – DRIB, WORC, etc.
Pilots are soaring there, nearly, but at a greater distance (7)

socialist
RED
Socialist newspaper is a cause of infuriation (3, 3)

socially acceptable
U (i.e. upper class)
Socially acceptable in top quarters to wear one of these? (6)

social worker
ANT
Petty officer gives mixed gin to social worker – how touching! (8)

society
S(OC)
Society standards as determined by philosopher (8)

society-girl
DEB
Society-girl, when broadcasting, looks very elegant (8)

soft(ly)
P
One soft drink and one beer? Just one light beer, please (4, 3)

so it's said
= homophone, e.g. 'Remained sober, so it's said' – STAID (i.e. STAYED, so it's said)
Nearly a trial, so it's said (5)

soldier
1 GI 2 NCO
Soldier on the road has the French belt (6)

(some) **soldiers**
1 MEN 2 RA (i.e. Royal Artillery) 3 RE (i.e. Royal Engineers) 4 TA (i.e. Territorial Army)
The soldiers have a meal, apparently just a salad (6)

some (of), (to) **some extent**
1 ANY 2 = 'burial', e.g.. 'some fever if endemic' – RIFE (i.e. some 'fever *if e*ndemic')
Bought some fine wool (originally from Sydney) (6)

somersault
1 = reversal, often in down clue, e.g. 'somersaulting sheep' – MAD, MAR, etc. 2 = anagram
Pat somersaults over Edward – she's got him weighed up! (5)

something
IT
Forget to order something (4)

something of
= 'burial', e.g. 'It's something of a tall order to get a duke' – LORD (i.e. something of 'a tal*l ord*er')
Drink is something of a special effect (3)

some time
HR (i.e. hour)
Spasm found some time in toe (5)

song
1 AIR 2 ARIA 3 LAY 4 ODE
Write a soft song for the dramatic production (4)

sort of square
T (i.e. T-square)
Old musical instrument has a back that ends in a sort of square (6)

so to speak
1 = homophone, e.g. 'Grain is in instalments, so to speak' – CEREAL (i.e. is SERIAL, so to speak) 2 indicates non-

literal or punning sense, e.g. 'Amateur on the waves, so to speak' (*Font.*) – RADIO HAM
You are (so to speak) taken out and enticed (5) (*Guard.*)

sound (like), **sound as if**
= homophone, e.g. 'sound lines of animals' – ROES
Rent paid sounds as if it should be greater (4)

sound unit
BEL (i.e. the measure for comparing intensity of noise, as in 'decibel')
Sound unit applied to a number of small things in this church building (6)

source (of)
indicates first letter of word or element, e.g. 'source of interest' – I, 'source of energy' – E
Matthew is source of envy of his friend at work (4)

south(ern)
S
Tales of the southern party members (7)

South Africa(n)
SA
Father Christmas is social worker in South Africa! (5)

South America(n)
SA
The great story of South America and the leaders of the Grand Alliance (4)

South Dakota
SD
I'd return to South Dakota, and almost die in torment, but I scorned this (9)

south-east
SE
Plant in the south-east is identical (6)

sovereign
1 L (i.e. pound) 2 = **king, queen** (which see)
Sovereign is in bed having lost blood (4)

Spaniard
DON
Beautiful boy a Spaniard is following (6) (*Font.*)

Spanish, in Spain
indicates Spanish word, e.g. 'the Spanish' – EL, 'Spanish gentleman' – DON, SENOR, 'spanish hero' – CID
This bend is called The Spanish Bow (5)

spasm
TIC
Article on spasms and grotesque acts (6)

speak
ORATE
Choose to speak for the voters (10)

speakeasy
= homophone, e.g. 'Record for right speakeasy' – WRITE
Sight speakeasy at this point (4)

spectacles
OO
Thanks to non-drinker, who has spectacles on, we can see the military display (6)

speed
1 MPH 2 RATE
Speed round, speed! It's urgent! (9)

sphere
O
Here's a sphere 'twixt west and east;
Here's misfortune, at the least (3)

spirit
1 ELF 2 GIN 3 RUM 4 SPRITE
Notes officer taking spirit – such propriety! (7)

spiteful woman
CAT
Spiteful women holding it back still (6) (*Times*, 25.7.81)

split
1 indicates inserted letter(s), element or word, e.g. 'Pole splits piece of wood' – LONG (i.e. N splits LOG) 2 indicates half a word or one with letter(s) missing, e.g. 'Tina split on disorganised worker – a real giant!' – TITAN (i.e. TINA split on disorganised ANT) 3 = anagram
Communion cup chap split with girl (7) (*S. Tel.*, 5.7.81)

spoil
1 MAR 2 = anagram
Spoil mixed grain after end of voyage, so have this spread instead (9)

spot (in)
= 'burial', e.g. 'Louse-egg spotted in furniture' – NIT
Bird spotted in the wilderness (4)

spouse
MATE
'E's bringing it back to 'is spouse, that's my guess (8)

spring
1 SPA 2 WELL
Spring line is out of the true for this springer! (7)

sprite
PERI ('a Persian fairy', says *Chambers*)
Sprite is here, and here my endless verse,
So see the time in which I run my course (6)

spy
AGENT
Graduate engages spy, reveals reddish purple colour (7)

(kind of) **square**
T
We came to a kind of square where there was much evidence of the recent rain (3)

staff
ROD
Reminder for first member of probationary staff (4)

staff officer
SO
The Staff Officer and the German Channel (5)

stamped addressed envelope
SAE
First form in stamped addressed envelope will be quite secure (4)

stand
= reversal, in down clue, e.g. 'stand on . . .' – NO, 'open stand' – NEPO
Girl gets dress at right stand (7)

standard
1 FLAG 2 NORM 3 PAR
Standard is high in this ecclesiastical district (6)

star
ACE
Look towards fellow star (4)

starboard
R
Floating mass of logs – starboard, aft (4)

start (of), **starter**
indicates first letter(s) of word or element, e.g. 'good start' – G, 'cheerful start' – CH, 'second starter' – S
Fascination could start to hurt (5) (*Guard.*)

start of an era
ADI (i.e. A.D. 1)
Start of an era in strange metal (6)

state
1 AVER 2 abbreviated name of American state, with some of most popular being: ALA, CAL, DC, FLA, ILL, MASS, MINN, NY, TEX, VA 3 = anagram
State I've come to is huge (7)

station
ST
Condition of station at Carlisle end (5)

staunch
STEM
Senior youth leaders staunch in their method (6)

steal
NICK
Steal the Spanish metal (6)

steamer, steamship
SS
Headland gives bearings to steamer (4)

stern
TAIL
Half of MS is written in stern eastern language (5) (*Obs.*, 12.7.81)

stick
1 GUM 2 JAM 3 POLE 4 ROD
Gold stick raised above officer (5) (*Guard.*)

stitch
SEW
Stitch back to start of trimming – in this direction? (4)

stomach
1 MAW 2 TUM
Put peg to stomach – it goes round and round (8)

stop
END
Five stop to offer goods for sale (4)

story
1 FABLE 2 LIE 3 TALE
First short story is very unoriginal (5)

strait
ST
Make sudden move, trapping seaman in strait (5) (*Obs.*, 12.7.81)

strange
1 RUM 2 = anagram
Strange, disorganised game, a real upheaval (7)

street
ST
Style of the street is quite unpretentious (6)

strike
1 BUTT 2 HIT 3 LAM 4 PAT 5 RAP 6 TAP
Scottish strike leads to a fight (5)

string
strictly speaking, could be any one of four strings of violin, i.e. G, D, A or E, but in practice (because of familiar 'g-string') is almost always G, although occasionally E
The string is out – it's quite painful (4)

strong(ly)
F (i.e. for *f*orte, or possibly for *f*orce)
Clear, strong air (4)

student
L (i.e. *l*earner)
Student points to shelter (3)

study
1 CON 2 DEN 3 READ 4 SCAN
Study a branch of learning – if you're good, it will be clear (10) (*Obs.*, 2.8.81)

study hard
CRAM
First student to study hard? Get away with you! (5)

stuff
PAD
Stuff the weed into the field (7)

stunning blow
KO
Stunning blow in the manner of an Australian bear-like creature (5)

subsequently
LATER
Great admirer I'd love subsequently (8)

such
SO
Such feet are easily cut (4)

(to) **suit**
FOR
A ceremony to suit a thousand (4)

sulphur
S
Sulphur on metal can cause irritation (4)

summer
1 ADDER 2 TOTTER
Fifty summers for us to go up and down (7)

sun
SOL (i.e. the Roman god of the sun, with Sol being the Latin for 'sun')
The Sun goes to Japan – exclusive! (4)

Sunday
S(UN)
Sunday for a superior meal (6)

Sunday school
SS
Girl for the French Sunday school (4)

sunk (in)
= 'burial', e.g. 'Vegetables sunk in Caribbean Sea' – BEANS (i.e. in 'Carib*bean S*ea')
Tile sunk in North Atlantic (3)

superior (to)
indicates element or word above another, in down clue, e.g. 'Soldiers superior to the people' – REPUBLIC (i.e. RE superior to PUBLIC)
Looks which show that gravity is superior to weapons (7) (*S.T.*, 5.4.81)

support(er)
1 LEG 2 PROP 3 indicates letter(s), element or word under another, in down clue, e.g. 'University man is supporter of a prohibition in desert' – ABANDON (i.e. DON is supporter of A BAN)
It's the right thing to support the Queen (6)

surgeon
1 BS 2 VET
Crowds round physician and surgeon (4) (*Obs.*, 18.1.81)

surprise
HA
Surprise regarding this timid creature (4)

Surrey
SY
Officer posted to Surrey, where he is very much at home (4)

surround
='straddle', e.g. 'The ceremony when soldiers surround it' – RITE (i.e. RE surround IT)
Farm vehicles surround hill crest in cases of fire (10)

Susan
SUE
Susan's half nude, the undressed kid! (5)

swallow
= 'straddle', e.g. 'Lou's swallowed tea' – LOTUS (i.e. LOUS swallowed T)
Woman turns and swallows one in the gangway (5) (*S.T.*, 19.7.81)

swear
AVER
Mean to swear when coming to mature years (7)

T

(to a) **T**
T
To seek advice fits a diplomat to a T (7) (*Obs.*, 2.8.81)

t'
T (mock North of England form of 'the', as 'trouble at t' mill')
Stepped on t' pole (4)

tail [see also next entry]
indicates last letter of word or element, e.g. 'dog tail' – G
Change head and tail, and this rogue would be a sailor (6)

tailed [see also previous entry]
1 indicates that letter(s), element or word follow another, e.g. 'copper tailed by first ruffian' – CUR (i.e. CU tailed by R) 2 indicates final letter of word is missing, e.g. 'tailed cat' – CA
Officer tailed by dogs, as it happens (6)

tailless
indicates that last letter of word is missing, e.g. 'tailless cat' – CA or PUS
Tailless monkey comes to former point (4)

take
1 R (i.e. *recipe*, Latin word meaning 'take' used in medical prescriptions) 2 indicates that one word or element 'takes' another, that is, is followed by it, e.g. 'he takes pupils' – HELL
Wine that she takes king on railway (6)

take aback
= reversal, e.g. 'I'm taken aback' – MI
Tim taken aback about the bishop's hat (5)

taken
LED
First skier taken to start of Grande Escarpe – on this? (6)

take in
1 = 'burial', e.g. 'we take in avenue' – WAVE (i.e. WE take in AV) 2 indicates that R (= 'take') is inserted in word, e.g. 'Cricketers take in annoying kids' – BRATS (i.e. BATS with R in)
Bob takes in pupil getting no marks (4)

take out
indicates that letter(s), element or word should be removed from relatively long word(s) to form smaller, e.g. 'Take nothing out of shoe for her' – SHE (i.e. take O out of SHOE)
Frenchman taken out of camp shows his hat (5)

take to heart
= 'straddle', e.g. 'he takes you to heart' – HUE
He takes girl to heart – Greek, she is (7)

take up
usually indicates that element or word in down clue is followed by another, reversed, e.g. 'she takes Ali up' – SHEILA
Bill takes up rubbish – and makes good show of it! (5)

talented
ABLE
Quite famous, though not talented (7)

tavern
1 INN 2 LOCAL 3 PUB
Both the tavern (the 'Half Lily') and the town get good media exposure (9)

tax
VAT
Tax on a container in Roman palace (7)

taxi
CAB
Southern Taxis – and the blacklegs who drive them? (5)

tea
1 CHA(R) 2 T
Dread making a mistake after tea? (6) (*S.T.*, 2.8.81)

tea-break
usually works out as ATE (i.e. anagram of TEA)
To begin in it I have a tea-break (8)

team
1 SIDE 2 XI
Like team in German-Italian alliance of 1936, for example (4)

tea-time
1 IV 2 V
Storm back after tea-time at home for this condiment (7)

technique
ART
Conquer by cunning but must change in love technique (8) (*S.T.*, 9.8.81)

Ted(dy)
ED
Influence Teddy, he's behaving in such an artificial way (8)

tee
T
Speed off from the tee – there's the line! (5)

teetotal(ler)
TT
Wait on a teetotaller to complete the course (6)

telepathy
ESP (i.e. extra-sensory perception)
Telepathy with religious ceremony, almost – there's real comradeship! (6)

ten (10)
1 TEN 2 X
Greek orthodox bishop listens, having ten in church (6)

terminate
END
Ring road to terminate at this continental port (6)

terriers (Terriers) [see also next entry]
TA (i.e. Territorial Army)
Terriers are first wet, then dry – all rather worthless (6)

Territorials, Territorial Army
TA
Army or Territorial Army, drawing blood? (5) (*Guard.*)

(voice-)**test**
ORAL
Pain-relief test making the Scottish retreat (8)

Texas, Texan
TEX
Synthetic rubber product sent from Los Angeles to Texas (5)

thanks, thank you
TA
Thanks to the horse, Teddy was closely followed (6)

that is, that's
IE
That's money, that is, 'The Club' (7)

that's right
YES
Points scored without touching the ball banned initially – that's right (4)

theatre
REP
Actor, say – place for me in right theatre coming up? (9) (*Times*, 29.8.81)

theatre of war
ENSA (i.e. the Entertainments National Service Association)
Commanding officer and MP arrive at theatre of war, and French retreat to make good the loss (10)

the end
Z
The end circle has points attached for the belt (4)

the old
YE
The old northern longing (3)

the one here
THIS
The one here allowed false Scottish emblem (7)

the ones here
THESE
Essays – the ones here – student's starting (6)

the ones there
THOSE
Tights are 'dishy' – I get in the ones there (9)

the one there
THAT
Straw roofing for the one there, the church (6)

there
usually indicates that answer is 'burial' in previous word(s), e.g. 'Copenhagen writer there' – PEN (buried in 'Co*pen*hagen')
London, England – made there! (4)

therefore
ERGO (term used in logic, Latin for 'therefore')
Port of London Authority, therefore, take in garden structure (7)

Theresa
TESS
Doubtful gain for Theresa, she's such a big girl! (8)

this
1 indicates that answer is first half of word or phrase, of which second half is word after 'this' in clue, e.g. 'this body is important' – SOME (i.e. 'this body' – SOMEBODY), 'this rose after the wars' – TUDOR (i.e. 'this rose' – TUDOR ROSE) 2 indicates that clue, or part of it, provides specific indication of answer, e.g. 'London, Paris . . . this is excellent' – CAPITAL (i.e. two examples, punning, then 'this' is the definition, non-punning)
This pet is a darling, Dad! (3)

this month
INST (old formal letter-writing jargon, short for 'instant')

This month everyone is to get set up and operational (7)

thoroughfare
1 RD 2 ST
Tear around the thoroughfare and you get a delay (6)

(a) **thousand (1000)**
M
Customs have a thousand metal containers (5)

(a) **thousand dollars ($1000)**
G (= 'grand')
Put a thousand dollars on this craft and you'll get an illicit profit! (5)

thrice
TER (as in 'tercentenary')
Thrice run round the balcony (7)

through
THRO
Cast through the opening week (5)

throw
LOB
Throw past the passage (5)

throw back
= reversal, in across clue, e.g. 'part thrown back' – TRAP
Catches fish, but throws ten back after start of supper (4)

throw up
= reversal, in down clue, e.g. 'throw up pan' – NAP
Throw up rod with my golf score (5)

thus
1 SIC 2 SO 3 = anagram
Alternative thus provided in tin for islander (8) (*S.T.*, 12.4.81)

tilt
CANT
Initially slight tilt, but not really enough (5)

time, The Times
several possibilities, among most popular being: AM, AGE, DATE, ERA, EVE, HOUR, T
Respect the time in changing the event (8) (*S.T.*, 9.8.81)

tin
1 CAN 2SN (Latin *stannum*)
Tin and silver are quite a catch! (4)

tip (of)
indicates first, or less often, last letter(s) of word, e.g. 'tip of iceberg' – I, 'filter-tip' – R
I got on tip of iceberg and nearly reached the sea! (6)

title see **decoration**

to
indicates letter, element or word is added to or joined to another, e.g. 'He goes to students – it's a place of torment' – HELL (i.e. HE goes to LL)
Pass to our blue or red, for example (6)

to a certain extent
= 'burial', e.g. 'Left-winger unprepared, to a certain extent' – RED (i.e. 'unprep*ared*' to a certain extent)
Nobleman belongs to social order, to a certain extent (4)

to and fro
= palindrome, e.g. 'blow to and fro' – TOOT
Canoe goes to and fro (5)

Tom
indicates reference to *cat*, e.g. 'Tom loses a little . . .' – PUS
Tom and family gather this flower (6)

top
indicates first letter(s) of word, usually in down clue, e.g. 'the top of the radiator' – RAD, 'the top' – T, 'top of the morning' – M
Tip-top covering for the roof! (6)

top grade
A (in American schools)
Concerning top grade round (5)

topless
indicates that first letter of word is missing, e.g. 'topless girl' – AL (i.e. GAL minus G)

Topless lass in Mediterranean is ready to attack on a broad front! (6)

(Mr) **Torme**
MEL (i.e. Mel Torme, the American popular singer and film actor)
A medley for Mr Torme and the French Angel (7)

torn
RENT
Father torn in his role as head of the family (6)

touch (of)
indicates a single letter of a word, usually the first, e.g. 'a touch of class' – C
Legal document with humour – and there's a touch of ribaldry in it (4) (*Now!*, 20.3.81)

town
CITY
Lack of provisions is a blemish on the town (8)

track
1 DOG 2 RY
Ancient house on a track (5)

trade union
TU
Trade union for the navy? That will be a change! (4)

trainees
OTC (i.e. Officer Training Corps)
Trainees in New Hampshire are in good nick! (5)

training
1 PE 2 PT
House-training gives confidence (4)

train(s)
1 RY 2 = anagram
Transport vehicle by train (5)

traitor
RAT
High-ranking man from car is to punish traitor (10)

transgress
SIN
Transgress against the king, becoming increasingly degraded as a result (7)

translate
1 TR 2 indicates foreign word, usually French, e.g. 'Translate the New Testament in this period of abstinence' – LENT (i.e. translate 'the' = LE+NT) 3 = anagram
Passage from article said to need translation (4) (*Guard.*)

transport
usually short word or abbreviation indicating method of transport, among most popular being: BR, BUS, CAB, CAR, CART, RY, TRAM, VAN
Transport the French messages (6)

trap
1 GIN 2 NET 3 = 'straddle', e.g. 'Grumble from man who traps nothing' – MOAN (i.e. MAN traps O)
Singular clicking instrument will mean you have to throw a trap (8)

travel
GO
Travel with Reg round to the ravine (5)

traveller
REP
Traveller comes to Broken Hill, and we have his account (6)

tree
among those most commonly found are: ASH, BAY, ELM, FIR, NUT, OAK
Tree in the mixed cover on top (6)

trial
TEST
Witness at trial (6) (*S.T.*, 2.8.81)

tribesman
DAN (not Daniel, but Jacob's fifth son in the Old Testament, the ancestor of the twelve tribes of Israel)
After us returning tribesman comes to African land (5)

trim
indicates word minus first and last letters, e.g. 'trimmed cloth' – LOT
To tour round trimmed linen is all in the day's work (7)

trouble
1 ADO 2 AIL 3 = anagram
After trouble dole out flattery (9) (*S.T.*, 19.7.81)

try
1 GO 2 = anagram
Try to do in return that which is worthy (4)

tuck in(to)
= 'burial', e.g. 'We tuck in to set pudding' – SWEET (i.e. WE tuck into SET)
Diana tucks into the meat after the end of the pie – I think I'll have to intervene! (7)

tune
AIR
Rock musical has hard tune (4)

turf
SOD
Turf over lair is wet through (6)

turncoat
RAT
Curse the dead turncoat! (4)

turn (over), **turn about, turn back** [etc.] [but see also next entry]
1 = reversal, e.g. 'turn stomach' – MUT, 'turn back the carpet' – GUR 2 = anagram
Turnabout Timothy goes to the East;
Of all the small creatures he's one of the least! (4)

turn up
= reversal, in down clue, e.g. 'we turn up' – EW
Sam turns up on the bed – that'll bring us luck (6)

TV doctor
WHO
TV doctor moves half left – that's complete (5)

twelve (12)
1 DOZ 2 XII
Having slept, the twelve went to the editor (5)

twenty (20)
1 SCORE 2 XX
No more than twenty died, it's emphasised (11)

twenty-five pounds (£25)
PONY (slang term for this sum)
£25 dog has special hair-do (4-4)

twice
1 BIS 2 indicates reduplicated letter(s), e.g. 'twice caught' – CC, 'is twice . . .' – ISIS
Twice cut round a cake (7)

twitch
1 TIC 2 = anagram
Are you the first sufferer to twitch? Do you live in the country? (6)

two hundred (200)
CC
Quite an event – 0–200 as I got on (8)

twopence (2p)
PP
I got twopence in the arena – that's excellent! (7)

two pounds (£2, 2lb)
LL
Bachelor gets two pounds for dance (4)

two-way
= palindrome, e.g. 'Two-way transaction' – DEED
Two-way watcher of the seas and skies (5)

(in) **Tyneside, Tyne and Wear**
NE
Hop over to Tyneside – you can make your arrangements by using this! (5)

type of boat
usually works out as U, but in theory could also be E or Q
Type of boat, silent repair vessel (7)

type of bomb
1 A 2 H
Type of bomb on board set all wrong. Whose property is it? (6)

tyro
L (i.e. *l*earner)
Stage of course for tyro, for example (3)

ultimate(ly)
indicates last letter of word, e.g. 'energy ultimately' – Y, 'ultimate say' – Y
Uncivilised fellow got birch ultimately (4)

ultimate letter
Z
Ultimate letter comes to an end, a match for ancient sacred writings (4-6)

(is) **unable (are unable)**
CANT
Virginia is unable to empty this (6)

uncle
SAM
Uncle's acting the strong man (6) (*Obs.*, 19.7.81)

unconscious
OUT
Margaret unconscious? Let's hope she won't do this (3, 3)

under
indicates that letter, element or word is after another, in a down clue, e.g. 'I'm under public relations – very correct, too' – PRIM (i.e. IM under PR)
The Editor's under strain – that's emphasised (8) (*S. Tel.*, 25.1.81)

understand
1 SEE 2 indicates that element or word follows another in down clue and is also reversed, e.g. 'We understood the evil, given the strength' – SINEW (i.e. WE = EW 'understood' SIN)
You once understood the splendour of the emperor (6) (*Guard.*)

understudy
indicates word starting CON in down clue, i.e. a word that is 'under CON'
Policeman is reliable understudy (9)

underworld
DIS (i.e. the Underworld in classical mythology)
Change of dress is underworld appearance (8)

unfinished
indicates element or word minus final letter, e.g. 'tea is unfinished' – TE, 'that is unfinished' – IDES (i.e. ID EST unfinished)
The French song is unfinished, and we can learn from this (6)

unhesitatingly
indicates word minus ER (usually final), e.g. 'mother unhesitatingly . . .' – MOTH
Unhesitatingly, the monk provides soup (5) (*Font.*)

union
1 TU(C) 2 indicates abbreviation of well-known trade union, among the most common being NUM, NUR and NUT 3 indicates reference to 'marriage' and possibly to element WED 4 indicates joining of two words or elements, e.g. 'union of man and bird' – MANDRAKE
First three members of Magicians Union get a large bottle of wine (6)

United Nations
1 BLOC 2 UN
Part of speech from 'Disagreement at the United Nations' (4)

United States
US(A)
In brief, Central and Southern United States will have an official enumeration of their inhabitants (6)

universal
U
Universal Mixed Ices, an international organisation, initially (6)

university
U
University egghead reveals the custom (5)

university man
BA
University man to study the philosopher (5)

unknown (factor)
X
This tool is an article unknown by the east (3)

unlimited
usually indicates word minus final letter, e.g. 'unlimited pay' – PA
Unlimited time, I would say, shows a lack of courage (5)

unpaid [see also next entry]
HON
Graduate gets half-ration (unpaid) for his feat of endurance (8)

unpaid debts
IOUS
Do return unpaid debts, it's offensive as it is (6)

up(wards), uphill
= reversal, usually in down clue, e.g. 'tips up' – SPIT, 'call-up' – ETIC
Woman who gives up her advantage (5) (*S.T.*, 9.8.81)

up and down
= palindrome, in down clue, e.g. 'Move quickly up and down' – BOB (notice that clue is exact definition of 'bob' anyway)
Seed goes up and down over it – what a lark! (5)

upbringing
= reversal, in down clue, e.g. 'Son's upbringing' – NOS
Her upbringing was by ear, on points, and she had to practise (8)

upper class
U
Upper-class member shows anger when he's a referee (6)

upset
1 = reversal, usually in down clue, e.g. 'upset the cart' – TRAC, 'upset can' – NIT 2 = anagram
If she's upset, I complain (5) (*S.T.*, 5.7.81)

Ur
indicates that answer is in some way 'primitive', 'original', 'very old', either for ancient city Ur or for German prefix *ur*-, as in 'Eve, the ur-woman', e.g. 'Urban on this tree?' – KNOWLEDGE (i.e. 'original ban' which was on biblical tree of knowledge)
Urgent – in two words (7)

uranium
U
Uranium found in mixed metal by northern town in France (5)

urge
EGG
Urge the director, a real intellectual (7)

US
indicates American term, word, name or spelling, e.g. 'US soldier' – GI, 'US prosecutor' – DA
US quarterdeck can be just the right place (8)

us
US
The responsibility is, quite literally, on us (4)

utterly
= homophone, e.g. 'utterly bored' – BOARD
Poet utterly excluded (4)

V

value
RATE
Note value of packing case (5)

vehicle
among most popular types are BUS, CAB, CAR, CART, TRAM, VAN
Vehicle in room on board (5) (*S.T.*, 5.4.81)

veil
= 'straddle', e.g. 'Fog veils river and one who lives there?' – FROG (i.e. FOG veils R)
Ran veiled by church, getting uplift! (5)

versus
V
The Glen versus The Lane (6)

very [see also next entry]
usually indicates a superlative, that is, a word ending in EST, e.g. 'very large' – BIGGEST, 'very 'efty' – UGEST
Book about animals is very good one to have on a train (8)

very (good)
V(G)
Sort of sombrero, very good in Worcestershire (10) (*Guard.*)

very large, very big
OS (i.e. *o*ut*s*ize)
Distorting the very big moral significance (5)

very little, very small
WEE
Beetle is very small and mostly detestable (6)

very loud(ly)
FF
After tea there is a very loud quarrel (4)

very quiet(ly)
PP
Love comes on very quietly, or comes on with a tune;
It comes at a convenient time – quite late or very soon! (9)

very soft(ly)
PP
Prescribe a very soft ointment (only half to be used, however) (7)

vessel
one of the most productive clue words, usually referring to some type of boat or utensil; among the most common are: ARK, BRIG, CAN, CUP, DISH, PAN, POT, SS, SUB, TIN, TUG, TUN, URN, VAT
Headquarters of French vessel (5)

veto
NO
Legal officer gets veto thanks to railway (6)

vice
SIN (often in form 'in vice' indicating letter(s) in SIN, or SIN itself as 'burial' in other letters)
Vice points to muscular strength! (5)

Vichy water
EAU (i.e. French for 'water')
Soft Vichy water points to a French red wine! (6)

victory
V
Base victory, I'll say (4)

Violet
VI
Violet comes to church and talks wildly, crazily – or is it the other way round? (4, 5)

violin string
GUT
Beginner gets in violin string, too many of them, in fact (4)

Virgil
indicates Latin word, e.g. 'Virgil's country' – RUS
Virgil's father, also a writer (5) (*Times*, 11.7.81)

Virginia
VA
Virginia points to the weathercock (4)

virtuous
PI
Virtuous, abstemious, and almost coming to church to get special allowance (8)

vitamin
could be any of letters A to E, but usually turns out to be BI
Vitamin store will provide hot wine drink (6)

volcano
usually ETNA
Gold seen on erupting volcano, that's very decorative! (6)

volte-face
= reversal, e.g. 'made a volte-face' – EDAM
Do a volte-face on deal, initially? That's strange! (3)

volume
1 CC 2 TOME 3 VOL
Point to religious volume as an ideal example (7)

volunteers
TA (i.e. the Territorial Army)
Ray joins island volunteers (5) (*Times*, 8.8.81)

vulgar(ly)
1 NONU (i.e. 'non-U') 2 RUDE 3 indicates colloquial or slang word, including one minus initial H, e.g. 'In vulgar parlance it is not a blemish' – TAINT 4 = anagram
She and I very vulgarly wander about (7) (*S.T.*, 2.8.81)

W

wager
BET
US soldier places second-class wager, but it leads to the gallows! (6)

want(ing)
indicates missing letter(s) in word, e.g. 'hero wants nothing' – HER (i.e. HERO wants O)
Nellie is back, wanting one. She's just the same person! (5)

War Office
WO
War Office advertisement for plant (4)

was first (to do it)
LED
Loosed a blow for France – was first to do it (9) (*Guard.*)

was leader (of)
LED
Peter the First was leader of great emperors, initially, and made a solemn promise (6)

waste
1 DESERT 2 LOSE
Note waste in cathedral precinct (5)

was the conductor
LED
Enthusiast was the conductor and produced a trumpet call! (6)

water
RAIN
Soft water is essential for reasoned living (5)

watering place
SPA
Watering place has record, even for this boy (8)

water-pipe
H
Water-pipe is very large at end of drive – maybe we'll need this? (4)

way
among most commonly used are AVE, LANE, PATH, RD, ROAD, ROUTE, ST (but note that 'in a way' could be anagram)
In Tyneside, is waylaid for one's savings (4-3) (*S. Tel.*, 18.1.81)

we
indicates plural answer, usually as word that completes proverb or saying, e.g. 'We should be seen but not heard, said our grandparents' – CHILDREN
We make light work of it – at least, many of us do (5)

weapon
ARM
Water-pipe weapon can cause damage (4)

we are
WERE
We are Wolverhampton Wanderers (10) (*Guard.*)

Webster('s)
indicates American word, phrase, name or spelling (as in *Webster*, the American dictionary), e.g. 'Webster's paint' – COLOR
Unpaid worker gets gold – that's Webster's privilege (5)

we hear
= homophone, e.g. 'She's sound as a bell, we hear' – NELL (i.e. we hear KNELL)
We hear, adds up on board! (7) (*S. Tel.*, 31.5.81)

weight
among most popular are: DRAM, G, LB, TON(NE)
Grace has lost weight – so she should stand a better chance of winning this! (4)

(Mr) Weller
SAM (i.e. Sam Weller, in Dickens's *Pickwick Papers*)
Exotic state to be in, like Mr Weller (5)

well-known lines
BR
Well-known lines of Mr Hardy: 'It keeps the raindrops from my head' (6)

Welsh
1 W 2 indicates Welsh word or name, e.g. 'Welsh son' – AP, 'Welsh town' – BARRY
Welsh jazzman near Shrewsbury (10) (*Guard.*)

went ahead
LED
Mother and I went ahead and sent the letter (6)

we read
= homograph (i.e. word spelled exactly the same as another), e.g. 'Lovely show, we read' – FAIR (i.e. FAIR, 'lovely' and FAIR, the 'show')
Fine French city, we read (4) (*Font.*)

west(ern)
W
Western snake has a nasty sting (4)

we would
WED
We would embrace closely, probably, if in this state! (7)

what a surprise(!)
MY
Burglar's tool a gem, I hear, what a surprise! (5)

what your best friend won't talk about
BO
Identify what your best friend won't talk about – it's just a harmless drug (7)

when
AS
When flanked by two escorts initially, relax! (4) (*Obs.*, 26.7.81)

where
usually indicates place-name in answer, often with no precise information regarding location, e.g. 'Where you can count sheep as they go through?' – RAMSGATE
Where a big white bird is on the water (7)

while
AS
Money caught while hot (4)

whim
FAD
Whim of editor lost its originality (5)

whip
1 CAT 2 = anagram
Whip a toothed instrument from the ancient burial place (8)

why (apparently)
Y
Why point to model before the affair is finished? (3)

wicked
1 BAD 2 EVIL 3 VILE 4 = anagram
Wicked in his generation? That's just playful talk! (8)

William, Will(ie)
1 BILL 2 TELL 3 WILL 4 WM
William has mixed gin and it has quite a powerful effect (7)

wine
usually turns out to be PORT
Kill-joy ruins the wine (10) (*Obs.*, 2.8.81)

wise men
1 MAGI 2 SAGES 3 SEERS
Wise men came first – it was like a miracle (5)

with
1 CON (i.e. Italian musical direction or prefix CON- as in 'construct') 2 indicates that one letter, element or word goes with or joins another, e.g. 'Man with a cure for treatment of hands' – MANICURE (i.e. MAN with I CURE) 3 = anagram
Run together with dog (6)

withdraw
= reversal, in across clue, e.g. 'withdraw money' – NEY (i.e. withdraw YEN)
Withdraw ace on king and first of two eights in this card game (6)

within
= 'burial', e.g. 'Indefinite number within doors as benefactors' – DONORS (i.e. N within DOORS)
Point to quarters within the house (4)

without
1 indicates that answer ends in LESS, clue usually being in form 'without . . .', e.g. 'without light' – SUNLESS, 'without Arthur' – ARTLESS 2 = 'straddle', e.g. 'Chap seems to exist without money all right' – BLOKE (i.e. BE without L+OK) 3 indicates missing letter(s), element or word, e.g. 'Escape without money leads to a brawl' – FIGHT (i.e. FLIGHT without L) (see also next entry)
Discussing without using bad language? Hell! (3)

without (the) **extremes**
indicates word minus first and last letters, e.g. 'work without the extremes' – OR
Dances, tra-la, without the extremes of our forefathers (9) (*Obs.*, 9.8.81)

with regard to
RE
Translate 'with regard to the Italian leader' (6)

(Mr) **Wodehouse**
PG (i.e. P. G. Wodehouse, the English humorist)
I'll get in Mr Wodehouse, you greedy thing! (3)

woman
1 HER 2 SHE 3 indicates girl's name (see **girl** 8)
Small building where woman will need a penny (4)

Women's Institute
WI
Women's Institute takes tea before church – but surely *this* woman is not one of their number? (5)

wood
usually indicates reference to **tree**, which entry see for common kinds

work
1 ERG 2 OP 3 TOIL 4 = anagram
Chose work with a man (5) (*S.T.*, 9.8.81)

worker
1 ANT 2 BEE 3 HAND 4 MAN
Worker gets the first supply of sugar (4)

workers
1 ANTS 2 BEES 3 HANDS 4 MEN
Workers get fish as a sign of welcome (9)

work hard
CRAM
Work hard by the nasty smell;
Here's a rhyme for you to tell! (6)

working woman
CHAR
Working woman married for her attractions (5) (*S.T.*, 9.8.81)

works
For a place of entertainment, Di's got the works! (5)

world
ORB
Take in the sailor's world (6)

world council
UN
In favour of veto on world council, judging by this part of speech (7)

wrinkle
TIP
Very fine wrinkle on upper end (6)

writer
1 NIB 2 PEN 3 indicates name of famous writer, with some of most common being, among others, AMIS, GIDE, LOTI, POE
Upholder of the law who discovers little licence in writer and artist (6, 9) (*S.T.*, 9.8.81)

writing
MS
Public relations is writing 'Spectra' (6)

writing fluid
INK
Doctor has writing fluid that can be taken internally! (5)

wrong
1 BAD 2 ERR 3 SIN 4 TORT 5 = anagram
Wrong the king and disappear without trace (4)

(in the) **wrong direction**
usually = reversal, e.g. 'put in the wrong direction' – TUP
Put lever in the wrong direction and have fun! (5)

(the) **wrong way**
usually = reversal, e.g. 'up the wrong way' – PU
Cutting was the wrong way in top of garment (6)

X
TEN
'XN' is a real game! (6)

yard (Yard)
1 CID 2 YD
Ran to the Yard? That's a bit off! (6)

year
1 AD 2 YR
Trade year suffers (6)

yellow
OR
Soft yellow touch for this picture of someone (8)

yellow pages
RAG
Yellow Pages are not worth considering to get this foreign dish (6)

you
1 U 2 YE
You get it coming back, this legendary ape (4)

you and I
WE
You and I 'ave to make cloth (5)

you and me
US
Object for throwing is a quoit, to you and me (6)

young
usually indicates short form of name, e.g. 'young Edward' – ED, 'young Elizabeth' – BET
Young Diana comes to the Italian detective, confused, and finds it difficult to understand him because of this (7)

young hero
ERIC (i.e. the schoolboy hero of *Eric, or Little by Little*, the famous school story by F. W. Farrar)
Information comes to young hero, but it doesn't relate to anyone in particular (7)

young lady
DEB (i.e. 'debutante')
There's something owing here, and the young lady has it (5)

young messenger
PAGE
Bump into young messenger while rushing wildly about (7)

young thing
BABE
Young thing is a beginner, and the result is total confusion (5)

young whelp
CUR
Young whelp has lots of creamy milk (4)

young woman
DOLL
Young woman has a right to get some money (6)

you old
YE
You old amateurs! What a joke! (4)

your (old) [see also next entry]
THY
Your note is just a plant (5)

your old [see also previous entry]
1 THINE 2 THY
A relative has your old indifference (6)

yours truly
ME
Yours truly and Bill returning to great place of pilgrimage (5)

Z

zero
1 NIL 2 O
Broken bale zero-rated when built up from raw materials (10)

a
Awkward name given to a flower – ANEMONE
Not a very 'awkward name', really: an anagram of NAME+'a' = ONE.

abandon
Cat abandons ship, going to Northchurch for a drink – PUNCH
This adventurous cat or PUSS 'abandons' SS ('ship') and adds 'Northchurch' disguised as N+CH. This gives the 'drink', or PUNCH.

(is) **able**
This clergyman is able to get on – CANON
The reverend gentleman thus CAN get ON. See also **disagreement**.

aboard
Equal value aboard for the masts and yards – SPARS
Here 'equal value' (PAR) is 'aboard' (in S . . . S) to give the SPARS that are the 'masts and yards' (see *Chambers*).

about
Puzzle about the bus – REBUS
RE here is 'about', so RE the BUS. A rebus, says *Chambers*, is 'an enigmatical representation of a name by pictures punningly representing parts of the word' – which sounds just the thing for a crossword solver.

above
Painter studies above board – CONSTABLE
In a down clue, you could actually see how the 'painter' CONS 'above' the TABLE.

abroad
Good place to spend the night abroad if camp fire is started – LIT
A good place to spend the night, of course, is a bed – in this case a French one, otherwise a bed 'abroad'. A solver's schoolboy or schoolgirl French should easily run to this!

absorb
Scotsman absorbs oxygen, lights up at night – MOON
So here he is, this Scotsman, out for a breather in the night air, a MON who absorbs O. The MOON, of course, 'lights up at night'.

abstainer, abstinent
Abstinent in commercial success? That's the lowest of the low! – BOTTOM
Thus the TT is in the BOOM – and you can't get much lower than BOTTOM!

Academy, academician
Second-class academician in first-class centre of learning! – BRAIN
'Second-class' (B)+'academician' (RA)+IN = BRAIN. It's a puzzler's 'first-class centre of learning' that enables him to take clues like this in his stride, of course! Compare the clues under **bust-up** and **water**.

Academy chief
Academy chief is oriental dignitary, which is commendable – PRA IS E WORTHY
In other words, PRA IS E WORTHY. Crossword setters are always pleased when they can 'translate' a word in a sequence of units like this.

acceptable
House has acceptable angled shape – HOOK
That is, the HO has an OK 'angled shape', the latter being a HOOK. For a more jaunty clue for this same word, see **all right**.

accommodate
Very poor eastern editor accommodated in New York – NEEDY
So an E ED is accommodated in NY.

accomplished
Accomplished turn is round head of class – that's good teaching! – DIDACTICS
A rather harder clue, perhaps. Here we have 'accomplished turn' – DID ACT+C ('head of class') with IS round it.

account
Account I should write quickly and send casually is bitter sweet – ACID DROP
Here we have AC+ID for the first word, with DROP defined as 'send (casually)'. And isn't an acid drop a bitter sweet?

accountant
Accountant comes back to tea, that's some-

thing done! – ACT
Here is our first reversal in operation, a CA 'coming back' – to T. And when he's done that, that's an ACT, or 'something done'.

acknowledgments of indebtedness
Stimulus gets acknowledgments of indebtedness, but they're not genuine – SPURIOUS
The common -IOUS ending usually works out as something to do with debts or IOUs, and here is a ponderous version for it. A SPUR, of course, is a 'stimulus'.

across the Channel
Life across the Channel (in the north) should provide plenty of drink – VINE
A nice French bucolic picture, with VIE, the French for 'life', taking in N.

act
Act very loudly and really take off! – DOFF
Simply DO+FF, with DOFF meaning 'take off'.

act(ion)
Was flat out in action, so got held up – DELAYED
If you LAY you were presumably 'flat out', and this then goes in DE . . . ED.

acting
Sam's acting the tough guy – SAMSON
Sam's acting means that SAM'S ON, and SAMSON was one of the great 'tough guys' of the Old Testament. (In the Book of Judges you can read how, among other exploits, he 'found a new jawbone of an ass, and put forth his hand, and took it, and slew a thousand men therewith'.) For a similar clue, see **uncle**.

actor
Actor caught short in passage – EXTRACT
Perhaps you weren't expecting that kind of passage? That's how crossword clues can catch you! The first two words of the clue provide the answer: 'actor caught short' is EXTRA CT.

actors
Outspoken actors on the air – BROADCAST
'Outspoken' is BROAD, 'actors' are the CAST, and 'on the air' is BROADCAST!

address
Address the people and you will get a sign – OMEN
O MEN gives you an OMEN.

admiral (Admiral)
Crazy admiral really *is* crazy – MAD
Well, 'admiral' is ADM, and if you obey the anagram indicator 'crazy' you will convert it to MAD, which *is* crazy! Compare the clue for this word under **bottom**.

admit
A number admit the truth, which is plain-spoken! – DOWNRIGHT
Which being interpreted is: 'a number' (D) 'admit' (OWN) 'the truth' (RIGHT).

(he) **admits**
He admits he's fit but in fact he's just the opposite – IMPROPER
He admits 'I'M PROPER' but he's actually IMPROPER.

advertisement
See advertisement and charge – LOAD
Quite straightforward, this one: LO, an AD! To load, after all, is to charge.

affirm
Revolutionary leader to affirm he's a crazy person – RAVER
The 'leader' of 'revolutionary' is R, and 'to affirm' is AVER. Thus we get our crazy RAVER.

afloat
Pat's afloat – I can see his gaiters! – SPATS
This image of a marooned bishop is obtained by PAT being afloat in S . . . S.

after
After do, this servile dependent achieves mastery – MINION
That is, DO+MINION will give you DOMINION, otherwise 'mastery'. But all you need for the answer is the MINION.

afternoon
'An Old Etonian in the afternoon . . .' That could be the first line of one! – POEM
Did this suggest a poem to you? Even if not,

you should have been able to arrive at the correct answer by putting the OE in the PM.

afterthought
Painter has an afterthought that strikes him – RAPS
So the RA has a PS, and 'strikes' is RAPS (see the entry **strikes**, where it also appears).

again
Unite again, trash! – REFUSE
To 'unite again' is to 're-fuse', of course, with 'trash' being the other sense of REFUSE. Puzzle setters enjoy employing a neat homophone like this. Compare this clue with the rather different one under **referee**.

against
Clergyman and I against the Queen – that's stimulating! – REVIVER
This suggestion of a rare legal case ('Cox and Box v. Regina', as it were) comes via a composition: REV + I V. ER, with a 'reviver' being a slang term for a stimulant (in *Chambers*, incidentally). Another setter might have capitalised on the word's potential as a palindrome.

agent
Unusual agent on ship, maybe one of a gang to force men to enlist – PRESS
The 'unusual agent' should have denoted an anagram of REP, this being on SS. A press gang, of course, forces men to join ships.

agreement
Eastern agreement or eastern hideosity ? – EYESORE
Here is another composite answer, its four elements being E+YES+OR+E. This is not as complex as it looks, since both the E's are the same, and the other two elements are direct 'copies' from the original clue.

air
Race in the air – then put this on to keep warm – MITTEN
The 'race' is the usual TT, here found in MIEN. Yes, normally you would put on mittens, but it can't be denied that even one mitten will keep one hand warm!

airline
Airline goes to the north, love, isn't it fun! – BEANO
Beware of slangy conversational clues like this: they invariably contain cryptic elements. This one is no exception, and we have BEA (the airline)+N (north)+O (love), with one definition (in *Chambers*) of BEANO being 'a jollification'. That *must* be fun.

airman
Trainee airman is worthy of tears – LACERATES
Admittedly rather a cunning clue here. The 'trainee airman' is the L ACE, 'is worthy of' is RATES and the 'tears' are not the expression of sadness that you may have thought they were, but the 'ripping' sort.

alack (!)
Married outside Israel, alack! – being improperly attached – MISRELATED
'Married' is MATED, and that goes round ISREL which is 'Israel' lacking its A. 'Improperly attached' is the definition of MISRELATED, of course.

Albert
Albert did not tell the truth – he was in league – ALLIED
AL LIED, and so was ALLIED, or 'in league'. A fairly easy one.

alcohol
Alcohol comes to Albert, and that's the lot! – TOTAL
Here's Albert again, still as AL. A TOT of alcohol comes to him, and that is his TOTAL or lot.

Alexander
Alexander to prepare for war? That's a dangerous sign! – ALARM
Here's another AL – Alexander, this time. To ARM is to 'prepare for war', so that if AL is to ARM we have an ALARM, or a 'dangerous sign'.

all but
Wanting all but few evicted – that's nasty – DEFECTIVE
A rather harder clue. 'Wanting' is the definition of the answer, DEFECTIVE. The rest is

an anagram, denoted by 'nasty', of FE ('all but few', i.e. 'few' minus its final letter) and EVICTED.

allow(ed)
Journey allowed for one of three? – TRIPLET
Simply: TRIP LET for this TRIPLET? Note that both 'allow' (present) and 'allowed' (past) will work out as LET.

all right
Hey, all right – I'll catch it! – HOOK
Not too contrived, I think. HO is to call to attract attention, just as 'hey' is. And a HOOK does catch things, of course. Compare another clue for this word under **acceptable**.

all up(!)
Ridicules love, in store, getting ring – it's all up! – POOH-POOHS
Here's the definition as the first word of the clue again. Then you have, working back from the end ('all up', as instructed), O in SHOP and HOOP, otherwise 'love in store' and 'ring'. Complex, but a nice image of a jilted, or jilting, bride.

almost
It's almost time, I would say, and I am not very brave – TIMID
TIM is 'almost time', and ID is how you would say 'I would'. Actually a rather touching clue, in fact. For a variation of this, see **unlimited**.

also
The second letter, also the second to last – that's crooked! – BANDY
The two letters, as you no doubt quickly spotted, are B (the second) and Y (the second to last)!

alternative
Special constable, 1st class, in alternative movie award – OSCAR
The 'special constable' is the SC, and he is A or '1st class', this all being in OR to produce the well-known movie award.

always
God embraces love, church poets always get comfort from it – GOOD CHEER
GOOD is God embracing love (GOD embracing O), of course, and CHEER is CH+EER, or 'church'+'always' (here the poetic version).

amateur
Talk to amateur in Kent – CHATHAM
Some clues featuring Kent indicate that SE ('south-east') is in the answer, but not here, since Chatham actually is in Kent. And have a CHAT to a HAM and you get this historic naval base.

ambassador
Ambassador goes to Cuba, mother of Paris is there – HECUBA.
Perhaps not a very felicitous clue, since what is a mythological character doing in Cuba? However, even if you didn't know that HECUBA was the mother of Paris in Greek mythology, you should have been able to get to her via His Excellency (HE) the ambassador and, of course, CUBA. (In fact a 'mother of Paris' could actually be a French mother, which makes the clue as a whole less incongruous.)

America(n)
Stigmatic padre, an American, very holy, too – PIOUS
The 'stigmatic padre' is Padre PIO, the Italian Capuchin friar (lay name Francesco Forgione) who was said to have received stigmata on his hands in 1902. 'An American', of course, is US, and the two together make PIOUS – which Padre Pio surely was.

American city
Merriment comes to American city, that's laughable – FUNNY
In other words, FUN comes to NY!

American soldier
Scotsman embraces American soldier – wonderful! – MAGIC
Here we have MAC embracing the GI, as in some great battle victory.

American uncle
Black American uncle thrown from ship – JETSAM
JET is 'black', and JETSAM is a word for

'goods jettisoned from a ship', here simplified to just 'thrown from ship'.

amid
Amid loud labourers little children see – INFANTS
Did you see the INFANTS? They were IN the F ANTS, or 'amid loud labourers'.

amidships
High sail amidships stays put – STOPS
There are some rarefied names of sails, but a TOPsail must be familiar to almost all puzzle solvers. This TOP then goes 'amidships', or in S . . . S, and thus 'stays put' or STOPS.

among
For look and see – the barefoot walker goes
Among the frozen fields and Alpine snows – SANDAL
This mock-Longfellovian couplet gives you a definition of SANDAL in the first line ('barefoot walker') and in the second line you have the actual word buried in the 'frozen field*s and Al*pine snows'.

amputate
Amputated thumb at pit-head, a real blow – THUMP
THUM is the 'amputated thumb', minus its final letter, and the P is the 'pit-head', or 'head' of the word 'pit'.

ancient
Hesitantly put on my ancient fur – ERMINE
'Hesitantly' is ER, and this 'puts on' or adds 'my' which is MINE as an 'ancient' form (like 'mine host'). So ER+MINE = ERMINE, the 'fur' of the clue.

ancient city
Endless fluid runs to oriental and ancient city – it's alcoholic! – LIQUEUR
The 'endless fluid' is LIQUID minus its last two letters. This then 'runs to' or joins E (oriental) and the 'ancient city' of UR. Compare the clue for this word under **fifty**.

ancient times
Twisted irony in ancient times, poetically cynical – BYRONIC
A rather more 'literary' clue, but nevertheless one that can be reached by means of the first cryptic half, with 'twisted' denoting an anagram of IRONY inside BC ('the ancient times').

and
A member of the House of Commons, and the Queen, and a state leader, and . . . and . . . – AMPERSAND
A clue like this should clearly indicate that there's something fairly contrived going on! To get your AMPERSAND, which is the sign '&' that stands for 'and', you build up A MP+ER+S (the 'state leader') and the last but one AND, with the final 'and' being the actual definition of the answer.

and not
A marsh, and not a resort – BOGNOR
Of course, Bognor (Regis) is a resort, even though the clue suggests otherwise. But there is actually no ambiguity: 'a marsh' is BOG, 'and not' is NOR, and you are left with 'a resort' – the definition of BOGNOR!

and so on
Half skip, and so on, to top of hill – that's a brief outline – SKETCH
Three elements to link together here: SK ('half *sk*ip'), ETC ('and so on'), and the 'top' of the word '*h*ill' – H. This would probably be a down clue.

anger
The Poles contain their anger, thanks to this fascinating woman – SIREN
The two 'Poles' North and South, are perhaps more often found the other way round, for a word starting with N and ending in S, but they serve perfectly well here as S . . . N to 'contain' IRE and so produce the SIREN who lured sailors to their death in Greek mythology. The clue could have used the more familiar sense of 'siren' if the second half had run: '. . . thanks to this factory hooter'. But the mythological mermaid makes the clue – and the answer – much more interesting. *Chambers*, incidentally, gives the actual definition ('fascinating woman') used in the clue.

Anglo-Saxon
Anglo-Saxon granted agreement – ASSENT
Chambers gives 'grant' as the sixth meaning

of 'send' (as in 'God granted her heart's desire'), and the past of this, sent, is added to AS to produce the ASSENT, or 'agreement'.

angry
Angry at the Spanish inn – HOTEL
Remember, even the smallest word in a clue can be significant for its cryptic message, and here 'the Spanish' produces EL to add to HOT ('angry'). And there's your HOTEL!

animal
Confused animal goes to church to get fruit – PEACH
This harvest festival robber is a 'confused' (i.e. anagrammatic) APE who goes to CH to get his PEACH. For two further clues leading to this same word, see **every** and **per person**.

answer
Hard answer for German boy – HANS
Not too hard an answer, though, for the English-speaking solver, who interprets 'hard answer' as H+ANS to get the boy with the typically German name.

antique
Note antique coat of arms, you can see the bird – GOLDCREST
It's probably best to leave the 'note', with its many possibilities, to the end, and concentrate on the rest of the clue. Once you have translated 'antique' as OLD and 'coat of arms' as CREST, you can then confidently add the note G to get your bird.

apparently
Didn't make contact in the fog apparently – MISSED
It's a matter of homophones here: MISSED ('didn't make contact') and MIST ('fog'). The fact that the latter is clued as 'apparently' leads you to the correct homophone of the two – MISSED.

appearing (in)
Girl appearing in violin dance – LINDA
Did you spot her, appearing in the 'vio*lin da*nce'? The clue-word 'dance' could temporarily mislead you into thinking that there might be an anagram involved (presumably of 'violin'). But the number of letters in the answer – 5, not 6 – should have steered you quickly away from this false trail.

apprentice
Apprentice gets pigment for furniture – LUMBER
So long as you knew that UMBER was a 'pigment', you should have had little difficulty in solving this clue, with its 'apprentice' being the initial L (for 'learner').

approach
Return approach by learner is regulated by sea currents – TIDAL
Here you have to 'return' ADIT and add L (for 'learner' again) to get the correct answer.

approval
Proprietor giving approval to Ronald – PATRON
In other words, the PATRON gives a PAT to RON! Note how it is in order for an answer to 'give' its component parts, just as it is for the constituent elements (more usually) to 'give' the answer.

arbitrator
Arbitrator at home with editor, made it more cultured – REFINED
So the REF was IN ('at home') with the ED, and that was 'more cultured' or REFINED.

archbishop
Archbishop returns to the five hundred, fully dressed – ROBED
That 'five hundred' is a giveaway for the final D. All you then have to do is 'return' EBOR and your archbishop will thus be correctly ROBED.

archdeacon
Archdeacon goes to tea, we hear, for escape – VENT
Probably you reached the answer via the cryptic elements (VEN goes to T) rather than the definition. But 'escape' is certainly a correct definition of VENT: *Chambers* gives it as the twelfth meaning in a total of eighteen.

archeological work
In archeological work northern worker is angry – INDIGNANT
The 'in' does not denote a 'burial', as it often

does – it is simply itself, IN! To this add the DIG and the 'northern worker' (N+ANT) to get the answer.

arena
First rate arena is drying out and warming up – AIRING
You can 'read' this straight through, seeing that an AI RING is AIRING. The 'out' and 'up' of the definition of AIRING are there to serve as mild decoys on the chance that you will look for an anagram or a reversal!

aright
Listen to him aright – HEAR
Here the definition comes first, so that HEAR is comprised of HE and AR ('him' and 'aright').

aristocratic
Aristocratic and knowledgeable man provides treatment – USAGE
If you correctly translated 'aristocratic' as U, you were off to a good start, and only needed to add your SAGE to get the answer USAGE, one of whose meanings is 'treatment'.

'ark
'Ark, the bird's 'ome – that's serious! – EARNEST
The first apostrophe here is significant, since it tells you to leave the initial H off HEAR. The second (in 'bird's 'ome') is simply to match it, and has no significance. So all you need do is add EAR to NEST to get the answer of EARNEST.

around
To rouse the guest, I ran around – STIR
This is the fourth type of 'around' clue listed, and the answer is thus both defined ('rouse') and 'buried' – in 'gue*st I r*an'.

arrive
Arrive on burst tyre at main channel of communication – ARTERY
Here you have the shorter abbreviation for 'arrive' (AR) followed by a 'burst' or anagrammatic TYRE. This gives your 'main channel of communication', which is exactly the definition given by *Chambers*, incidentally.

article
Biting article of Scottish origin – TARTAN
The 'article' is AN and it is 'biting', or TART. True, the definition part of the clue does not give the exact meaning of TARTAN, but if you consider all the traditional things that are 'of Scottish origin', a tartan would surely be among them!

artillery
Artillery I'd attack – RAID
Quite a nice neat clue here, although the 'I'd' is really a giveaway for a word ending in -ID. We could have had an anagram of ARID to get this answer, but neat anagrams are not very exciting. Like a 'short', they are more exciting with something added.

artist
Instruct artist in metal – TRAIN
A short clue structured much like the last one: definition plus two cryptic elements. Here, though, the latter are not next to each other but one within the other: the RA is in the TIN. For an identical 'burial', but a different idea, see **man of art**.

art master(s)
MA
A long coat for the art master? Aren't they the limit! – MAXIMA
As you can see, a MAXI for the MA. Notice that the definition part of the clue, although not very direct, contains 'they' to denote a plural answer.

arts supporter
Arts supporter follows Welsh, furtive fellow! – WEASEL
No doubt the slightly unnatural word order ('Welsh furtive' instead of 'furtive Welsh') indicated to you that something rather contrived was happening. However, the order is acceptable, and gives you the EASEL following the W that stands for 'Welsh', the two elements producing the WEASEL who is the 'furtive fellow'.

as before
The Spanish road in chaos, as before – yet this is the land of the Spanish conquerors! – ELDORADO
It is always nice when the cryptic part of a

clue and the definition part match or blend so closely, as they do here with the two Spanish references. So here we have 'the Spanish' (EL) followed by an anagram of ROAD ('in chaos') and ending in the DO that is the 'ditto' or 'as before' of the clue. In fact the Spanish 'the' for once actually produces a genuine Spanish 'the', since ELDORADO (or EL DORADO, as two words) means 'the gilded'. (See the word in *Chambers* for its rather curious origin.)

ascend(ing), in the ascendant
School's reputation in the ascendant – ETON
The name of Eton College is probably the most versatile there is when it comes to cryptic clues. Here it is reversed (NOTE) to give the meaning 'reputation'. The name can also produce the anagram TONE – another 'status' meaning!

as it were
Sequence of words given in docking procedure, as it were – SENTENCE
The phrase 'as it were' should have warned you that the 'docking procedure' was very likely nothing to do with ships or spacecraft. Nor was it, since the reference is the legal one, with 'sequence of words' being the actual standard definition of SENTENCE.

aspiration
Mother's aspiration is rather a muddle – MASH
Otherwise MA'S H, with MASH being a 'muddle'. But if you hadn't known about 'aspiration' being H, you might have found the clue rather more baffling!

assembly
Base assembly needed for this game – FOOTBALL
A good example of an unexpected meaning. 'Base assembly' suggests something you have to put together before you can play this game. Instead you have FOOT as the 'base' and not a BALL for a game but one that is an 'assembly' (for dancing). Hence, incidentally, the term 'assembly room' as an alternative way of saying 'ballroom'.

assistance
A number get assistance from this servant – MAID
A nice straightforward clue. M ('a number', actually 1000) get AID from the MAID.

assistant
Assistant in Rolls is robber – RAIDER
Here is the AIDE in his RR, producing the required RAIDER.

astern
Handle is hard astern – HAFT
It's convenient that a genuine naval phrase, 'hard astern', can actually serve as a cryptic clue like this – H+AFT. A glance in *Chambers* will confirm that a HAFT is 'a handle'. ('Hard astern' as a naval term just means 'full astern'.)

as they say
Floor is something worth writing about, as they say – STOREY
A pun, of course, on the homophones STORY and STOREY. Note that the definition of STORY is quite accurate, since a story is not only something that is written, but – to a journalist – something that is worth writing *about*.

as well as
Mountains along west coast of South America, as well as east and south – ANDES
Only the first half of the clue is geographically accurate! The 'east' and 'south' were added to get the final two letters of ANDES.

at
At piano I'm the best – TOP
The hardest part of this otherwise very easy clue is the 'at' meaning TO. Yet look up 'to' in *Chambers* and you'll find 'at' as its tenth meaning (of a total of nineteen). The 'piano', of course, gives the final P.

'at
Soft 'at is sign of approval – PAT
In spite of the rather strange image of the clue (some kind of secret signal?) its cryptic elements are straightforward enough, with a P 'AT giving a PAT.

at home
Senior officer at home getting money – COIN
The CO is IN to get the COIN!

at last
Tom home at last, as the great book tells – TOME
The 'great book' or TOME is reached via TOM and the last letter of 'hom*e*'.

at rest
Shed blood of many at rest – BLED
A slightly harder clue. 'Shed blood' is the definition of BLED, while 'many at rest' is to be read as L ('many') in BED. The 'shed blood' of the clue should be given a face value of 'the blood that has been shed' rather than 'he – or someone – shed the blood', since 'at rest' presumably already means 'dead', 'killed'. However, it could also be taken to mean, 'He (say) shed the blood of the many people who were resting'.

attempt
Friend has an attempt but it's insignificant – PALTRY
It's easy when you see the answer: PAL has a TRY but it's PALTRY!

attention
Attention in off-stage area is tiring – WEARING
In other words, it is EAR in WING, the latter being 'off-stage area'. And although we usually talk of a stage's 'wings', in the plural, there are in fact two – one to the left of the stage, and one to the right.

Attila
Attila's in the way, let's move him over – SHUNT
Another 'burial', with Attila the HUN being in the ST or 'street' (the 'way').

attorney
Attorney and politician are 'wet' – DAMP
That is, the DA and the MP are DAMP. Note the careful use of the quote marks: in the clue they are used to indicate a slang or jargon word, but in the answer, or as applied to it, they simply single out the definition required. A similar clue is used for **district attorney** (which see). Which do you find more satisfying?

audience
Noisy audience is scared – FEARS
The thing to do here is to make the breaks at the right points in the clue: 'noisy' (F) + 'audience' (EARS) = 'is scared' (FEARS). Thus the 'is' properly goes with 'scared', not with 'audience'.

auditor
Auditor is after a penny as it's expensive – DEAR
So the EAR is after a D, which is DEAR. In many crosswords today D appears as 'old penny', to distinguish from P. In this clue, however, 'old' would spoil the face value of the words.

automation pioneers
Automation pioneers, and a number from the country – RURAL
An acceptable enough clue to produce the required answer. Notice that the 'a' is significant, before the 'number' that produces the final L.

autumn
Autumn, with its own endless untilled land – FALLOW
This rather mournful clue produces its answer by means of taking FALL ('autumn') and adding 'own endless', otherwise OW, to it.

available
Beer available in physical training – PINT
Notice that the 'in' of the clue does not produce the IN of the answer: that is provided by 'available', which is 'buried' in PT.

avenue
Quit avenue in sheltered side – LEAVE
First the definition ('quit' = LEAVE), then the cryptic elements, with AV 'buried' in LEE, the 'sheltered side'. '*On* sheltered side' would read more naturally, but we specifically need 'in' to get the desired 'burial'.

average
Average college lecturer gives remission of

punishment – PARDON
PAR is 'average', a 'college lecturer' is a DON, and a 'remission of punishment' is a PARDON. Q.E.D!

award
Prince gets award for investigatory work – PROBE
Thus the PR gets an OBE for his PROBE.

away
Sick fitter remains, but pines away – so end it all! – TERMINATE
This sort of clue takes a bit of getting used to, and you may have to stare at the words for a while before the penny drops. It works like this : 'sick' denotes an anagram, in this case of FITTER REMAINS – but before you work this you have to remove the letters that spell FIRS, i.e. 'pines away'! When you have done all that, you should end up with TERMINATE, to 'end it all'.

B

bachelor
Fruit for the bachelor goes straight down – PLUMB
The PLUM for the B goes PLUMB, with B here represented by the 'bachelor' element in such tities as BA or BM. Compare this clue with the rather different one under **chimney**.

back and forth
Holy woman goes back and forth – NUN
Not too difficult, I think, especially once you correctly 'read' 'back and forth' to denote a palindrome.

back from
Back from America, is Eli sojourning in Europe? – SILESIA
Here is a neat reversed 'burial', with SILESIA to be found in 'Americ*a is Eli s*ojourning'.

back(ing)
An Italian lute contains this backbone – ULNA
Here we have another tricky combination of a reversal that is also a 'burial'. So the ULNA is not actually a *back*bone anatomically (it is in fact a bone in the fore-arm), but a bone that goes back, i.e. is a reversal. And the 'Itali*an lu*te' contains it as a 'burial'!

backslide
Tim's backsliding before hard worker – SMITH
Reverse TIM'S so that he 'backslides' to SMIT, then add the H of 'hard' to get the SMITH or 'worker'.

back(ward), from the back
Backward kid goes east to the ditch – DIKE
Another reversal, with 'backward' KID going to the E to reach the DIKE or 'ditch'.

backwards or forwards, backwards and forwards
This instrument goes round and round as well as backwards and forwards – ROTOR
It's not quite such a versatile instrument as the clue seems to suggest, though! A ROTOR certainly goes 'round and round', but it only goes 'backwards and forwards' as a palindrome. Compare the clue under **revolver**.

bad
Bad head – a symptom of this? – ILLNESS
The unexpected meaning again. 'Bad' and ILL more or less coincide in their senses, but the 'head' is not part of the body but a headland or NESS. However, a 'bad head' could be a symptom of an ILLNESS.

bad grade
Bad grade in first half of German – it's a pointer – FINGER
The clue as a whole suggests some kind of unsatisfactory school report, but it will actually produce a FINGER if you take the three elements and add them together: F as the 'bad grade', IN as itself ('in') and GER as the 'first half of *Ger*man'.

ball
Drunkard has ball in street – SOT
It doesn't matter how you understand 'ball', whether as the sports item or as a slang 'good time' ('have a ball'), so long as you interpret its cryptic value correctly as O. Then you will get your SOT or 'drunkard' by having an

O in the ST. Compare the clue under **go into**.

base
Frame to relieve spinal base – EASEL
Were you stuck? Take a gamble: if 'frame' is the definition, you could look up 'relieve' in *Chambers* to see if you can get a four-letter word which with L (the 'spinal base', or last letter of 'spina*l*') would mean 'frame'. Sure enough, as the fifth sense given, you find 'ease'. But is an EASEL really a 'frame'? Let's cross-check in *Chambers* again: easel, 'the frame for supporting a picture . . .'. So that's it, and we can write EASEL with confidence.

base metal
Soft base metal here – a whole flood of it! – BORE
Here we have a B ORE producing a BORE, the latter in the special sense of 'tidal flood', as the famous Severn bore. Compare the clue under **rock**.

battalion
A senior officer in the battalion can be usually found at breakfast – BACON
Otherwise A CO in the BN. Note that the first word (A) is important for the correct composition of the answer, and that the definition does not have to be an absolutely direct one (compare the general way TARTAN was defined in the **article** clue). For quite a different sort of clue for this word, see **university man**.

batting
Father batting? That hurts! – PAIN
PA IN? That's a PAIN, which 'hurts'!

battleship
A battleship wrecked – what a bungle – MASH
This is simply an anagram of A HMS ('a battleship') which gives the 'bungle' or MASH. Compare the clues for this same word under **aspiration** and **be quiet**.

beam
Beam reflected to Pole – quite a story! – YARN
A reversal of RAY ('beam')+N ('Pole') will give you the answer. At its face value, it doesn't matter how you understand 'Pole' in the clue, whether geographically, as a nationality, or even electrically!

bearing
Chicken loses bearings but finds her baby – CHICK
In other words CHICKEN loses EN (its 'bearings' of east and north), and thus gets her baby CHICK.

beast(ly)
Little beasts do break up the organisation of crime – DORMICE
The 'little beasts' are the DORMICE, of course, who can also be reached by means of DO (a word in the clue)+the anagram ('break up the organisation') of CRIME.

beat
Tandem song, having no beat, is out of fashion – DEMODE
To get the answer here, join DEM and ODE, the former being 'tandem' that has 'no beat', i.e. 'no word meaning "beat",' i.e. 'minus TAN', and the latter being 'song'.

beauty
Beauty queen has love and endless phone calls for brave Greek – BELLEROPHON
We have four elements to string together here: 'beauty' (BELLE)+'queen' (R)+'love' (O)+'endless phone' (PHON). All that 'calls for' or demands the definition 'brave Greek', who is BELLEROPHON. Did you get him?

become
Become good man – or even more than that! – BEST
The message to be understood here is: BE a ST (a saint), to get something that is 'even better' than 'good' – which is BEST! Compare the clues under **Goodfellow** and **highway**.

bed
As bed, very fashionable – ASCOT
AS COT makes the fashionable annual horse race meeting of Royal ASCOT.

bee
Bee is on edge of glass – upper edge – BRIM

So the B is on the RIM, that is, the BRIM. Compare the rather different clue under **edge**.

beer
Knock back a beer for a royal treat – REGAL
'Knock back' indicates a reversal, so LAGER becomes REGAL, which is 'royal'. The final 'treat' is not just to go with 'royal' in the clue, but also hints that the word needs to be 'treated' in some way. (In another clue, it might well indicate an anagram.)

before
Caught before a beginner – that's corny! – CEREAL
In this quite short answer (defined punningly as 'corny') we have four cryptic elements: C ('caught')+ERE ('before')+A ('a')+L ('beginner').

before noon
A wee tipple for GP before noon – DRAM
That is, the 'GP' or DR, in the AM ('before noon'), has a DRAM, defined by *Chambers* as 'a small drink of alcoholic liquor' or 'a tipple'.

beginner
Mixed team is joined by rustic beginner, which makes it less exciting – TAMER
'Mixed' indicates an anagram, so that we have TAME ('mixed TEAM') joined by the 'beginner', or first letter, of 'rustic', which is R. The 'less' in the clue hints that a comparative word ending in -ER is probably what's needed.

beginning
Naturally beginning to clear up causes deep depression – NADIR
Here we have the 'beginning' or first two letters of '*na*turally' followed by the reversal ('up') of RID ('to clear'). This gives the NADIR, or 'deep depression'.

behead
Cad beheaded a river creature – OTTER
But where's the 'cad'? He's the 'beheaded' ROTTER, who gives the OTTER! For a different kind of clue leading to this word, see **dram**.

beheaded king
First the beheaded king, then his small sister – and then the gun carriage – CHASSIS
Of course, in another clue, a 'beheaded king' could well work out as ING. Here, however, it is CHAS, who is followed by his 'small sister', or SIS. The 'gun carriage' meaning of CHASSIS (see *Chambers*) was chosen here to match the general funeral procession image of the clue as a whole.

behind
Game bird has the narrow crest in behind part – RIDGE
The 'game bird' here is the PARTRIDGE, with the PART actually given as the last word of the clue. So all you need is RIDGE, defined as 'narrow crest'.

behold
Behold the feathers of the bird,
And then the noise of cows is heard – LOWING
This rustic rhyme should steer you fairly obviously to the answer: LO the WING will give you the 'noise of cows' that is heard.

bend
Bend over upside-down tin to get one – UNIT
Put U ('bend') over the 'upside-down' or reversed TIN and you will quickly get your UNIT – the 'one' that is the last word of the clue.

beneath
Beneath the rug a lock you'll see
And there's the bed for you and me! – MATTRESS
Did you see, in this down clue, the TRESS ('lock') under the MAT ('rug')? The 'you and me' of the second line of fairy-tale verse is not personal, of course; it just means 'for everyone', 'as we all understand it'. A mattress, incidentally, actually *is* a bed as well as forming part of a bed (see *Chambers*, who does not even define it in the second sense).

Benedictine
Benedictine in charge of French island – he lives there! – DOMICILE
A rather nice clue, with an agreeable image (Mont-Saint-Michel, say). To interpret: the

DOM is IC the ILE (French for 'island'), while a DOMICILE is the place where a person legally lives. (It is a place, not a person, so the 'he' of the clue refers back to the 'Benedictine', and the indicator of the dwelling-place is 'there'.)

be painful
Question is painful; answer is 'flinches' – QUAILS
The QU AILS, therefore, and the 'answer' (both to the 'question' mentioned in the clue and the clue itself) is QUAILS. The quote marks round 'flinches' single it out as a definition – and also as a quoted 'answer' to the 'question' mentioned in the first part of the clue.

be quiet
Mother, be quiet, give us the potato! – MASH
You can easily divide it: MA+SH = MASH. We clued this same word somewhat differently under **aspiration** and **battleship** (which see, for comparison).

beset
I'm beset by the French fruit – LIMES
I hope you didn't start thinking of French words for types of fruit: it's the French for 'the' that you want (LES), and you then 'straddle' that round IM (I'm) to get the LIMES. For another version of this clue, see **put in**.

beside
Beside the Spanish mountain range – ATLAS
In earlier clues, we have had EL as 'the Spanish'. Now we have LAS (actually the feminine plural 'the', as in 'Las Vegas', the American city, whose name means 'the fields'). We precede this with AT ('beside') and so get the well-known mountain range.

besiege
Teetotallers besiege tree trunk to get drink container! – BOTTLE
One would hardly expect *teetotallers* to do this, but no matter – perhaps they were parched with thirst! For our purposes, the TT 'besiege' or are 'buried' in the BOLE, thus getting their BOTTLE.

betting
Betting on a champion chaser to get real glitter! – SPARKLE
Not so easy, of course, if you have not heard of ARKLE, the famous racehorse winner of the 1960s, but the chances are that the solver, with his good – or at any rate better than average – general knowledge, will know of him, and add his name to SP ('betting') to get the SPARKLE that is the answer (as defined as 'glitter').

biblical town
Holy man has gone to biblical town – gone over to get fish – STURGEON
The three cryptic elements here are the 'holy man' (ST)+the 'biblical town' (UR)+'gone over', i.e. an anagram of GONE (GEON). And there's your fish!

big bell
The big bell loudly rings for Law Society beginners – they're so silly! – TOMFOOLS
Here there are four cryptic elements. 'The big bell' (TOM)+'loudly' (F)+'rings' (OO)+'Law Society beginners' (LS, the 'beginners' of '*L*aw *S*ociety'). And that takes us to the TOMFOOLS who are 'so silly'.

big timekeeper
Big timekeeper has little time for criminal – BENT
Put another way: BEN has T ('little time') for a 'criminal' who is BENT.

bill (Bill)
Bill Stringer makes an agreement – ACCORD
If a suspicious name like this occurs in a clue, that is, a name you've never heard of before, treat it with caution! Here it provides the cryptic elements we need for the answer: 'Bill' is AC and 'Stringer' is a definition (in a way) of CORD. The complete word is defined as 'agreement'.

bind
Big vessel binds baby ones – POTTIES
A clue with a somewhat ambiguous image. What is this 'vessel' – a ship or a pan of some kind? It is the latter, really, since it is a POT which TIES 'baby ones', these being 'baby pots' or POTTIES. (You can regard these as

either small-size pots or pots for babies – it doesn't matter.)

bird
A boy and a bird – and another bird – TOMTIT
TOM is the 'boy', TIT is the 'bird', and the TOMTIT (defined by *Chambers*, rather oddly, as 'the blue or other tit') is 'another bird'. (Note the not altogether random use of the word 'another' in the clue, in the light of *Chambers*'s definition!)

bird home
Me with a bird home? That's the lowest of the low! – MEANEST
ME with A NEST? That's the MEANEST.

bishop
Bishop goes to Bible city to get the sweet smell of sanctity – ODOUR
So Bishop ODO goes to UR, and gets the 'ODOUR of sanctity'. (See *Chambers* for the uses of this phrase, which seems to have come into English from the French.)

bit
The French bit is painful – LESION
Here is 'the French' again, once more as LES. With ION ('bit') this makes LESION, defined by *Chambers* as 'a hurt' or 'an injury or wound'.

(a) **bit of**
A bit of novelty indoors for these contributors – DONORS
The 'bit' here is the first letter of '*n*ovelty', N. This goes 'indoors', or in DOORS, to give the answer of DONORS ('contributors').

(a) **bit off,** (a) **bit short**
Rafter not in actual use, being a bit short – SPAR
'Not in actual use' is SPARE. This is 'a bit short', so it loses its final E. And the resulting SPAR is the 'rafter', as defined.

black
Black Jack goes back for a kid who deserves a smack! – BRAT
This jingling clue unfolds as follows: 'Black' (B)+'Jack goes back' (RAT, i.e. a reversal of TAR, who is a sailor or 'Jack') = 'kid who deserves a smack', the definition of a BRAT.

bloomer
A rude stare is a bloomer! – ASTER
One of the many anagrams possible for this flower or 'bloomer', in this case STARE (which is 'rude', i.e. an anagram). Among other possibilities which could perhaps have been used here are RATES, TARES (in the biblical sense of 'weeds') and RESAT (i.e. 'sat again').

blow
Blow true, false delight – RAPTURE
This quasi-Shakespearian clue is more of a tease. 'Blow' is RAP. This is followed by 'TRUE false', i.e. an anagram of TRUE, which here is TURE. Then we have the definition of the answer, 'delight'. The comma may have put you off. Remember to ignore punctuation!

blue
Man's blue tale – HISTORY
So not 'blue' in the sense you may have thought of. 'Man's' is HIS, 'blue' is TORY, and, of course, 'tale' is the definition of HISTORY.

bluff (Bluff)
Tough and bluff, showing obduracy – HARDNESS
Rather an unexpected answer, perhaps. But 'tough' is HARD, and a 'bluff' is a NESS or headland (!), this giving the HARDNESS, defined as 'obduracy'.

blushing
Poor Vera, blushing, swore it was true – AVERRED
Never mind, we can spare her blushes, since 'poor' (i.e. anagrammatic) VERA gives us AVER, the 'blushing' is RED, and 'swore it was true' is the definition of AVERRED. A clue like this is meant to act on the solver's emotions and put him right off!

board
Pennon showing king has boarded ship – STREAMER
Once you realise that 'boarded' means 'buried in', you can put the 'king' (R) in the

'ship' (STEAMER) and get the 'pennon' (STREAMER).

Bob
Bob made his mark and went ahead fast – SPRINTED
'Bob' is almost always S (for 'shilling'). Here he 'made his mark' or PRINTED, and 'went ahead fast', or SPRINTED.

bodyguard
The fool has a bodyguard in the south as they're all murderers – ASSASSINS
This longish answer has no less than five cryptic elements. But they all follow quite naturally: 'the fool' (ASS) has 'a' (A) 'bodyguard' (SS) 'in' (IN) 'the south' (S), and have their definition as a single word: 'murderers'.

bolshie (Bolshie)
Bolshie player helps to make paint – RED LEAD
The clue would have been harder, of course, if the elements had not split up neatly into two words. So we have 'Bolshie' = RED and 'player' = LEAD (i.e. the leading actor or actress) producing the RED LEAD which, says *Chambers*, is 'an oxide of lead . . . used in paint-making'.

bolt
Taff to bolt back with bit of cheese on toast – WELSH RABBIT
'Taff' is WELSH ('Taffy was a Welshman', after all), and he has 'bolt back', i.e. a reversal of BAR with a BIT. This gives the cheese on toast that is often called Welsh rarebit but here, in this answer, is spelled in its original (and actually more correct) form of WELSH RABBIT.

book(s)
First poem in book with bit of a choice – OPTION
Did you untangle all the cryptic elements? 'First *p*oem' is P. This is 'in' or 'buried' in 'book', in other words, OT, and followed with 'bit' giving ION. So OPT+ION = OPTION, or 'choice'.

boozer
Boozer has 51 to 100 at the counter – in this part, anyway! – PUBLIC BAR
'Boozer' is PUB, '51' is LI and '100' is C (of course), and 'counter' is BAR. This gives PUBLIC BAR – which is part of the boozer aforementioned!

border
Border in a town and port in northern Italy – RIMINI
Most of this clue is devoted to the geographical description of the town that is the answer. But the cryptic elements are there, too: 'Border' is RIM, 'in' is IN, and 'a' is I.

born
Was she born in sin, taken aback? – NELLIE
'She' often indicates a girl's name, and here it is. How do we arrive at it? It's a matter of a 'burial'. 'Born' here is NEE, and in this is 'buried' a reversal of 'sin' or ILL. And there is NELLIE.

boss
Mixed-up boss comes to Queen for special flag – DUSTER
'Boss' here is STUD, which when 'mixed-up' or anagrammatised becomes DUST. It is followed by 'the Queen' (ER) to form DUSTER. This is a slang term for a flag, especially as the 'Red Duster', which is the Red Ensign flown on British merchant ships.

bother
It's ripped – bother! And this will only cause more damage! – TORNADO
The cryptic elements are in the first half of the clue ('ripped' and 'bother'). These combine (TORN+ADO) to form the answer, the TORNADO which will 'cause more damage' (than a mere rip, that is). Compare the clue under **rent**.

both ways
Miss Derek to look both ways. She's a forgetful girl – BO PEEP
The names of film actor and actresses feature reasonably frequently as cryptic elements. Here we have BO Derek, who is to 'look both ways', otherwise PEEP (a palindrome, hence 'both ways'). And BO PEEP, of course, 'forgot her sheep'!

bottom
Mother sits on bottom of bed – is she angry? – MAD

MA sits on bottom of 'be*d*', i.e. on D. If she is MAD she could be 'angry'. For a different type of clue leading to this word, see **admiral**.

bounder
Bounder gets points over Civil Engineer, that's his downfall! – CADENCE
To spell it out: CAD gets EN (the 'points' of the compass) over CE, getting a CADENCE which is, among other things, 'the fall of the voice'.

bowled
Bowled and not exactly youthful – was he blindfolded? – BANDAGED
B AND AGED are the three elements you will need to get BANDAGED ('blindfolded').

box
'Box, brown' – that's the old military way! – SPARTAN
Although to put the adjective after the noun is indeed a peculiarity of military English, here it is used so that we can have TAN after SPAR and so get SPARTAN, with 'the old military way' being a reference to the disciplined and militaristic people of Sparta in ancient Greece.

boy
James the scholar boy – MASON
What was that we said about film stars? Here now is James MASON, whose name is comprised of MA ('scholar') and SON('boy'). A clue that is probably all the more effective for being brief. Compare the clue under **old lady**.

(the) **branches**
Southern branches lead to sort of square on this highway – STREET
Put another way, S TREE leads to T ('sort of square'), with STREET being a 'highway'.

break
Ball breaks cup – that's a blow – COUP
'Bury' O ('ball') in CUP and you get COUP, which is a 'blow'. The clue conjures up a mishit tennis ball during tea on the lawn.

breather
Breather in middle of exercises, then a dive – PLUNGE
The physical exertions are not as great as they seem, for there is just a PLUNGE, produced by a LUNG 'buried' in PE.

brief(ly)
Brief moment on the French spot – MOLE
It doesn't matter what kind of 'spot' the clue suggests, so long as its definition is used for the answer (MOLE) in conjunction with the two cryptic elements: 'brief moment' (MO) on 'the French' (LE).

bring back
Bring back the employer to me, then we can continue – RESUME
Which being interpreted is: reverse the USER to ME so that we can 'continue' or RESUME.

bring in
Here are the bears, now bring in the horse – what rogues they all are! – BEGGARS
To sort out this circus act, you must 'bury' GG ('horse') in BEARS, thus getting the BEGGARS, who are here defined more playfully than directly.

British
British, i.e. French cheese – BRIE
As it stands, the clue is rather a puzzle. But it does at least provide us with the two cryptic elements, BR and IE, that we need for the 'French cheese'.

British island
British island reverts to holy man, it's quite damp – MOIST
We had a holy man on an island before (see **Benedictine**). This one is a saint (ST) to whom 'British island reverts', i.e. the IOM is reversed. So we get MOI+ST – which is MOIST or 'quite damp'!

British Museum
A pupil goes into the British Museum to find some peace – BALM
Another 'burial' here, with 'a pupil' (AL) going into the BM to get BALM, or 'peace'.

broach
Reversed nail broaches vat – that's courageous – VALIANT

And here is a reversed 'burial', with LIAN (NAIL 'reversed') 'broaching' VAT.

brother
Brother NCOs are quite wild – BRONCOS
You can 'read' this clue straight from left to right: BRO NCOS. A 'bronco', says *Chambers*, is a 'half-tamed horse' – hence 'quite wild'.

brown (Brown)
Brown turned, 'I've an African man here' – NATIVE
This clue, that sounds like a line from a schoolboy yarn, has a reversal of TAN followed by the common IVE produced from 'I've'. And there is the native African man.

brushworker
Quick getaway for brushworker in Britain – GRAB
The RA is in GB, producing a GRAB, or 'quick getaway'.

brute
Up and away! There's a brute in there! – PANDA
The final 'there' of the clue should have indicated to you that the answer was a 'burial'. You will find it in the first part of the clue, where the PANDA is hidden in 'u*p and a*way'.

Buddhist priest
Buddhist priest introduces religious scholar, getting Greek letter – LAMBDA
So the LAMA 'introduces', i.e. 'straddles', a BD, and the result is the Greek letter of the alphabet LAMBDA.

burn
Burn fifty in one – SINGLE
Quite a neat clue: SINGE ('burn') with L in gives you SINGLE, defined as 'one'.

(for) **Burns**
Baby for Burns – BAIRN
A simpler clue, leading to a Scottish 'baby' or BAIRN. (The clue could have been even shorter, as 'Burns baby', but this produces an undesirable image, so is best avoided.)

bury
King buried in tomb with one brass instrument – TROMBONE
You will almost certainly have quickly guessed that the 'brass instrument' is the defining part of the clue. This means that the first part is cryptic, and it can be 'cracked' as R buried in TOMB with ONE. And there is your TROMBONE.

bust-up
Bust-up in nerve centre – BRAIN
Or BRA+IN = BRAIN. Of course, in another clue 'bust-up' would have indicated a reversal, but do this here and you get the unlikely letter-group TSUB. Compare the clues under **Academy** and **water**.

busybody
Bring in the busybody, it's urgent – IMPORTANT
Another 'read-through' clue: IMPORT the ANT.

butter
After tea is announced, the butter runs along the rails – TRAM
Beware of innocent-looking words ending in -ER (see Appendix IV, page 288)! This 'butter' is a RAM, and after T he makes a TRAM, which 'runs along the rails'.

by the sound of it
Being there with gifts, by the sound of it – PRESENCE
When dealing with a pair of homophones like this, make sure you enter the correct one, especially when they both have the same number of letters. So it's PRESENCE you should enter here, not PRESENTS, since the homophone indicator 'by the sound of it' follows 'gifts', not 'being there'. You therefore want a word that *sounds* like the definition of 'gifts', and this is PRESENCE.

Caesar
Caesar's force in unusually poor condition – PROVISO
'Caesar's' should have alerted you to a Latin

word, in this case VIS ('force'). That is 'buried' in POOR 'unusually' (i.e. as an anagram) and will then give you the PROVISO, defined as 'condition'.

California
California goes French on endless draught of liqueur! – CALVADOS
The three elements here are CAL ('California'), VA ('goes French') and DOS ('endless draught', i.e. DOSE), all combining to give the 'liqueur', CALVADOS. The clue could also have indicated DOS as a French word ('back French' or 'French back'), but VA, as a verb, is easier to manipulate.

Cambridge town
Fifty-four come to Cambridge Town – they're a rowdy lot! – LIVELY
The 'fifty-four' could hardly be anything other than LIV. Add ELY ('Cambridge Town') to this and you get 'rowdy' – LIVELY. The 'town' is given a capital here to suggest the name of a football club, since that is what the clue as a whole seems to describe.

can
Little Viola can, she's capable of anything – VIABLE
No real mystery here. Probably the cryptic side of the clue will come more readily than the definition, so that you will add 'Little Viola' to 'can' (ABLE) and then see that VIABLE is defined as meaning 'capable of anything' (not precisely so in *Chambers*, but acceptably enough).

cancel
Track had first train cancelled producing extreme anxiety – RACK
A deliberately imposing clue to produce the answer – just 'cancel' the first letter of TRACK and you get RACK, here defined as 'extreme anxiety'.

Canonbury district
Drove car round Canonbury district, checked on broadcasts – MONITORED
The hardest part of this clue is deciphering 'Canonbury district' as NI. Once you get that, you can readily see how whoever he was MOTORED round NI and MONITORED.

cap
Baron caps us, and we all go home in this – BUS
Such an easy answer justifies a rather vague description of BUS. But the cryptic elements, B 'caps' (i.e. precedes) US, should leave you in little doubt that you have the right word.

capital
Shuns every small Cossack hamlet except Western Siberian capitals – ESCHEWS
A rareish but enjoyable type of clue, where the answer is literally spelt out in the 'capitals' or first letter of all the words. So 'shuns' is the definition of ESCHEWS, and the seven letters that comprise it can be found in the first letters of the next seven words, starting with '*e*very'!

captive
Trace captive queen in row of houses – TERRACE
Take the word TRACE, insert a 'captive' ER, and you have a 'row of houses' or TERRACE. Compare the clue for this word under **thrice**.

card
Threaten the fellows with a card – MENACE
The definition comes first, then the MEN with the ACE to support it.

care of
'Care of North Street' can get you a policeman – CONSTABLE
Four cryptic elements here: CO+N+ST+ABLE ('can') – and there's your CONSTABLE. We clued this same word quite differently under **above** – see also **understudy**.

caricaturist
West African caricaturist is spiteful – WASPY
The capitals of 'West African' should have indicated the possibility of an abbreviation. Then it was simply a matter of adding WA to the 'caricaturist' SPY to get WASPY, or 'spiteful'.

carry
Scotsman carries little Sarah to get the fish – SALMON

The important thing here is to interpret 'carry' correctly. Here, in this down clue, it means that 'Scotsman' will *follow* or 'carry' 'little Sarah', in other words MON follows SAL. And there's the fish. SALMON is a nice word to clue since you can do so many things with it, including a 'burial' ('colos*sal mon*key', 'na*sal mon*ologue' and the like), an anagram (SLAM ON, LAM SON, NO ALMS), a homophone ('Sam on the fish, I hear') and other cryptic dodges galore ('mixed earth between poles', 'several in beauty parlour', and so forth).

case
Where to sort out vegetable case – PORTSEA
The 'vegetable' is the PEA, which is a 'case' or a 'straddle' for 'sort out', ORTS. This produces PORTSEA. You don't need to consider *why* it's PORTSEA, all you need to know is that the answer is the name of a place, and 'where' in the clue tells you that.

cash
File has top-class cash for Russian monk – RASPUTIN
Yes, *that* sort of 'file'! So RASP has U TIN for the notorious RASPUTIN.

cat
Low noise of cat grabbing ball at home – MOOING
The face value of the clue strains the imagination somewhat, but is effective enough to produce the punning 'low noise' definition and the cryptic MOG 'grabbing' 'ball at home' (O+IN). Consider how else this word might have been clued, with Chinese vases, mixed gins, spectacles and love-ins!

catch
Drunkard catches cold living north of the border – SCOT
And serve him right, too, this SOT who carelessly 'catches' C 'north of the border' between England and Scotland.

cathedral city
Half London went to cathedral city, maybe they felt in need of company? – LONELY
Half LONdon went to ELY, of course.

caught
Caught, and, I'd say, quite fair – CANDID
C+AND+ID – 'quite fair' as a clue, too, wouldn't you say?

celebration
A celebration about love – ADORE
Quite a neat clue, although one might normally hesitate to celebrate *about* something. But I think we can accept it, and so reach the definition 'love' (ADORE) via A DO RE, or 'a celebration about'.

censor
He comes to censor with doctor for a large number of victims – HECATOMB
Not so fair? Well, admittedly harder than the last clue, and you might have to check on the exact meaning of HECATOMB (*Chambers*: 'a great public sacrifice: any large number of victims'). But perhaps the cryptic elements helped, so that HE came to CATO with MB.

central heating
Shed has central heating as it is a home for pets – HUTCH
HUT has CH. A clue that makes good 'straight' sense and also provides the correct clue elements to lead to the answer.

centre
Exact centre of map – it has significant meaning – PITH
Did you spot the 'burial'? It is the 'exact centre' of 'ma*p – it h*as' (two letters before and two after), and is defined as 'significant meaning'.

centre of gravity
Centre of gravity holds zero reading and it stops the wheel – COG
The clue is meant to blind you (temporarily) with technology, so that a few seconds elapse before you discover that CG 'holds' O, and see that a COG 'stops the wheel'.

century
A double century – and mixed post as indication of approval? – ACCLAIM
A cricketing scene here, I think, but one that readily gives A CC and 'mixed' LAIM ('post') to produce the deserved 'indication of approval', or ACCLAIM.

(a) **certain amount** (of)
A certain amount of duplicity is allowable – LICIT
The 'burial' here is in the single word 'dup*licity*', a 'certain amount' of which gives 'allowable', or LICIT.

certainly
Most shy, certainly, in bed – COYEST
'Most' often indicates a superlative ending in -EST, as it does here (see **most** as a clue entry), so the definition, 'most shy', leads to COYEST, otherwise cryptically clued as YES ('certainly') in COT ('bed').

champion
Forbidding champions make ugly faces – GRIMACES
But not too 'forbidding' a clue, I hope. All you need are the GRIM ACES, or 'forbidding champions', to get the GRIMACES, or 'ugly faces'!

(Mr) **Chaney**
Mr Chaney comes to scholar in capital city – LONDON
All too easy, really, when LON comes to DON.

Channel Isles
Disturbances in Channel Isles with signs of impact by blunt instruments – INCIDENTS
These fearful goings-on are not as bad as they sound: the definition, 'disturbances', is built up by the three elements IN ('in'), CI ('Channel Isles') and DENTS, pompously clued (to put you off) as 'signs of impact by blunt instrument'. (The definition of DENT is not the *Chambers* one, which is confusingly – and even misleadingly – given simply as 'a notch'.)

chap
A chap gets a notice back for a girl with a lovely name – AMANDA
In other words, A MAN gets DA ('notice back') for AMANDA. The 'lovely name' is really an optional extra here, although it has a genuine significance for the classically inclined, since the name AMANDA is Latin for 'lovable'! Note that the first 'a' of the clue is essential to the answer, but the second ('*a* notice') is of no consequence at all.

chaps
Chaps go down these hills – MENDIP
Self-explanatory, really. Note that 'these hills' implies that the answer needs to precede the word 'hills', not replace it. That is why there is no final S on MENDIP. (There can't be, since here MEN is plural.)

chapter
Dean and chapter meet in some confusion at the ball – DANCE
I have to confess a special attachment to this clue, not only for its neatness (in combining 'dean and chapter' so agreeably) but also for its enjoyable image (solemn clerics caught on the hop, so to speak). The entire answer, defined as 'ball', is an anagram ('some confusion') of DEAN and C (for 'chapter').

character(s)
Nude characters pursued by Communist bore – ENDURED
Another nice clue. The letters of NUDE, rearranged (as individual 'characters') as ENDU, are 'pursued' or followed by the RED Communist, with 'bore' being the definition of ENDURED.

cheat
Cheat the railway – here's a small boat – DORY
Perhaps you had to check that DORY actually *was* 'a small boat' (it is also a fish), but the two short cryptic elements, DO the RY, should have helped to lead you to it.

chemist
Caught a chemist in the service stations – CAMPS
Not a 'burial', as it might at first appear, but a straight 'read-through' of three elements (C+A+MPS) with 'service stations' being one definition (not in *Chambers*) of CAMPS.

chief
Chief, I've a document here – ARCHIVE
It's true that the answer is more common in the plural, but it *does* exist in the singular, and is here arrived at by a combination of ARCH and IVE.

child
Completely childless colleague – ALLY

Get it? 'Completely' is TOTALLY, 'childless' is TOTALLY less TOT, 'colleague' is ALLY!

children
Noisy children run quickly about – FLITTER
Quite straightforward, once you see that 'noise' is F and 'children' LITTER.

children's nurse
Bachelor and children's nurses together – that's crazy! – BANANAS
BA+NANAS = BANANAS, or 'crazy'. The word is in *Chambers* (in the *Supplement* to the 1977 edition).

chimney
Chimney, surrounded by lead, is quite vertical – PLUMB
As you would probably expect it to be. But no matter, this LUM, or Scottish 'chimney', is surrounded by PB, otherwise 'lead'. Compare this clue with the one under **bachelor**.

(a) **choice word**
Prepare a choice word – 'entrance' – DOOR
Although an easy answer, not such an easy clue, especially if you haven't cracked 'a choice word' as OR. The 'entrance', with its quotes, is also off-putting. And is it '*en*trance', to do with entering, or 'entr*a*nce', to do with a trance? Tricky. Well, 'prepare' is one of the senses of DO (the thirteenth of the eighteen given by *Chambers*) and with OR you have the first and more common type of 'entrance' to define DOOR.

choose
Choose the French onions in brine – PICKLES
Here it is 'choose' = PICK+'the French' = LES that give the 'onions in brine' definition of PICKLES. Incidentally, if six letters had been indicated for the answer, instead of seven, you could have quite correctly entered PICKLE, since LE is still 'the French'.

Christian dispensation
A Christian dispensation for this worker – ANT
A+NT = ANT. Note that the definition here is the standard cryptic one for ANT, rather than a dictionary-type one. This is really because an 'insect' could hardly merit 'a Christian dispensation'.

Christmas
Christmas is all wrong when you're on your own – LONE
Don't allow yourself to be mesmerised by the moral message, however true. Read the clue again to see where the cryptic content must be. There it is, in 'all wrong', denoting an anagram of 'Christmas', i.e. of NOEL. This produces the answer LONE, 'on your own'.

Christopher
Christopher's central heating is very vulgar aesthetically – KITSCH
That is, KIT'S CH is KITSCH! It's not defined quite like this by *Chambers*, but to have put 'pretentious and inferior' or 'in bad taste' (as *Chambers* suggests) would have rung false in the clue, since central heating is hardly either of these, normally. But it could *look* unduly showy, and that's why 'very vulgar aesthetically' was the definition chosen.

chuck
Charity chucks it, being cautious – CHARY
It doesn't matter whether you understood 'Charity' as an organisation or the name of a girl, so long as it or she 'chucks', i.e. omits IT, you will get the correct answer of CHARY.

church
Scholar comes to church and we see his sign of authority – MACE
The MACE is actually a ceremonial staff used as a 'sign of authority'. To get it, the MA comes to the CE. Compare the clue for this same word under **expert**.

church dignitary
Address the church dignitary – 'What's cooking?' – OVEN
The incongruous question put to the dignitary justifies the cryptic elements of 'address' (O) and VEN. The question mark is not only essential anyway to indicate the question; it can also suggest to the solver that 'what's cooking' may in fact be the definition part of the clue, as indeed it is.

churchman
Churchman is also editor, so examined and corrected – REVISED
REV IS ED, so REVISED. No more need be said for this straightforward 'read-through' clue.

church service
Is 'collect' a church service? – MASS
No, it isn't – but it is a definition of MASS (as 'the troops were massing'). So here we have a clue with two definitions, the only cryptic aspect being the quite different senses of MASS defined. (Solvers interested in word origins may like to know that the 'church service' MASS is not so called because people 'collect' or congregate for it, but because in the Roman mass the priest ended the service with the words *ite, missa est*, meaning 'go, [the congregation] is dismissed'.) Compare the clue under **service**.

cigarette
Cigarette sent back to returning umpire – he's the foreman! – GAFFER
We have two reversals here, indicated respectively by 'sent back' and 'returning'. So reverse GAF and REF, put them together, and you get the 'foreman', or GAFFER.

circle
Get the black circle – BRING
Yes, I know, the definition of 'get' is properly 'fetch', not BRING. But we all use BRING as 'fetch' – and look up 'fetch' in *Chambers* and you will see, as the first two meanings given, 'to bring: to go and get'. So BRING it is! The 'black circle' is the B RING, of course. The clue suggests some kind of game in which one shoots or aims at a target.

circuit
This animal ran about two hundred circuits – RACCOON
'Two hundred' could hardly be otherwise than CC, which will have given you a start. So 'two hundred' is CC, 'circuits' is OO, and RAN goes 'about' these to produce the 'animal', a RACCOON.

city (City) (district) (of London)
Tea-time delicacy in city hide-out – ECLAIR
Was the clue to your taste? An ECLAIR is a 'tea-time delicacy', and this one was got from an EC LAIR.

Civil Defence
Painter is back in Civil Defence – he's a real joker! – CARD
RA is 'back' or reversed in CD – and a 'joker' can certainly be a CARD. (There appears to be a connection, in fact, between the playing CARD and the human CARD or witty person. Perhaps the wit was someone who had a 'good CARD' to play.)

Civil Service
There's work in the Civil Service for the police – COPS
So there's OP in the CS for the COPS. (For OP see **work**, if necessary.)

clamour
Clamour in oil well is continuing – RIDING
DIN in RIG is RIDING. But 'continuing'? Yes, this is a possible definition of RIDING, in the slang sense, as 'I wanted to change that, but let it ride'. This sense is not given in *Chambers*, but it is in other dictionaries, such as *Collins English Dictionary*. Admittedly, we don't often use it with the -ING ending, but the actual sense makes the word fair game for this clue!

Clara
Clara comes to the Queen for a tea-time spread – BUTTER
The definition part of the clue is semi-punning, but Clara BUTT and ER are the two cryptic ladies who can otherwise guide you to the correct answer.

clasp
A Pole clasps me – so be it! – AMEN
The two kinds of Pole, N and S, turn up fairly frequently. Here A N(orth) 'Pole' 'clasps' ME to get the traditional interpretation of AMEN, 'so be it'. We could have clued this as 'A Pole clasps me – that's the last word!' but somehow this is less convincing.

classy
Sit in classy costume – SUIT
Quite a nice neat clue, with U 'buried' in SIT to get the necessary SUIT.

cleaner
Cleaner brings two notes for the cost – CHARGE
A professional clue-writer will avoid using the all too handy 'note' more than necessary. Here, however, the 'two notes' are fairly limited as the two letters that complete the CHAR or 'cleaner' to make the CHARGE or 'cost'.

clergyman
Clergyman, in love with the German Queen, is all of a tremble – DODDERER
Not too many cryptic elements for you, I hope! The first two involve a 'burial' – O in DD – and you then have two more: 'the German' (DER) and 'Queen' (ER). These give a DODDERER who is 'all of a tremble'. Notice that 'Queen' has a capital to indicate ER ('the Queen') rather than just R ('a queen'). And if you object that there *is* no German Queen, allow me to suggest that the DD actually fell for a beauty queen!

climbing
Climbing cat goes on the tile, moving by touch – TACTILE
A 'climbing' CAT in this down clue is a reversed one, so we have TAC on the TILE, giving TACTILE, which is 'moving by touch'.

clique
The 'Back Rodney' clique is in Wessex – DORSET
'Back Rodney' to get DOR, add 'clique' (SET), and you have the Wessex county of DORSET. (Wessex, apart from the literary setting of Thomas Hardy's novels, chiefly in Dorset, was the Kingdom of the West Saxons which corresponded to Hampshire, Dorset, Wiltshire, Berkshire, Somerset, Avon and Devon.)

close, closing
Constituent at close of day may be Conservative or Labour – PARTY
No doubt 'constituent', in view of the clue as a whole, put you on a political track. Yet 'constituent' is a good definition of PART, and if you add the 'close' or last letter of 'day' to it you get a PARTY, political or otherwise.

clothing
Rumpled clothing makes me lose my temper – RAGE
Where's the 'clothing'? It's GEAR, 'rumpled' or turned into an anagram. This gives RAGE, which is to lose one's temper.

club
Old soldier has small coin to join upper-class mixed club – CENTURION
The definition is the 'old soldier' (actually a Roman one), who has a CENT to join the U anagram of IRON ('club').

(the) **C.O.**
The C.O. comes up to a recruit, and is very hot-tempered – COAL
The C.O. comes up to A 'recruit' or learner (L), and that makes COAL, which is 'hot-tempered' (i.e. brought to a hot temper or state).

coach
Coach comes to a headland – that's its job – BUSINESS
Thus the BUS comes to I ('a') NESS, which is its BUSINESS.

Cockney (says)
Primitive weapon is of the Cockney school – ARROW
An ARROW is a 'primitive weapon', and 'ARROW is a 'Cockney school', minus its initial H.

code
Trainee follows the code for a bit – MORSEL
The 'trainee' is the learner (L), who follows the MORSE. That gives the MORSEL, or 'bit'.

coin
Coin-op favourite, a darling girl – POPPET
The 'coin' is P, which plus OP and PET ('favourite') gives the 'darling girl'.

cold
Cold sailor gets a taxi – CAB
Or the C AB gets a CAB. A nice clue with a straightforward answer.

college
Famous college is back with quite a large number – NOTED

Otherwise ETON 'back' with D, which is five hundred, or 'quite a large number'.

colonel
Colonel brings back the rope – that's terrific! – COLOSSAL
You may have wondered how the 'rope' would work out. As you can see, it's a LASSO, here 'back' after the COL to get COLOSSAL, defined as 'terrific'. Perhaps the comment on the colonel's action in the clue is more ironic than approving.

colour(ed)
Scholar coloured, being undressed – BARED
The BA went RED. Of all the colours, RED is easily the most useful for puzzles since it can be used for a number of words that end in -RED or start with RED-.

coloured fluid
Coloured fluid in ship's basins – SINKS
Notice that the 'S at the end of 'ship's' means 'is' here, that is, INK in SS 'is' SINKS.

come back (to)
Mr Runyon makes a comeback – he's always on the move – NOMAD
It's simply a matter of reversing the first name of DAMON Runyon, the American writer, to get the NOMAD who is 'always on the move'.

come round, come around
He comes round fish, being in place of concealment – HIDE
The little ID is a handy fish, as here, when HE 'comes round' it. Some other common ways of clueing ID are **self** (which see), 'I'd', 'I had' or 'I would', of course, and 499 (see **consequence**).

come to
Holy man comes to a king – and it was this that led him – STAR
You probably solved this Christmas-tide clue without 'reading' the cryptic elements. Yet they are there, for ST comes to A R.

come up
There's a prohibition order on young Roger coming up to North Wales town – BANGOR
Rather an obvious clue, with a BAN on ROG ('young Roger') reversed. The little word 'to' here means 'these cryptic elements amount to the following definition'.

commanding officer
Commanding officer at home to get some money – COIN
You no doubt recall a similar clue for **at home**. Once again, the CO is IN to get his COIN. The 'commanding officer' is most useful for beginning clues leading to words starting CO-.

commercial
With commercial backing, engineers are bold – DARE
The RE have DA 'backing', or reversed, so they DARE.

Commie
Commie and German worker dismissed from work! – REDUNDANT
The RED UND ('and German') ANT are REDUNDANT. In the excitement, don't misread 'Commie' as 'Connie', which could legitimately lead to CON.

commit(ted)
I'm committed to the editor, so charged – IMPUTED
Perhaps the cryptic elements (IM PUT to the ED) are easier here than the definition, since 'charged' can be taken a number of ways. Here it is IMPUTED, more or less as 'accused' or 'ascribed'.

common(ly)
The common fool – he'd put a coat on! – CLOTHED
The CLOT – HE'D got CLOTHED! 'Common' is needed to denote the slang word CLOT.

Common Market
Gravity about rioting Common Market country – GREECE
That is, G RE ('about') 'rioting' or anagrammatic EEC. For the record, GREECE *is* a member of the EEC, joining it in 1981. The clue would have lacked conviction if it had featured a country that was not actually part of the EEC.

common sense
He and I have common sense – is that so terribly wicked? – HEINOUS
A straightforward 'read-through', so that HE and I have NOUS. 'He and I', in another clue, might legitimately have led to WE.

Communist
Tedium for Communist in capitalist commercial activity – BOREDOM
BOREDOM for the RED in BOOM. The word 'capitalist' is justified in order to give a suitable contrast to 'Communist' in this politically slanted clue, and also since a BOOM is normally something one associates with a western or 'capitalist' society. No wonder the RED felt out of place in it!

companion
Shrewd painter comes back to companion – ARCH
Taken 'cold' this clue seems to offer two possible definitions. But is it 'shrewd' or 'companion'? In the event, of course, it is 'shrewd', with the 'companion' being CH added to the RA ('painter') who 'comes back' as AR.

company
Prison company work – COOP
These three nouns run nicely together in the clue to provide COOP ('prison') CO ('company') and OP ('work'), with the definition thus preceding the two cryptic elements.

comparatively
British possessor, yet has comparatively dark skin – BROWNER
That 'comparatively' should have immediately signalled a word ending in -ER. With that information, you can quickly obtain the rest of the answer either from the definition ('comparatively dark skin') or the two cryptic elements – 'British' (BR) 'possessor' (OWNER).

competition
Weight competition has easy elegance – GRACE
Many weight competitions or contests do not have 'easy elegance' (GRACE), but this one does – perhaps because the 'weight' is such a little one (G)!

complaint
Doctor's complaint is pneumatic – DRILL
This clue cheats a little, since 'pneumatic' is meant to suggest 'pneumonia'. However, 'pneumatic' *could* have a medical sense since it means 'relating to air, gases or wind' – and even if it does not, there is no harm done. (Who said he was a doctor of medicine?) Anyway, the DR has an ILL, and this is the DRILL which (here) is a 'pneumatic' one.

component(s)
Five engine components found scattered at end of the day – EVENING
A harder clue, with its misleading cryptic possibilities – the answer does not start with V, for example, and 'end of the day' is not Y (for once). Instead, we have an anagram ('scattered') of V+ENGINE, and that turns into EVENING, which is the 'end of the day'!

compound
London prison compound moves to northern town in France – PENTONVILLE
At first glance, it is not so easy to distinguish the definition in the clue from the cryptic elements. As it turns out, it is the name of the 'London prison' you want, not that of a 'northern town in France'. The longish answer is built up from four cryptic elements: PEN ('compound') TO ('to') N ('northern') and VILLE ('town in France'). 'Moves' simply indicates that the PEN has to 'move' to join the next element.

comprise
Set comprises mined elements, mixed, which form a deposit – SEDIMENT
The 'deposit' or SEDIMENT is obtained from the SET which 'comprises' or 'straddles' the anagram ('mixed') of the letters ('elements') of MINED. Not too involved, I hope.

conceal(ing)
George, the rascal, conceals anaesthetic liquid – ETHER
This *is* a 'burial', so that 'Georg*e, the r*ascal' conceals the ETHER.

concealed
Mythical monster concealed rare flower – ORCHID
This is not a 'burial' but a 'read-through', with the 'mythical monster' being an ORC. He HID ('concealed') the 'rare flower' or ORCHID.

concerned with, concerning
Retirement is concerned with an agreeable excursion or a party – RETREAT
No, not that sort of 'retirement'! The RETREAT is RE ('concerned with') a TREAT, here deliberately defined in such a way as to suggest the other sort of 'retirement'.

concert
Concert exercises are performed at once – PROMPT
A clue like this owes its success to its ability to mask its definition – will the answer be a word for 'concert', 'concert exercises', 'performed at once' or 'at once'? Where are the cryptic elements, if any? We know they lie in 'concert' (PROM) and 'exercises' (PT), but it may take a little thought to identify them correctly. PROMPT, incidentally, is defined by 'performed at once', the precise wording of the word's second sense in *Chambers*.

conclusion
For the record, retaliatory attack has speedy conclusion – DIARY
An unexpected answer to this military-style clue. Yet a DIARY is kept 'for the record', and DIAR is a 'retaliatory' or reversed RAID, finished off with the 'conclusion' or last letter of 'speedy'.

condition
Tom's back condition is a recurring subject – MOTIF
At least you get off to a good start here, with 'Tom's back' giving MOT. Add IF for the 'condition' and you will find your MOTIF, or 'recurring subject'. I hope that 'recurring' did not lead you to spend too much time looking for a reversal! See also **doctor**.

conducted
Greek character conducted, made a heap – PILED
The 'Greek character' is the old faithful PI, who 'conducted' (LED) and so 'made a heap', or PILED.

(in the) **confine(s) of**
Tax collection for five in the confines of the field – LEVY
Rather an unusual image here (a medieval tax-gatherer at work, perhaps?), but a clue that clearly tells you to put V 'in the confines' of the LEY.

confused type
Confused type of church musical composition – PIECE
Not specifically ecclesiastical, as it turns out, since 'church' is there simply to give you CE after the PIE. Of course, in many clues, 'confused' will indicate an anagram, so that 'confused type' could be PYTE or ROTS ('confused SORT').

consequence
Add 504 to 499 and the consequence is a pay-off – DIVIDEND
So this is your answer, not 1003! It's simply a matter of getting the Roman numerals right: '504' is DIV, '499' is ID, 'consequence' is END, and there's your richly deserved 'pay-off' or DIVIDEND.

Conservative
5+99 = Conservative gain – VICTORY
After this and the previous clue, numeral-type clues will hold no terrors for you. This one adds V to IC to produce TORY, the total making the 'gain' or VICTORY.

conspirator
Conspirator, an artist, the cause of many a purge – CASCARA
CASCA+RA gives you the 'cause of many a purge'. You may groan at the pun, but it serves fairly enough as a definition.

constituent of
Seize the constituent of Newton Abbot – NAB
This 'burial' is not very hard. Of course, the 'constituent' need not necessarily be a political one; we could have a culinary 'constituent'. Did you know that a peg, for example, is a constituent of a chocolate eclair?

consumed
Patrol leader consumed dish – PLATE
The hungry Boy Scout was the PL or 'patrol leader' who ATE the 'dish', which is a PLATE. 'Leader' here does not indicate a first letter, as it sometimes does, so that PL is the abbreviation of '*p*atrol *l*eader'.

contains, container, content
Fear not, the river is content – ARNO
I'm not too sure how a river, except a personified one, can be 'content'. But no matter, 'fe*ar no*t' has the 'content' or 'burial' that we need to produce this Italian one.

continental (Continental)
First class – the continental beer – ALE
An easy 'read-through' clue, with 'continental' denoting the expected French word (LE, 'the'). For a rather different sort of clue, see **something of**.

continue to
Continue to carry box – CARTON
So CART ON the CARTON.

contribute (to)
New agent contributes payment – WAGE
The 'burial', of course, is in the 'ne*w age*nt'.

cooler
Soldiers in cooler attempt – INFANTRY
INFANTRY IN FAN TRY – a 'read-through' clue.

copied
Medical man copied and assumed a casual pose – DRAPED.
The DR APED, so DRAPED.

copper
Copper Street sounds like Milky Way! – CURD
That 'sounds like' immediately suggests a homophone. And there it is in the 'way' of 'Milky Way' and the 'whey' that is CURD. And if this pun didn't give you the answer, the two cryptic elements of 'Copper Street' (CU+RD) will have done.

coppers
Coppers in Southern Region find a woman's under-garment – SPENCER
So that's what these apparent railway police were after – the SPENCER that was 'a woman's short under-garment, formerly over-jacket' (says *Chambers*). No doubt you had little problem over the 'burial', with the 'coppers' or PENCE being in the 'Southern Region' or SR.

copy
Typed top copy is found on recording instrument – TAPE
But a tape is not a recording instrument, you protest? Quite so – but a TAPE 'is found on recording instrument', the tape-recorder, is it not? The 'typed top copy' also cryptically leads to TAPE, since you have the 'top' or first letter of 'typed' and 'copy' meaning APE.

core
Tap core of the earth in pitfall – TRAP
Not too involved, I imagine. The 'core of the earth' is its middle letter, and this goes 'in' TAP to get the TRAP that can be a 'pitfall' (see *Chambers*, if necessary).

(this) **corner**
Corner street provides cosy home – NEST
In this case it's the north-east (NE) 'corner', which with the 'street' (ST) makes your NEST or 'cosy home'. You can take 'corner street' at its face value to mean what you wish. Perhaps it is a street in the corner of a town, or a hidden one – or even one forming a corner?

Cornwall and Devon
Urge to come to Cornwall and Devon for a change – SWITCH
The only thing here is to be sure to make ITCH ('urge') 'come to' SW by following it, rather than preceding. The 'change' is the definition, of course.

(that's) **correct**
Acid for President of the United States? That's correct – PRUSSIC
The PRUSSIC 'acid' can be seen in the three cryptic elements: PR ('President'), US ('United States') and SIC ('that's correct'). If you don't like the clue, see it as the President wanting the acid!

corroded
Silver corroded, Ruby? – AGATE
Probably the silver did not corrode, or was not corroded. But for our purposes AG ('silver')+ATE ('corroded') will make AGATE, which is a 'ruby type' (*Chambers*). I originally planned the clue as 'Silver corroded ruby', but since this seemed to be chemical nonsense I decided to turn 'ruby' into a woman (for some reason, she suggests a housemaid) and use the question mark to suggest to the solver, 'Is this the correct answer?'

costly fiddle
Costly fiddle led astray, shooting beyond and short of the target – STRADDLE
The longish second part of the clue is the definition, with the first part containing the cryptic 'costly fiddle' (STRAD) and 'led astray' (DLE).

councillor
A councillor, on my return, gives a word like Ernie – ACRONYM
This word should be in the vocabulary of every solver! It means 'a word formed from the initial letters of other words' (*Chambers*), and the clue contains the familiar ACRONYM 'Ernie' (which actually stands for '*e*lectronic *r*andom *n*umber *i*ndicator *e*quipment', the machine that deals with Premium Bonds). Of course, the usual cryptic elements are there as well to lead you to the word: 'a' (A) 'councillor' (CR) 'on' (ON) 'my return' (YM).

count
Conservatives count leaderless nation – but they can't count all the stars here! – CONSTELLATION
In fact a straight 'read-through' clue: 'Conservatives' (CONS) 'count' (TELL) 'leaderless nation' (ATION, i.e. 'nation' less its 'leader'), and an indirect definition.

counter
Counterweight in the farmyard – BARTON
Did you know this word already? If not, the cryptic elements – more definitions, really – in 'counterweight' (BAR+TON) should have led to it. There are lots of English villages called BARTON (including Barton in the Beans in Leicestershire), with the name originally meaning 'barley enclosure', as it did for the 'farmyard' word.

country
Uninteresting, second-rate country – BLAND
A 'second-rate country', or B LAND, can be 'uninteresting', which is one sense (not in *Chambers*, in fact) of BLAND.

county
County cricketer takes in pupil, thus getting a special blue – COBALT
The 'county cricketer' is not the name of a sportsman but a CO BAT. He 'takes in' L ('pupil') to get COBALT 'blue'.

couple
A couple of hundred points will give you admittance – ACCESS
'A couple of hundred' is ACC, of course. Then we actually have three 'points' (ESS) to gain our ACCESS, or 'admittance'.

court
Court quite a number among the trees – WOOD
'Court' in the clue at its face value need not necessarily mean WOO, as it does here. 'Quite a number', however, is D (actually 500) and 'among the trees' defines WOOD.

cover
Five per cover fulfilling the necessary conditions – VALID
Be ready for 'per' to represent A sometimes, as it does here. Otherwise the clue is regular: V A LID is VALID, one definition of which (taken word for word from *Chambers*) is 'fulfilling the necessary conditions'.

crack pilot
Crack pilot sets off from South Pole into cosmos – SPACE
'Sets off from' here implies 'follows, goes after', so that the ACE follows the SP, and that turns 'into' SPACE, which is the 'cosmos'. Compare the quite different clue under **resort**.

crash into
Albert crashes into house, and wins this aura of sanctity! – HALO

Otherwise AL 'crashes into' HO to win his HALO. The clue as it stands suggests a kamikaze driver, but is acceptable, I think, to produce the required 'aura of sanctity'.

creature
Sinister creature went off – LEFT
'Sinister' means 'left' (i.e. not right), the abbreviation for which is L. This is followed by the 'creature' which is an EFT (actually a newt – believe it or not, the words are related). The outcome is the other type of LEFT, 'went off'.

credit
Credit for us? Hard in this dense mass of people – CRUSH
Don't let the question mark put you off or interrupt the flow of cryptic elements (CR+US+H). A CRUSH is defined as the 'dense mass of people'.

crew
Means to see the crew about agreement – EYESIGHT
Here, in this rather unexpected 'burial', the EIGHT are 'about' YES ('agreement'), giving 'means to see'.

cross
Did she make Socrates cross, diffusing the pain round philosopher's head? – XANTHIPPE
A rather erudite clue. Still, we reach this exotic classical name from the cryptic elements. 'Cross' is the initial X, and 'diffusing' indicates an anagram of 'the pain'. This turns out to be ANTHIPE and goes 'round philosopher's head', otherwise 'buries' the 'head' or first letter of '*p*hilosopher', which is P. And there is XANTHIPPE, who was actually Socrates' wife! (The name – and its definitions – are in fact in *Chambers*.)

crowd
Crowd I'll say is able to move – MOBILE
You should have no problems with this clue so long as you correctly interpret 'I'll say' as ILE.

cunning
Former president is cunning – deliberately! – EXPRESSLY
Thus the EX-PRES is SLY.

Cupid
Tender Cupid flies back – SORE
Just a simple reversal ('flies back') and its definition ('tender'). Compare the clue under **sulphur**.

currency
Same currency for the dean – DOYEN
'Same' is DO (i.e. 'ditto') and here the currency used is YEN. DOYEN has the basic meaning 'dean' (via the French).

current
Current account is first class return for those who live in this traditional suburban avenue – ACACIA
Notice how each AC is clued differently: the first as 'current', the second as 'account'. 'First class return' is a reversal of AI, of course. And who has not heard of the archetypal ACACIA 'avenue', the typical middle-class suburban street?

current fashion
Current fashion points to a soft kind of talk – GOSSIP
Only 'kind of talk' is the definition. The remainder of the clue contains the four cryptic elements: 'current fashion' (GO) 'points' (SS) 'a' (I) and 'soft' (P).

curtailed
Curtailed dog or where he comes in – DOOR
That is, 'curtailed dog' (DO)+'or' (OR). 'Curtailed dog' sounds like some sort of pun involving curs and their tails, but this is simply a red herring. Perhaps we can literally understand the two words as meaning 'cut dog short' (or 'dog cut short'). Come to that, he need not be a real dog, but a rogue or 'cur'. Compare the clue for this word under **choice word**.

custom
Examine each custom – PERUSE
Simply a definition ('examine') and two cryptic elements, also near-definitions – 'each' (PER) and 'custom' (USE).

cut (out)
Cut out article from Indiana for this country – INDIA
Yes, that sort of 'article'. 'Cut out' AN from INDIANA to get INDIA.

D

Dad(dy)
Dad has six lions in the tents – PAVILIONS
Quite a nice 'read-through' clue, so that PA has VI LIONS in the PAVILIONS or 'tents'.

daily
Daily mass has special influence – CHARM
The M is the abbreviation for the physics type of 'mass', in fact, but we can add it to the 'daily' or CHAR to get CHARM, otherwise 'special influence'.

dandy
Dandy returns with mangled fish – is that why he looks so solemn? – PO-FACED
An agreeable clue with a cartoon-type image (one of the early *Punch* drawings, perhaps, with caption to match). What we have, apart from the definition ('looks so solemn'), are a reversed FOP (who 'returns') and an anagrammatic or 'mangled' DACE. Notice that for cryptic clueing purposes the hyphen in a hyphenated word can be ignored.

Daniel
Daniel follows us up to this Middle East country – SUDAN
Thus DAN follows US 'up' (i.e. reversed). To make it harder, this clue could have been simply 'Daniel follows us up-country', with no indication of the country's location – or indeed as to whether it even *was* this kind of country. Compare the clue under **tribesman**.

darling
Darling pupil comes in – so hide! – PELT
I must confess to a soft spot for this clue, with its unexpected PELT (yes, *that* sort of 'hide'!) The 'pupil', of course, is the L, who 'comes in' PET, or 'darling'. The picture, I think, is of mischievous schoolchildren waiting to bait teacher's pet.

day
Day One is over – DONE
Short and sweet, so that D ONE is DONE. For a different sort of clue, see **there**.

(the) **day before**
It's common the day before Railway Day – EVERYDAY
Read right through here, with the definition coming first. So 'common' (EVERYDAY), then 'the day before' (EVE), 'Railway' (RY) and 'Day' (DAY)! In the USSR there actually is an annual 'Railway Day', on the first Sunday in August.

day of victory
Day of Victory – right, I go,
Turning makes my head spin so – VERTIGO
The whole of the first line of this celebratory couplet consists of the cryptic elements (VE+RT+I+GO), with the definition in the second. The general image conveyed seems to be a jubilant dance (as in London streets on VE Day, in fact, 8 May 1945).

dead
Dead – with a mask of fine linen – DAMASK
A virtual giveaway here, with every letter of the answer spelled out in the clue.

deadly
Deadly gin doctored, making him collapse – FELLING
'Deadly' is FELL and 'gin doctored' is an anagram of GIN – the usual ING. Notice how the verb ending of the clue ('making') matches that of the answer (FELLING).

death
Death in the arena is heart-breaking – RENDING
END in the RING is RENDING.

debtor
Dead debtor has an endowment – DOWER
Once again, D represents 'dead', with the 'debtor' being an OWER, and a DOWER being a dowry or 'endowment'.

debt(s)
Endless vice and debts make him ill-tempered – VICIOUS
'Endless vice' is VIC less its 'end' (E), and the 'debts' are the IOUS to add to this.

decapitate
Looks after the meeting and still lives even when decapitated! – PRESIDES
The face value of the clue may be over-contrived for some tastes (its humour is offset by its lack of credibility), but it is effective

enough for its cryptic content: if PRESIDES ('looks after the meeting') is 'decapitated', i.e. loses its first letter, you get RESIDES, clued as 'lives'.

December
December – note Roman confusion of the ten-day tales – DECAMERON
Initially, perhaps, the clue seems to hint at something to do with the Roman calendar, in which December was originally the tenth month (hence its name, the Latin for 'ten' being *decem*). But in fact the 'ten-day tales' are the definition of the DECAMERON, which was, as *Chambers* tell us, 'Boccaccio's book of a hundred tales, supposed to be told in ten days' (the name is actually Greek for 'ten days'). But you can check all this after arriving at the word cryptically: 'December' is DEC, and 'note Roman confusion' indicates an anagram of a 'note' (E) and ROMAN (as AMERON).

declare
Mick goes over to declare he's a nonconformist – MAVERICK
A 'straddle', as you can see, so that MICK 'goes over' AVER. A MAVERICK, says *Chambers* (in its second definition of the word), is 'one who does not conform'.

decoration
Decoration on the king is anti-metathetical and pro-theistic – CHRISTIAN
This clue is designed to put you off altogether! Actually, it works through quite reasonably. 'Decoration' is CH (Companion of Honour, 'king' is R, 'is' is IS (!), 'anti-metathetical' is an anagram (a 'metathesis' – see this in *Chambers*, if necessary) of ANTI, i.e. TIAN, and these four elements make CHRISTIAN, which is 'pro-theistic', or 'for God'! So long as they don't come up too often, clues like this are fair game and should not be beyond a solver of good average ability (and some experience of this sort of thing).

deep
Deep freezer – ICEBERG
A clue as short as the last one was long. It's a pun, of course, with an ICEBERG being a 'freezer' of the 'deep', i.e. the sea.

defeat
Defeat after tea, so hurry off quickly – TEAR OUT
The unexpected word-break may temporarily halt you. But then you'll spot that a ROUT after TEA gives TEAR OUT, or 'hurry off quickly'.

deflated
Marriage god found among deflated hairy men – HYMEN
A weird image, it's true (a primitive jungle tribe and its rites, perhaps), but if the 'hairy men' are 'deflated', i.e. have AIR removed, you'll get HYMEN, the god of marriage in Greek mythology!

degree
Girl gets a degree (I) with her study – MAIDEN
The MAIDEN who apparently got a first class degree can be seen in MA+I+DEN ('her study').

deity
Deity holds love, is kindly – GOOD
The biblical-style clue declares that GOD 'holds', i.e. contains O and is GOOD ('kindly').

delayed
Pass a special law, for member is delayed – LEGISLATE
The 'member' here is not MP but LEG, adding IS LATE to give the answer defined as 'pass a special law'.

deliver
Eddie comes back to deliver mixed gin – is he making fun of us? – DERIDING
A reversal (ED to DE), an unexpected meaning (RID = 'deliver'), and an anagram ('mixed' GIN to ING), followed by a definition ('making fun') to produce the answer.

demon
Demon donkey goes east, there's no way out of it – IMPASSE
IMP+ASS+E give you the IMPASSE. I hope you found your way out of the cryptic snares.

demonstrate
Young Alastair demonstrates the festivities – GALAS
The GALAS are 'demonstrated' by 'Youn*g Ala*stair'. (Perhaps the 'young' initially led you to look for a short form of 'Alastair'? A false trail, I fear.)

depart
Inspire novice to depart when I'm melancholy – IMBUE
To reach your objective here, defined as 'inspire', the 'novice' (L) needs to 'depart' from I'M BLUE.

department
The Department for First Defence is in East London – DEPTFORD
It may be helpful to know that the unobtrusive 'for' plays an important part in this clue, enabling you to link DEPT (via FOR) with D ('First *D*efence').

depend
China depends on prize secured by pirate – CUP-HOOK
Not the country but crockery! The 'prize' is the CUP, of course, and the 'pirate' is Captain HOOK, of *Peter Pan* notoriety. And the 'china' 'depends' or hangs on this CUP-HOOK.

depression, depressed
Mad life in France leads to depression, that's obvious – EVIDENT
Here you have an anagram ('mad') of the French for 'life', VIE, followed by the 'depression' or DENT, which is EVIDENT or 'obvious'.

Descartes
Descartes got married and began a fresh lease of life – RENEWED
RENE WED, therefore and RENEWED his life. For the record, the great French philosopher never actually married.

desert(er)
Deserter – one on a fixed allowance – RATION
An easy clue to read through, with the 'deserter' or RAT 'one' (I) 'on' (ON) a RATION, or 'fixed allowance'.

despatched
Agreement as despatched – ASSENT
Otherwise ASSENT AS SENT! For a slight variation, see **since**; for a greater variation, see **Anglo-Saxon**.

detailed
Girl detailed to go across – BRIDGE
It is BRIDGET, of course, who is the 'detailed' girl (minus her 'tail' of T).

detective
Detective has drink, getting something to do with building – TECTONIC
Not a very common word, true (it means 'pertaining to building', says *Chambers*), but the 'detective' gives you a good start with his TEC and you can sort through the few words beginning thus (under a column in *Chambers*) to find the TONIC that gives you the answer.

detectives
Drink for detectives of the Queen – CIDER
More tecs and their drinks! But these 'detectives' are the CID and, with ER, you can see that this time their drink is CIDER.

devil
The devil has a tune, but this will make it worse! – IMPAIR
The IMP has an AIR, but if we IMPAIR it we 'make it worse'. So, according to this clue, the devil does *not* always have the best tunes.

devotee
Devotee has exciting stay – in imagination only – FANTASY
Did you spot 'exciting' correctly as an anagram indicator? If so, you'll have had little difficulty in combining FAN and anagrammatic STAY to get FANTASY, 'in imagination only'.

devour
Chum sees me devour 'at – MATE
My MATE sees ME 'devour' AT. And if you found that a difficult clue – perhaps you may find the one under **source of** more straightforward.

dial?
Unable to move? – LAID UP

Yes, this answer was given you in the clue entry. But it was included as an example of the uses of the question mark – in this case really reversing the process and giving you an 'answer' to which you have to supply the 'clue'. Perhaps it's one of the clues you'll have to . . . gum?

diamond(s)
Diamonds smuggled in this old Sussex port to reach this Isle of Wight one – RYDE
You have two place-names to deal with here. If you 'smuggle in' or 'bury' D ('diamonds') in RYE (the 'old Sussex port') you will get the Isle of Wight one (RYDE). It's a not unrealistic situation, and both the ports are on the south coast! Note that RYE has to be called 'old' since although it was once indeed a flourishing port (one of the famous Cinque Ports) it is now nearly two miles inland. It was, incidentally, also famous for its smuggling, which agreeably adds to the credibility of the clue.

Diana('s)
Diana's flower is a calamity – DISASTER
Poor Diana. But at least her 'flower' was a real one, and not a river as it might have been in another clue.

(old) **dictator**
Old dictator rang round when making his assault – RAIDING
How considerate of him. Although you see that really you have a 'burial' here, RANG 'round' IDI.

died
Mr Chaney died on the 'Capital' – LONDON
In other words LON Chaney 'died' (D) ON = the 'capital' of England, which is LONDON. As far as I know, the famous American film actor did not die on this ship (if that is what it is) or any other. You met Mr Chaney before in another clue leading to this same answer (see the entry under his name).

diminutive
Diminutive person has first-class return to ancient middle east country – PERSIA
PERS is an abbreviated or 'diminutive' PERSON, who with a reversal or 'return' of AI ('first-class') gets PERSIA. It is called 'ancient' since this was the country's former name – today it is Iran.

dine
Hundreds dine, eating this – MEAT
'Hundreds' might have been CC, perhaps, but here it is M (actually 1000, or ten 'hundreds'). The rest is straightforward, I think.

dined
The good man dined in Mississippi or Missouri – STATE
Were you caught into looking for a 'burial'? There isn't one! 'Mississippi and Missouri' are there merely to serve as a 'definition by example' of a STATE. The first four words of the clue give you the cryptic elements: 'the good man' is ST and 'dined' is ATE.

diocese
Jolly jaunt for priest in diocese – SPREE
That is, a SPREE for the PR in the SEE.

diplomatic letters
Used for securing, or in diplomatic letters – CORD
OR in CD is the CORD that is 'used for securing'. Compare another way of clueing this word under **lot**.

direction
Information from all directions – NEWS
A rather corny one, this, but still valid. Not all that long ago, there were people who liked to believe that the word NEWS originated from a combination of the four points of the compass, which represented the four quarters of the world from which information or NEWS comes.

director
Director to get curtailed funeral hymn – DIRGE
So the 'director' or DIR, + to 'get curtailed' or GE, = 'funeral hymn' or DIRGE.

dirty
Reports tell of dirty times – MESSAGES
The 'reports' are the MESSAGES (MESS+AGES, or 'dirty times'), with 'tell of' really meaning that you can 'tell', from the information given, how the word was devised.

dirty dog
Dirty dog is with veterinary surgeon and gives a jump – CURVET
As you can quite easily see, the CUR is with the VET (here given his full title in an attempt to sidetrack you), and that 'gives' or produces the answer CURVET, which is actually 'a light leap of a horse' (*Chambers*).

disagreement
Churchman has the power to comprehend disagreement – CANON
No, the division is not CAN+ON, since there is no indicator of a reversal (of 'disagreement' or NO). The significant word is 'comprehend' which indicates a 'burial'. So 'has the power', or CAN, is to 'comprehend' NO. This gives you the CANON who is the 'churchman'.

disc
Employees break pole with disc – PEOPLE
No doubt you were looking for the usual N or S 'pole'? But here, for once, what you actually need is the word POLE. Your instruction is to 'break' or make an anagram of this, together with the 'disc', which here is EP. So POLE+EP turns into PEOPLE, who are the 'employees'! (The definition is perfectly valid: in *Chambers* it is the tenth meaning of the word given out of a total of twenty-seven.) Compare the clue for this word under **energy**.

discover
In Parma, I zealously discover a cereal – MAIZE
I am not sure how 'zealously' one can actually 'discover' something, but clearly some word with ZE is necessary if MAIZE is to be clued by a 'burial' like this (in 'Par*ma, I ze*alously'). Perhaps some other word than 'discover' would have been better, such as 'obtain' or 'produce'.

disease
Disease weeded out in this unhealthy place of growth – HOTBED
As frequently, it's the unassuming word that is important here. In this clue the significant word is 'out', which tells you that 'weeded' (HOED) must be 'out', i.e. outside 'disease' (TB) – or, if you prefer, that TB must have HOED 'out'. Once you have cracked that, your HOTBED, or unhealthy place of growth, will follow easily.

disfigure
Disfigure lines of vegetables – MARROWS
MAR ROWS, of course. (Even though officially called a 'vegetable marrow', the marrow is actually a fruit. But most people cook and eat it as a vegetable, so it would be most misleading, or at any rate over-pedantic, to clue it here as 'fruit'.)

disheartened
Disheartened day amid misfortunes, leading to happy episodes – IDYLLS
That is, 'disheartened' DAY, without its middle A, 'buried' in ILLS, or 'misfortunes'.

dismissed
King dismissed! Riot ensues! – ROUT
'Riot' may have suggested an anagram, perhaps – although in fact it is simply the definition of ROUT. Add 'King' (R) to 'dismissed' (OUT) and RIOT 'ensues'.

disorientated
Queen, disorientated, comes to church after a gin cocktail, slaking her thirst – QUENCHING
The second of two royal scandals, it seems! However, this clue has an unexpected element, in that 'queen' does not mean the usual ER or R (or even HM) but is the actual word QUEEN. She is 'disorientated', so loses one E, thus becoming QUEN. She then 'comes to church' so adds CH, and 'after' this is a GIN 'cocktail' or anagram – the usual ING. And so, after much excitement, you arrive at QUENCHING, 'slaking her thirst'.

dispense with
Player dispenses with pupil, being the one who has to find the fee – PAYER
The PLAYER 'dispenses with' or loses his 'pupil' (L).

display
Lord Erpingham displays his system – ORDER
The 'display' indicates a 'burial', of course, and there it is in 'L*ord Er*pingham', giving the answer ORDER. As far as I know there is

no actual such lord, although Erpingham is real enough as a village in Norfolk.

dispute
Bird box dispute ! – SPARROW
The exclamation mark indicates something special here, and certainly things are not what they seem. This is no squabble about possession of a bird box, but the name of a 'bird', derived from 'box' (SPAR) and 'dispute' (ROW). The number of letters may have helped you get the bird (or the ROW given in the entry), but did you straightaway see why it was in fact a SPARROW?

dissipated fellow
Arouse once more terrible awe in a dissipated fellow – REAWAKE
'Terrible' or anagrammatic AWE is 'buried' here in the RAKE, or 'dissipated fellow'.

district
District to take up weapons for this mass of flying insects – SWARM
'Take up' is literal here, and does not indicate a reversal. Thus the SW is to ARM for the SWARM.

district attorney
District attorney meets British politician – a 'wet' – DAMP
When the DA 'meets' the MP you get your 'wet', or DAMP. 'Wet' or soft-line MPs appeared in British politics in the Conservative government of the early 1980s.

ditched
Flier ditched noisily, and as a result he's now flat on his back – LIER
Did you 'ditch' correctly? This FLIER 'ditched noisily', that is he lost his F, and so became a LIER, who is 'flat on his back'.

ditto
Launched in sea exercises – mountain exercises ditto – TORPEDO
Quite a nice 'read-through' here, with the indirect definition first. A TORPEDO is 'launched in sea exercises', and is 'mountain' (TOR) 'exercises' (PE) 'ditto' (DO)!

divide
He divides conservative thinking – THEORY
HE thus 'divides' or is 'buried' in TORY to produce the THEORY or 'thinking'. Only purists would consider the small 'c' of 'conservative' as unacceptable, I think.

divine
O divine son, thou hast a better chance – ODDS-ON
You get good value in this clue, with your cryptic presentation in the first three words (O DD SON), a definition *and* something of a pun in the last three words, and a quasi-biblical flavouring – of no significance whatever for working out the answer – in 'thou hast'. Didst thou get it right?

divinity
Divinity protects ancient city and is represented in bottle-like fruit – GOURD
The 'bottle-like fruit' must be the definition – it is almost too obvious! Otherwise you have GOD who 'protects' or 'straddles' UR. No doubt God did indeed protect this ancient biblical city.

do
Do in for business agent – FACTOR
It's a 'burial' again – ACT ('do') in FOR. You may object that there is no verb 'to do in for' (to 'do for' and 'do in', yes, but 'do in for'?). My reply is that in this clue someone is to 'do in' someone 'for', i.e. on behalf of, the 'business agent'!

doctor
Doctor has endless quarrel – it's his constant theme! – MOTIF
We clued this same word before, under **condition**. Perhaps you recalled it when solving this clue. It's straightforward – the MO has an 'endless' TIFF, which is a TIF. With 'doctor' in the clue you have quite a wide range of possibilities – see this entry in the first half of the book.

dog
Dog has tail cut short – CURTAIL
I couldn't resist this one, I'm afraid. It reads straight through, with one semi-definition, one actual word, and a final proper definition.

dog-end
Sold dog-end in grass! – RETAILED
Remember that 'grass' often works out as the handy REED in which things can be conveniently 'buried'. Here you have a 'dog-end' or TAIL in it.

do it yourself
Abstainer is into do-it-yourself with a merry tune – DITTY
A 'burial', of course, with the TT 'into' DIY. The clue defines DITTY as 'with a merry tune' (not just 'a merry tune') since a 'ditty' means both words and music, or even, as *Chambers* puts it, 'a little poem to be sung'.

dollar
New dollar hits the headlines – NEWS
That is, NEW S. This same word was clued differently under **direction**.

(it's) (what's) **done**
Places regularly visited – the done thing in Hants – HAUNTS
Otherwise U ('the done thing') in HANTS

don't, doesn't
PLA doesn't do this with bombs or trees – PLANT
You have all the letters of the answer in front of you, in fact, in 'PLA doe*sn't*'. The 'trees' were not strictly essential to the clue, but I added them to make the overall presentation fairer. For two quite different clues for PLANT, see **hill dweller** and **in short**.

don't fail (to)
Don't fail to use a heavy blow – DOUSE
In other words DO USE 'a heavy blow'. *Chambers* gives three separate entries for 'douse', and 'a heavy blow' is the definition in the second one. (The other two are respectively 'to plunge into water' and 'to extinguish'.)

don't know
Don't know half of Alick's birds – DUNNOCKS
With DUNNO for 'don't know', note that the final 's' of 'Alick's' is counted for 'half' purposes. Although frequently it's the first half of the word that is used, there is no reason why it should not be the second, as here. A DUNNOCK is a hedge-sparrow.

don't make changes
Don't make changes, kid, put this on your head – STETSON
A combination of STET ('don't make changes') and SON ('kid') produces the broad-brimmed felt hat designed, apparently, by an American hatmaker called John STETSON.

Dorothy
Dorothy and the youth leaders are quite crazy! – DOTTY
The 'leaders', as often, are the first letters of words, in this case of '*t*he *y*outh'.

double
Do double time? Editor put a stop to it! – DOTTED
DO+'double time' (TT)+ED = DOTTED. The definition is a punning one, of course (a 'dot' is a 'stop', e.g. a full 'stop'), hence the exclamation mark.

double bend
Double bend on river will give you a ducking – SOUSE
It's high time we had the name of a river, and here now is the handy OUSE. Put a 'double bend' or S on it and you get your 'ducking' (one of *Chambers*'s definitions, in fact).

doughboy
Scoffed at doughboy going to bed – GIBED
You need to know this American military slang term, of course, in order to translate it correctly as GI. He goes to BED to give you the answer (defined as 'scoffed at').

draft
Fail to notice draft is in – MISS
Even the little 'is' can be important, as here, where it goes 'in' the MS or 'draft'. This gives you MISS, defined as 'fail to notice'.

dram
Mix the dram reluctantly for this slippery customer! – OTTER
'Mix' indicates an anagram. Here it is of TOT, to which ER ('reluctantly') is added to get the 'slippery customer'. Yes, I know, an

OTTER is not actually a 'customer', but it's used here as a general slang term for a human or animal (like the countryman I once heard who said of an escaping fox in a hunt, 'He *were* a funny job!'). For another clue for the same creature, compare **behead**.

dress
Dress right, going with a girl – ROBERTA
Just a 'read-through': ROBE+RT 'going with' A. For another clue for ROBERTA, see **stand**.

dressed
She came in dressed – and we arrived at the same moment – CLASHED
SHE came in CLAD – and we CLASHED!

drink
Hard drink healthy? Sounds like hard water! – HALE
Your definition here is supplemented by a homophone, so that HALE 'sounds like' 'hard water', which is an over-simplified way of saying 'hail'! The first half of the clue is made up of H ('hard') and ALE ('drink'), with 'healthy' being the definition, of course.

drive(n) from
Truck is driven from Vancouver and you lose the lid – COVER
There are three operations in this clue to be carried out. First the 'truck' or VAN must be 'driven from' or removed from VANCOUVER, then 'you lose', i.e. 'lose U' or remove the U from COUVER, and finally 'lid' must be interpreted as COVER, which is what you are left with!

driver
Dead body means car has shaken driver – CARRION
Not quite as grisly as it sounds, since CARRION is an animal's dead body. Getting the CAR is easy; it may be a moment or two before you realise that 'shaken driver' means an anagram of IRON (a 'driver' in golf).

driving place
Long seat is fixed driving place – SETTEE
Golf again. A 'fixed driving place' is a SET TEE, which, as a SETTEE, is a 'long seat'.

drop (off) (a bit)
Name-dropping car salesman out to get villains – RASCALS
A favourite *Sunday Telegraph* device. Take CAR SALESMAN, 'drop' or omit the letters of NAME from it (thus leaving CARSALS), put this 'out' as an anagram (RASCALS) and there are your 'villains'!

drop aitch(es)
Insinuator, that chap, dropping aitches in the meantime – INTERIM
Two words drop their aitches here: HINTER ('insinuator') and HIM ('that chap'). Join these, minus their aitches, together and you get 'meantime', INTERIM.

drove (car)
Mum, in this state, drove crazily and very hard, having nothing in! – MOTHERHOOD
Not too complex, I hope. 'Drove' is MOTORED. That must be turned into an anagram ('crazily') and include HH ('very hard') and O ('nothing'). And there is the 'state' that 'Mum' is in!

drum
Soft, a drum, a big brown beast will come! – BEAR
B+EAR for the 'big brown beast'. The image is that of a circus, perhaps. (The B on pencils, meaning 'soft', as here, stands for 'black'.)

drunk(ard)
Drunk and in love – looks black! – SOOT
A SOT with 'love' (O) in. A drunken love affair could indeed have black prospects.

dry grass
Noticed no dry grass – NOTED
TED ('to spread as new-mown grass, for drying', says *Chambers*) is one of the few rareish words (like 'adit') seized on gratefully by crossword compilers. See also **college** and **journalist**.

duck
Duck on Scottish river, right in it, too, is another sort of bird! – OSPREY
The 'duck' should at least have given you the letter O to start the 'bird', even if you were not at first sure about the implication of

'another sort' (a girl's name, perhaps?). But I hope it didn't take too long before you came up with the correct 'Scottish river', the SPEY, to insert an R in it ('right in it') and complete the answer. Compare the clue under **huge**.

dug
Dug right into a real feast! – TREAT
'Dug' is TEAT. With 'right' (R) in, you have a 'real feast' or TREAT. Note that the little word 'into' has a dual function: the 'in' half tells you to insert 'right' in TEAT, the 'to' half indicates that TEAT with R 'in' will take you 'to' the answer!

dull
Marriage in dull church – MATCH
A 'read-through', not a 'burial': a MATCH in a MAT CH.

(in) **duplicate**
It's crazy to duplicate the General Assembly – GAGA
'Duplicate' or repeat the GA ('General Assembly') for the 'crazy' answer.

duplicating machine
Sure upset about duplicating machine going wrong – ERRONEOUS
Well-known trade names occasionally find their way into clues, as here, especially when they are in the dictionary (RONEO is in *Chambers*, for example). In this clue, you have an anagram ('upset') of SURE 'about', i.e. 'straddling', RONEO. That gives the answer, defined as 'going wrong'.

during
Proper scare for king during fight – FRIGHT
'During', of course, means 'in', so also denotes a 'burial'. Here the 'king' (R) is 'buried' in the FIGHT.

dusky damsel, dusky maiden
Dusky damsel doesn't feature in sports programme – EVENT
'Dusky damsel' (or 'dusky maiden') has really become a compilers' cryptic cliché to denote EVE. Here she adds NT ('doesn't') to make the EVENT, a 'feature in sports programme'.

Dutchman, Dutch boy
Dutch boy takes tea in south of England – HANTS
HANS 'takes' or 'straddles' T to get this southern county. HANS is also quite often clued as 'German boy'.

'e
'E 'as 'is 'at, so will 'e do this to it if 'e's wrong? – EAT
Most of the words with the missing aitches here are red herrings, simply designed to blend in with the essential ones. These are the first word and the fourth, so that E 'as 'is AT, which 'e may EAT if 'e's wrong'! I 'ope you got the 'int.

each
Authority given for each young lady with one on – PERMISSION
Another straight 'read-through' clue, with the definition as the first word. Like many clues of this type, the answer is much more prosaic than the solver may have been led to expect! The four cryptic elements of the word are, of course, PER+MISS+I+ON.

ear
With ear pinned back, pupils see these sea birds – GULLS
Or with LUG 'pinned back' (reversed) LS ('pupils') 'see' GULLS. The 'see' is directed at you, the solver, since if you have handled the first half of the clue correctly, you will 'see' the answer.

earlier
Not quite right in earlier performance – INEXACT
Yet another 'read-through', and again with the definition first ('not quite right'). The elements here are IN+EX+ACT.

early
Doctor gets in early, having a brolly – GAMP
Thus the GP 'gets in' or 'straddles' AM ('early'). The clue uses 'brolly', not 'umbrella', to denote a similar slang word for the answer.

early evening
Called in the early evening, having lots of angry things to say – RAVING
'Called' is RANG, and it 'straddles' VI ('early evening').

earth
Earth round this district is level – DIRECT
That is to say, the DIRT round EC. 'Level' here means DIRECT in the sense 'to aim', as of a gun.

east(ern)
To the east there's a peninsula – TOE
Well, a 'peninsula' is a TOE of land! You don't like it? I can't refer you to *Chambers*, but in view of the geographical flavour of 'to the east' (TO+E) I feel it's justified. Perhaps an exclamation mark could have been used at the end of the clue to indicate the liberty taken.

eaten
United force, having eaten special food supply, enters note – FEDERATION
Notice that the 'note' (E) has to be 'entered' between the two elements (FED and RATION), not in an individual word. This is quite in order.

eat(ing)
Holy man eats very little pudding – SWEET
Or a ST 'eats' ('straddles') WEE. Quite a nice neat clue, in fact, with the holy man setting a good example by not indulging.

ebb(ing)
'Ebb Tide' or 'I Go to the Italian Leader' – EDITORIAL
I hope this clue didn't seem too ingenious. It is intended to convey a chapter heading in an old-style autobiography. 'Ebb Tide' gives a reversal of TIDE, which is EDIT. The next two words in the clue provide OR and I, and 'to the Italian' is AL (the Italian for 'to the'). The 'Leader' is the EDITORIAL, thus.

echo
Waterfall echo makes horse stop – REIN
A punning definition of RAIN to be used as a homophone ('echo') for REIN, which 'makes horse stop'. A mountain waterfall might actually have an echo at a particular point near it – and this could frighten a horse!

'e'd
Reverse of coin 'e'd shadowed – TAILED
Fairly straightforward, with "e'd' one of a number of devices used to obtain the common ending -ED.

Eddy, Edward
Eddy points to paradise – EDEN
The two 'points' (E and N) are convenient here to follow ED. Compare the clue under **retreat**.

edge
The top, where the water is – note the edge – BRIM
Do you prefer this clue for BRIM or the one we used for **bee** (which see)?

edgily, edging
Screen with red centre and unusual rose edging – REREDOS
A 'burial' here – or a 'straddle', if you prefer, since RED in the 'centre' has an anagrammatic or 'unusual' ROSE 'edging'. For a different sort of image altogether, see **large**.

editor
William comes to editor, having sent his account – BILLED
BILL comes to the ED. The 'having' may refer to 'William' in the clue, but it really signals to the solver that if you join BILL and ED you 'have' the answer, as defined in the remaining words of the clue. Compare the quite different clue for this word under **misfortune**.

Edward
Edward has acknowledgments of debts – how boring – TEDIOUS
So TED has his IOUS, which is 'boring'. Although the clue is actually a kind of exclamation, it does not deserve an exclamation mark, since it does not contain any surprising or difficult feature.

effort
Country workers produce peas – with an effort – PEASANTRY
In a way, clues that actually give you a word 'neat', as PEAS and AN in this one, are harder to solve, since the solver does not expect this much charity! (But perhaps that is

an argument for the compiler to resort to this, on occasions.) So in this clue there are virtually no real cryptic elements – just a definition ('country workers') and a synonym ('effort' for TRY).

egg
I egg on boss in photo workshop – STUDIO
The important thing here is the order – it's not easy trying to find a word starting with 'I egg'. So first you need the 'boss' (STUD) and 'on' that you put IO ('I egg') to get the STUDIO.

Egyptian goddess
When crown is placed on Egyptian goddess, that's the turning point – CRISIS
This would probably be a down clue, so that the 'crown' (CR) would actually be put 'on' the 'Egyptian goddess' (ISIS) underneath it. The 'turning point' is the CRISIS, of course, this being the strict sense of the word (which is actually Greek for 'decision').

eject
The EEC engine stops, and sots are ejected – oddly, for not much British money! – EIGHTEEN PENCE
A somewhat cumbersome clue, but its lengthiness is justified by the longish two-word answer. It's a *Sunday Telegraph* speciality again, where a group of letters has to be removed from a phrase which is then anagrammatised. Here you need to take the whole of THE EEC ENGINE STOPS, 'eject' or remove SOTS (making THEEECENGINEP), and then rearrange these letters ('oddly') to form the answer. EIGHTEEN PENCE, for those who may have forgotten (or perhaps the younger solver!), was a common pre-decimalisation term (pre-1971, therefore) for one shilling and sixpence – in present terms 7½p!

Eleanor
He met Eleanor by the river where Abraham dwelt – HEBRON
HE met BRON, of course, to get the name of this biblical river. ('Eleanor' looks something like a biblical name, but there is no person so called in the Bible. It is actually a form of 'Helen'.)

elected
Jack and Paul elected to supply the waterproof cloth – TARPAULIN
Too obvious? Well, at least you had 'Jack' and 'elected' to interpret.

electroplated
Electroplated? Och, it's no a wee while! – EPOCH
I must confess I'm not quite sure under what precise circumstances a Scot would make this query and comment, but it was the OCH that caused it (with the rest of the clue 'Scottified' to match it). An EPOCH is a long period of time, 'no a wee while'.

elevated
Albert is elevated by the French boy's voice – TREBLE
Where is 'Albert' in all this? There he is – BERT 'elevated' (in this down clue) or reversed. LE is the usual 'the French', of course. The clue conjures up a French church service, perhaps, with a solo *jeune choriste*.

eleven(th)
Poisonous to the eleventh century – TOXIC
A straight 'read-through', with all apparent, I think.

Eliot
About Eliot . . . these are his practical ones! – CATS
A reference I am sure you will have recognised, to T. S. Eliot's *Old Possum's Book of Practical Cats* (with its subsequent musical spin-off of the 1980s, *Cats*). 'About' is CA, the abbreviation of Latin *circa*.

elite army group
Elite army group go to Kent after German, yet find Englishman! – SASSENACH
All is made plain when the SAS go to the SE ('Kent' is in south-east England) NACH (German for 'after') the SASSENACH (actually a Scottish word for an 'Englishman', but a third nationality in the clue would have been rather overwhelming). I think it is reasonable to expect the solver to know this German word, even if he or she never learnt German at school.

Elizabeth
Jack goes to Elizabeth, the religious leader – ABBESS
An easy clue, with its two elements and straightforward definition.

'em
I rid 'em, stop 'em all rushing about in the afternoon – POST MERIDIEM
Some compilers delight in long anagrams, so here is one for you to try. You may not have realised for a moment that it *was* an anagram. There are two indicators, however – 'rushing about', and the somewhat contrived appearance of the first five words (often a sign of an anagram). The answer, obviously is the Latin abbreviation 'p.m.' (for 'afternoon') spelt out in full. (Notice that it does actually end in M. Some people feel that the final letter should be N, no doubt by confusion with 'meridian'. But the anagram will ensure this comes out right.)

embarrassed
Confused country girl got embarrassed, looked angry – GLARED
Anagrammatic GAL got RED. 'Country' to indicate a non-standard version of 'girl'. In other clues this could have been omitted, but here an anagram is involved, and without it the solver might try to form an anagram of 'girl' or some girl's name.

embrace
Man embraces girl to get the stone – MALACHITE
MALE 'embraces' or 'straddles' A CHIT. MALACHITE is actually a green mineral, but it is used for ornaments, vases and so on, and I think we can legitimately call it 'stone'.

eminence
His Eminence is in charge – it's quite an important event – HISTORIC
Quite an enjoyable clue, with a happy run of elements.

employ(ment)
Mother has employment in Kent, being a sort of contact healer! – MASSEUSE
The order of the elements is important here – what goes 'in' what? As you can see, the breakdown is: MA ('mother') +S ('has')+USE ('employment'), and then 'in' this (between MASS and USE) goes SE ('Kent'). Rather a more complex cryptic arrangement than usual. The exclamation mark indicates the hideous pun that has been perpetrated.

empty
Tailless cat goes on empty road – he's quite a character! – CARD
Did you think it was a Manx cat? Not really, just a 'tailless' CAT, i.e. a CA. He goes on an 'empty' ROAD, or RD, to show he's a 'character' or CARD. We clued this same word quite differently under **Civil Defence** (which see) – but also compare **man of account**.

encage
Judge returns and encages bird – but he also hunts down birds of another kind! – FOWLER
The 'judge' is the REF, who 'returns' (as FER) and 'encages' or 'straddles' the OWL. A FOWLER, of course, hunts wildfowl – quite different birds from the OWL.

encircle
Men encircle little Lolita to get fruit – MELON
An easy clue (MEN 'encircle' LO) once you realise that LO is a pet form of 'Lolita' (with this itself being a pet form in origin of 'Dolores'). The clue conjures up a Spanish or South American(?) market scene, with child fruit sellers.

enclose
Father enclosed right leg – PROP
It does not have to be *his* leg, in fact – the 'leg' of a table or workbench would do just as well! But either way, you get POP 'enclosing' R ('right'). Compare the clue at **publicity man**.

enclosure
Has tumbledown enclosure to put in shape – SHAPEN
'Tumbledown' is an anagram indicator, here used to change HAS to SHA. This, plus PEN ('enclosure'), gives you the desired answer.

encountered
Military commander encountered a heavenly body! – COMET

Take the clue as you wish, so long as you 'read' it correctly to produce the COMET – which is perfectly accurately defined at the end of the clue. Compare the clue under **meteorological**.

(at the) **end** (of)
Young bird has no end of elegance – CHIC
So the CHICK has 'no end' and becomes CHIC, which relates to 'elegance'.

endless(ly)
He protests about endless belt – REBEL
In fact a 'read-through' clue, with the definition first ('he protests') then the two elements that make the word – 'about' (RE) and 'endless BELT' (BEL without its T).

energy
Energy in love with the French race – PEOPLE
PEP with O in with LE ('the French') which is 'race' (PEOPLE). Compare the clue under **disc**.

enfold
Torn sheet enfolds apprentice coming to king, giving some protection – SHELTER
This poor, meagrely-clad 'apprentice' is simply the L ('learner') in the answer. Around him is a 'torn' (anagrammatic) SHEET as he comes to the 'king' (R). This gives the 'protection' or SHELTER of the answer.

engage (in)
Bill engages redhead and a worker – splendid! – BRILLIANT
Thus BILL 'engages' or 'straddles' R (the 'head' or first letter of '*r*ed') with 'a' (I) 'worker' (ANT), and that is 'splendid', or BRILLIANT.

engineer(s)
Went underground in the Engineers – but was given the job – HIRED
HID ('went underground') with the RE ('Engineers') 'in' or 'buried'. Note that 'Engineers' is given a capital to suggest special ones (and even the word itself as part of a title).

English, England
English ogre raving to feed on blood! – ENGORGE
A nice gory clue, which actually suggests the 'Fee-fi-fo-fum' children's rhyme. The answer is reached via ENG ('English') and ORGE ('OGRE raving').

Englishman's castle
First meal in Englishman's castle for Frenchman – HOMME
You may occasionally find a foreign word – in this case a French one – as the actual answer to a clue. Here is an example, with 'first meal' (M, the first letter of 'meal') being 'in' 'Englishman's castle' (HOME). A 'Frenchman' is a French 'man', which is HOMME. That is well within the capacity of the average solver!

engulfed (by)
Cricketer engulfed by river – we had a serious discussion about it – DEBATE
That is to say, a BAT was 'engulfed' by the DEE. The 'about it' at the end of the clue is a non-significant tailpiece or 'make-weight'.

enmesh
Songstress enmeshed in Kremlin network – LINNET
Once you appreciate that 'enmeshed' denotes a 'burial', the rest is easy, and you won't have to look too hard to find your 'songstress'.

ensconce
Bird ensconced in a better nest – ERNE
The 'burial' is not hard to see in the 'bett*er ne*st'. What is interesting here is that the answer could equally well have been TERN. In this particular crossword, however, TERN would not have checked with the crossing letters, so had to be ERNE (a word for an eagle).

enter (in), **entertain**
Priest entertained by Roman Catholic memorial – RELIC
The 'priest' is ELI, who is 'entertained' by the RC, getting a 'memorial', or RELIC.

entrance
Tailless arrow flies to entrance – I claim it as mine – ARROGATE
The 'tailless' ARROW (or ARRO) 'flies to' or

joins on to the 'entrance' (GATE). To ARROGATE something is to claim it as one's own.

envelop
Fog envelops royal leader – is this what he turns into? – FROG
The FOG 'envelops' or 'buries' the 'royal leader' (R, the first letter of '*r*oyal'). Folk tales and fairy tales tell of a frog who changed into a prince (a 'royal leader'), or a prince who changed into a frog.

epoch
Fine feathers for a fine epoch – PLUMAGE
Or quite neatly, PLUMAGE for a PLUM AGE. The clue echoes the proverb, 'Fine feathers make fine birds'.

equal (to), **equality**
Head of state, equal to king, is a bright, lively fellow – SPARK
'Head' of 'state' (i.e. its first letter, S) 'equal' (PAR) to 'king' (K) is a SPARK – a 'bright, lively fellow'!

equipment
Equipment, at end of game, is sent up – KITE
The definition should be enough ('is sent up') to support the cryptic elements (KIT+'end of gam*e*').

'er
Send 'er a wall-chart – POSTER
A rather too transparent clue!

erect(ion)
Pole erected at end of passage, giving escape – ELOPE
In other words, POLE 'erected' or reversed (as ELOP) at 'end of passage' (E), producing ('giving') ELOPE ('escape').

'e's
Pot 'e's smashed – how 'e drinks! – TOPES
'Smashed' is an anagram indicator, as might be expected, so that POT 'E'S re-emerges as TOPES, 'drinks'. The second "e' is simply to back up the first one.

essay
Harshly criticise essay – there's food for thought! – PANTRY
I hope this sense of PAN ('harshly criticise') did not prove too elusive (it's the sixth and last of this verb given in *Chambers*). 'Essay' is TRY, of course, and 'for thought' simply means, at the end of the clue, 'think about it (to get the correct answer)'.

(the) **establishment**
Power for the establishment – FORCE
A 'read-through' for you, with the definition first and the unobtrusive FOR vital to the answer.

etc.
Working well if fine, etc. – EFFICIENT
There is no actual direct anagram indicator in this clue, but the final ETC suggests an artificially concocted word.

European
European tailless mice are controversial – POLEMIC
A POLE is a 'European', and with 'tailless' MICE (that is, MIC), forms the answer, defined exactly as in *Chambers* ('controversial').

even
Unable even to find a place to eat – CANTEEN
No great difficulty over this 'read-through' clue: CANT+EEN = CANTEEN. ('Find' is simply a guide to the solver: 'interpret this correctly and you will find the answer'.)

every
Soft – every fruit – PEACH
An easy 'read-through': P+EACH making the 'fruit'. Compare the clue under **per person**.

everyone, everything
Quiet, everyone – I *will*! – SHALL
Yet another 'read-through': SH+ALL giving the answer. Somewhat unusually, '*will*' is italicised in the clue to emphasise its importance (it is the definition, of course). It also indicates the natural stress that the speaker of this sentence would have probably put on the word.

evidence of liability, evidence of debts
Irreverent rascal has evidence of debts – IMPIOUS

The single definition is 'irreverent', with 'rascal' (IMP) forming the first half of the answer.

evil
Destroy the king's evil – KILL
Notice that the apostrophe S after 'king' does not appear as a letter in the answer. It merely indicates that the 'evil' (ILL) 'belongs to' or follows the 'king' (K). There actually was a disease nicknamed the 'king's evil', which was supposed to have been healed by a touch of the king. (It was a form of scrofula, or tuberculosis.)

exam(ination)
Bad-tempered exam at the end of the day – TESTY
The 'end of the day' is the Y that follows the 'exam' (TEST).

examine
Examine the island – plenty of sand and gravel there! – CONCRETE
It's simply a matter of getting the right 'island' to add to CON ('examine'). 'Sand and gravel' (with cement, of course) are two basic constituents of CONCRETE.

excellent
Both are excellent in public relations – PAIR
A simple 'burial' (AI in PR) to give the answer (defined as 'both') in this rather neat clue.

excerpt(s) (from)
Excerpt from 'Measure for Measure' needs to be improved – REFORM
A more unexpected 'burial', right in the middle of 'Measu*re for M*easure'. If you REFORM something, it will usually 'be improved'.

exclude
Tasty morsel can be had from two birds, excluding the tern – TITBIT
The 'two birds' are, of course, the TIT and the BITTERN, but 'excluding the TERN' the latter becomes simply BIT. And there is the 'tasty morsel', or TITBIT. (The word seems to have nothing to do with tits, the birds, even though tits welcome titbits!)

exercise(s)
Approve business exercises – ADOPT
Be prepared for versatility when it comes to the meanings of words! 'Business' here means 'fuss', 'busyness', not its normal 'commercial activity', so it translates as ADO. 'Approve' has the special sense used when you 'approve' or ADOPT a resolution or decision made by a committee, for example. But at least the 'exercises' are the predictable PT.

exhibition
Mothers' Union came to exhibition to get something different – MUTATE
So the MU came to the TATE, and that gives MUTATE, when you 'get something different'.

exist
Exist on tea for a wager – BET
Short and sweet, both clue and answer.

exists
Equality exists for the capital – PARIS
There was a chance you may have been sidetracked into thinking of financial matters (with 'equality' and 'capital'), but as you can see the answer really *is* a 'capital'.

exotic
Six learner drivers go east and come to this exotic town – VILLE
Not really 'exotic', of course, but simply the French for 'town'. The word is spelt out quite nicely by the 'six learner drivers' (VILL) who go 'east' (E).

expel
Risk of empire is having one expelled – IMPERIL
Here you have to 'expel' or remove 'one' (A) from IMPERIAL ('of empire') to get 'risk', IMPERIL.

expert
Mike's the first expert, he carries the mark of authority, too – MACE
We clued this same word differently under **church** (which see). This time it is 'Mike's the first' (i.e. the first letter of '*M*ike') plus ACE ('expert') that reveals it.

explosive
Explosive at high temperature – HEAT
Or HE AT HEAT. A dangerous situation, but an easy clue to solve.

expose
Sid exposed article – or so he maintained – SAID
The 'article' is the usual A, which SID 'exposed' or 'straddled'.

extra large
Award for extra large vehicle – OSCAR
Perhaps you recalled the **alternative** clue, which also led to OSCAR? This clue is rather more straightforward, however, with no 'burial'.

extreme(ly), extremists
Extremely modest way to return to university and do no work! – PUREST
The 'extremely' suggests the superlative -EST ending, with 'extremely modest' producing the actual answer. Note the lengthy way PU is clued ('way to return to university', i.e. go UP). 'Modest' is the eighth definition of 'pure' out of the seventeen given by *Chambers* – and 'pure' is the eighth of ten for 'modest'!

extremity
A thousand in extremity – well, a good volume, anyway! – TOME
An exclamation mark to indicate the groan-provoking pun, with the answer also cryptically clued by the M ('thousand') in the 'extremity' (TOE). Compare **at last** and **introduction**.

eyesore
Nasty environment – real eyesore there – STYE
Another pun, but no exclamation mark since it is more academic than entertaining (after all, a STYE actually *is* an 'eyesore'). The answer is 'buried', of course, in the 'na*sty e*nvironment'.

fabulous bird
Fabulous bird, a department head in bed – dressed in silk, too! – BROCADED
A 'burial' of three elements (ROC+A+D, the latter being '*d*epartment head') in BED, with the final 'too' of the clue indicating that the definition, as usual, is an extra clue to the answer.

face
Note it has round face, this watch, although no hands – DIGITAL
A harder clue – at least, as far as its cryptic content goes. Be sure to interlock the elements correctly: 'note' (G) 'it' (IT) 'has round', i.e. has round it, 'face' (DIAL), with a DIGITAL watch, of course, having 'no hands'.

fair
Limit study on fair – CONFINE
A 'read-through': CONFINE = CON on FINE.

fair bit of
Fair bit of noise among workers, so pours oil on – ANOINTS
To interpret: 'fair bit of NOISE' (NOI, in fact) 'among', i.e. 'buried' in, 'workers' (ANTS), with the definition completing the clue.

fairy
Takeover threat by the Chinese? The cowardly fairy left – THE YELLOW PERIL
The first half of this clue provides the definition (see 'yellow peril' in *Chambers*, if necessary), with the second half providing the cryptic content ('cowardly' = YELLOW, 'fairy' = PERI, 'left' = L).

fall sideways
Cat falls sideways, having itches. What are its plans? – TACTICS
So the CAT 'falls sideways' (as TAC) and it has 'itches' or TICS. The rest is the definition.

famous person
Famous person returned, getting date mixed

up, and then sallied forth – EMANATED
You have a reversal (NAME to EMAN) and an anagram (DATE to ATED) to give your answer, also defined as 'sallied forth'. 'Then' at its face value in the clue means 'next', 'after that'; to the solver it really means 'so', 'in that case', indicating that the first part of the clue can be equated with the second (the definition).

farewell
Turkish warrior gives farewell to the king – TATAR
A simple combination of elements to produce the 'Turkish warrior'.

Fascist leader
Down-graded Communist receives Fascist leader – REDUCED
Note that the 'Communist' RED is not the first three letters of the answer, but the first two and the last, since he 'receives' or 'straddles' the DUCE. It would take a very 'down-graded' Communist to receive a Fascist leader in real terms, I feel!

(-)**fashion**
Marine-fashion call to arms – ALARM
In other words, an ALARM A LA RM ('Royal Marines'). For another way of clueing ALARM, see **Alexander**.

fashionable, the fashion
Fashionable bird points to prisoner – INTERNEE
The TERN is rather a handy 'bird' (remember how we used him in the **exclude** clue?). Here we have a straightforward 'read-through' – IN ('fashionable') TERN ('bird') EE ('points') to INTERNEE ('prisoner').

fast
Fast time nothing! It's slow! – LENTO
The paradox is meant to confuse you! Once you can see that it's *that* sort of 'fast time' and that 'nothing' means O, the rest is easy.

father
Father swallowing bird's bone – FEMUR
Quite a difficult clue, until you 'read' it correctly as FR 'swallowing' EMU, which is the 'bone' or FEMUR. The apostrophe S thus means 'is'.

favourite
I'm the favourite to go to America, and I have a real incentive! – IMPETUS
IM the PET to go to the US. 'I'm' can suggest the missing or understood word that is the answer (as 'I'm a viewer', which could be EYE). Here it actually represented the letters IM.

FBI types
Among Atlantic Treaty leaders top-class FBI types require increase – AUGMENT
A 'burial' here, as 'among' indicates. So the U GMEN go 'among' the '*A*tlantic *T*reaty leaders' (AT) to get 'increase', or AUGMENT.

feature (of) **(feature in)**
Concise – a feature of better sermons – TERSE
The 'bet*ter se*rmons' have a fairly easy 'burial' to spot.

federal agents
Federal agents are in a fit – it's just a fabrication! – FIGMENT
The 'G-men' again. (The 'G' actually stands for 'Government'.) Once again they are 'buried', and in their FIT produce a FIGMENT, which is a 'fabrication' of the imagination. (The definition is direct from *Chambers*.)

(the) **fellow**
Fellow has two articles, one inside the other – but he's uncivilised! – HEATHEN
HE thus has 'two articles' (AN and THE), 'one inside the other' (ATHEN). The solver need not trouble to exercise his imagination unduly as to what the articles were, as the clue stands – the main thing is that the fellow offended against the rules of etiquette by placing the articles so, out of ignorance!

fellows
Notice passes round fellows, to get more fellows to come to tea for a change! – AMENDMENT
This college decree (as one may perhaps see it) is more straightforward than it looks. The AD ('notice') 'passes round' or 'straddles' the MEN, getting more MEN to come to T for

the AMENDMENT which is a 'change' designed to improve.

female
Female and French – and fit to go to bed – SHEET
A clue that is not nearly as bawdy as it looks, since 'female' is SHE, 'and French' is ET, and a SHEET is 'fit to go to bed' – or is even something you 'fit to go to bed' (with also a suggestion of 'fitted' sheets). And in fact any hint of impropriety in the clue can be avoided if you simply picture a very tired Frenchwoman.

feminine
A feminine or backswept frizzy hairstyle – AFRO
The three cryptic elements are 'A' (A) 'feminine' (F) and 'or backswept', i.e. reversed (RO). And there's your AFRO 'frizzy hairstyle'.

festivities
Festivities, with count in charge – it's out of this world! – GALACTIC
A quite enjoyable 'read-through' with a hardly original pun: GALA with CT IC. The answer is the adjective of 'galaxy', which is certainly 'out of this world'.

(a) **few**
A few of the Irish are reluctant – AVERSE
Perhaps not such an easy clue, although it reads through quite nicely: A+V+ERSE ('or the Irish'). For quite a different type of clue for this word, see **poem**.

fifty (50)
Fifty-one go to head of queue on French back street to get Benedictine – LIQUEUR
Yes, rather a contrived clue, but the situation is (just) imaginable, and it does give the LI going to the 'head of *qu*eue' (QU) on 'French back street', i.e. the French for 'street' (RUE) reversed! 'Benedictine' was chosen for this particular LIQUEUR in the hope that some solvers might treat it cryptically as DOM (see its entry)! Compare the clue under **ancient city**.

final
I'm going to cup final – aren't I naughty! – IMP
A puckish clue, with 'cup final' being the P that is the final letter of 'cup'.

find
Find green plant on Greek mountain for Greek girl – CRESSIDA
That is, find CRESS on Mount IDA for CRESSIDA. The famous loved one of Troilus actually belongs to medieval mythology, not classical. She was a 'Greek girl', though, so qualifies for the clue.

find in
Find money in Omar Khayyam – MARK
A 'burial', of course. You could 'find money' in this well-known Persian poet if you exploited his 'Rubáiyát' somehow (perhaps produced a TV version of it) – or if you discovered an old ten shilling note in between the pages of a copy bought in a second-hand bookshop!

fine
See fine appearance! – LOOK
Some of the neatest clues are the short, cryptic ones like this. 'See' is LO, 'fine' is OK, 'appearance' is LOOK.

finish
Like an infant not finishing cold food – CHILDISH
The 'cold' that is 'not finishing' is CHILL, of course. With the DISH ('food') it makes CHILDISH ('like an infant'). Note the economy of this clue, with no superfluous words.

finished
Started at Land's End, finished in Kent port – DOVER
A sail up the Channel, perhaps? For the solver, the 'Kent port' is reached via 'Lan*d*'s End' (i.e. the 'end' of 'lan*d*') and 'finished' (OVER).

firm
Firm has fifty bonds for its associates – COLLEAGUES
CO has L LEAGUES ('bonds'). An unexpected meaning of 'bonds', perhaps, but perfectly fair here!

(at) **first,** (in the) **first** (place), **firstly**
Firstly, Satan's prime responsibility is to encourage some little devils – SPRITES
The important words here are 'firstly', which is the instruction to the solver, and 'little devils', which is the definition of the answer. The remaining seven words are simply there to give you the seven letters of SPRITES – the first of each, starting with '*S*atan's'. We had a similar clue with a 'spell-out' like this for **capital** (which see). This type of clue is something of a speciality of the *Sunday Telegraph*, from which both were taken.

first-class
First-class railway is nice and open, too – AIRY
A straightforward clue, with the traditional AI for 'first-class', and RY for 'railway'.

first lady (First Lady)
First Lady surrounded by students, all equal – LEVEL
EVE 'surrounded by' LL ('students'). For another clue, good use might have been made of the answer's value as a palindrome.

first piece
First piece in long aerobatics display – LOOPING
The 'first piece' (OPI) is in LONG, giving the 'aerobatics display' or LOOPING. 'First piece' could also legitimately indicate P – just as 'first class' and 'first lady' (above) could indicate respectively C and L, and 'first rate' and 'first woman' (below) R and W.

first rate
It's first rate in the Royal Navy, but you get wet! – RAIN
So it's AI in the RN. The solver can take 'but' to mean that the definition that follows ('wet') is nothing to do with the being in the Navy. To have had 'and' here would have fitted awkwardly with the 'first rate' of the start of the clue. Compare **sloth**.

(the) **first woman**
The first woman – right? – to put on weight for a football club – EVERTON
You probably guessed that the strategically placed 'right?' was a compiler's device. It was, of course, to get the R in the correct place, between EVE ('the first woman') and the 'weight' (TON) she puts on.

fish
Fish rises at slight twitch of a beginner – that's efficient! – PRACTICAL
A number of fish names can conveniently 'rise' or reverse, and here it's the CARP, at the 'slight twitch' (TIC) of 'a beginner' (AL).

fitting
Advertisement fitting skill – and the power to vary one's skills, too – ADAPTABILITY
You can probably 'read' this clue right through quite easily, the definition being the whole of the second half (after the dash).

five (5)
A 'five' at end of revue for French nude in Champs-Élysées – AVENUE
Otherwise AV ('a "five"') at 'end of revu*e*' (E) for 'French nude' (NUE) in the AVENUE des Champs-Élysées, as the official name of this famous Paris street goes. The prepositions here ('at', 'for', 'in') can be fairly literally interpreted, but at least the whole of the cryptic part of the clue is 'in' the answer.

five hundred (500)
Ban the Five Hundred, they're a real gang! – BAND
An easy clue, with 'ban' exactly as it is in the answer.

five hundred and one (501)
501 trucks for the couches – DIVANS
You're not likely to get much more of a giveaway than this!

five hundred pounds (£500)
Beast took in £500 – it's a real fraud – SWINDLE
The SWINE 'took in', i.e. 'straddled', DL ('£500').

flag
Note flag on hospital – it's quite attractive – FAIRISH
'Note' (FA) 'flag' (IRIS) on 'hospital' (H). The -ISH ending of the answer is defined by 'quite'.

Fleet Street area, Fleet Street district
During the day, the Fleet Street area looks pretty rotten – DECAY
Quite literally 'during the DAY'. The clue is not a difficult one.

flier
The 'Seafoam Flier' skims over it – SURFACE
'It' being what is skimmed over, not what does the skimming! SURF is 'Seafoam', of course, with ACE the 'Flier'. The name suggests a hydrofoil craft of some kind, perhaps.

(getting) **floored**
Lout holds note, floored, and prevents us getting in – LOCKOUT
The 'note' is thus C, which with KO ('floored'), is 'held' by LOUT.

flower
Flower power? – TORRENT
Quite a neat pun, with the question mark indicating that things may well not be what they seem, even though the words do have a meaning. The 'flower' is a stream, of course, or even a dam. Compare the two other clues for this word, under **mount(ain)** and **opposite**.

fluorine
Fluorine, released from lift, started a fire – LIT
Simply LIFT with F ('fluorine') 'released' or removed. It is doubtful that fluorine would in fact be present in a lift, or even that it would start a fire. That doesn't matter too much, since we don't know the precise circumstances of this particular gas escape!

fluter
Fluter making sweet music in orchestra – PHILHARMONIC
PHIL the 'Fluter' combines with HARMONIC ('in harmony', so 'making sweet music') in a word that is used as part of the name of many orchestras round the world, including the Royal Philharmonic, London Philharmonic and New York Philharmonic.

flutter
First letter provides flutter – and there are 25 more to complete it! – ALPHABET
We have to understand 'first letter' on two levels here. First as 'first letter of the Greek alphabet', which is ALPHA, then as 'first letter of the English alphabet'. As the latter it will be regarded as A and thus have '25 more' letters to 'complete' the sense of ALPHABET. The 'flutter' is BET, of course. Compare the quite different clue under **record**.

flying saucer
Flying saucer goes round Pole to land, remove article, and give display – UNFOLD
A rather complicated manoeuvre to produce a relatively simple answer. As you can see, the UFO has to 'go round' the Pole (N) to LAND, remove 'article' (so that it becomes LD), and finally give 'display' or UNFOLD.

fold
Applaud a hundredfold! – CLAP
Quite concise, this clue, with both cryptic elements clued by a single word ('hundredfold').

follow(ing)
Irishman followed by Ronald as a sponsor – PATRON
The clue would have been slightly harder as 'Ronald follows Irishman as sponsor', but it would still have produced PAT 'followed by' RON. Ronald also contributed to this word when we clued it under **approval**.

fool
Fools, two of them, and a land of murder – ASSASSINATION
Doubtless the 'two fools' were something of a giveaway here, and a glance at the length of the word (13) confirmation of the solver's good guess! Compare the clue for **bodyguard**.

foot
One foot behind – AFT
Easy, of course, when you know about the 'foot' or FT, but take the clue 'cold' and it may mesmerise for a while. The compiler, of course, hopes it will!

football body
United Nations football body has a right – but this is not right! – UNFAIR

The four cryptic elements are UN+FA+I+R, of course.

footnote
'Abscinds' (see footnote) – LOPS
If the compiler is feeling in a vindictive mood, he may occasionally come up with a clue like this (not too often, one hopes). The idea is to harass the poor solver, who will probably have to seek refuge in his dictionary. If it is *Chambers*, as it often will be, under 'abscind' he will find 'to cut off'. Well, to 'lop' is also to cut off, so that must be right! But of course it is possible to get the correct answer via the cryptic part of the clue, with 'see' = LO and 'footnote' = PS. A quick glance in the dictionary will then confirm that he is right – and doubtless feeling extra pleased for having handled such a forbidding clue so confidently. (The bracketed part of the clue is also a harassment, since, of course, there is no actual footnote for the puzzled solver to refer to.)

for
Medicine for weight (99) – TONIC
The 'weight' is, of course, the TON, with the cryptic '99' in brackets actually the Roman numeral IC. If this was a person's weight in pounds (it's just on 7 stone) he or she would probably need a TONIC!

forbid
Article to forbid university man to give up – ABANDON
A nice 'read-through': A+BAN+DON = 'to give up', ABANDON

force
A force to imitate with wide-open mouth? – AGAPE
Another 'read-through', this time A+G+APE = AGAPE. A much more recondite clue would have been 'Brotherly love is a force to imitate' (which perhaps makes better sense than the clue just given). Try *Chambers* if in doubt.

for each
For each change there is variation on a theme – PERMUTATION
A slightly abstruse clue but a perfectly fair one, with PER being 'for each' and MUTATION being 'change'. A PERMUTATION, says *Chambers* (among other things), is 'any one possible order of arrangement of a given number of things taken from a given number'. Of course, we are not obliged to use this definition in the clue.

foreign (sort of) **accent**
Very sharp salesman turned up, with a foreign sort of accent – PERACUTE
The answer is defined as 'very sharp' (*Chambers*'s definition precisely), and the 'salesman' who 'turned up', i.e. reversed, is a REP. That leaves you with the ACUTE, 'a foreign sort of accent'.

foreign(er)
Foreign word I've put means 'reason' – MOTIVE
As you can see, the 'foreign word' doesn't mean this at all – it means MOT (the French for 'word'). MOTIVE, however, does mean 'reason'.

Foreign Office
Foreign Office to the right and – er – that's the Market Place – FORUM
So long as you appreciate that 'er' is UM you'll have little difficulty in understanding this hesitant guide. You may, of course, need to check that 'Market Place' is FORUM, but *Chambers* will confirm that this is in fact what the word (originally Latin) means.

for example
Poor people are Grade Two, for example, having an assortment of rags – BEGGARS
A more complex clue. 'Poor people' is the definition of BEGGARS. Then you get the cryptic elements. 'Grade Two' is B, 'for example' is EG, 'an assortment of rags' is GARS (an anagram of RAGS). For a different type of clue for this same word, see **bring in**.

for instance
Dog guide, for instance – POINTER
The clue is deliberately 'woolly' (is 'dog' a noun or a verb?) to put the solver off the track. In fact both words are nouns, giving different definitions of POINTER, the first being the game-dog and the second, more allusively, a 'guide' that is a hint or suggestion (a POINTER to the answer, if you

like!). As such, there is no normal cryptic element in the clue.

former(ly)
Former operation was accurate – EXACT
A straightforward clue: EX+ACT = EXACT. Compare the clues under **old** and **out**.

fortissimo
Sally by a fortissimo fighter and talismanic character – SALADIN
What kind of 'Sally' exactly – a sortie or the girl's name? The latter, in fact with 'fortissimo' here being DIN. SALADIN (not to be confused with 'Saracen'!) is not in *Chambers* since he was a historic figure – the famous twelfth-century Sultan of Egypt who fought the crusaders. But he was also famed as a 'character' in Walter Scott's *The Talisman*, hence 'talismanic'. All this sounds rather high-flown, but the solver can reach his quarry from the cryptic elements (SAL by A DIN), and will surely have heard of him anyway.

fortune
Where Arthur stopped and came to a fortune – CAMELOT
It is simply a coincidence that this literary and historical clue follows the one above! It's probably easier, since the solver is on home ground here, with CAMELOT being the famous site (wherever exactly it was) of King Arthur's court and palace. The answer can also be arrived at cryptically, of course, since it is where Arthur CAME to a 'fortune' or LOT.

forty (40)
One in forty in ease, I hear, in banishment – EXILE
This is a 'double burial', which the solver may occasionally encounter. Furthermore, it is a 'burial' of cryptic elements: 'one in forty' is I in XL (XIL), and this is 'in ease, I hear', or in E . . . E. This gives the 'banishment' or EXILE. But although rather complex, the instructions are quite clear, and if followed carefully will lead to the correct answer – which is, of course, additionally defined.

forty-nine (49, '49)
Dossier for the 49 in Further Education – FILE
A much more straightforward clue than the one above, with a simple 'burial': IL ('49') in FE. Notice that the capital letters of 'Further Education' indicate that an abbreviation is required.

found
George found a railway using this mathematical system – GEOMETRY
A direct 'read-through' clue, so that GEO MET a RY to get his 'mathematical system'.

four (4)
Act Four, I feel, should be rewritten, to give something that's far from boring – ACTIVE LIFE
'Act Four' gives you ACTIV virtually free of charge, with 'should be rewritten' clearly indicating an anagram (of I FEEL). Perhaps the rest of the clue is rather tame. Since the theme of the clue is a play, I would prefer to see a definition on the lines of 'to give something that's quite different from this submissive death'.

frame
Lees framed the Poles using these pieces of photographic equipment – LENSES
One more 'burial', with LEES 'framing' the familiar 'Poles', N and S.

(of) **France (in France)**
Calm swim, backstroke, in lake in France – PLACID
Did you think of the name of a French lake? A red herring, I fear, since the actual answer is defined by 'calm'. It is comprised of two cryptic elements – a 'swim, backstroke', which is a reversed DIP, and 'lake in France', which is the French for 'lake', LAC. The latter is 'buried' in the former, to give P-LAC-ID. By a curious coincidence, the answer *is* the name of a lake, but not a French one – Lake Placid, in the United States (north of New York).

free
Horseman to free the Queen – RIDER
An easy combination of definition ('horseman') and two cryptic elements (producing RID+ER).

French
Abject misery of the French couple – DESPAIR
You can't start the cryptic side of the word without that innocent-looking 'of the French' which gives you DES. 'Couple', of course, is the normal English PAIR.

French girl
I got involved with French girl on centre of gliding ground – MILLED
A rather curiously located romantic entanglement (if that is what 'involved' means here), but a clue that is perhaps justified for springing the unexpected definition 'ground' (MILLED) on the unsuspecting solver. 'Involved', in cryptic terms, actually means that 'I' is buried in MLLE ('French girl'), with the esoteric 'gliding' necessary to provide the final letter D ('centre of gli*d*ing'). In his determination to use 'ground' in this clue, the compiler somewhat restricted his choice of preceding words.

Frenchman
Frenchman is mixed-up idle fellow. That's something new! – MODERN
Here you have to translate 'idle fellow' (DRONE) before turning it into an anagram ('mixed-up') and putting it after 'Frenchman' (M).

Frenchwoman
Confused girl embraces Frenchwoman in the candle-light – GLIMMER
Blind man's buff, perhaps? Anyway, you need to make an anagram ('confused') of GIRL and 'straddle' it ('embraces') round MME ('Frenchwoman'). That will give you your GLIMMER or 'candle-light'.

French writer
Turgid essay reveals the French writer – GIDE
GIDE is one of the more popular French writers for crossword purposes, usually as part of a longer word in some form. Here he is 'neat' – and 'buried' in 'tur*gid e*ssay'.

Friday
Friday goes on for ever, and I'm alone in the world – FRIENDLESS
Not too depressing a clue, I hope. It simply signals that FRI is ENDLESS.

friend
Friend in Rome holding diamond could be Anna, for example – PALINDROME
A specialised word, of course, but one all too familiar to crossword solvers! There is one in the clue, of course – 'Anna, for example' – but there is also the usual cryptic definition, with PAL IN ROME 'holding', i.e. 'straddling', the 'diamond' (D).

from
To get the bird, extract redhead from cattle-herd – DOVE
That is, 'extract' or remove the '*r*edhead' (R) from the DROVE. A novel variation on the 'benighted damsel' theme.

from east to west
Star goes from east to west? Rubbish! – RATS
Maybe a rather quaint equivalent to 'rubbish' or 'nonsense', but quite in order for the purposes of our reversal here. (*Chambers* says RATS expresses 'contemptuous incredulity'.) See also **retire**.

from either end
Erected from either end – PUT UP
Ignoring the word-break, a pure palindrome, of course.

from the sound of it
End of European race, from the sound of it – FINISH
Not a gloomy prophecy of doom but a simple pun, with 'end' defining the answer, and 'of European race' its homophone, FINNISH.

front (of)
Front beds are quite empty – BARE
The 'front' or first letter of '*b*eds'+ARE. It doesn't matter whether you think of them as bedroom beds or flower-beds, either will do for the sense of the clue and its answer.

frost (Frost)
Violation of law about frost – CRIME
'About' here is C, combining with the 'frost' or RIME to make the CRIME, defined in the first half of the clue.

fruit
Source of rejected mixed fruit – FOUNT
Why 'rejected'? This is simply a reversal indicator for OF, so that you get FO with 'mixed fruit', i.e. an anagram of NUT (UNT). FOUNT is defined as 'source'.

funny
Note funny soft bit – CRUMB
That is, C+RUM+B ('soft'), a CRUMB being a 'bit' of something. You can imagine what you like for the face value of the clue – a musical phrase, perhaps, or a piece of unbaked cake?

fuss
Fuss for the navy men, the first overall dressing – ADORNMENT
Quite a satisfactory clue, since the first occasion when a ship was to be 'dressed overall' (decorated with all her signal flags from bow to stern) would in fact be a time of increased activity, if not actual 'fuss'. Anyway, the first seven words of the clue provide the cryptic elements: 'fuss' (ADO), 'navy' (RN) 'men' (MEN) '*t*he first' (T).

G

gallery
Condition of south gallery – STATE
An easy 'read-through', especially once you know that 'gallery' is TATE. Compare the four other ways we can clue this word, under **dined, martyr, show** and **station**.

game
Pane broken during game – a sign of how little it cost – CHEAPNESS
Otherwise PANE 'broken' in CHESS. Note that 'a sign of' is there to indicate a noun for the answer: if the definition wording had been merely 'not worth much', say, this would have suggested an adjective (CHEAP).

game body
Game body of learners on double bend collapses – FALLS
No great complexity here, with the 'learners' being the LL and the 'double bend' the S.

(a) **garden**
Prior article found by detective next to garden before tea – ANTECEDENT
A slightly contrived clue, on account of its four cryptic elements: AN found by TEC next to EDEN before T. As an adjective, ANTECEDENT is defined as 'prior'.

gather (round)
Bands gather round it – they're robbers, too! – BANDITS
All the letters you need are right there in front of you, and, with the direct definition, you cannot fail to solve this clue in record time!

gee
Gee, I'm allowed to have half a glass of gin and lime! – GIMLET
Chambers will confirm, if required, that a GIMLET is 'half a glass of whisky, gin, or vodka, and lime-juice'. Possibly you thought this latter half of the clue contained the cryptic elements? In fact they are in the first half, with 'Gee, I'm allowed' working out as G+IM+LET. The clue could have used the more familiar GIMLET in its clue (the tool) but that would have been – forgive the pun – rather a bore.

general
Mixture of snow and rain is general, in a way – SLEET
Otherwise 'General' LEE in a ST ('way').

George (the writer)
Quick, George, it's treacherous – SAND
'George' here simply completes 'quick'. Notice that the definition ('treacherous') does not apply to the answer, for once, but the word formed from two clue words. All the solver does is to supply the second half of the word defined.

Georgia
Yacht race is exciting treat in Georgia – REGATTA
Once you have spotted that 'exciting' is an anagram indicator, and that GA ('Georgia') goes in it (rather than the other way round), you will have little difficulty in getting your 'yacht race', or REGATTA. It is TREAT, of course, that is anagrammatised as RETTA.

German
Young people gather round the German pals – BUDDIES
'The German' is DIE, of course, but how about the 'young people'? These are the BUDS that 'gather round' or 'straddle' DIE, making 'pals', BUDDIES. The 'young people' clue is rather a liberty, perhaps, but *Chambers* does define 'bud' as 'a young person (as a term of endearment)'. (This is not apparently the same as the American 'bud', which is the same as 'buddy' – our plural answer – and comes from a childish or Negro version of 'brother'.)

get
I'm getting it to eat, funnily – you do the same – IMITATE
As you can see, a reasonably easy clue, really: IM getting IT to EAT 'funnily' (= ATE).

get in
Church singer somehow not getting in car – CANTOR
The anagram indicator here is 'somehow', referring to NOT. This 'gets in' the CAR (as NTO) to produce the 'church singer'.

get round
Rodney gets round middleman – and gets his way! – ROAD
Both ST and RD (or ROAD, as here) can be 'way'. Perhaps the most obscure element here is the 'middle man', which is A (the 'middle' of 'm*a*n'). 'Rodney' features fairly regularly in cryptic clues as ROD.

giant
Giant is muddled – he is the first person saying there are no gods – ANTITHEIST
Quite a hard clue, especially as 'muddled', although indicating an anagram, relates not to 'giant' but to TITAN, its synonym. This rearranges to ANTIT, and you then have an easier second half: HE IS '*t*he first'. An ANTITHEIST is, of course, the opposite of a 'theist', who believes in a god or gods. You may well have been misled into trying to combine an anagram of 'giant' with a possible answer of 'agnostic', especially since the letters of each coincide. (Pedantically, I should perhaps say that this would have been the wrong answer anyway, since an 'agnostic' is not someone who says there is no god but one who says it is impossible to *know* whether there is a god.)

gin
Sir Robert's back with gin cocktail, and he's oblivious to the world! – SLEEPING
'Sir Robert' is Sir Robert PEEL, the English statesman who instituted the Irish constabulary (and improved the British), so 'Sir Robert's back' means that PEEL'S back, complete with S, giving SLEEP. The GIN 'cocktail' is the easiest part of the clue.

ginger (Ginger)
Was anxious about Ginger – CARED
'About' being CA, as it often is. A more boring clue would have had a 'car coming to the editor' for this answer.

gipsy (fellow)
Gipsy points to ravine – CHINE
The word may be a local one (most CHINES are on the Dorset coast) but it's in the dictionary and can fairly easily be reached by means of 'gipsy points' (CHI+NE).

girl
Master takes girl pupil in marriage – MARITAL
As can be readily seen, MA takes RITA+L. Notice that 'in' denotes the answer to be an adjective: 'in marriage' is MARITAL, just as 'in the house' is 'domestic'.

give (him, etc.)
Give artist a basin for the plant – RADISH
Give RA a DISH, of course. The only thing with a 'give' clue is to be sure that the elements of the word are joined in the right order. Compare the clue for this word under **soldiers**.

give(n) permission
I came in to give permission for the dressing – TOILET
An obvious 'burial' of I in TO LET (with the removal of this same letter from the answer here a favourite vandalism of jokers on trains, and elsewhere). The clue might have had 'come', not 'came', but purists will say that, since 'I' is being treated as a word (or a letter), any present tense verb should end in S (i.e. 'I

comes in'). But this would clearly be out of the question!

give over
Give over, lad – 'e's a part of t'scenery in t'North! – DALES
A clue that some might regard as over-ambitious. 'Give over' indicates an anagram of LAD 'E'S; 'part of t'scenery in t'North' is meant to suggest Yorkshire speech (with its clipped form of 'the'), and so point to a well-known Yorkshire feature – its DALES. The answer is defined conventionally as well, of course ('scenery in the North'). How did you fare?

glasses
Lord Provost in glasses on his circuit – LOOP
A fairly simple 'straddle' (or 'burial').

globe
Cricketer goes round the globe – presumably on this? – BOAT
'Cricketer' quite often turns out to be BAT, although BAT itself, as a word or element, can be many things beside 'cricketer'. Compare the clues under **grasp** and **hole**.

glove
Sent back glove packed in grass – REMITTED
MITT in REED, of course. MITT could also legitimately be clued as 'hand'.

go (to)
Father goes to tent to get certificate – PATENT
Commentary superfluous, I think!

god (God)
Theft of 'God and the Church of England' (New York) – LARCENY
At its face value, the clue tells of the theft of a theological work (published in New York), perhaps. Here the 'god' is LAR, which with the CE and NY makes the necessary LARCENY.

go(ing) north
Mat's going north for the day to this Lincolnshire town – STAMFORD
So in this down clue MAT'S produces STAM ('going north'), which with FOR and D ('the day') produces the attractive market town of STAMFORD (worth a visit for more than Mat's one day, in fact).

go into
Ball goes into road – maybe this drunk was responsible! – SOT
Colourful, but simple as a cryptic clue. The SOT behaved similarly when we clued him under **ball**.

gold
Gold piece goes round – ORB
A straightforward 'read-through'.

good
A small number after a good instrument – PIANO
I am not too happy about the second 'a' in the clue, which personally I would have omitted. Still, quibble apart, we get 'a' (A) 'small number' (NO) after 'good' (PI) correctly enough to give us the 'instrument'.

Goodfellow (good fellow)
ST
Be a good fellow: give the utmost – BEST
The message is, BE a ST (or 'saint'), and 'give the BEST'. See **highway** for quite a different kind of clue to produce the same word, and also compare the clue under **become**.

good man, good person
The good man, a boy at heart, quietly comes to a halt – STOP
An example of how even a common word can be clued in an interesting way. 'A boy at heart' is the O (the 'heart' of 'b*o*y') that joins the 'good man' (ST) to 'quietly' (P).

good queen
Good queen has a horse, excellent to back, in the old country – BESSARABIA
What did you first think of for 'horse'? It will not necessarily be one of the four possibilities listed under **horse** in the first part of the book. Here it is ARAB, which follows 'good queen' BESS and is itself followed by 'excellent to back', otherwise a reversal of AI. BESSARABIA is 'the old country' since it no longer exists as an independent administra-

tive territory with clearly defined borders, but is a region in the USSR (by the Black Sea).

go outside
Men go outside to help a girl – MAIDEN
MEN 'go outside' AID, of course. We clued the MAIDEN quite differently under **degree**, and will clue her a little differently under **hold**.

go round
Mr Crosby goes round the end, bowing – BENDING
No prizes offered for who 'Mr Crosby' is. He 'goes round' the END quite conveniently to give us his 'bowing' or BENDING.

go up
Roy goes up to the king in northern city – YORK
A simple reversal in this down clue, so that ROY 'goes up' (as YOR) to the 'king' (K). We could have had a similar, although more elaborate clue, to produce YORICK. Perhaps you would like to devise one?

governor
Governor returns with a table that can be drawn up towards the body – RETRACTABLE
A more complex clue. The 'governor' is (President) CARTER, who 'returns' as RETRAC with TABLE. The rest of the clue ('that can be . . .') is a definition of the answer (based closely on one in *Chambers*).

go west
Boy goes west to meet girl who lost a dollar in this Texan town – DALLAS
One of the hardest sorts of clue you will find, since – twice – you have to carry out two operations instead of one. For a start, although you know that 'goes west' indicates a reversal, it is not the letters of 'boy' that reverse but those of his synonym LAD. Similarly, it is not enough to know that 'lost a dollar' means 'lost letter S': you also have to find a word or name (with an S to lose, of course) representing 'girl'. It is in fact LASS. But at least you have 'Texan town' to help you on your way to the well-known DALLAS. Compare the clue under **here**.

grab
Happy Jo's grabbing you! – JOYOUS
'You' might have been the letter U. But actually it's YOU in full, so you have quite a straightforward 'burial'.

graduate
Graduate has a wry grin, coming to the edge – MARGIN
Or MA has a 'wry' (anagrammatic) GRIN, which 'comes to' MARGIN.

grand
Grand lad is bright and cheerful – GLAD
An easy 'read-through': G LAD is GLAD.

grasp
Cricketer grasps the ball – that's a smack! – BOAT
Well, a 'smack' is a fishing BOAT! Compare this clue with the one under **globe** and then with the one under **hole**. You may have found this marginally the hardest.

grass
Girl in grass given a feast – REGALED
You can easily see the 'burial' here.

grass land
Ban on grass land for this crop – BARLEY
No 'burial', just two mini-definitions and a direct indicator ('this crop').

gratitude
Welshman expresses gratitude very loudly at end of play – TAFFY
The three cryptic elements, of course, are 'gratitude' (TA), 'very loudly' (FF) and 'end of play' (Y). You may well have remembered TAFFY from the derogatory nursery rhyme, 'Taffy was a Welshman'.

grave inscription
Grave inscription on N. Yorks town – RIPON
A fairly straightforward 'read-through' clue (RIP+ON), with, however, the 'N' of 'N. Yorks' designed to mislead you. Ripon actually is in North Yorkshire!

gravity
Single person displays longer lack of gravity – LONER

A weightless bachelor astronaut, perhaps, or the only person unable to stop laughing? Either way, he or she 'displays' (to you, the solver) LONGER with a 'lack of gravity', i.e. minus G. Thus you have the LONER.

great
Great run-in causes low throaty noise – GRUNT
Not too bizarre a clue, I trust, to produce this straightforward 'burial'. (You can imagine the clue as the end of a race, maybe, or of a mass jog.)

great man
Great man in bed produces cigar! – CHEROOT
This Churchillian image is yet another 'burial', with the HERO in his COT. The exclamation mark could perhaps be dispensed with, but is really just a triumphant flourish to the clue.

Great North Road
Great North Road leads to noted Yorkshire valley – could be a real bitch! – AIREDALE
'Noted' here is RE, and the 'Yorkshire valley' is DALE (see **give over**, for more about this). The exclamation mark here is much more justifiable, since it indicates the rather dreadful play on words ('bitch' the dog – the AIREDALE terrier, here – and 'bitch' the slang term for a difficult situation or problem). Note that the AIREDALE actually *is* in Yorkshire (the valley of the river Aire), with the region being the place of origin of this particular breed of dog. For a different kind of clue leading to the same animal, see **jolly good**.

great number
A great number found love and then separated – CLOVE
That is, 'a great number' (C, or a hundred) found LOVE and then CLOVE. Another clue for this word might have used the better-known 'flower-bud' sense, of course, but 'separated' enabled us to have two contrasting verbs.

Greek letter, Greek character
In the past, this Greek character was a supporter of the pope – PAPIST
A 'burial' of the 'Greek character' PI in the PAST, giving a 'supporter of the pope', or PAPIST.

green (Green)
For all to see, making love on green – OVERT
A 'read-through', with the definition first.

grip
Friendly kid grips pole – KIND
The usual 'pole' (N) 'buried' in KID and making 'friendly'.

g-string
Novice in g-string – that's rather too much of a good thing! – GLUT
Another simple 'burial', with the L a 'novice' this time. Compare the clue under **violin string**.

gun
Game beauty, holding a gun – BAGATELLE
Quite a neat clue, with the ambiguity of 'game' a good teasing factor. In fact, as we can see, it's actually the definition, and precedes the 'burial' of 'a gun' (A GAT) in the 'beauty' (BELLE).

gunner(s)
Fanatic gunners make an offer – RABID
A definition and two cryptic elements to make up this clue.

Gwynne
Prudence and Gwynne with a strong fabric – PRUNELLA
That is to say, PRU and NELL with A = PRUNELLA, defined by *Chambers* as 'a strong silk or woollen stuff, formerly used for academic and clerical gowns and women's shoes'.

hail
Hail! The king is coming here! – HITHER
Admittedly a rather tortuous clue. In fact it is a 'read-through', with 'hail' (HI), 'the' (THE) and 'king' (R) being 'coming here'

(HITHER). The clue well deserves its two exclamation marks, the first of which is justified on sense grounds anyway.

half (of) **(half a)**
No half-term report! – NOTE
NO+'half-term' (TE) makes NOTE, which is a 'report' in that both words can denote an official statement or account of something.

half a dozen
Half a dozen cars close to the church – VICARS
An allusive definition, but if VICARS aren't 'close to the church', who is?

half-day
A half-day can be continental – AFRICAN
You probably weren't expecting this answer! Yet there it is ('continental'), the product of 'a' (A) 'half-day' (FRI) and 'can' (CAN).

half (a) **score**
Occupies half a score workers – TENANTS
TENANTS here must be understood as a verb ('holds as a tenant'), in order to match 'occupies'. The 'half a score workers' are TEN ANTS, of course.

Hampshire town (Hants town)
Bachelor goes to Hants town – it's like paradise! – BLISS
Not a very big town, in fact (compare its crossword rival, DISS, under **Norfolk town**), but quite a handy one for words involving the letters LISS.

harbour
Soldier harbours boy on a hill – Roman soldier, that is – GLADIATOR
As you can see, the GI 'harbours' a LAD on A TOR. It's agreeable that the clue is able to accommodate both types of 'soldier'.

hard
Guard hard edge – HEDGE
A fairly concise clue, with HEDGE not in its basic meaning ('row of bushes') but in a more specialised sense (*Chambers*'s fourth verb out of five).

Hardy heroine
Hardy heroine stands astride almost empty river – perhaps she will bring it to the Test? – TEMPTRESS
Contrived, maybe, but an obvious 'straddle' of TESS over the 'almost empty river' (EMPT+R) and the pun on the river 'Test' too good to overlook. Note that as 'Hardy heroine', TESS will lose much of her impact if she occurs anywhere other than the first word in the clue, since 'Hardy' must always have a capital H. As the first word, the exact import of 'Hardy' can be conveniently hidden.

harker (Harker)
Reginald Harker is to put in harness again – REGEAR
So that REG EAR is to REGEAR ('put in harness again').

Harry
Wave the silver one, Harry! – AGITATE
It doesn't matter how you understand 'one' in the clue (a wand? a hat?), so long as you 'read' it as I in the answer to link AG ('silver') and 'Harry' TATE.

has
Victor has debts – that's bad – VICIOUS
A fairly obvious clue of the type $x+y = z$. Compare the clue we had for VICIOUS under **debt(s)**.

hat
So, hat is quite strong – SOLID
But supposing you did not know that 'hat' here was LID? SO, of course, combines with it to form the answer, defined as 'quite strong'.

have
Writers have one on old age benefit – PENSION
ON here is used as two important letters in the answer, with the 'writers' being the PENS. The 'one', of course, is I.

he
He is in Red House, where bad boys stay – REMAND HOME
Otherwise MAN is in RED HOME.

H.E.
Shelter for H.E. round bottom of mine – TENT

You could even interpret 'H.E.' as 'His Excellency' here and still get quite good sense! It works out as TNT, of course, which is 'round', i.e. 'straddles', 'bottom of min*e*' (E). This would almost certainly be a down clue.

head
E is for Intellectual! – EGGHEAD
This is to operate a kind of role reversal, with the answer being a cryptic 'clue' for one part of the actual clue – EGGHEAD, of course, is the 'head' of '*e*gg' (hence 'E'), as well as an intellectual. The exclamation mark indicates that something special is going on here.

head away
Pickets head away cyclists – TRIKERS
If 'pickets' (STRIKERS) 'head away' they become TRIKERS – who are certainly 'cyclists', even if three-wheeled ones! Should a word like this be used if it cannot be checked in most standard dictionaries? Where it can be confidently deduced, as here, I think this is quite fair, especially as it is a comparatively well-known word (at least, 'trike' is). What would *not* be reasonable would be to have a rare or highly specialised word, one that was not in the ordinary dictionary because of its rarity or narrow usage.

head chopped off
Head chopped off flower further down – LOWER
All this clue says is: FLOWER minus F = LOWER!

headless
Headless corpse is battered – it's a real mystery – POSER
A more ingenious clue. 'Headless' CORPSE is ORPSE, which when 'battered' (as an anagram) is POSER – a 'real mystery'!

head of
Sam goes to head of police with the French specimen – SAMPLE
By now (if you have been working through these clues at all) you'll be all too familiar with 'head of . . .' meaning 'first letter of . . .', and 'the French' being LE or LES. Here they both are, so that SAM goes to P with LE. A 'specimen', of course, is a SAMPLE.

head office
Head office uses these buildings – HOUSES
Too 'transparent', perhaps, but quite a valid clue.

head over heels
Tom tumbled head over heels and went to her – after all, she *is* a boy's best friend! – MOTHER
A reversal followed by a direct 'copy', MOT+HER. I imagine most solvers will have heard that 'a boy's best friend is his mother'. (The quotation is actually the title of a popular song.)

head to tail
Bud and I head to tail in beer, as good speakers should be – AUDIBLE
Almost an over-ingenious clue ('head to tail in beer'?), but one presumably necessary to produce AUDIBLE ('as good speakers should be'). The most obscure part is 'Bud and I head to tail', which is BUDI rearranged ('head to tail') as UDIB. This then goes 'in' 'beer' or ALE.

hear(d), (from what one) **hears**
Mangle heard in the belfry – WRINGER
I am not too sure under what circumstances a mangle would ever be actually heard in a belfry, but at least the clue produces the homophonic pair needed for the answer. Notice that 'heard' here relates to 'in the belfry' – or rather to the RINGER 'heard' there – as well as to 'mangle'. It thus plays a dual role.

hearing aid
Be wary of loud hearing aid! – FEAR
A 'read-through', with the definition first. For a somewhat similar clue, compare **organ**.

heart
Cop in heart of Florida has a big haul – CROP
'Heart of Florida' (R) in COP makes the 'big haul'.

hearten
Black man, heartened with tea, has plenty of drive – MOTOR
MOOR is often associated with 'black man' in cryptic clues (*Chambers*'s definition is, 'a dark-coloured person generally, a Negro').

Here with his central 'burial' ('heartened') of T, he has 'plenty of drive', which of a MOTOR can be taking 'straight' (as 'motive power') or punningly.

heartless
Editor, the heartless guy, is irritable – EDGY
A fairy easy composite clue, with 'heartless' GUY minus his 'heart' (U).

Heath
Point Heath noticed – SPOTTED
No doubt initially you thought of the usual 'point of the compass' letter (N, S, E or W) for 'point'. For a change, however, it's SPOT! (The two words are very close in meaning, whether as noun or verb, and after all in billiards the 'spot' is the 'point' on the table from where a ball is played.) The rest of the clue is straightforward, of course.

heath(er) (Heather)
Stick close about Heather – CLING
With 'about' as C, this is an easy clue.

heat source (source of), **heat**
Avoid heat source in hospital – SHUN
A clue that's slightly more tricky than it seems, since 'source', independently, can indicate the first letter of a word. Here, therefore, 'heat source' could mean H. In fact, as we know, it means SUN, which with 'hospital' (H) in, becomes SHUN ('avoid').

heavyweight
Heavyweight forces needed for this gripping and lifting instrument – TONGS
TON+GS makes this 'gripping and lifting instrument' (the definition is exactly that of *Chambers*).

height
Glide-round at height gives great pleasure – DELIGHT
Did you appreciate that 'round' was an anagram indicator? You thus need to rearrange the letters of GLIDE (as DELIG), add 'height' (HT), and so get your 'great pleasure', or DELIGHT. For a more complex clue for this word, see **lose**.

held (in)
Examination held by me to get sense of discipline – MORALE
Or an ORAL 'held' by ME. One may perhaps debate the exact definition of MORALE, but 'sense of discipline' must be acceptably close, even if it does not tell the whole story.

Helen
On the stroke of a bell, the king came to Helen – KNELL
The convenient 'king' (K) at work again, to join NELL 'on the stroke of a bell'. ('On' since KNELL means either 'the stroke of a bell' or 'the *sound* of the stroke of a bell'.)

hell(ish)
Hellish company in this music and dance club – DISCO
Just a 'read-through' again, with the first two words providing the two elements of the answer. Compare the clue for this same word under **works**.

help
Amateur help is applied – LAID
L (for 'learner') AID is thus 'applied' or LAID.

help(s) to make
Dancing girl's performance helps to make astronaut cheerful – NAUTCH
There it is, of course, 'buried' in the last two words of this rather esoteric clue. 'Nautch-girls' are professional dancing women in India. ('Nautch' is a Hindi word meaning 'dance'.)

Henry
A fish for Henry I, on the other hand – HALIBUT
'On the other hand' is BUT, of course, added to HAL I to produce the 'fish'.

Herbert
Record it, Herbert – the words will remind us of him – EPITAPH
A slightly harder 'read-through', with 'Herbert' here turning out to be APH. An EPITAPH (not to be confused with an 'epigraph') is an inscription on a tombstone.

here
Found all a senator's letters here in Texas – DALLAS

Yes, it's Dallas again (compare **go west**), with the fairly obvious 'burial' in 'foun*d all a* senator's'. 'Letters', of course, refers to the 'buried' letters that you need for the answer.

Hertfordshire town (Herts town)
Note sent to South Herts town – it covers the bare essentials! – G-STRING
A 'read-through' clue with the all too obvious pun. TRING is actually a West Herts town, but we can't have everything in a cryptic clue. (Perhaps we should have reclued the word as 'Forces go to Herts town'. But then we'd have to rephrase the definition!)

(with) **hesitation, hesitantly**
From the starting point, child hesitantly goes to the top! – TEETOTUM
An agreeable clue, especially in view of the unexpected use of 'top' (as the definition). It is a straight 'read-through', otherwise: TEE+TOT+UM. For a different clue, see **stomach**.

he would
Eat up, he would, when pressed – PUSHED
That is to say, in this down clue: PUS ('eat', or SUP, 'up', i.e. reversed) and HED ('he would'). 'When' means 'upon which', in other words 'and now, having got that'.

hide, hidden
Celebrity hides in Latin America – NAME
If ever there was a 'burial' indicator, this is it. And you can easily see the 'celebrity' in 'Lati*n Ame*rica'.

(good) **hiding**
Charles loses points, and gets a good hiding, being a false pretender – CHARLATAN
There is a satisfactory pseudo-historical ring about this clue! What it actually tells the solver is that CHARLES 'loses' ES ('points') and gets A TAN, with the CHARLATAN being the 'false pretender'.

high class
Artist got in high-class, highly seasoned stew – RAGOUT
The expected RA for 'artist' and GOT with 'high-class' or U in it to make the 'highly seasoned stew'. For a clue with a difference, see **yellow pages**.

high explosive
The proposal is: put high explosive in hill, then bring me back – THEOREM
A definition, a 'burial' and a reversal combine here to produce the answer.

high priest
High priest surrounded by strong smell – it must be gas! – HELIUM
We could have had a more familiar HUM to 'surround' ELI, but this one nicely fits the answer.

high tension
Set up high tension? Correct! – RIGHT
'Up' does not denote a reversal, as it frequently does, it is simply part of the phrase ('set up') that leads to RIG.

highway
To live on the highway is most satisfactory! – BEST
In other words, to BE on the ST ('street'). You doubtless recall the way we clued this same word – quite differently – under **Goodfellow**. (And compare the clue under **become**.)

hill
The tale of a hill in Surrey – STORY
No doubt several Surrey hills have a tale to tell, but all we need here is the 'burial' of TOR in SY, a frequent abbreviation for 'Surrey'.

hill dweller
From half-plot hill dweller to full-root earth dweller! – PLANT
A deliberately teasing clue: what's all this about hill dwellers with half a plot and earth dwellers with full roots? The latter, as is now apparent, is the definition of the answer, worded in such a way as to echo the cryptic first half. 'Half-plot' is half the word PLOT (PL), together with 'hill-dweller' (ANT) making PLANT.

hint
Hairdresser almost gets hint that there is to be an outdoor party – BARBECUE
'Hairdresser almost' is BARBE, of course, and he 'gets' his 'hint' or CUE. 'That there' (as they say) is to be a BARBECUE. The

definition is rather vague (no mention of food, for example, which is an essential ingredient of a barbecue), but clear enough to support the correct solving of the cryptic elements.

(on) **hire, hired**
Amateur actor hired for village – HAMLET
HAM is LET for the HAMLET, or 'village'. Compare the clue under **permit**.

His Excellency
His Excellency is in a pet – it's a fraud! – CHEAT
Of course, it all depends how you understand 'pet'!

hit
Officer hit in half an hour – what an outcry! – CLAMOUR
The 'half' should have flashed a warning light. For once it's the second half of a word, not the first, as it usually is. So the 'officer' (CO) has 'hit' (LAM) in (as CLAMO) and is followed by 'half an HOUR' (UR).

hold
Men hold a fish for the girl – MAIDEN
The 'fish' being the convenient little ID. Compare the clues under **degree** and **go outside**.

hold up
Beam of light holds up the French race – RELAY
'Race' is clearly RELAY, but how about the rest? The 'beam of light' is the RAY, and this 'holds up', i.e. contains a reversal, of 'the French' (LE). We could have avoided this reversed 'burial' by switching languages, like this: 'Beam of light holds the Spanish race'. But that is not what this entry is about – nor is it such a convincing clue.

hole
Hole in bat? Better than hole in this! – BOAT
We have clued BOAT before (see **globe**, for example), but this clue is perhaps more imaginative, if only for its allusive definition.

holy man
It's a strain, having a holy man about the ship – STRESS
The 'about' does not denote a burial – this clue is a straight 'read-through' with the definition first, then ST+RE+SS.

Holy Writ
Humbug about Holy Writ – CANT
And this 'about' is CA, which with NT ('Holy Writ') makes CANT, or 'humbug'.

home
Team member sends thanks home to team leader – CAPTAIN
The 'team member ' is the CAP (*Chambers*: 'membership of a team symbolised by a cap'). He sends 'thanks' (TA) 'home' (IN) to get the 'team leader', or CAPTAIN. The solving of this clue is perhaps as satisfying as the compiling of it.

Home Guard
Home Guard, surrounding article, are undecided – HANG
Yes, 'Home Guard' (HG) surrounding 'article' (AN) is clear enough – but 'undecided'? If something 'hangs' it is 'undecided' (*Chambers*'s eighth definition of the verb out of a total of sixteen, incidentally), so 'are undecided' is HANG. (The word is most familiar in this sense of a thing that 'hangs' in the balance.)

honour
Honour your leader, and do this, too! – OBEY
The 'honour' is OBE, 'your leader' is the 'leader' of 'your' (Y). And if you honour your leader, surely you must OBEY him?

horrific
Horrific change in the hanging rope – HALTER
A 'halter', says *Chambers*, is 'a rope . . . for hanging criminals', so this is the definition, otherwise cryptically clued by 'horrific' (H) 'change' (ALTER).

horse
Horse cloth – although not for horses, even when produced by spinners! – COBWEB
A 'horse' is a COB (at any rate here), and a 'cloth' is a WEB (*Chambers*: 'a whole piece of cloth as woven in the loom'). This makes a COBWEB, 'produced by spinners'!

horseplay
Horseplay over a TV horse (of a sort) – a disreputable fellow – RAGAMUFFIN
Did 'over' or 'of a sort' suggest an anagram – of 'TV horse', perhaps? Alas, no there is no anagram, simply a RAG ('horseplay') 'over' (i.e. on top of, in this down clue) A MUFFIN, the reference being to the famous 'Muffin the Mule' of children's TV fame. ('Of a sort' was necessary since strictly speaking a mule is not a horse, but the offspring of a donkey and a horse.) And these elements combine to make the 'disreputable fellow', or RAGAMUFFIN.

hospital
Negative terminal at hospital, in disguised form – CATHODE
The CATHODE is the 'negative terminal', and the cryptic part of the clue is provided by 'at hospital' (AT+H) 'buried' in 'disguised form', which is CODE. A clue of medium difficulty.

hot
Is this where hot love comes to me? – HOME
It might not be, of course, but it could be – and as far as the cryptic elements go, it is, since 'hot love' (H+O) comes to ME here!

hot and cold
Team game is hot and cold – nothing between them – on this scale – HOCKEY
That is, H and C with O between them on a KEY (which is a 'scale' in the musical sense).

hotel
Third-class hotel has a bar – you can get a mineral there, too – CINNABAR
A C ('third-class') INN with A BAR will get your 'mineral' CINNABAR. Quite a straightforward 'read-through', in fact. Cinnabar is actually a mineral consisting of mercuric sulphide.

hour
Hour One: 'Sharp on Smooth' – HONE
A rather mysterious clue – a secret military operation, perhaps? – which does, however, provide the two cryptic elements (H+ONE) and an allusive definition. A HONE, says *Chambers*, is 'a smooth stone used for sharpening instruments'.

house
House in London district covers a good number of feet – SHOE
Not square feet, however, as the clue suggests! This is a 'burial', of course – HO in SE.

howler
Sat between Alfred and Ian – what a howler! – ALSATIAN
A three-part cryptic composition: SAT between AL and IAN, with the 'howler' of the clue meant to suggest a mistake or blunder rather than the ALSATIAN who, as a dog, is a 'howler'!

huff
Learner in huff having to speed – PELT
It is surprising how frequently a short one-letter 'burial' as here, will provide a satisfying clue. A learner driver forced to 'speed' (or PELT) could well be in a huff (an L in a PET). For another way of clueing this word, see **darling**.

hug
Where one girl hugs another – PENANG
As we see, PEG 'hugs' NAN. The only clue that this is a place-name is 'where', which may not satisfy some solvers. Personally, I would have compiled a more specific clue, such as 'One girl hugs another in the east', this being not only a more precise geographical description but a more misleading one (could 'east' indicate E in the word?).

huge
Bird has huge victim – OSPREY
The OSPREY has an OS PREY. Indeed the fish that is usually the prey of this bird could actually be a 'huge victim'! (It is apparently simply a coincidence that the name of this bird of prey suggests the word 'prey': it does not seem to derive from it.) See also **duck**.

humble
Humble rank at the end of the court – BASE LINE
'Rank' in the sense of 'row', as in a LINE of soldiers, and with a BASE LINE being the line at the end of a tennis court. 'Humble', of course, is BASE. The clue at its face value is meant to suggest a lowly position in a royal court.

humorist
Humorist and her decline – WITHER
Not a failing female comedy writer, but simply WIT and HER making WITHER, which is to 'decline' (so defined by *Chambers* as the third of four senses).

humour
Holy man has humour in his northern, twisted way:
'My power's in my reins,' he quipped, 'for more than just one day!' – SWITHIN
The first line of this curious couplet contains the obviously cryptic elements. It also contains the definition, which is 'holy man' (SWITHIN was a saint). 'Humour in his northern, twisted way' denotes a 'burial' of WIT ('humour') in an anagram of 'his northern' (i.e. HIS+N), with 'twisted way' indicating this anagram. We thus have WIT in SHIN. The second line has more precise information about this particular 'holy man' who had 'power in his reins' 'for more than just one day'. St Swithin, of course, was said to have had the power to bring rain for forty days. All this is rather involved, but some solvers may well have to cope with this sort of clue – indeed, may positively enjoy doing so!

(a) **hundred (100)**
A hundred at the Pole – sounds like 'chin chillers'! – CATS
Apart from the excruciating pun, the answer can be reached via the cryptic first part of the clue, with 'a hundred' (C) 'at' (AT) 'the Pole' (S). Chinchillas, says *Chambers*, are 'a breed of rabbits, *or of cats* [my italics], with soft grey fur'. Compare the clue under **Eliot**.

hungry
Hungry cat could need a thicker one – COAT
The CAT has nothing (O) inside, so contains O. If in this state he might well need a thicker COAT to keep warm.

huntress
Can huntress have a boy-friend? She is prepared to have a try! – CANDIDATE
CAN DI have a DATE? A CANDIDATE, of course, is someone who is 'having a try' for a position or qualification, as by means of an examination.

Hunts
Navy man after his ship in Hunts. Could he be wearing one of these? – MESS JACKETS
That is to say, JACK after SS in MEETS. A Navy man might well wear a mess jacket, although he could hardly find his ship in this inland county! (Let us just say he was trying to find out where it was located, while staying or living in Hunts.)

hurried
Arthur hurried to get some – RANSOME
The solver will surely have heard of Arthur RANSOME, the English children's writer. In this clue he cornily RAN to get SOME.

hurry
After tea, hurry to get fellows' leader – he's a burglar! – THIEF
A 'read-through' clue: after 'tea' (T) 'hurry' (HIE) to get '*f*ellows' leader' (F). And there's the 'burglar'.

husband
Warrant Officer with her husband – only she can have one! – WOMAN
An easy clue, revealing the WO with her MAN, making the WOMAN who alone is capable of having a husband. There are in fact servicewomen of the rank of Warrant Officer in the Army (WRAC) and RAF (WRAF).

hush
'Hush! Out!' is the cry – SHOUT
A peremptory order to leave a library, perhaps. The cryptic elements of the clue are easily 'read'.

hydrant
Hydrant in Wales can send up columns of water! – WHALES
Put an H (for 'hydrant') in WALES, and you get WHALES, known for their ability to 'spout' columns of spray.

hydrogen
Much obliged for hydrogen in containers – THANKS
H in TANKS produce THANKS – for which some people say 'much obliged'.

hypocrisy, hypocritical stuff
Noisy, hypocritical stuff about strike – CLAMANT
CLAMANT is 'noisy', or cryptically CANT ('hypocritical stuff') about LAM ('strike').

I

I
I am in a love part, being a bird – ORIOLE
Although not too happy about the 'am', perhaps, we can see I in a 'love part' (O+ROLE) to get the necessary ORIOLE.

I am
Meaning I am left with? – IMPORT
I hope you were left with this meaning, easily deduced from IM and PORT ('left') and clearly defined ('meaning').

Ian
Schoolboy sends note back to Ian – ETONIAN
This clue could have been varied as 'Schoolboy returns note to Scot', for example. As it is we can easily see the 'schoolboy' (ETONIAN) sending his reversed NOTE (ETON) to IAN. We commented on the versatility of this particular school for crossword purposes under **ascend**, as well as using it (predictably) under **college**.

I'd
While waiting, I'd got in Mr Crosby – BIDING
Obviously ID got in BING. We used the 'Old Groaner' before, under **go round**.

if (with)
Wild fear, if one's taken in by copper – PANIC
'If' is AN, here, so 'if one' (AN+I) is 'taken in' or 'buried' by the 'copper' (PC), thus producing 'wild fear' (PANIC).

if not
Circling, if not gripping with the teeth – ORBITING
In a nutshell, ORBITING, OR BITING! The clue suggests a ferocious wolf, perhaps.

I had
Objectives I had with jumble sale – IDEALS
Fortunately, there are many useful words as anagram indicators. Here we have 'jumble', so that ID+EALS ('jumble' SALE) gives the 'objectives'.

I have
The others I have are impatient – RESTIVE
Just a 'read-through' again: REST+IVE = RESTIVE.

Illinois
Illinois in Surrey? That's stupid! – SILLY
So it is – although the 'burial' of ILL in SY is sensible enough.

I'll say
Doctor came round, I'll say, and made inaccurate diagnosis – MISLED
The clue sounds like a cover-up for a crime, even a murder. Note that although 'I'll say' produces ISLE, these letters do not have to have their regular pronunciation in this word – that is to say, you have correctly interpreted 'I'll say' as ISLE but you are merely inserting the four letters that make this word in MD ('doctor came round').

illuminated
Illuminated some part of the prayer book – LITANY
A straightforward 'build-up' clue: LIT+ANY ('some') gives 'part of the prayer book', or LITANY.

I'm
I'm ashen-faced having to put body on stake – IMPALE
A slightly grisly clue – I *would* be pale doing this – but one that quite neatly produces the required answer, defined as 'to put body on stake'.

imitate
'Page to imitate the king' – headline in this? – PAPER
A 'read-through' clue: 'page' (P) 'to imitate' (APE) 'the king' (R). This might make a headline in some local PAPER, if only to describe a pantomime performance.

impertinence
Such loud impertinence is over-smart – FLIP
This ('over-smart') is *Chambers*'s second definition of the adjective FLIP. In this clue we also have it as a compound of F ('loud') and LIP ('impertinence').

imprison
Judge imprisons evil leader with reluctance – maybe possession of this caused the sentence? – REEFER
As I am sure you correctly deduced, REF 'imprisons' '*e*vil leader' (E) with ER ('reluctance'). A REEFER here, of course, is a cigarette containing marijuana.

impudent talk
Obliterate censored word of second-rate impudent talk – BLIP
To BLIP a word is to 'obliterate' it as a means of censorship, for example on a tape or TV programme. The meaning is not given in *Chambers* (even in the *Supplement* of 1977), and is missing, too, from other dictionaries, but it is almost certainly known to the solver and the word can anyway be arrived at via B+LIP ('second-rate impudent talk').

in(to)
Backward in composition, and in severe trouble – RETRO
'Backward' does not indicate a reversal, as it often does, but is simply the definition of the answer, made more precise by 'in composition', so that RETRO, when 'in composition' with the rest of the word, or with a complete word, means 'backwards' (as in 'retrogression' or 'retro-rocket'). But why 'in severe trouble'? The answer is a 'burial' – it is 'in' 'seve*re tro*uble'!

in addition
Set down learner driver, in addition – LAND
To LAND somebody or something is to 'set them down'. The answer is also a compound, of course, of L ('learner driver') and AND ('in addition').

in advance
Allowance made in advance in Devon – CREDITON
So that CREDIT ('allowance made') is 'in advance' (ON) in CREDITON, the pretty town in Devon. (Another good Devon town for a cryptic clue, which the reader may care to devise for himself, is Honiton.)

in a vessel
Found on the shore and in a vessel – SANDS
A classically simple clue, with 'and' used for the important three letters that go 'in a vessel' (in S . . . S). For a different kind of 'burial' for this word, see **in part**.

in a way
In the forefront of domestic heating recession, in a way! – GRATE
'In a way' here is used as a pun indicator. Note that the clue otherwise lacks any standard cryptic elements – there is no anagram or 'burial' involved, for instance.

in both directions
The language of Malabar is written in both directions – MALAYALAM
I think I actually first encountered this word in a crossword clue, and have come across it not infrequently since. Some languages may be written 'in both directions' (early Greek was, going first right to left then left to right in alternate lines), but MALAYALAM is not one of them (except punningly!).

in charge
Man in charge is afflicted by mental illness – MANIC
It's a sad state of affairs when the MAN IC is MANIC.

include
Scouts' camp invariably includes a dish of sea-food – SCAMPI
Not fish and chips, therefore, as one might expect, but the SCAMPI 'included' or 'buried' in 'Scout*s' camp i*nvariably'.

in connection with
Come round again in connection with dog – RECUR
Once you have spotted that 'in connection with' is RE, the rest is easy!

incorporated
Royal consort incorporated in press – PRINCESS

A direct 'burial' of INC in PRESS. Compare the clue for this word under **newspapers**.

indeed
Committed indeed to be sent as an agent – DEPUTED
That is, PUT ('committed') in DE . . . ED, which is to be 'sent as an agent', or DEPUTED. Strictly speaking there is nothing to stop a compiler from using a number of words starting IN- as 'burials' (e.g. 'inside' in SI . . . DE, 'intake' in TA . . . KE), but mercifully this doesn't happen too often. 'Indeed' is a conventionally recognised cryptic indicator of this kind.

(an) **indefinite number**
Aborigines – an indefinite number at four points – NATIVES
The answer is made up of four elements: N ('an indefinite number') AT ('at') IV ('four') and ES ('points'), all this being defined as 'aborigines'.

indisposed
Doctor indisposed after mixed gin? That's boring! – DRILLING
Quite an enjoyable clue, with the three cryptic elements (clueing DR+ILL+ING) followed by a not too hideous pun. At its face value, the exclamation ('that's boring!') nicely suggests a familiar situation ('Is he? That's nothing new!').

in favour (of)
In favour of the test – PROOF
The little 'of' is thus essential to the answer: PRO+OF = PROOF ('the test').

infiltrate
Engineers infiltrate river – they're the very best – CREAM
The only question here is, which 'river' do the RE ('engineers') 'infiltrate'? The definition (and number of letters available) should have quickly led to the CAM.

information
Get information in at . . . But he will know! – AGENT
You must have suspected an artifice here, with the sentence breaking off like this. And quite right you were, for the 'information' (GEN) is 'buried' in 'at' (AT). This produces the AGENT who will know how the sentence would have finished! See also the clue at **male**.

in good condition
Suit of clothes abroad and in good condition – OUTFIT
The definition comes first here, of course, so that an OUTFIT is OUT ('abroad') and FIT ('in good condition').

ingredient (of)
One third of an eclair is ingredient of pie. Like a bit? – PIECE
Not too involved, I hope. 'One third of an eclair' is EC ('one third' of ECLAIR). This is an 'ingredient' of PIE. And there ('like a bit') is PIECE! Compare the quite different clue under **confused type**.

in grip of
In charge of learner in grip of ice – cool and to the point! – ICICLE
A pun that might be better forgotten, but at least 'in charge of learner' (IC+L) 'in grip of' or 'buried' in ICE will get you the ICICLE that you need.

initial(ly)
Evangelical Alliance initially came to Kent to give freedom from pain and rest from work – EASE
'Initially' indicates the first letters of the '*E*vangelical *A*lliance', who came to 'Kent' (SE) to give the two definitions of EASE (the first and second of *Chambers*'s six).

inlaid
Sets of armour inlaid with gold for wooers! – SUITORS
A grand, romantic clue. The 'sets of armour', as can be seen, are the SUITS, and they are 'inlaid with gold', i.e. contain OR. This gives the SUITORS or 'wooers'.

inn
Silence in the inn, everyone – here's a game for you! – PUSHBALL
How quickly did you get the 'game'? SH in the PUB+ALL are the elements you need for it.

in operation
Uprush of liquid in operation for man in operation! – SURGEON
Otherwise a SURGE ('uprush of liquid') ON ('in operation') for the SURGEON. Quite a nice clue, agreeably confusing.

in order
Corner on reversing in order – NOOK
A 'corner' is a NOOK. This consists of ON 'reversing' (NO) and 'in order' (OK).

in part
On the seashore in part of Hants and Sussex – SANDS
A 'burial', of course, in 'Hant*s and S*ussex'. These two adjacent southern coastal counties in fact have a number of SANDS. Compare the clue under **in a vessel**.

in respect of
Sailor to return in respect of infant – BABY
A reversal of AB ('sailor')+BY ('in respect of') produces the BABY, or 'infant'.

insect
Scottish insect not commonly found – SCANT
That is, a SC ANT, which is 'not commonly found' or SCANT.

in short
Port authority, in short, doesn't get equipment – PLANT
The 'port authority' is the PLA, or Port of London Authority. 'In short' applies to this, although in fact 'doesn't' is also abbreviated (as NT). Compare the clues under **don't** and **hill dweller**.

inside
Left inside with no clothes on? Roar! – BLARE
A 'burial' that is easily spotted in this clue (which could describe an imprisoned streaker).

insolence
Cold insolence deserves this over the ear – CLIP
Not a very difficult clue, with 'Cold' the usual C.

intelligence
Uri, when bending, has intelligence, but the result is disastrous! – RUINOUS
This clue is obviously about Uri Geller, the man who could – or convinced some of us he could – bend metal objects purely by his NOUS or thought processes. (The result of his experiments often *was* disastrous, in fact.)

intelligence department
Intelligence department get their strength back! – VIM
Just a simple reversal, but quite an effective one, as it happens.

intend to
150 intend to make a demand – CLAIM
The Roman numeral here is CL, which with AIM ('intend to') gives CLAIM ('make a demand').

interior
Repair French mill's interior with an eastern shrub – PATCHOULI
A harder clue for the solver who claims that it's all too easy! 'Repair' is PATCH, 'French mill's interior' is OULI (the middle letters of the French for 'mill', *moulin*), and the 'eastern shrub' is the PATCHOULI ('a labiate shrub of S.E. Asia', says *Chambers*). 'Eastern' was designed to mislead you into thinking in terms of a letter E somewhere.

international organisation, international agency
Part of speech that needs no international organisation! – NOUN
Yes, *that* sort of 'part of speech', devised here by NO+UN.

interrupt
Sid, embarrassed, interrupts meal – a wrong way to set about things! – MISDEAL
'Sid' is often in demand for an initial reversal (a word starting DIS-). Here, however, he is 'embarrassed' or anagrammatic (as ISD) in the MEAL which he 'interrupts'. The second half of the clue is a gentle pun.

in the morning
In the morning, lawyer comes to worker, and he's insistent – ADAMANT

Doubtless you had little difficulty here. The DA is 'in' the AM and comes to the ANT.

in the place of
Former head of country in the place of department head – FORD
The reference, you will hardly need telling, is to President FORD – otherwise clued as 'in the place of' (FOR) '*d*epartment head' (D).

in the way of
Page in the way of the establishment at royal residence! – PALACE
Once you know that 'in the way of' is ALA you can use it to join up 'page' (P) and 'the establishment' (CE, or Church of England) at the PALACE. Remember, however, that often 'in the way' can indicate a 'burial' in R . . . D or S . . . T.

in this place
Stick advertisement in this place – ADHERE
Otherwise ADHERE AD HERE!

in this way
In this way clergyman comes to quarters – wet through! – SODDEN
A 'read-through' of no great complexity: SO+DD+EN ('quarters') = SODDEN.

into a mess, into a muddle
The Spanish get into a muddle, resulting in high spirits! – ELATION
That is: EL ('the Spanish') get INTO A 'muddle' or anagram (ATION), resulting in their 'high spirits' or ELATION.

introduce
Introduce First Lady to James the Fair – BLOND
In other words, 'introduce' or 'bury' the first letter of '*L*ady' (L) to James BOND (did you realise?), making him 'fair' or BLOND.

introduction (to)
Tom has introduction to Eric, the bookmaker – TOME
As now apparent, TOM has the 'introduction to' or first letter of *E*ric, this 'making' the TOME, or book! Compare the clue under **at last**, and then the rather different one under **extremity**.

intrusion
With her intrusion, small creatures become little angels – CHERUBS
Or with HER 'intrusion' (into the 'small creatures') CUBS become CHERUBS. The clue suggests the entry of some tyrant aunt at a children's party.

invert, inversion
One gent has inverted hat on – how industrious! – DILIGENT
You can see the 'one gent' easily enough. But his 'inverted hat'? That's his inverted LID! This makes him DILIGENT, or 'industrious'.

involved (in)
Apprentice involved in fight – this was the best way to escape! – FLIGHT
The 'apprentice', of course is the L (for 'learner') who is 'involved in' the FIGHT.

Ireland
Supporter in Ireland giving sidelong look – LEERING
The 'supporter' is the LEG, in which is 'buried' ERIN. The rest, of course, is the definition.

Irish
Clergyman, Irish – that's back to front! – REVERSE
I must admit I enjoyed this clue – which itself is a little 'Irish'. Still, 'back to front' or not, the elements are in the correct order for the answer – REV+ERSE.

Irish hill
Befuddled Nat, 'twixt Irish hills,
A trumpet hears – a sound that thrills! – TARATANTARA
The unusual word (or perhaps not all that unusual?) is in *Chambers*, where, together with the shorter and more familiar 'tarantara', it is defined as 'the sound of a trumpet'. The first line of this mock-romantic couplet clues it cryptically, with 'befuddled Nat' (TAN) being between 'Irish hills' TARA and TARA.

Irishman
Irishman in a film – PATINA
A clue that looks deceptively simple – until

you begin to wonder what the 'film' is. In fact the answer is not a 'burial' of PAT (in 'film', for example) but a straight 'read-through': PAT IN A PATINA, this last word being a 'film', of course – although perhaps not the one you originally expected.

iron
Iron discipline – and a cane to enforce it! – FERULE
FE+RULE for the 'iron discipline', which gives a FERULE, defined by *Chambers* (where you may have had to check it) as 'a cane or rod used for punishment'. (This is not to be confused with a 'ferrule', such as you get on an umbrella.)

is
'The South' is the subject of my dissertation – THESIS
Just a reminder that a 'link-up' of elements like this can be formed from the smallest and most innocent of words, here: THE+S ('south')+IS.

I shall
I shall enter this side of the stage, if agreeable – WILLING
Otherwise ILL enter the WING. A simple 'burial'.

island, isle
An island and a rocky boat – what a place to be in! – MANITOBA
As now revealed, MAN, with A = I, and a 'rocky' or anagrammatic BOAT. It is a shame that MANITOBA is not officially a state, as the clue would have read that much more convincingly with 'what a state to be in'. But Canada has only provinces and territories, not states, with Manitoba being a province.

island retreat
Way island retreat is established – STABLE
ST+the reversal of ELBA, of course. In fact any island could have a 'retreat' (some others are ANOI, NAM and MUR), but ELBA is the most popular for the common ending -ABLE.

issue
Justification concerning one issue – REASON
The definition first, then the three cryptic elements (RE A SON).

it
Please bring us back to it! – SUIT
Is this what you expected? To 'please' a person is to SUIT him, of course. And to get the word, bring US 'back' to IT. For a more conventional clue, perhaps, see **classy**.

Italian
The Italian boy's first – that's easy – GLIB
A nasty, almost unfair clue! Yet GLI *is* one of the Italian words for 'the' (it's used before certain masculine plural nouns), and as such should really form part of a solver's foreign vocabulary. Here it is followed by '*b*oy's first' (B) to make GLIB, which is defined as 'easy'.

item
Item No. 1 is back – it's a liquid preparation for the skin – LOTION
That is, LOT NO I, with the latter phrase being 'back' or reversed.

it's said
Stronger than nature, it's said – NURTURE
But perhaps you did not know the proverb ('Nurture is stronger than nature')? If so, this is unfortunate, although some existing letters (in an actual crossword) could suggest the complete word to you, and in fact there is a reference to the proverb in *Chambers* (under 'nurture'). The implication is that a person's up-bringing ('nurture') is more influential than his inherited personality ('nature').

I've
I've got in the doctor for him – he's often very low! – DIVER
IVE in DR, of course. The suggestion of something cryptic here is made by the rather artificial order of the words – we would be more likely to say 'I've got the doctor in'.

I will
The odds are on I will have a fall! – SPILL
That is, the SP ('odds', or *s*tarting *p*rice) are on ILL. And these two elements 'will have a fall' or a SPILL.

I would
Arena I would enter for cycling – RIDING

Another routine 'burial' – ID in RING. For a harder clue for RIDING, see **clamour**.

J

Jack
To one side of Jack is a piece of timber – ABEAM
Not the expected AB or TAR, but simply a nautical term, so that for 'Jack' the sailor 'to one side' is ABEAM (defined cryptically as 'a piece of timber').

Japan (perhaps)
Ban in Japan for this vegetable? – BEAN
Easy, really – BAN with E in!

jay (Jay)
Jay is sick when kept in these places of captivity – JAILS
As you can see, J ('Jay') AILS when kept in the JAILS. 'Jay' could be a person (male or female, in fact) or the bird.

jerk
Account of half roll, half back jerks, makes impressive gymnastic display – ACROBATICS
These gymnastic terms are also impressive, although their authenticity ('half back jerk'?) is highly suspect! They are in the clue, of course, to provide some necessary cryptic elements, and altogether these spell out as follows: AC ('account') RO ('half *ro*ll') BA ('half *ba*ck') TICS ('jerks'). The result is the 'impressive gymnastic display' – ACROBATICS!

jet
Jet speeds and goes overseas – MIGRATES
A straightforward 'read-through', as so often: MIG ('jet') RATES ('speeds' – the noun, that is), and MIGRATES ('goes overseas').

jockey
Medical man comes to jockey, a trouble-maker – MOLESTER
Thus the MO comes to LESTER to get the 'trouble-maker'.

jog
Jog by a revolutionary riot along the French pavement – TROTTOIR
We finish up with a French word, but one surely known to most solvers. (Note that for once 'the French' does not lead to LE or LES.) The cryptic elements, of course, are 'jog' (TROT) and 'revolutionary' RIOT (TOIR).

John
John, why is he such a cruel person? – BULLY
'John' = BULL, and 'why' = Y. The combination makes a 'cruel person', or BULLY.

join
Fish join in the drink! – HADDOCK
The 'split' could have been HAD+DOCK, but here it's the 'burial' of ADD ('join') in the 'drink' (HOCK). Compare the same word clued under **owned**.

join(ing)
Cup-bearers have the cheek to join the Royal Society – SAUCERS
A typical cryptic pun for the definition – and then the clue of 'cheek' (SAUCE) 'joining' or combining with the 'Royal Society' (RS).

jolly good
Terrier is jolly good about the valley – AIREDALE
In other words he is AI RE the DALE. This particular dog has been clued before, you may remember – see **Great North Road**.

Jolson
Bring a drink to Mr Jolson in the main entrance! – PORTAL
To put it concisely: Bring a PORT to AL in the PORTAL.

Jonson
Jonson has one son, a real source of joy – BENISON
As you can easily see, BEN and I SON, which is a BENISON (properly a benediction or blessing – but is not that a 'source of joy'?). Ben Jonson in fact had more than one son, but surely each was a 'real source of joy' or BENISON.

Josephine
Reply about Josephine and the At Home – REJOIN
To REJOIN is to 'reply', of course, and the three cryptic elements that comprise the word are RE+JO+IN (the 'At Home').

journal
Fancy, a journal in Japan! – IMAGINE
Every word is significant here, with the definition first, then 'a' (I) 'journal' (MAG) 'in' (IN) 'Japan' (E, i.e. the east).

journalist
Not the journalist that wrote the report – NOTED
Or – NOT the ED that NOTED! Compare the clues we had for this word under **college** and **dry grass**.

jug
Holy jug or wholly pot! – STEWER
Heaven preserve us from too many clues like this! Still, they do occur (compilers cannot always resist the temptation), so let's analyse it. 'Holy' (as well as the more frequent 'holy man') gives ST; 'jug' gives EWER; a STEWER is something that is 'wholly' or entirely a 'pot' (a stewpot, of course).

junction
Junction needs oil to work – TOIL
In this case the T 'junction', so that the T needs OIL to 'work' or TOIL. Compare the clue under **nearly fifty**.

junior
Junior has one in a pot – JAR
To your relief, JR has A ('one') in a JAR.

K

Kay
Kay in her family circle – KIN
Short and sweet – 'Kay' (K) 'in' (IN) her 'family circle', or KIN.

keep
Keep moving, stupid! – GOON
That is, GO ON, GOON! *Chambers* defines *goon* as, first, a 'hired thug' (US slang), and, second, a 'stupid person'.

keep quiet
Over-hasty gunners keep quiet – RASH
Another brief combination, with the definition first, and the answer made up of RA+SH.

Kent
Drive off car in Kent – SCARE
Quite literally, CAR in SE, making SCARE, which is to 'drive off'.

kill
Modishly original in attempt to kill – TRENDY
TRENDY is 'modishly original', here with 'to kill' (END) in 'attempt' (TRY). Don't let the word order put you off for the 'burial': 'in attempt to kill' means 'in TRY you must put END'.

killer
Killer comes to king, result is a sticky end! – GUNK
GUN comes to K, giving what *Chambers* defines as 'unpleasant dirty sticky material'.

king
King Edward is a man who favours sweeping changes – RED
Not reasonable, you say? Well, a RED is a revolutionary, who favours widespread reforms, however they are brought about. The short answer is made up from R and ED ('King Edward').

King George
Seize King George and the snake – GRASP
As can be seen, GR and the ASP make 'seize' or GRASP.

Kingsley
Kingsley South? That's wrong! – AMISS
The clue is meant to suggest a wrong railway station (or parliamentary constituency, perhaps). The word is comprised, of course, of AMIS+S.

King's Square (king's square)
Poles in King's Square presumably have a white one? – SKIN
The clue is designed so that you can't immediately be sure what kind of 'Poles' are meant. So a 'white' what? Following the

cryptic elements, and arriving at S . . . N with KI 'in', we can see that 'Poles' are the natives of Poland, who as East Europeans will 'presumably have a white SKIN'.

kiss
Love and a kiss for Diana cut short by this university scholar! – OXFORDIAN
Poor Diana. Here we have 'love' (O) and a 'kiss' (X) 'for' (FOR) DIANA 'cut short' (DIAN), making the spoilsport 'university scholar' or OXFORDIAN.

knight (Knight)
Very much wanted to be a knight. Indeed! – DESIRED
Get it? SIR in DE . . . ED, giving DESIRED, or 'very much wanted'.

knock back
Knock back two rums and you could have the symptom of a dicky heart – MURMUR
A warning against drinking – 'knock back' i.e. reverse 'two RUMs' and you could have a MURMUR. Why 'could' have, when you *do* have? Well, you 'could' have if you solve the first, cryptic section of the clue correctly. If you do not, you won't have!

knockout
This drink is a knockout back in the establishment! – COKE
A 'knockout back' is KO reversed. This is 'in' the 'establishment' or CE (Church of England). And there is your drink – a trade name, true, although well-known and found in many dictionaries, including *Chambers*.

L

label
Label on the French picture – TABLE
Compilers occasionally take slight liberties, but never so much as to be inaccurate. 'Label' is TAB, 'the French' is LE – but is 'picture' really TABLE? The answer is, yes, it is – although, of course, not in the best known sense. In a case like this, check in *Chambers* to see whether the answer you have arrived at (cryptically) does actually have the sense as defined. Do this with TABLE, and you will find the word defined, in the fifth of over twenty senses, as 'a picture'! You now have proof that you were correct – and, also important, your faith in the accuracy of the compiler is reassured.

laboratory
Docket shows that laboratory is L-shaped – LABEL
With the definition first: LABEL shows that LAB is EL (the usual cryptic reading of 'L-shaped'). For a completely different kind of clue for this word, see **Lincoln**.

lack(ing)
Rail for back door lacking nothing – ROD
The 'back' DOOR is, of course, the reversal of it. If this 'lacks nothing' it omits O, so we have ROD. And that is the 'rail'.

ladder
To harden, I get a ladder up the top of Everest – INURE
Another reversal in this down clue, so that I get a 'ladder up' (a reversed RUN) the 'top' or first letter of '*E*verest'. To INURE, of course, is 'to harden'.

lady
The lady's a goddess – HERA
HERA ('the lady's a') make HERA, the Greek 'goddess' who was the equivalent of the Roman Juno.

lake
Softly circle round the lake,
You will thus still water make! – POOL
It's not often that you will find a word clued cryptically letter by letter. This one is, however, so that P is 'softly', O is 'circle', O is 'round' (!), and L is 'lake'. The second line of the rather mysterious couplet gives you the definition, of course ('still water').

Lancashire town (Lancs town)
Ride to Lancs town, then to Kent one – CANTERBURY
It's easy, as they say, when you know how: CANTER to BURY, then to CANTERBURY. For once, 'Kent' does not mean SE. ('Kent one' in another clue could have worked out as SEA!)

large
The Queen turns round twice before the multitude on the large screen – REREDOS
Which is to say that ER 'turns round' or reverses twice before D ('the multitude', actually 500) with OS ('large') 'on'. This gives the REREDOS that we clued quite differently under **edgily**.

largely
Sweet largely takes soft range – SWEEP
SWEET 'largely' is SWEE. This takes 'soft' (P) to mean 'range', SWEEP.

large number
Points to large number of monkeys – CAPES
A tricky clue, since 'points' suggest the usual compass 'points' (N, S, E, W) and the definition of the answer appears to be 'monkeys'. In fact the clue can be translated like this: 'Points' (CAPES) can be broken down 'to' 'large number of' (C) 'monkeys' (APES). 'Cape' is defined in *Chambers* as 'a head or point of land . . .'.

last
Split U.N. atom in last large quantity – MOUNTAIN
A clue of medium difficulty, perhaps. 'Split' indicates an anagram of U.N. ATOM, which here is MOUNTA. 'In last' means that the answer has IN last. And that makes a MOUNTAIN, which can mean a 'large quantity' (*Chambers*'s fourth sense of five).

last letter
Last letter sent to the Queen 'with love' means nothing – ZERO
As now apparent, Z ('last letter') 'sent to' or joining ER ('the Queen') with O ('"with love"') means ZERO, or 'nothing'!

last letters
Note the last letters – they really hold your attention – GRIP
G+RIP gives GRIP, to 'hold your attention'.

last word
Foretell the last word in this condition – PREDICAMENT
A 'burial' of AMEN ('the last word') in PREDICT ('foretell'), to get a PREDICAMENT, or 'condition'.

late
Disinter the late cardinal – EXHUME
EXHUME the 'late' (EX) 'cardinal' (HUME), the latter being anything but 'late' when he was appointed the Roman Catholic Archbishop of Westminster in 1976.

late monarch
Late monarch buried in the lines when this military flag flies – BANNER
ANNE is thus 'buried' in BR (British Rail!), when you will get the 'military flag' or BANNER.

lawful
The child is lawful, that's understood – IMPLICIT
The IMP is LICIT, and that's IMPLICIT.

lawgiver
Lawgiver gets note. It says 'Goodbye for now' – SO LONG
This cryptic message is devised by SOLON ('lawgiver') getting G ('note').

Lawrence
Lawrence is into jazz – it's really hot! – STEWING
Otherwise TE is into SWING, which makes STEWING ('really hot'). Experts may say that there is a difference between SWING and 'jazz', but I think we can use *Chambers*'s definition of 'swing' here (supported by other dictionaries): 'jazz music with impromptu complications'.

lawsuit
Run after head of house in lawsuit – CHASE
To CHASE is to 'run after', of course, and this is composed of 'head of *h*ouse' (H) in 'lawsuit' (CASE).

lawyer
Lady lawyer visits me – DAME
A simple clue, with the DAME ('lady') a combination of DA ('lawyer') and ME ('me').

layer
Rock layer, for example, goes back to this famous megalithic complex – STONEHENGE
You were warned about the 'layer' here being HEN, of course! Without this information,

the answer might perhaps have been harder to deduce. As it is, we have a combination of STONE ('rock'), HEN ('layer') and GE ('for example goes back'!) to get the 'famous megalithic complex', as I have seen it described, of STONEHENGE.

lead
Herbert in first-class lead, having self-possession – APLOMB
Thus LOM ('Herbert') is in APB ('first-class lead'). A clue containing 'lead' will almost certainly take advantage of the word's different meanings and pronunciations.

leader
'Famous orchestra leader disappears', the notes declare – ALLEGE
The 'famous orchestra' whose 'leader' has disappeared is, of course, the HALLE. So we have ALLE followed by 'the notes' (GE) to get ALLEGE, 'declare'.

leaderless
Leaderless crowd come to end of rally – they're very noisy – ROWDY
A 'leaderless' CROWD is ROWD. This comes to 'end of rally' (Y) to be ROWDY, or 'very noisy'.

leading light
Leading light approaches king,
And so you see a naked thing – STARK
This Christmas carol-type couplet has its cryptic content in the first line, where 'leading light' (STAR) 'approaches' or joins 'king' (K). The definition, of course, is in the second line.

leaf
Leaf on tree and French fringe – PELMET
A vaguely artistic clue which uses the elements P+ELM+ET ('and French') to produce the PELMET or 'fringe'.

learned person
Learned person and apprentice boy get together in a song – BALLAD
The elements that the solver needs to 'get together' for the BALLAD or 'song' are: BA ('learned person'), L ('apprentice'), and LAD ('boy').

learner
Striking weakness about a learner – FLAILING
If we analyse this, we can see that the 'striking' (FLAILING) is a 'weakness' (FAILING) about a 'learner' (L).

learning
Learning about Busoni variation – it's slower than Mach one – SUBSONIC
A deliberately abstruse clue. 'Learning' is SC. This 'straddles' BUSONI 'variation' or anagram, which here is UBSONI. And that makes SUBSONIC which means 'below the speed of sound' and so is 'slower than Mach one' – Mach 1, which actually *is* the speed of sound. 'Variation' suggests a musical composition, perhaps, especially since Busoni was a famous composer. It's too much to hope, of course, that the solver will misread 'Mach' as 'Bach'!

leave
One I leave in New York is responsible for crime – INIQUITY
It is important here to arrange the elements correctly. 'One' is the initial I. Then 'I leave' (I QUIT) goes in 'New York' (NY), to give a composition of I+N – IQUIT – Y. All this is 'responsible for', or leads to, INIQUITY, or 'crime'.

leave out
Friend leaves out the king, the devil! – FIEND
A well-known 'letter-drop' (like the TOILET that is TO LET). The FRIEND 'leaves out' R ('the king') to get the FIEND, or 'devil'.

left
Left at it, so due for allowance – LATITUDE
Quite a complex clue: L ('left')+ATIT ('at it')+UDE ('so', i.e. anagrammatic DUE) for 'allowance', defined as LATITUDE.

left and right
Turn for information, left and right – REFER
The first three words of this clue are the definition, the last three are the single cryptic

indicator (of a palindrome). The two should be enough to produce the answer.

left hand
Left hand as in the flick – LASH
The 'flick' or LASH being LH ('left hand') with AS in!

leftist
Trained second-grade leftist – BRED
Otherwise BRED a B RED.

leg
Leg on top of the table? Could be after two or three of these! – PINT
That is, PIN ('leg') on 'top of the *t*able' (T). Compare another clue for this word under **available**.

legislator
The French legislator is a source of illumination – LAMP
LA+MP is a LAMP, with LA being a change from the usual LE reading of 'the French'. Compare a different clue for this word under **mile**.

Leonard
Leonard comes to tea in fast time – LENT
The best thing about this clue is its unexpected definition – much more satisfactory than the past tense of 'lend', for example.

less
Loveless Romeo, in confusion, gets what Oliver wanted – MORE
ROMEO is 'loveless' so loses an O (but keeps the other). The result is ROME, which as an anagram ('in confusion') makes 'what Oliver wanted' – MORE. (Oliver, of course, is Oliver Twist.)

let it stand, let it remain
The French let it remain in ruins – yet it's the most recent! – LATEST
LA ('the French')+TEST ('let it remain', i.e. STET, 'in ruins').

letter
Swordsman, as it were, points to letter – SWALLOWER
A SWALLOWER ('points' to 'letter', or SW to ALLOWER) is a kind of 'swordsman', even if an unconventional one.

lettuce
Lettuce planted by journalist – he made a fuss of it – COSSETED
That is, the COS SET by the ED, which he COSSETED, or 'made a fuss of'.

liberal
Liberal standard to balance – LIBRATE
A rather rarer word, but one that can, of course, be checked in the dictionary. The two cryptic elements for it are LIB ('liberal') and RATE ('standard').

lid
Circle or lid of box – ORB
An ORB is a 'circle', here cryptically devised by 'or' (OR) 'lid of *b*ox' (B).

lie in
American Veteran leaders lie in state and all the officers and men are there – NAVY
As you can see, we have a 'burial' here: AV ('*A*merican *V*eteran leaders') 'lie in' NY (New York 'state').

lieutenant
Graduate lieutenant in charge – of ship in this fleet? – BALTIC
This answer is made up of three cryptic elements – BA ('graduate'), LT ('lieutenant') and IC ('in charge'). The Baltic Fleet exists as part of the Soviet Navy – maybe one of its ships does have a 'graduate lieutenant in charge'. (Not with a BA, however.)

light
Street light is out of place – STRAY
A handy combination of elements: ST ('street') RAY ('light') is STRAY ('out of place').

like
Rise, like money – ASCENT
Here we have an ASCENT ('rise'), which is AS CENT ('like money').

limb
For horse-flies, put top part of cream over limbs – CLEGS
'Top part of *c*ream' is C (its first letter). Put

this over LEGS ('limbs') and you have CLEGS, which are 'horse-flies'.

limit
Despatch to south limit – SEND
With the definition first, this is a straight 'read-through' clue (with S for 'south').

Lincoln
Students in Lincoln make a record – LABEL
'Students' (LL) have 'Lincoln' (ABE) in, which devises a LABEL, as a gramophone record is often called (from its 'label' with its title and the name of the manufacturing company). This sense is not in *Chambers*, either in the main dictionary or the 1977 *Supplement*, but it should be known to most solvers (who can anyway derive it from the cryptic elements). For the most traditional kind of LABEL, see the clue under **laboratory**.

line
French 'iron line' is in fact a cross-channel service – FERRY
Misleadingly – but not unfairly! – only the French for 'iron' is needed, not 'line' as well. We thus have FER+RY ('line') to get the 'cross-channel service' or FERRY. (The English Channel is not specifically meant here, since a ferry can take you across any channel.)

lines
Lines on last letter are copper in colour – BRONZED
That is, BR ('lines') ON ZED are BRONZED.

linesman
Linesman has sort of square – and there's another! – POET
Perhaps an unexpected answer? Here a 'linesman' is the name of a writer, POE. He has a 'sort of square' (T) – thus making a POET, who is another 'linesman'!

liquid
Sulphur liquid from the earth – SOIL
'Sulphur' is S, and here 'liquid' is OIL. These two elements give SOIL, or 'earth'.

liquor
Penny on liquor – can you beat it? – DRUM
Quite a nice clue. D on RUM, of course, gives the answer. Note that it is not always necessary to clue D as 'old penny' simply because the term is no longer used in the language.

list
No list is worth considering – NOTABLE
An easy 'read-through': NO TABLE is NOTABLE. For a slightly harder clue, see **talented**.

listener, listening device
Approaches northern listeners – NEARS
A short and easy clue, with the definition first.

little
Go round the hospital a little way – that's the spirit! – GHOST
Analysing as usual, we have: GO 'round' H ('hospital')+ST (a 'little' street). This gives GHOST – and 'that's the spirit'!

little fellow, little demon, little devil
Little fellow to go on the stage – that's a blow – IMPACT
This is the straightforward equation IMP+ACT = IMPACT.

little woman
Little woman not half keen – that's funny! – JOKE
JO + KE = JOKE, of course. Note that both 'half' and 'not half' can indicate that only half a word is required as a cryptic element. In this case (KEEN), 'half' would indicate that you need the first half of the word, and 'not half' (which makes better sense here) that you do not need the second!

live
A gentleman in love lives as a god – OSIRIS
Notice that here you have a 'burial' in between two elements or words, rather than in the middle of one. Thus, 'a gentleman' (SIR) is in 'love' (O)+'lives' (IS), so that the element order works out correctly as O – SIR – IS.

local
Local student is her announcer – PUBLISHER

That is, PUB ('local') + L ('student') + ISHER ('is her'). A PUBLISHER publishes, of course, and one of the main meanings of 'publish' is 'to make public' – or 'to announce'. (*Chambers* gives the 'announce' meaning of 'publish' as the third of eight – in fact, before the 'book' sense.)

loch
Seaman's leader in vessel on loch's huge expanse – VASTNESS
As can be seen, 'seaman's leader' (S) is in 'vessel' (VAT) on 'loch' (NESS), and all that 'is' (represented by the apostrophe S) 'huge expanse', or VASTNESS.

lock (of hair)
Diana's lock of hair is in a sorry state – DISTRESS
DI'S TRESS, obviously. But why shy away from such a satisfying clue?

locker
Donald has got on top of the locker, silly ass! – DONKEY
Again, the obvious combination: DON has got on top of the KEY ('locker'), and so is a DONKEY or 'silly ass'.

lodgings
Hurry along to lodgings for the lively celebrations! – SHINDIGS
The familiar 'read-through' clue, but leading to a rarer word, perhaps. To SHIN is to 'hurry', and this goes 'along to' or joins DIGS ('lodgings'), making the 'lively celebrations' or SHINDIGS. (The definition is that of *Chambers*.)

London area
London area tea service – SET
The 'tea' (T) goes with the 'London area', of course – although SET could actually be used of a 'tea service'.

(a) **long time**
Officer at home a long time – is this something he's made up? – COINAGE
CO IN an AGE, with COINAGE in its sense of 'a newly invented word or phrase'.

look
Lingering look in different directions – SLOW
An unexpected answer? Still, SLOW is 'lingering', and its cryptic definition is 'look' (LO) in 'different directions' (S . . . W).

looking glasses
It's forbidden to fasten a loop onto the looking glasses – TABOO
All is made plain, since if you fasten a 'loop' (TAB) onto the 'looking glasses' (OO), you get a TABOO, which is 'forbidden'. (See also **loop**, below.)

look out
He keeps a look out in Donhead North – WARDEN
A slightly involved cryptic entanglement. A WARDEN is someone who 'keeps', and the word is devised from 'look out' (WARE) with '*D*onhead' (D) 'in' it, followed by 'North' (N). There are two villages called Donhead (St Andrew and St Mary) in Wiltshire, but no actual 'Donhead North'. But that needn't matter for our vigilant WARDEN!

loop
Measure loop for size of page – QUARTO
That is, 'measure' (QUART) 'loop' (O). It was only when I had devised this clue that I realised its possibly macabre image – that of preparing a noose to (presumably) hang a page! However, not all solvers will see it this way, I am sure. (Try reading the sentence out to someone and ask him or her what it suggests.)

lop
Lop tree, lop more – what a thrill! – TREMOR
Well, once you appreciate what 'lop' means, you will have no problem. So 'lop' TREE and 'lop' MORE and you get TRE+MOR which is a 'thrill' (*Chambers*'s third sense of the word out of five). As it stands, the clue suggests a crazed woodsman.

lord
Proceed, Lord Rich! – GOLD
This short clue has a short combination: GO+LD=GOLD. Yes, 'gold' is not an exact synonym of 'rich', nor 'rich' of 'gold', but their overlap of identity is clear, I think.

Los Angeles
Direct fix in Los Angeles – PLAIN
'Direct' is PLAIN, 'fix' is PIN, and in this goes LA ('Los Angeles').

lose
The Hidalgo's lost love has turned up. That'll please him! – DELIGHT
An involved clue – what's the significance of the 'Hidalgo'? The answer is an anagram. Take the letters of THE HIDALGO'S – but then 'lose' from them the letter OHAS ('love has'). This gives TEHIDLG, of which the anagram is DELIGHT – and 'that'll please him'! If you tackle a *Sunday Telegraph* crossword, you must expect occasional clues like this. Compare the rather easier clue under **height**.

lose (your, his, its) **head**
Noblemen make precious things lose their head – EARLS
That is, you will get EARLS if you 'make PEARLS lose their head'.

lose heart
Diver loses heart, gets all tangled – it's dreadful – DIRE
So DIVER loses 'heart', i.e. middle letter (V), gets all tangled, i.e. is anagrammatised (DIRE), and that's 'dreadful'! So a happy issue (for the solver, anyway) out of this particular affliction.

(a) **lot** (of)
Bind a lot of corn with copper – CORD
To CORD something is to 'bind' it, and the word is made up of COR ('a lot of' CORN) and D ('copper', i.e. the old penny). Compare the clue under **diplomatic letters**.

loud
Kind of musical instrument, a loud lute – FLUTE
Which is a 'loud' (F) 'lute' (LUTE). So not a lute after all.

love
Bob in love – that's a mistake! – BOOB
BOB 'straddles' O, which is a BOOB! Compare the clue under **rebound**.

loveless
Loveless hero gets confusing clues – and he's such a strong man! – HERCULES
A 'loveless HERO' is HER (without O), and this is followed by 'confusing' or anagrammatic CLUES (CULES). And there is the 'strong man', HERCULES.

lover (before)
A special message for lover before journalists – EXPRESS
So here is an EXPRESS ('a special message' – *Chambers*'s definition) for the EX+PRESS ('journalists'). 'Before' here really goes with 'lover', but it will do no harm if it is understood as EX 'before' PRESS, since the position is correct.

low
Low ridge-top is broad heathland – MOOR
Slightly cryptically: 'low' (MOO) '*r*idge-top' (R) is MOOR.

low-down
Class has low-down on America – GENUS
A GENUS is a 'class', and it has GEN ('low-down') on US ('America'). GEN could also be used as an adjective in some clues, e.g. 'low-down hat' (GENTILE).

lower
Lower undergarment is primrose – COWSLIP
COW+SLIP = COWSLIP, which is a species of 'primrose'.

L(-shaped)
Man visits L-shaped church – CHAPEL
If we hadn't been using 'L-shaped' here, I would have clued this word, 'Man visits the Spanish church'. The elements are the same, but the cryptic definition of EL is more likely!

lubricate
About to lubricate ring – COIL
An easy 'read-through' clue, with 'about' here C.

lurk (in)
Doctor lurks in study, the devil – DEMON
As you can see, the MO 'lurks' in his DEN. Compare the clue under **moment**.

M

MacTavish
Cried like MacTavish: 'nice to see you!' – GREETED
To a Scotsman, to GREET is to weep – hence 'cried' as the definition here.

made a meal
Jack made a meal and people came to tea, the result being less all round – ABATEMENT
We have four elements here: 'Jack' (AB) 'made a meal' (ATE) and 'people' (MEN) came to 'tea' (T) – the result being ABATEMENT, or 'less all round'.

made a mistake
Umpire made a mistake, did this to rules – REFERRED
The REF ERRED and REFERRED. Normally, of course, this would be quite in order!

magazine
Picture that is in magazine – IMAGE
This IMAGE or 'picture' derives from 'that is' (IE) with 'magazine' (MAG) in.

magistrate
Magistrate a Communist? Well, looking rather shabby, anyway – DOG-EARED
DOGE A RED? Note the unexpected division (but unaltered order) of the elements in the answer.

main(ly)
Volume is mainly in stream – BOOK
A 'volume' is a BOOK, of course – but 'stream'? Oh yes, BOOK is 'mainly' or mostly in BROOK! (I was initially tempted to clue this as 'Mainstream volume' but felt this was a little too unclear.)

make a meal
Make a meal on half a tray? What a feast! – TREAT
The exclamation is not ironic – a 'feast' *is* a TREAT. In the cryptic first half of the clue, it is important to get the elements in the right order: 'make a meal' (EAT) goes 'on', i.e. follows 'half a' TRAY (TR). This would thus have to be an across clue (in a down clue 'on' would mean 'on top', 'above'). For a different kind of 'feast' (but the same TREAT), see **dug**.

make a mistake
Make a mistake and you get sent on this! – ERRAND
'Make a mistake and . . .' – ERR AND . . .

make hay
Scholars make hay – get properly thrashed – BASTED
Thus the BAS TED ('make hay'), so getting BASTED, literally 'beaten with a stick'. As it stands the clue can be taken metaphorically: 'Scholars throw things into confusion – get soundly beaten in the game'.

make notes
The fathers make notes when going by – PASSING
As we now see, the PAS SING when PASSING. The 'fathers' in the clue could be monks or just ordinary Dads.

male
A male detective – AGENT
Short and to the point – and every word significant. But compare the clue for this word under **information**.

man
Man in charge in mischievous mood – MALICE
Did you at first think the answer was MANIC ('man in charge')? Wrong number of letters, for a start! It's a little more subtle than that, actually: 'man' (MALE) 'in charge in', i.e. containing or 'straddling' IC. So MALICE is the 'mischievous mood'.

managed
Although confused, Marti managed to get the boat – TRIMARAN
MARTI, 'although confused' (i.e. TRIMA) 'managed' (RAN) to get the 'boat', TRIMARAN!

manipulate
Robbers to manipulate in bands! – BRIGANDS
In other words, the BRIGANDS are to RIG in BANDS.

man of account
Man of account has his way – he can be a joker at times! – CARD
'Man of account' or CA, has his 'way' or RD – and he can be a 'joker' or CARD. For a variation on this clue, see also **Civil Defence** or **empty**.

man of art
Can man of art enter the series? – TRAIN
A somewhat unexpected answer. The cryptic section of the clue tells you to 'enter' RA ('man of art') in TIN ('can') in order to get the TRAIN or 'series'. As always, make sure the elements interlock correctly. Compare the clue under **artist**, where we used the same 'burial' for a different idea.

man of no spirit
A man of no spirit – tipsy Scot to achieve it! – ATTAIN
And a rather devious clue here. 'A' (A) 'man of no spirit' (TT) 'tipsy Scot', i.e. anagram of IAN (AIN) to 'achieve' (ATTAIN). Note that as it stands, the clue does *not* imply that a 'tipsy Scot' is to become a teetotaller – it means that a spiritless or feeble man who happens to be a tipsy Scot is to carry out some endeavour or exploit!

man of the cloth
A man of the cloth in charge of the tea – or is he hooked on the stronger stuff? – ADDICT
A 'read-through' clue, with the elements being A+DD+IC+T.

(the) **man's**
Man's conservative account – HISTORY
Just two elements here, with the definition last – HIS TORY HISTORY. See also **blue** and **politician**.

manuscript
Main manuscript by Lock found in a sewer – SEAMSTRESS
Once again, a 'read-through', with the 'sewer' being the definition. The elements are: SEA ('main'), MS ('manuscript') and TRESS ('Lock').

Manx
Manxman joins East-West emergency inflation measure! – MAE WEST
A 'Manxman' is a MAN without a tail, or MA. He joins 'East-West' (E WEST) to get the MAE WEST which is the 'emergency inflation measure' – more precisely, an inflatable life jacket as used by American servicemen in the Second World War and so called, explains *Chambers*, 'from a supposed resemblance, when inflated, to an American actress of that name'.

Manx race
Forecaster includes the Manx race, the dog! – SETTER
In other words, the SEER ('forecaster') includes the TT ('Manx race') which is the 'dog' or SETTER.

many
Many a mile for mother – DAM
The answer perhaps might have been MAM (although presumably a cross-check of the first letter would establish whether it was or not). As it is, the word is DAM, clued as 'many' (D) 'a' (A) 'mile' (M).

March
March to a gold flower – MARIGOLD
Rather obvious perhaps – but the 'obvious' clues are often the most elusive. Here, of course, the elements are MAR ('March') I ('a') GOLD ('gold').

mariner
Mariner achieves results – TARGETS
'Mariner achieves' is obviously TAR GETS. 'Results', of course, is the definition of TARGETS (*Chambers*'s sixth sense of the word out of a total of ten given).

Marines
Tea is given to the Marines in Gateshead – very nice! – CHARMING
And now a more complex clue. 'Tea' is not the usual T but CHA (not CHAR here, you notice). So it's a 'read-through' clue: CHA is given to the RM IN G ('*G*ateshead').

married
Walk delicately when married in church! – MINCE
This clue, like the previous one, has 'in' not indicating a 'burial'. It's simply there to provide two letters of the answer. So the defini-

tion comes first ('walk delicately') then the cryptic elements in order: M ('married') IN ('in') CE ('church'). A 'read-through' again, in fact.

marry
Marry a redhead – or her mother! – MATER
Perhaps not what you were expecting? The answer is clued cryptically by the two elements MATE ('marry') and R ('redhead'), with the definition following.

marsh, marshy ground, marshy place
Paddy Marshfoot – BOG-TROTTER
One of the harder clues in this book, if only because of the off-putting brevity of the clue with its strange-sounding and unfamiliar name (apparently). Where is the definition? Indeed, *is* there a definition? There is – the first word. BOG-TROTTER is a nickname for an Irishman (check in *Chambers*, if required), hence 'Paddy', a more polite nickname for him. This is followed by the two cryptic definitions: 'marsh' (BOG) and 'foot' (TROTTER). Don't be put off by the fact that these two elements appear in a single word! Probably the indication of the number of letters in the hyphenated answer told you that something special was involved.

martyr
Public martyr consumed – STATE
The image is that of a burning at the stake, perhaps. The unexpected definition of STATE ('public') may have put you off (the adjective is intended, as in a STATE holiday). The two elements are 'martyr' (ST) and 'consumed' (ATE).

Marxist
Colour of Marxist study – REDDEN
The definition here is 'colour' (i.e. to blush or REDDEN). Then you have the two straightforward cryptic elements: RED ('Marxist') and DEN ('study').

mass (Mass)
A mass in church is the ultimate perfection – ACME
Not too hard to disentangle, really: 'a' (A) 'mass' (M) in 'church' (CE). Notice that only the 'mass' (M) goes in the CE, not the A.

massage
Rub hard, namely, massage – SCRUB
No, the RUB does not start the answer! It's the definition that comes first ('rub hard'), then the two elements: 'namely' (SC) and 'massage' (RUB).

master
Physical education master gets a respite – PEACE
Otherwise the PE ACE gets some PEACE!

material
Material increase means renewed spell of action – REPRISE
'Material' (REP) 'increase' (RISE) means 'renewed spell of action' (*Chambers*'s exact definition, incidentally) of REPRISE.

mathematical symbol
Mathematical symbol's next to 'ton' to indicate type of engine – PISTON
A 'bluff' clue, which aims to sound more technical than it is! As we see, it is simply PI'S next to TON to indicate a PISTON engine.

mature
Look closely at mature members of the nobility – PEERAGE
In other words: 'look closely at' (PEER) 'mature' (AGE) 'members of the nobility' (PEERAGE).

Mauretanian
Mauretanian soil is largely uncultivated – MOORLAND
As we can 'read through': the MOOR LAND is MOORLAND (which is 'largely uncultivated').

me
Bring the silver back to me, sport! – GAME
'Silver' is AG, which here is 'brought back', or reversed, to ME – so that a GAME is a 'sport'!

meadow
Tom returns to the meadow with his team – a mixed bunch – MOTLEY CREW
How useful 'Tom' can be. Here he returns (as MOT) to the LEY, with his CREW, forming the 'mixed bunch' or MOTLEY CREW.

meal
Rushing the meal on the cooker – TEARING
'Rushing' is the definition of TEARING. 'Meal' and 'cooker', of course, provide the two elements TEA and RING.

measure
U.S. Navy officer to measure the mark – ENSIGN
The 'U.S. Navy officer' is the answer, ENSIGN. This word is made up of EN ('measure') and SIGN ('mark'), with 'to' simply indicating 'ENSIGN' amounts 'to' EN+SIGN.

Mediterranean
River flowed to the Mediterranean – as I thought – DEEMED
'Flowed to' simply indicates 'joined' of the two elements. So the DEE 'flowed to' the MED, and that was 'as I thought', or as I DEEMED.

meet
Boy meets girl – but what an affected way to to talk! – LA-DI-DA
That '2-2-2' was a giveaway, I fear! Still, we do have 'boy meets girl' to get LAD meeting IDA, as well as the definition ('affected way to talk') to consider, so it's not quite an open and shut case.

member
If backing genuine member, it's a danger-signal – FIRE-ALARM
All is now revealed: IF 'backing' (FI) 'genuine' (REAL) 'member' (ARM) is a FIRE-ALARM or 'danger-signal'.

member of the order
Member of the order is given an order – and this will help him to keep things in order! – BROOM
The aim of the clue is to bemuse. I hope it didn't succeed, and that you got the BRO given his OM, thus getting a BROOM which will 'help him to keep things in order'!

members of
Regard as members of fraternity – RATE
It's about time we had another 'burial', and here it is in 'f*rat*ernity', with the answer defined as 'regard as'.

men
One to greet the men in harmony – AGREEMENT
Quite an involved clue, but once you have sorted out the cryptic elements and realise that 'greet' and 'men' are 'giveaway' words, you have: A+GREET, with the latter 'straddling' MEN, and the whole word being defined as 'harmony'.

meritorious order
Concerning meritorious order in capital – ROME
The tricky word here is 'in'. This is not a 'read-through' clue, but a 'burial', with 'meritorious order' (OM) 'buried' in 'concerning' (RE) to get the 'capital' or ROME. The clue should be mentally divided as follows: 'Concerning – meritorious order in – capital'.

merry
Recognise the merry bunch – NOSEGAY
Actually a 'read-through': NOSE ('recognise' – *Chambers*'s third sense of the verb out of eleven), GAY ('merry') and NOSEGAY ('bunch').

metal
Metal on metal forms a hidden obstacle – SNAG
SN (in fact 'tin') on AG ('silver') forms a SNAG or 'hidden obstacle'. Compare the clue under **tin**.

meteorological
Officer in charge of the Meteorological Body found in space – COMET
The break-down of the answer is CO ('officer in charge') and MET ('meteorological'), giving COMET, a 'body found in space'. Compare this clue with the one under **encountered**.

middle (of)
Acted dumbly with me in the middle – MIMED
That is, MIMED with ME in the MID. Consider how easily this clue could have been, 'I'm in the Mediterranean, acted dumbly'!

Middle East
Tried to get aid in the Middle East – AIMED
This is a little like the last clue and answer, with the 'burial' here being 'Middle East' (ME) in the 'aid' (AID). Again, the clue should be divided as follows: 'Tried – to get aid – in the Middle East.'

middling character
Biblical personage took middling character from the chosen people – ELITE
How about this? The 'biblical personage' is ELI, who 'took' or removed the 'middling character' (the middle letter) 'from THE', i.e. removed the H, getting TE. And there is the ELITE or 'chosen people'.

mile
Mile in the circuit, but also travelling light! – LAMP
M in the LAP, which is (or could be) a 'travelling light', in other words a LAMP. See also **legislator**.

military (man)
Transported for military exercises – RAPT
RAPT is 'transported', with the word composed of RA ('military') and PT ('exercises').

military commander
Desirable residence offered for military commander, teetotaller, mature – COTTAGE
An enjoyable clue, reading like a 'house to let' advertisement. The definition comes first, of course – is not a country COTTAGE a 'desirable residence'? Then come the elements: CO ('military commander') TT ('teetotaller') AGE ('mature').

Military Police
Obtain information from someone by backing up the Military Police – PUMP
To PUMP someone is to 'obtain information' from him. In this case the solver 'obtains his information' by 'backing UP', i.e. reversing it, and adding the 'Military Police' (MP).

mimic
Northern mimic talks through this, as it were – NAPE
'Northern' is N, 'mimic' is APE. And NAPE, says *Chambers*, as well as other dictionaries, is 'the back of the neck'. A 'northern mimic', or indeed any mimic, would be quite likely to 'talk through the back of his neck', or talk a lot of nonsense!

mincemeat
In this country festivities include really high-class mincemeat – GUATEMALA
A moment's analysis of GUATEMALA ('this country') will reveal that GALA ('festivities') includes 'really high-class' (U) and 'mincemeat', i.e. an anagram of MEAT (here, TEMA).

mine
A bit of embroidery the company put in a mine – PICOT
When you have 'the company put in a mine', you have the CO put in a PIT. This 'burial' produces the PICOT that is 'a bit of embroidery' (actually a raised knot).

mineral
Mineral the German used to get a light – TINDER
The break-down of the clue is: 'Mineral' (TIN) 'the German' (DER) 'used to get a light' (TINDER).

mining engineer
Get the vessel to the mining engineer – what a performance! – PANTOMIME
This clue works out very satisfactorily: Get the PAN TO the MIME, and you have a 'performance' or PANTOMIME.

minister
It's hell to minister to swell – DISTEND
DIS is 'hell' (in classical mythology) and TEND is 'to minister'. Both these give DISTEND, or 'swell'.

ministry
Money earned in the ministry can cause trouble – INCOMMODE
Possibly not what you were expecting. 'Money' is not the name of some kind of currency but INCOME, since the full cryptic phrase is 'money earned'. In this goes the 'ministry' or MOD, and this 'burial' gives INCOMMODE, or 'to cause trouble'.

minor
Minor church to imitate leader's first place of worship – CHAPEL

A more complex clue for this word than we had under **L(-shaped)**. The definition is not 'minor church' but 'place of worship'. We thus have a straight 'read-through' that goes as follows: 'minor church' (CH) 'to imitate' (APE) '*l*eader's first' (L) 'place of worship' (CHAPEL).

minor highway
A minor highway in another country – ABROAD
As can be seen, this is A B-ROAD ABROAD!

minus
Public vehicle is broken – minus junction – BUS
It's what's missing here that's important. 'Broken' is BUST, which 'minus junction' or without T is BUS, a 'public vehicle'. Compare the rather different clue under **cap**.

mirror
Hands swap mirror – PAWS
Once you know that 'mirror' indicates a reversal, the rest is fairly easy, since PAWS, of course, are 'hands' (as in 'Get your paws off!').

mischief-maker, mischievous kid
Where ringleader brings in mischievous kid, a real cry-baby! – WHIMPERER
A fairly involved 'burial': WHERE+R ('*r*ingleader') 'brings in', i.e. 'buries', IMP ('mischievous kid'), the result being a WHIMPERER or 'real cry-baby'!

misfortune
'Misfortune in Bed' scheduled – BILLED
Could this be the title of a film? Whatever it is, it works out as ILL in BED, which gives BILLED, or 'scheduled'. Compare the clue for this word under **editor**, which is quite different.

miss(ing)
He arranges for opera singer to miss gym workout – ORGANISER
Quite a hard clue, which may need to be read more than once before 'the penny drops'. 'He arranges' is a description of ORGANISER. The cryptic section of the clue indicates that OPERA SINGER must 'miss' or omit 'gym', i.e. PE, giving ORASINGER. This then needs a 'workout' or rearrangement as an anagram – which is ORGANISER!

Mississippi
The Queen in Mississippi is the equivalent of a ruler in North Africa – EMIR
A much easier clue. 'The Queen' is ER. With 'Mississippi' or MI in, this gives EMIR, 'a ruler in North Africa'.

Missouri
Missouri bird is native of America – MOHAWK
MO is 'Missouri', and of course a HAWK is a 'bird'. A MOHAWK, says *Chambers*, is 'an Indian of an Iroquois tribe of New York State', so a 'native of America'.

mistake
Mistake among misguided Conservatives getting to govern by fear – TERRORISE
This is a 'burial': 'mistake' (ERR) among 'misguided', i.e. anagrammatic, 'Conservatives' or TORIES (TORISE) gives 'to govern by fear', or TERRORISE.

Mister
The painter, Mister Halfgood, is a strict disciplinarian – RAMROD
That strange name should have alerted you to something cryptic. The clue is a 'read-through': 'The painter' (RA) 'Mister' (MR) 'Halfgood', i.e. half GOOD (OD), is a 'strict disciplinarian' or RAMROD. (*Chambers*'s third sense of the word of a total of three.) Compare the clue for this word under **perch**.

model
Kleenex for model kids! – TISSUE
Not an advertising slogan but a combination of a definition ('Kleenex') and two cryptic elements: 'model' (T) and 'kids' (ISSUE). The well-known trade name will surely be familiar to solvers, even though it is not in *Chambers*. (It is in most other dictionaries, however.)

modern (style)
Location of building where modern-style clothes can be found – ADDRESS
The 'read-through' order is the same as in the last clue. First the definition ('location of

building'), then the cryptic elements: 'modern style' (AD) and 'clothes' (DRESS).

Mohammad
The African country where Monsieur Mohammad comes from? – MALI
A fairly easy clue, with once again the definition followed by the two cryptic elements: 'Monsieur' (M) and 'Mohammad' (ALI).

moment
Energetic person has a moment in study – DEMON
Thus the DEMON ('energetic person') has a MO in his DEN. Compare the clue under **lurk**.

monarch
Monarch, having power, grows old – and rushes about wildly – RAMPAGES
The last three words of the clue suggest an anagram, but there is none here. The cryptic elements are: 'monarch' (R) 'power' (AMP) and 'grows old' (AGES) – and those final words, as you can see, are in fact the definition. The general image of the clue is a crazy, senile king, or some kind of 'mad monarch'.

Monday
Shakespeare character gets it coming back on Monday – TIMON
IT 'coming back' or reversed is TI, of course, and this on MON gives TIMON, the hero of Shakespeare's play *Timon of Athens*.

money
Good man brings in the money – it's just a day's work! – STINT
The 'good man' is the ST ('saint') who provides the first and last letters of the answer. He thus 'brings in' or 'straddles' the TIN or 'money', providing the STINT that is defined as 'a day's work'.

money owing
Edward has money owing – what a bore! – TEDIOUS
An easy clue, really. TED has IOUS which is TEDIOUS, or 'a bore'. No doubt you recalled the similar clue under **Edward** when solving this.

monkey
Monkey wandered around and recovered – IMPROVED
All is revealed when you see that the IMP ROVED and IMPROVED!

Monsieur
Monsieur to come back to his family saying 'Je reviens', for example – MOTTO
I hope that this clue didn't prove too complex to solve. The cryptic elements came first: 'Monsieur' (M) TO 'come back' (OT) 'to' (TO) his 'family saying' (MOTTO), with the example of a MOTTO (a French one, as befits 'Monsieur') to give additional aid. The actual French motto – whose words may be familiar from their association with a brand of perfume – means 'I return'. This, again, is perhaps appropriate for a Frenchman coming back to his family, as the clue says!

monster
Monster stayed concealed in rare flower – ORCHID
This is a minor variation on the clue for the same word under **concealed**. This time, however, the 'monster' (ORC) 'stayed concealed' (HID) *in* the flower – in the other clue he actually hid it. 'In' is meant to suggest a 'burial', but there is no 'burial' here.

monster's home
London river monster's home showing rapidity of motion – FLEETNESS
The 'London river' is the FLEET (which gave its name to Fleet Street). This, together with 'monster's home' (NESS), gives 'rapidity of motion', or FLEETNESS.

month
Almost a full month for this bird by the sea! – FULMAR
'Almost a' FULL is FUL; 'month' is MAR; a FULMAR is a seabird or 'bird by the sea'!

Morecame
'E's coming back to Morecambe – now ain't that hard to understand? – ESOTERIC
Was this clue hard to understand? ES is ''E's' OT is 'coming back' TO, Morecambe is ERIC. This all gives ESOTERIC, meaning 'hard to understand'.

more than half
More than half the Indian tribe are in town, and this is the total that can be accommodated – CAPACITY
'More than half the Indian tribe' means 'more than half' the APACHES, i.e. APAC. This is 'buried' in 'town' or CITY to give the CAPACITY, the 'total that can be accommodated'.

morning
Cried having spent the morning in writing – SCREAMED
The definition is first, here, with 'cried' giving SCREAMED. The cryptic section of the clue involves a 'burial': 'morning' (AM) in 'writing' (SCREED). I am not sure about 'spent', which has no significance for the solver. Perhaps the clue might have been more straightforward as 'Cried when writing in the morning'.

most
Fairest and most wonderful – FINEST
A clue that for once has no standard cryptic element but simply two definitions, since both 'fair' and 'wonderful' can mean FINE. The 'superlative' ending (-EST) of the answer is made clear enough by this means.

most (of), **mostly**
Mostly hard birds – all of them rapacious – HARPIES
'Mostly' HARD is HAR, 'birds' is PIES, and the two cryptic elements together make the HARPIES, who were the 'rapacious' birds of classical mythology.

mother
She's a lady of quality, and twice a mother – MADAM
This 'lady of quality', or MADAM, is 'twice a mother' since she is MA and a DAM!

Mothers Union
Holy man has Mothers Union in – it's a matter of obscene talk – SMUT
Shame on the Mothers Union! But as you can see, it's only a simple 'burial', since the 'holy man' (ST) 'has in' or 'straddles' the 'Mothers Union' (MU).

motorway
Glide smoothly in two directions up the motorway – SWIM
To SWIM, here, is to 'glide smoothly'. The word is formed from the 'two directions' (SW) and 'up', or reversing, the 'motorway' (MI).

mount(ain)
A mountain high is torn asunder here,
And then a stream of water doth appear – TORRENT
Another 'heroic couplet' (of sorts). No doubt you can see the arrangement. The 'mountain high' is the TOR which is 'torn asunder' or RENT. This makes the TORRENT or 'stream of water' that 'doth appear' when both cryptic elements are joined.

mountain lake
The mountain lake is half starting to lose its lustre – TARNISH
There are three cryptic elements here: TARN ('the mountain lake') IS ('is') and H ('*h*alf starting'). This gives TARNISH, which of a metal, for example, means 'to lose its lustre'.

mountain pass
The official formula is in favour of getting to the mountain pass – PROTOCOL
The 'official formula' is the definition of PROTOCOL, which is devised from the three elements PRO ('in favour of') TO ('to') and, of course, COL ('mountain pass').

Mr
The gunners came to Mr Shaw with the silver – what an odd assortment! – RAGBAG
An unexpected division of cryptic elements. The RA ('gunners') came to GB ('Mr Shaw', i.e. George Bernard Shaw, the playwright) with the AG ('silver'). That produced the RAGBAG or 'odd assortment'!

multitude
Multitude came to the Spanish inn – HOSTEL
Otherwise the 'multitude' (HOST) came to 'the Spanish' (EL) 'inn' (HOSTEL). Not really a difficult clue.

mum
Black mum loses her head – such perplexity! – BOTHER
Perhaps you wondered at first what the precise significance of 'loses her head' was? 'Mum' is MOTHER, who 'loses her head' to become OTHER after 'black' (B). And there is the BOTHER or 'perplexity'.

muscular twitch
Devotee has a muscular twitch – he's almost *too* enthusiastic – FANATIC
So the FAN has A TIC, which makes him a FANATIC! The word 'fan' in this sense ('devotee') is actually an abbreviation of 'fanatic' in origin, so we are really using one and the same word here. For cryptic purposes, however, this is quite in order.

musical group
Musical group sound great. Are they going to go abroad? – EMIGRATE
A cunning homophone here, with 'sound great' giving GRATE to follow the 'musical group' or EMI. To EMIGRATE, of course, is 'to go abroad'.

musicians, musical group
Member of musical group has this on the sleeve – ARMBAND
'Member' here is ARM. Followed by BAND ('musical group') this gives ARMBAND, which is worn on the sleeve. The clue was devised in the hope that 'sleeve' in this context might suggest 'gramophone record cover'.

mute
Take mute out – now make a really loud noise! – SHOUT
Quite a neat clue, in fact. You literally 'take' the two elements SH ('mute') and OUT ('out') and so 'make a really loud noise' or SHOUT! Compare the clue under **hush**.

my goodness (!)
Second letter from Ealing misdirected. My goodness, that's casual, and as a man, I'm not sure I'm going to wear it! – NEGLIGEE
A rather long clue, but one that is perhaps worth it, if only for its entertainment value. It is also fairly complex, and unfolds as follows: 'Second letter from EALING' giving ELING (i.e. minus the second letter) which is 'misdirected' or rearranged as NEGLI. To this is added GEE ('my goodness'). The rest of the clue is a punning definition: NEGLIGEE is 'casual', and since it refers to clothes worn by a woman, it needs a man to say 'I'm not sure I'm going to wear it'. ('Wear', as it stands, has the slang sense of 'put up with'.)

myself
Enter myself in run. That could be my undoing! – RUIN
A nice straightforward clue after the last rather involved one. Enter 'myself' (I) in RUN and you get RUIN, or 'undoing'.

N

name
Name or number, that's the rule – NORM
'Name or number' spells out the three elements N+OR+M (the latter being the Roman numeral for 1000), and a NORM is a 'rule'.

namely
Beetle (namely, Egyptian) – SCARAB
The SCARAB, says *Chambers*, is the dung-beetle, especially 'the sacred beetle of the ancient Egyptians'. 'Egyptian' in the clue, however, is not so much for the 'beetle' in the answer as to supply the ARAB that follows the SC ('namely'). Loosely, Arabs are the people of north Africa, including Egypt, with, in fact, the official name of Egypt being the 'Arab Republic of Egypt' and Egyptian being an Arabic language. I mention all this to support the use of 'Egyptian' in the clue to produce ARAB!

nation
The first nation to have a railway – it's quite a network – TRACERY
'Network' is clearly the definition of TRACERY, but how about the first part of the clue? This provides the cryptic elements: '*t*he first' (T) 'nation' (RACE) to have a 'railway' (RY). The clue as a whole is thus not such a 'network' after all.

national
International organisation provides national love – NATO
'National love', or NAT+O, is provided by NATO, an 'international organisation'!

naval personnel
A party for the naval personnel after tea looks very attractive – ADORNMENT
To spell it out: A DO ('a party') for the RNMEN ('naval personnel') with 'tea' after (T), gives you the ADORNMENT that 'looks very attractive'. Compare the clue under **fuss**.

navy
A commanding officer joins the navy – a real Heart of Oak – ACORN
As you can see, A CO joins the RN, giving the 'Heart of Oak' that is the ACORN. By a happy coincidence (exploited here!), 'Heart of Oak' is the name of a famous sea shanty and naval march.

Nazi troops
Famous revolutionary leader met Nazi troops on board – and they worked out their moves here – CHESSBOARD
Did this clue enable you to 'work out your moves'? The 'famous revolutionary leader' is CHE (Guevara). He met the 'Nazi troops' (SS) on BOARD (so not SS, for once – which we've just had anyway!) You 'work out your moves', of course, on a CHESSBOARD.

nearly all
On the road to this town, said the poet, you have nearly all the shoes – SANDALS
'On the road to MANDALAY' (as Kipling wrote), and the name of this town has 'nearly all' (ANDAL) of the 'shoes' that are the SANDALS of the answer.

nearly fifty
Work to nearly fifty – TOIL
A short 'read-through' clue: 'Work' is TOIL, from TO ('to') and IL ('nearly fifty', or 49). For another way of arriving at this answer, see **junction.**

necessary to
Protective cover – necessary to prevent him bleeding – THIMBLE
It's some time since we had a clue 'burial' like this. There it is, in 'preven*t him ble*eding'. This gives the THIMBLE, defined as a 'protective cover'.

neckwear
Standard neckwear for these celebratory occasions – PARTIES
'Standard' is PAR, 'neckwear' is TIES. These together make the 'celebratory occasions' or PARTIES.

never-never
Fashion leader is never-never on top of digging when installing this ornamental structure in the garden – FISHPOND
Not too obscure, I hope! '*F*ashion leader' is F; 'is' is IS; 'never-never' is HP; 'on' is ON; 'top of *d*igging' is D, and these five elements give the FISHPOND as defined in the rest of the clue.

new driver
New driver comes to a quiet part of the racecourse – LAP
Each letter of this three-letter word has its clue: L is 'new driver', A is 'a', P is 'quiet'. A LAP, of course, is 'part of the racecourse'.

news
It can be said of any member of the class – which is news to Eric – GENERIC
GENERIC, says *Chambers*, means 'applicable to any member of a group or class'. And that's basically the definition here, with the answer also cryptically clued as 'news to Eric', or GEN to ERIC. For another clue leading to this word, see **young hero**.

newsman
Diana and The Five meet newsman – maybe he did this to escape? – DIVED
As can be seen, DI and the V meet the ED, who DIVED! Admittedly, it's usually the other way round, with the interviewee wishing to escape the newsman. But doubtless this newsman was intimidated by the formidable 'Di and The Five'.

newspapers
Newspapers contain almost an inch for Lady Diana – PRINCESS
That is, the PRESS contains an INC ('almost

an INCH'). Lady Diana, the solver will hardly need reminding, became the PRINCESS of Wales (in 1981) when she married Charles, the Prince of Wales, the heir to the British throne. Compare the clue under **incorporated**.

newt
Roll over the newt – he's not right! – LEFTIST
There's a 'straddle' here: 'roll' (LIST) 'over' the 'newt' (EFT), making a LEFTIST, who is certainly 'not right'!

New Testament
Affected use of religious phrases about the New Testament – CANT
This clue is a more solemn version of the one we used for the same word under **Holy Writ**, which see, if necessary, for the two cryptic elements that combine in the answer.

New York
'A Saint in New York' is unpleasant – NASTY
This mock play, film or book title has the necessary cryptic ingredients for the answer: 'a saint' (AST) in 'New York' (NY). This makes NASTY, which is 'unpleasant'.

niche
Order for goods is in niche – INDENT
An INDENT is the same as an indenture, that is, an 'order for goods'. Here the INDENT is 'in niche', with 'niche' being DENT.

Nick
Left Nick rather drooping – LIMP
'Left' (L) 'Nick' (IMP) 'rather drooping' (LIMP). So a 'read-through' clue with the definition last.

nickel
Pinch nickel and penny! – NIP
To 'pinch' is to NIP, 'nickel' is NI, and 'penny' is P. A short and fairly easy clue.

night(-)flier
Night-flier on the staff – BATON
As you no doubt quickly spotted, 'night-flier on' gives BAT+ON, and that is the 'staff' or BATON.

nil
Two of the French get nil – DUO
Perhaps a little trickier than most clues for very short words. 'Two' here is the definition, of course, with DUO consisting of the two elements DU ('of the French') and O ('nil').

nine (9)
He'll return by the 9.5 for the city, ruined – NINEVEH
I think I might have clued this, 'He'll return *after* 9.5 . . .', since 'by' is a little ambiguous. But no doubt the compiler deliberately arranged such ambiguity! The elements, thus, are '9.5' (NINE+V) 'by' which 'HE'll return' (as EH). This gives the 'city, ruined', the definition of the Biblical city of NINEVEH. The best word in the clue is probably 'ruined', which at its face value suggests a 'broke' businessman, to the solver seems to indicate an anagram, but in actual fact turns out to be part of the correct definition of the answer!

nine-nine-nine (999)
999 to beat – in a single blow? – IMPULSE
'999' is IM, and 'beat' is PULSE, the two combining to produce the IMPULSE or 'single blow' (*Chambers*'s fifth meaning of the word, out of a total of eight.)

ninety (90)
90 in two directions followed by two double bends – that's too much! – EXCESS
The image here is of some crazy car chase or race. Analysing the answer (defined as 'too much'), we see: '90' (XC) in 'two directions' (E . . . E) followed by 'two double bends' (SS).

ninety-nine (99)
Graduates get 99, that's the standard minimum – BASIC
Put another way, the BAS get IC, which is BASIC!

no
Certain enjoyment when no plea is entered – SURE
'Enjoyment' clues PLEASURE, which with 'no PLEA entered' is SURE, or 'certain'!

no good
Typical Kentucky voice says airline is no good – TWANG
As you can see (and almost hear) a TWANG ('typical Kentucky voice') says the TWA ('airline') is NG ('no good'). The Kentucky accent is noted for its TWANG or nasal sound.

noise
A big noise in dwelling – ABIDING
There is a 'burial' here, of course, with 'noise' (DIN) in 'a big' (ABIG). The result is ABIDING, defined as 'dwelling'.

noisy, noisily
Resist the noisy one! – FACE
'Resist' defines FACE, which is cryptically clued as 'noisy' (F) 'one' (ACE). See also **star**.

non-alcoholic
To tease Albert the non-alcoholic is coarse – RIBALDRY
A 'read-through': to RIB AL the DRY is RIBALDRY (which is 'coarse').

non-drinker
A non-drinker in command? That's a tall story, in a way! – ATTIC
The first half of the clue provides the cryptic elements: A+TT+IC. An ATTIC, 'in a way' (i.e. punningly), is a 'tall story'. (Originally, as *Chambers* reminds us, an attic was not just a single skylighted room in the roof but a whole story, or storey, 'above the cornice of the main part of an elevation', the term being an architectural one.)

non-flier
Medical men gather round non-flier as he hesitates – DEMURS
So the DRS ('medical men') 'gather round' or 'straddle' the EMU ('non-flier'), as he DEMURS, or 'hesitates'. Precisely what he was hesitating to do (jump?) is left to the solver's imagination!

nonsense
Loud nonsense, hotheaded chatter – FROTH
'Loud' is F, 'nonsense' is ROT, '*h*otheaded' (as you probably suspected) is H, and the resulting FROTH is 'chatter' (*Chambers*'s second definition of three for the word).

non-U
Fat, but firm if non-U – SET
'Fat' is SUET. This becomes SET or 'firm' if it is 'non-U' or minus its U!

noon
Drinking bout – noon in bed! – BEND
No doubt one leads to the other. A BEND is a slang word for a 'drinking bout' or spree, and here it is cryptically clued as 'noon in bed', otherwise N in BED. See also **pole**.

no one
No one points to the racket – NOISE
'No one' (NOI) 'points' (SE) to the 'racket', or NOISE. Compare **north**, below.

Norfolk town
Norfolk town nearly gets a badge, but we have to disguise that – DISSEMBLE
In other words, DISS nearly gets an EMBLEM (which is EMBLE), and that gives to DISSEMBLE or 'disguise'.

norm (Norm), normal
I'm normal, Edward, I made it known – IMPARTED
A fairy easy 'read-through', once you know that 'normal' is PAR. So IM+PAR+TED = IMPARTED ('made it known').

North America(n)
Female North American red – HENNA
HEN is 'female', NA is 'North American', and HENNA, of course, is the 'red' dye or pigment so called.

north(ern)
Northern French river will provide a row – NOISE
The 'Northern' (N) 'French river' (OISE) will provide a 'row' (NOISE) rather than a 'row' in a boat! Compare **no one**, above.

Northern Ireland
Combination of Northern Ireland and Church of England is delicate – NICE
Delicate, indeed. The rather complex-sounding clue is quite a simple 'combi-

nation', as can be seen: NI+CE is NICE, defined in this sense as 'delicate'. See also **we read**.

not
String not the way to make a telephone call! – RING
STRING – but 'not the way', i.e. minus ST ('street' or 'way'), so becomes RING, defined as in the clue!

not altogether
Long-legged king not altogether annoyed – RANGY
RANGY means 'long-legged', here arrived at via 'king' (R) and 'not altogether annoyed', otherwise 'not altogether ANGRY', otherwise ANGY!

not drinking
Not drinking in time of prosperity, that's the fundamental thing – BOTTOM
'Not drinking' (TT) in 'time of prosperity' (BOOM) gives you BOTTOM, punningly defined as 'a fundamental thing'. Compare how this same word was clued under **abstainer**.

note(d)
Note insect on part of shield – CANTON
The 'note' here is C, which with 'insect' (ANT) and 'on' (ON) makes the CANTON, or 'part of the shield' (in heraldic terms).

noted orchestra
Arranged for mixed drams to go round noted orchestra – MARSHALLED
A nice image of an alcoholic rehearsal break, say. The 'burial' (or 'straddle') is rather unexpected here, with 'mixed' (i.e. anagrammatic) DRAMS 'going round' the HALLE, a 'noted orchestra'. This gives MARS-HALLE-D, defined as 'arranged'.

not entirely
Not entirely pleased over the three points, but that's just the way it turns out – HAPPENS
'Not entirely pleased' means 'not entirely HAPPY' (so HAPP). This goes over 'the three points' (ENS), making HAPPENS, which is 'just the way it turns out'.

not half
Snake makes horse rage – not half! – COBRA
The 'snake' is the COBRA, which 'makes' if you analyse it, COB ('horse') and RA ('RAGE – not half'). No doubt a snake, and especially a cobra, would indeed make a horse rage!

nothing
Smell nothing grim – ODOUR
Three significant words: a definition, and two cryptic elements (O+DOUR, or 'nothing' and 'grim'). For a different type of clue for ODOUR, see **bishop**.

nothing short of
The fearless broken by nothing short of perdition – INTREPID
'Fearless' defines INTREPID, which otherwise is cryptically clued as an anagram ('broken') of PERDITION with 'nothing short', i.e. minus O. (You could also regard the answer as an anagram of PERDITIN, thus.)

notice
2nd-class notice is not good – BAD
A nice, easy clue (I hope). '2nd-class' (B) 'notice' (AD) is 'not good' (BAD).

not in
Church dignitary not in a study – DEN
In other words DEAN with A 'not in'.

not long
Correct public relations officer not long through – PROPER
PROPER is defined as 'correct', and cryptically clued as 'public relations officer not long' (PRO, i.e. the abbreviated form) and 'through' (PER). Compare the clue for this word under **support**.

not out
Growth not out to double – INCREASE
'Growth' is INCREASE, devised from IN ('not out') and CREASE ('to double' or fold).

not quite
Anger not quite nice in tending to promote peace – IRENIC
The cryptic elements are IRE and NIC, clued as 'anger' and 'not quite NICE'. The word is

defined as 'tending to promote peace', and, of course, IRENIC can be checked in this sense in a dictionary, if necessary.

(I'm) **not sure**
River steamship? I'm not sure. What a brute! – POSSUM
Here we have PO ('river'), SS ('steamship') and UM ('I'm not sure'). These elements combine to give the 'brute' POSSUM (better known, perhaps, as the opossum).

novel
Novel vessel in this town! – NEWARK
Or, as a pun, a NEW ARK in NEWARK.

novice
Novice nearly over state of passion – LOVE
A suggestion of 'the spirit is willing, but . . .', here. 'Novice' is L, 'nearly OVER' is OVE, and that gives the 'state of passion', or LOVE.

now
Now the day is over, and he's home from work! – DAD
A clue with a touch of an evening hymn. But it actually is evening, and DAD is 'home from work', this being one of his characteristic daily roles. The first part of the clue leads to DAD as 'now' (AD) with 'day' (D) over it!

number
A pathetic number in dead-end occupation – IMPASSIVE
'Apathetic' defines IMPASSIVE, which is cryptically clued as 'number' (IV) in 'dead-end occupation' (IMPASSE).

numbers
Magazine numbers have top sales, producing these large liquid assets! – MAGNUMS
'Magazine' (MAG) 'numbers' (NUM) have 'top sales' (S, i.e. first letter of 'sales'). These elements produce the MAGNUMS which properly are large wine bottles (or bottles of wine).

O

object
Object to me coming back? What a thing! – ITEM
In other words, 'object' (IT) to ME 'coming back' or reversed (EM). This gives an ITEM or 'thing' (not the *Chambers* definition, but the common one, which is in fact in other dictionaries, such as *Collins English*).

objection
First presentations of foreign objections – DEBUTS
DEBUTS are 'first presentations' of a kind, and here they are cryptically clued as 'of foreign' (DE, the French for 'of') and 'objections' (BUTS).

obligations
Kick out the obligations, they're false – SPURIOUS
More simply, SPUR the IOUS, they're SPURIOUS! We had a somewhat different clue for this word under **acknowledgments of indebtedness**. See *Chambers* under SPUR for 'kick out', if necessary.

observe
Observe it's true (though it goes out),
Explain to me what it's about! – CONSTRUE
To 'observe' is to CON, and this is followed by 'IT'S TRUE (though IT goes out)' – in other words, by STRUE. The result is CONSTRUE, which is defined as 'explain' (with a small amount of padding to fill out the second line of this riddle-me-ree rhyme.).

obstacle
1001 and 50, and 51 obstacles – but they're quite small, if weighty – MILLIBARS
With near-rounded numbers like this, you can be sure there will be some Roman numerals in the answer. There are, of course: '1001' (MI) and '50' (L) and '51' (LI) 'obstacles' (BARS). These are the MILLIBARS that are 'quite small' (the thousandth part of a bar, in fact), but 'weighty' since they measure atmospheric pressure, i.e. the 'weight' of the atmosphere. (The 'bar' part of the word

actually derives from the Greek for 'weight', *baros*.)

obtain
Friend obtains allowances – BUDGETS
To put it another way, BUD ('friend') GETS BUDGETS.

ocean
To cause sick feeling in Aunt, 'e tosses about the ocean – NAUSEATE
The definition comes first ('to cause sick feeling'), then the cryptic section, with an anagram ('tosses about') of AUNT 'E 'straddling' the 'ocean' or SEA.

October
Devise something for a month (October) – DECOCT
No, not CONCOCT – that's too long, for a start! One of the meanings of DECOCT is 'devise', and here the word is itself 'decocted' from 'a month' (DEC) and the bracketed 'October' (OCT).

odds
The odds are on her going to Japan, maybe. That will be a real field of activity – SPHERE
That is, the SP ('odds') are on HER going E (east, or 'Japan, maybe'). One of the many meanings of SPHERE is 'field of activity'.

of course
They're animals, of course! – HORSES
Just a pun (of course).

(go) **off**
I feel a cold shiver. Lad goes off to get a sheet. That's cold, too – ICE-FLOE
One of the celebrated *Sunday Telegraph* 'doctored anagrams' again. The anagram indicator is 'shiver', and the letters for it are contained in I FEEL A COLD. However, LAD 'goes off' (i.e. these three letters drop out), so we are left with I FEECOL. This is rearranged to form ICE-FLOE, defined allusively as 'a sheet that's cold'. A good 'value for money' clue!

offence
Graduate offence – in the dock – BASIN
As can easily be seen, we have a BA SIN in the BASIN ('dock').

officer
Officer points to ice-cream! – CONE
'Officer' (CO) 'points' (NE) to 'ice-cream' (CONE). A fairly easy transformation.

offspring
A time for the ocean to bring forth her offspring – SEASON
A rather poetic clue, with the definition first, of course ('a time'), and the two elements clued as 'the ocean' (SEA) and 'her offspring' (SON), with the remaining words simply a 'link'.

of yours
Doctor of yours seems rather weary and worn – MOTHY
MO+THY ('of yours') = MOTHY, otherwise moth-eaten, or ravaged by time and care.

old
Demand and obtain old part of play – EXACT
The definition comes first, then the two elements: EX ('old') ACT ('part of play').

old Bob
Old Bob has a friend for his excursion – SALLY
The 'friend' is not SALLY, of course! 'Old Bob' is S, 'friend' is ALLY, and together they make a SALLY, or 'excursion'.

old boy
Watch the old boy start the game of tennis – OBSERVE
Which is, of course, OBSERVE the OB SERVE.

old city
Old city gentleman calling for immediate attention – URGENT.
A fairly easy 'read-through': UR ('old city') GENT ('gentleman') is URGENT, as defined.

old convict
Old convict loves the north – and this lake by the sea – LAGOON
To interpret: 'Old convict' (LAG) 'loves' (OO) 'the north' (N). *Chambers* defines a

LAGOON as 'a shallow lake, especially one near or communicating with the sea'.

old copper
Old copper craftwork for a type of weapon – DART
D ('old copper') ART ('craftwork') for a DART, which is a 'type of weapon'.

old copper coin
He values old copper coins? So right – ASSESSOR
The definition comes first ('he values'), then the three cryptic elements: 'old copper coins' (ASSES) 'so' (SO) 'right' (R).

old English
Get hep and twist round old English bridgehead – that's where you'll find the moon goddess! – PHOEBE
A longish and seemingly involved clue, but logical enough. If you get HEP and 'twist' it round 'old English bridgehead' (OE+B) you will find PHOEBE, the 'moon goddess'!

(in an) **old-fashioned** (way)
The lady 'as, in an old-fashioned way, what's very fitting – SHEATH
'The lady' is SHE, and "as, in an old-fashioned way' is ATH (i.e. HATH without its initial H). That gives a SHEATH, which could be described as 'very fitting'.

old king
Absurd old king in charge confounding ours – LUDICROUS
A straightforward 'read-through', with the definition first ('absurd'): LUD ('old king') 'in charge' (IC) 'confounding', i.e. making an anagram of OURS (ROUS).

(the) **old lady**
Old lady comes to son – he's a builder – MASON
Of course, MA comes to SON, who's a MASON. (I nearly clued this, 'The old lady's acting, James!') For quite a different clue, see **boy**.

(the) **old man**
The old man's a real brick, allowing me to go abroad – PASSPORT
In other words PA'S a SPORT! The rest of the clue, it goes without saying, describes the function of a PASSPORT.

old money
A small cubical piece – old money, that is – DIE
In this clue, it may be difficult at first glance to tell which is the cryptic section and which the definition. In fact, as we know, the definition comes first (as word for word in *Chambers*, in fact), and then the cryptic elements: 'old money' (D) 'that is' (IE).

old pence, old penny
Benefactor puts old English penny on French gold – DONOR
That is, the DONOR puts D ON OR ('French gold').

old priest
Old priest gives kiss to a king – could it be the kiss of eternal life? – ELIXIR
The four cryptic elements come first: 'old priest' (ELI) gives 'kiss' (X) to 'a' (I) 'king' (R). Then follows the allusive definition, with an ELIXIR being, as *Chambers* says, 'a liquor once supposed to have the power of indefinitely prolonging life'. There is something mystic about the image of the clue.

omen
Specify like an omen – ASSIGN
Or ASSIGN AS a SIGN.

on
A dog on the line – it makes me break out into a hot sweat – CURRY
Were you expecting this? The cryptic elements, of course, are CUR ('dog') and RY ('line'). The fact that the definition talks of a 'hot' sweat (not the usual cold one) should have alerted you to some special antic here – after all, a CURRY makes you do just that!

on board
Condescends to take work on board, apparently – STOOPS
'Condescends' defines STOOPS, and this is followed by the cryptic 'burial' (indicated by 'apparently'): 'to take work' (TO+OP) 'on board', i.e. 'buried' in S . . . S.

once
Once having tea out, get leave of absence – EXEAT
Decoding: 'once' (EX) 'having TEA out', or an anagram of it (EAT) gives EXEAT, 'leave of absence' (at a school or college, for example). There may still be some private schools where an exeat is still required for precisely this.

one
Does one member have this power? – AMP
An easy 'break-down' of elements: A+MP = AMP.

(from what) **one hears**
Students read attentively and sweat buckets, from what one hears – PORE
Notice that the actual homophone (i.e. what 'one hears') is not the answer. So here you need PORE ('read attentively'), not POUR ('sweat buckets'), which sounds like it. The confusion is perhaps compounded here by a misleading association with 'sweat pores'. (The two types of 'pore' – 'read closely' and 'sweat-gland' – have nothing in common.)

one of the family
To help like one of the family before tea – ASSIST
That is, to ASSIST 'like' (AS) 'one of the family' (SIS) before 'tea' (T).

oneself
People round oneself getting it back – that's a successful manoeuvre – NEGOTIATION
Was your solution of this clue a successful manoeuvre? There is a reasonably complex 'burial': 'people' (NATION) round 'oneself' (EGO) getting IT 'back' (TI), otherwise N – EGO+TI – ATION. The definition follows, of course.

one side of
One side of wig is soft – there's a thin piece of hair there – WISP
'One side of WIG' is W (although it could have been G), and it 'is' (IS) 'soft' (P). This WISP is 'a thin piece of hair'.

only
This mountain only a cairn? That's silly! – GORMLESS
As explained in the first half of the book, 'only' can mean that the *missing* half of a word+LESS should be written. So CAIRNGORM which is 'only a CAIRN' is GORMLESS – and that means 'silly'! If purists point out that the Cairngorms are a range of mountains, and that therefore the clue should be plural, I shall pedantically retort that this clue relates to one of the mountains in the range, which is (individually) called Cairn Gorm!

onset
Onset of cold followed by climb leads to muscular trouble – CRAMP
'Onset of cold' is C (its first letter), which followed by 'climb' (RAMP – regard the two words as verbs) leads to 'muscular trouble' or CRAMP.

on the contrary
Does she go in for high society? On the contrary – DEBUTANTE
A DEBUTANTE does not 'go in' for high society – on the contrary, she 'comes out'! (A groansome pun – but think how much more agreeable it is to solve this sort of clue than one crammed with cryptic clues. Or perhaps you prefer that?)

open(er), opening
In the present era it provides an opening – ADIT
A rare word, but one beloved of compilers (who more frequently use it in combination with other letters or elements). Here it is cryptically clued as AD ('the present era') and IT ('it'), with its definition following. Compare the clue under **translate**.

opening of play
Opening of play on Victoria's preparations for battle – ACTION STATIONS
'Victoria', of course, provides the STATION (with her apostrophe S the final S). The first half of the cryptic section consists of ACTI ('opening of play') ON ('on'). The latter half of the clue defines ACTION STATIONS.

operation
Hush – operation in store – SHOP
This clue is more subtle than it looks. 'Store' is SHOP, of course. But consider the first

half. You can take it as two cryptic elements: 'hush' (SH) and 'operation' (OP). Or else you can take it as a 'burial', with the SHOP being 'in' 'Hu*sh* – *op*eration'! Either way, you'll arrive at the correct answer.

opposite
Flower of the rush? No, quite the opposite! – TORRENT
In other words, not 'flower of the rush' but 'rush of the flower'. With 'flower' often working out as a stream or river, here is your TORRENT! Compare the clues under **flower** and **mount(ain)**.

or
One of the chosen or one who chooses – ELECTOR
Quite a neat clue. 'One of the chosen' is (one of) the ELECT, 'or' (OR) 'one who chooses', ELECTOR.

organ
Beware the loud organ! – FEAR
'Beware' is FEAR, and the cryptic elements are F ('loud') and EAR ('organ').

orient(al)
Oriental beasts figure in concise saying – EPIGRAM
Not so straightforward, maybe, if only because of the 'beasts'. These are the PIG and the RAM which follow 'oriental' (E). This makes an EPIGRAM, which is, says *Chambers*, 'any concise and pointed or sarcastic saying'.

originate (from)
Fox in each case originating from Eastern Nubia – note ears – colossal! – FENNEC
The answer can be found by 'originating' or reading the first letters of all the six words in the clue starting '*f*rom *E*astern *N*ubia . . .'. Note how the compiler has taken care over the authenticity of the information: the FENNEC is found in North Africa, where the Nubian Desert is, and it is noted for its long ears. 'In each case' seems slightly superfluous, but doubtless invites the solver to consider the importance of all the words of the clue, 'in each case'.

(the) **others**
I'm dejected, with a hundred others captured – CRESTFALLEN
Perhaps rather an unusual clue, with unexpected cryptic elements. We have 'dejected', of course, as the definition, then the rest of the clue to build up the answer: 'a hundred' (C) 'others' (REST) 'captured' (FALLEN).

other things
Five other things half hint at the heroic – VALIANT
Or 'five' (V) 'other things' (ALIA) 'half HINT' (NT) give the 'heroic' or VALIANT. Compare the clue we used for this same word under **broach**.

ouch
Salute the warrior chief . . . ouch! Is his bark worse than his bite? – BOW-WOW
Rather contrived, but here it is: 'salute' (BOW) 'the *w*arrior chief' (W, the first letter of 'warrior'), 'ouch' (OW). A BOW-WOW is a dog – whose bark could be 'worse than his bite'!

our
The sword our defence – ARMOUR
A nobly simple clue! The ARM OUR ARMOUR.

out (of)
Out of play, to be precise – EXACT
'Out of' is EX, and 'play' is ACT, which is EXACT, or 'precise'. Compare the way we clued this word under **former** and **old**.

outfit
Outfit I'd find too severe – RIGID
Add RIG ('outfit') to ID ('I'd) and you'll 'find' RIGID, which is 'too severe'.

outhouse
Pressed back up to outhouse – PUSHED
As you can see, the definition comes first ('pressed'). This is followed by the cryptic elements: 'back UP' (PU) to 'outhouse' (SHED). Compare the clue under **he would**.

out of bed
Surrey redhead out of bed – how sweet! – SYRUP
Rather obvious, but concocted from 'Surrey'

(SY) '*r*edhead' (R) and 'out of bed' (UP), the resulting SYRUP being 'sweet'.

out of work
Out-of-work policeman mislays the ends – CLOSES
A difficult clue, really. 'Out-of-work policeman' is COP minus OP, so C. This is followed by 'mislays' (LOSES) to make CLOSES, or 'ends', both treated as nouns.

outside
Dump the drunk outside the house – SHOOT
Also not too straightforward. To 'dump' can be to SHOOT, so that is the definition. A 'drunk' is a SOT, and he is 'outside', or 'straddles', the 'house' or HO. And that is the cryptic section of the clue.

outsize
Outsize tea brought to rich bird – OSTRICH
OS ('outsize') T ('tea') brought to RICH – and there's the 'bird', or OSTRICH.

outskirts
Officer comes to outskirts of Rome, then the centre – CORE
So the CO ('officer') comes to 'outskirts' (first and last letters) of ROME (RE), which gives the CORE, or 'centre'.

over
Meal about over – REPAST
A neat clue. 'Meal' is REPAST, 'about' is RE, 'over' is PAST. In other words we have the definition followed by two cryptic elements. For a more straightforward clue see **sapper(s)**.

overdraft
Challenged lawyer with overdraft – DARED
'Challenged' is the definition of DARED, which is a composition of 'lawyer' (DA) and 'overdraft' (RED).

overhead railway
Is stylish overhead railway a real one? – MODEL
'Stylish' is MOD and 'overhead railway' EL. The question mark hints at a doubt – so the MODEL is not, in fact, 'a real one' but an imitation.

overlooking
Hill overlooking the church – there's a lamp there – TORCH
The 'hill' is a TOR, and the 'church', as usual, is CH. This gives the 'lamp' or TORCH.

overture
Make open, touching overtures to her – maybe she will become one ultimately? – MOTHER
The 'overture', or inital letters, are those of '*m*ake *o*pen *t*ouching', and these (MOT) are joined to HER to make someone who may ultimately become a MOTHER if she responds to the 'overtures' and accepts the implied proposal of marriage! Compare the clue under **head over heels**.

overturn
Lorry overturned by a gate – perhaps the driver found it difficult to do this? – NAVIGATE
An 'overturned lorry' is a reversal of VAN, which is NAV. This is followed by 'a gate' (I+GATE), making NAVIGATE – which the driver may have 'found it difficult to do' in view of his overturned lorry!

owned
Owned waterway for fish – HADDOCK
An easy 'read-through' clue about someone who HAD a DOCK for HADDOCK.

Oxford Street
Oxford Street illuminations are the outstanding features – HIGHLIGHTS
One more 'read-through', with 'Oxford Street' being HIGH and 'illuminations' working out as LIGHTS. This gives HIGHLIGHTS, defined as 'outstanding features'.

oyster
As another possibility, change the oyster – ALTERNATIVE
In other words, as an ALTERNATIVE, ALTER the NATIVE.

P

page
Page and king in church – king's son, too! – PRINCE
In spite of the 'in', not a 'burial' but a straight 'read-through' clue: 'page' (P) and 'king' (R) 'in' (IN) 'church' (CE), which is a PRINCE or 'king's son'.

painter
Painter comes to Pennsylvania town, showing he has this greedy, grasping nature – RAPACITY
Another 'read-through', so that the RA ('painter') comes to PA ('Pennsylvania') CITY ('town'). The definition is of RAPACITY.

pair
Pair chosen to order men a drink – COCOA
The CO here is the commanding officer, who is 'chosen to order men'. There are a 'pair' of him (COCO) followed by 'a' (A), this producing the COCOA that is defined by the last word of the clue.

pale
First pale we see comes to the east,
And then we see the moon decrease – WANE
In this romantic couplet, the first line contains the cryptic elements ('pale' or WAN comes to the 'east' or E), and the second line the definition ('we see the moon decrease' or WANE).

papers
Officer has lots of papers – give him this to keep him cool – COMPRESS
The 'officer' (CO) has 'lots' (M, literally 1000) of 'papers' (PRESS) – so give him a COMPRESS!

parapsychology
Parapsychology in Virginia is redirected to an emperor of Rome – VESPASIAN
Otherwise ESP in VA with IS 'redirected' (as SI) and AN, giving the 'emperor of Rome', or VESPASIAN. Admittedly the clue seems a curious blend of past and present, but with ESP many unusual things are possible!

parking
Parking is all right up to a point if you can shove in like this – POKE
The elements here are P ('parking') OK ('all right') and E ('point'). The definition of POKE, of course, is 'shove in'.

Parliamentarian
One Parliamentarian is a bit of a devil – IMP
I am sure you can easily see the elements here, getting the small equation I+MP = IMP (a 'bit of a devil'). For a more whimsical clue, see **final**.

parliament(ary)
Parliament and monarch celebrate with this drink – HOCK
An easy 'read-through' here (although perhaps not so easy if you didn't know about HOC being 'parliament'). So it's HOC+K making HOCK, a 'drink' to celebrate with.

parson
Is parson upset concerning the translation? – VERSION
The reversal indicator here is 'upset', of course, applying to 'is parson' in the form IS REV. This gives VERSI, which with 'concerning' (ON) makes the VERSION or 'translation'.

part(s) (of)
Physician, heal thyself; result, in part! – HEALTHY
A neat 'burial' here ('*heal thy*self'), indicated by 'in part' and defined allusively by 'result' (i.e. if the physician heals himself, the result will be HEALTHY).

particle
Areas about gravity particles – REGIONS
This is simply a pseudo-scientific clue, giving the solver a definition ('areas') and three cryptic elements: 'about' (RE) 'gravity' (G) and 'particles' (IONS).

partly
Elizabethan architecture partly regarded as a promoter of lawlessness – ANARCH
A highly unlikely situation, if one thinks of it, but actually a ruse for offering a 'burial' ('Elizabeth*an arch*itecture') indicated by 'partly' and defined by the rest of the clue.

part of theatre
Part of theatre has central heating set up – PITCH
The definition of PITCH is 'set up' (*Chambers*'s second meaning of the word out of a total of sixteen). This is composed by the combination of PIT ('part of theatre') and CH ('central heating').

part of the Bible
He's over-zealous about a large part of the Bible – BIGOT
A BIGOT is 'over-zealous', and the word is 'about' or made up of 'large' (BIG) and 'part of the Bible' (OT).

party
Ron has a party, and chooses this music for it – RONDO
As can easily be seen, RON has a DO and chooses a RONDO for it.

pass
Pass on the mark – COLON
'Pass' is COL, which with ON makes a COLON, or punctuation 'mark'.

past
Struggle past New York – AGONY
A good example of how clue words can change their parts of speech in the answer. 'Struggle' is (probably) a verb in the clue, but a noun (AGONY) in the answer, while the first of the two cryptic elements that comprise it is a preposition in the clue ('past') but an adverb (AGO) in the answer. The other element, however, remains as a noun ('New York', or NY)!

patriarch's birthplace
An excursion to patriarch's birthplace – TOUR
Or a TOUR TO UR! The 'patriarch' in question, of course, is Abraham.

pay(ment)
Pay a penny and have something to eat – FEED
A misleadingly simple-looking clue, perhaps. 'Pay' is FEE, and 'penny' is D, this giving FEED, which is to 'have something to eat'.

peg (Peg)
Put the peg on this seat – SETTEE
Rather obvious, but a little thought may be required before you see that you need to SET the TEE on the SETTEE! For another clue leading to this answer, see **driving place**.

pelt
Pelt the ringleader as well! – FURTHER
Quite a hard clue, with 'as well' the unexpected definition. The cryptic elements are FUR ('pelt') THE ('the') and R ('*r*ingleader').

pen
Pen the French way – STYLE
'Pen' is STY, and this, followed by LE ('the French'), makes STYLE, defined as 'way'.

pence
Sixpence for a bigwig – VIP
An answer that is an abbreviation does not necessarily have to be indicated as such. Here the familiar VIP (defined as 'bigwig') is cryptically clued as 'sixpence' (VI+P).

pence once
Pence once on carpet means unsellable article – DRUG
Thus D on RUG means a DRUG (as a 'drug on the market').

penetrating
Look for pole penetrating shed – HUNT
The 'pole' here is N, and it 'penetrates' or is 'buried' in the HUT ('shed'). This gives HUNT, defined as 'look for'.

penniless
Brings into operation penniless specialists – EXERTS
First the definition, 'brings into operation', then the single cryptic section with its 'penniless specialists' or EXPERTS minus letter P!

Pennsylvania
It's quite a stretch running from one pole to another in Pennsylvania – SPAN
A SPAN is 'quite a stretch', and it is formed here by 'running from one pole to another', or expanding S . . . N to contain 'Pennsylvania', or PA.

penny
Penny on your first horse? – PONY
That is, 'penny' (P) 'on' (ON) 'your first' (Y) 'horse' (PONY). A child's 'first horse' might actually be a PONY, of course.

people
Change for people in our time – AMEND
To 'change' a thing is to AMEND it, and the word is cryptically clued by the 'burial' of 'people' (MEN) in 'our time' (AD).

perch
Creature on perch stays quite straight and still – RAMROD
The 'creature' or animal here is a RAM. He is on a 'perch' or ROD, making a RAMROD which is proverbially a thing or person that stands 'straight and still'. Compare our other clue for it under **Mister**.

perform
Perform blue dance. Do it twice! – DOUBLE
The suggestiveness of the clue is rapidly dispelled when you see that 'dance' is actually an anagram indicator! So the cryptic elements are DO ('perform') and UBLE (BLUE 'dance'). This gives DOUBLE, to 'do twice'.

perhaps
Mean well, perhaps, with the 'phone call – SPARING
There are two cryptic elements here. SPA is 'well' (qualified by 'perhaps'), and RING is the 'phone call'. The whole word SPARING is defined as 'mean'.

(a) **period**
A period to celebrate, removing all traces of the past – ERASING
Seen another way, an ERA to SING, which makes ERASING, defined in the second half of the clue.

permit(ted)
Radio operator permitted in this village – HAMLET
So a HAM is LET in the HAMLET. A straightforward clue with no 'burials' or anagrams.

per person
A penny per person for this fruit – PEACH
Once again, an easy 'read-through', with a P EACH for the PEACH!

(a) **person**
Cold person has ice-cream! – CONE
C for 'cold', with ONE being the 'person'. The result of this chilly clue is thus an 'ice-cream' or CONE. For a more heated clue leading to CONE, see **officer**.

personality
RAF man has personality that is decidedly ill-natured – ACID
The AC ('RAF man' or aircraftman) has an ID ('personality') that is thus ACID ('decidedly ill-natured').

Philadelphia
Stamp collection from Philadelphia at Cambridgeshire town – PHILATELY
The three elements here are PHIL ('Philadelphia') AT ('at') and ELY ('Cambridgeshire town'), the whole being described as 'stamp collection' (this to be understood more as 'the collecting of stamps' than 'a collection of stamps'). The rather awkward 'at' in the clue (instead of the more natural 'in') is necessitated by the use of this little word as a cryptic element.

physical education
Genuine physical education included in the change of law – REPEAL
'Genuine' is REAL, and this 'includes' or 'straddles' PE ('physical education'), giving a REPEAL or 'change of law'.

physical training
Gunners' physical training has me spellbound – RAPT
In other words the RA PT has me RAPT. Note that the apostrophe after 'gunners' plays no part in the cryptic aspect of the clue. Compare the clue under **military** (man).

piano
Piano work is quite explosive! – POP
P for 'piano' and OP for 'work' produce POP, which is 'quite explosive' (but not very). For a different sort of clue, see **this**.

piece(s)
Attack with pieces of stone – ONSET
A happy combination of definition and anagram here, with the ONSET or 'attack' being made by the 'pieces' or letters of STONE.

piece of
Piece of metal covered in powder – TALC
There's the 'burial', of course, in 'me*tal co*vered', the definition of TALC being 'powder'.

piece of wood
Lots of pieces of wood needed for this footwear – CLOGS
'Lots' is C (100 as a Roman numeral) and the 'pieces of wood' are the LOGS. Together they give the CLOGS, 'footwear' that are indeed often made of wood, or at least have a wooden sole.

piggery
Way of coming to the piggery? That's unobtrusiveness, if you like! – MODESTY
Otherwise a MODE coming to the STY, giving MODESTY, which 'if you like' (since it can be defined in different ways) is 'unobtrusiveness'.

pilot officer
Bright light reveals pilot officer in the way – SPOT
A SPOT is a 'bright light', among other things, and here it is formed by a 'pilot officer' (PO) 'buried' in the 'way' (ST).

pinch(ing)
Robber in Italian city pinching coin – TURPIN
The 'robber' is Dick TURPIN, of course, the notorious highwayman, and here he appears in the 'Italian city' of TURIN, 'pinching' or 'straddling' a 'coin' (P).

pipe
Checked the pipe outside the cupboard – REPRESSED
An apparently innocuous clue, but actually a devious one! It first defines the answer ('checked') then gives the cryptic elements – a 'pipe' (REED) 'outside' or 'straddling' the 'cupboard' (PRESS, *Chambers*'s eighth sense of the word out of a total of nineteen).

(the) **piper**
Piper goes to the Spanish doctors – PANEL
A PANEL can mean a group of 'doctors', of course. The word comprises the elements 'piper' (PAN) and 'the Spanish' (EL).

pirate
Sea leader pirate trembled! – SHOOK
'Sea leader' is S (the first letter of '*s*ea') and 'pirate' is HOOK. These together make SHOOK, or 'trembled'.

(kind of) **pistol**
Lied about pistol, resulting in discharge – DELIVERY
The clue opens with an anagram: LIED 'about'. This gives DELI, which is followed by VERY ('pistol'). The result is DELIVERY, defined as 'discharge' (as in delivering or discharging a shot).

pitch
Rough fellow has a double pitch! – TARTAR
A TARTAR is a 'rough fellow', and this one has a 'double pitch', or TAR twice!

place
Flower place, by the sound of it, is actually pygmy place! – LILLIPUT
LILLIPUT 'by the sound of it' is 'lily put' or 'flower place'. Actually, however, it is a 'pygmy place', since it was, as *Chambers* puts it, 'an imaginary country described by Swift in his *Gulliver's Travels*, inhabited by pygmies'.

place of flowers
Place of flowers hit – place of uproar! – BEDLAM
'Place of flowers' is BED, and 'hit' is LAM. The combination of the two gives BEDLAM, a 'place of uproar'.

place of retirement
Dressed – or came back to place of retirement? – ROBED
ROBED is defined as 'dressed', and cryptically clued as OR 'came back' (RO) to 'place of retirement' (BED). Compare the way we clued this word under **archbishop**.

players
Support the players in the rear! – BACKSIDE

BACK the SIDE, in other words, with the resulting BACKSIDE (not necessarily a 'rude' word, by any means) being defined as 'rear'.

(it's a) **pleasure**
Back payment results in pleasure when in the red – REFUND
A 'burial' here, as can be seen, with a REFUND, or 'back payment', being FUN ('pleasure') in the RED.

plot
Examined in favour of plot – PROBED
A 'read-through' of no great complexity: 'examined' (PROBED) 'in favour of' (PRO) 'plot' (BED). In other words, the definition followed by two cryptic elements.

Pluto
Pluto can cripple! – DISABLE
Reading the clue literally, DIS is ABLE to DISABLE!

pocket(ed)
Doctor has pocketed extravagant fee, resulting in delay – DEFER
The 'doctor' is the DR. He has 'pocketed' or 'straddled' an 'extravagant' or anagrammatic FEE (as EFE). The result is the verb 'delay', or DEFER.

poem
A poem's here, you soon will find:
To state its sense I'm disinclined – AVERSE
We had to have a couplet for this cryptic element! 'A poem's' A VERSE, of course, and the answer is defined ('disinclined') in the second line of the rhyme. ('Disinclined', incidentally, is the basic sense of AVERSE given by *Chambers*.) Compare the clue at **few**.

poet
Poet to write back to glamorous film star – BARDOT
The 'poet' is the BARD, here. After him you must 'write back' or reverse TO, giving the final name, BARDOT, of the 'glamorous film star'. (She need not have been 'glamorous', but the adjective helps to make the definition more specific.)

point
The fat gives point to decorations – OBESE
'Fat' is OBESE, of course, with the word cryptically clued as 'point' (E) 'given' or added to 'decorations' (OBES).

pointless
Pointless poem on 'Last Ship' ceremony – POMP
Not too cryptic a clue, I hope. A 'pointless' POEM is one without E, so POM. This has 'Last Shi*p*', otherwise the last letter of 'ship' (P), to make POMP, defined as 'ceremony'.

pole (Pole)
Pole in bed, subject to tension – BEND
Here the 'Pole' is N. He is in BED, making the verb BEND, defined (exactly as in *Chambers*) as 'subject to tension'. For another type of 'bedtime' clue for this word, see **noon**.

police group
Control police group on points – POSSESS
To POSSESS is here defined as 'control', with the cryptic elements being 'police group' (POSSE) with 'points' on (SS).

police(men), police department
Ran to the police rank – RANCID
RAN to the CID gives RANCID, which is 'rank'!

politician
The life story of his politician – HISTORY
Or, of course, the HISTORY of HIS TORY. Compare the clues under **blue** and **man's**.

poor actor
Poor actor gets imitation bed – HAMMOCK
Or, of course, the HAM gets a MOCK HAMMOCK.

popular
Teach popular class – INFORM
Three significant words, the first the definition (to 'teach' is to INFORM) and the other two the cryptic elements ('popular' is IN, and a 'class' is a FORM).

port
Isolated port on the east – LONE
LONE is 'isolated', and the word is made up of L ('port') ON ('on') and E ('east'). For

quite a different kind of clue leading to LONE, see **Christmas**.

portent
Surrenders position regarding portents – RESIGNS
The definition is first here ('surrenders position') and the two elements follow – 'regarding' (RE) and 'portents' (SIGNS).

posh
Posh top Scot is the fellow to live in ideal society! – UTOPIAN
First, the three cryptic elements: U ('posh') TOP ('top') and IAN ('Scot'). Then, of course, the definition, with a UTOPIAN being an inhabitant of Utopia, regarded generally as the name of a place or state of ideal perfection (based on Sir Thomas More's satire *Utopia* written in Latin, although the name is Greek for 'not a place', i.e. 'nowhere').

position
Hanger-on gets equal top position – PARASITE
A PARASITE is a 'hanger-on', often quite literally, and the word is clued cryptically by the three elements 'equal' (PAR) 'top' (A) and 'position' (SITE).

possessed
Chief cook possessed sort of fish – CHAD
'Chief *c*ook' denotes the first letter of 'cook'. This C is followed by HAD ('possessed'), making the fish known as a CHAD.

post office
Put forward a plan in favour of the Post Office for the south east – PROPOSE
The definition comes first ('put forward a plan'), and the word is then analysed as 'in favour of' (PRO) 'the Post Office' (PO) and 'the south east' (SE).

(a) **pound (£)**
Sweetmeat – I had a pound to be eaten, to tell the truth – CANDIDLY
The 'burial' here is indicated by 'to be eaten', so that 'I had a pound' (ID+L), is 'eaten' by 'sweetmeat' (CANDY). The resulting CANDIDLY is defined in the last four words of the clue.

preserve
Preserve the oriental sugar plant – CANE
To 'preserve' is to CAN, and 'oriental' is E. This makes a CANE, or 'sugar plant'.

president
Entrance of president or church leaders – PORCH
A PORCH is an 'entrance', here composed of P+OR+CH, '*p*resident OR *ch*urch leaders'. ('Leaders' relates to the first two letters of 'church' rather than to 'president'.)

(the) **press and TV**
Press and TV come to hill, and there is someone who can act as a go-between – MEDIATOR
Once you know who the MEDIA are, you can easily make them come to the TOR to make a MEDIATOR, or 'go-between'.

press association
Press association take advantage of the interval – PAUSE
Put another way, the PA USE the PAUSE.

press men
Press men return for drinks here – PUB
Just a single cryptic element and its reversal, or 'return'.

(old) **priest**
Priest is on lake, appearing to be in a state of meditation – REVERIE
The 'priest' here, of course, is the REV, and he is on 'lake' ERIE, producing a REVERIE, or 'state of meditation'. Both clue and answer have an agreeably peaceful air about them.

primate (Primate)
Primate is unknown, but this is the culminating point of his career – APEX
The 'primate' is the APE, who is 'unknown' (X), making the APEX, or 'culminating point of his career' (although an apex can be the culminating point of anything, in fact).

prime part
Remain prime part of day by the spring – DWELL
The 'prime part of *d*ay' is D, which by the WELL makes DWELL, defined as 'remain'.

prince (Prince)
Prince Andrew gets a smack on the palm – PANDY
Not necessarily *the* Prince Andrew, of course. 'Prince' gives P and 'Andrew' is ANDY. This makes a PANDY, a word defined by *Chambers* as 'a stroke on the palm as a school punishment'. (The word apparently derives from the Latin imperative *pande*, 'hold out!')

prisoner
Prisoner comes to Queen and gets beer – LAGER
Rather an easy 'read-through' clue, with the LAG coming to ER to get the LAGER.

problem
Problem account of subtropical tree – SUMAC
The 'problem' is a SUM, with the 'account' being the abbreviated AC. This gives the SUMAC, or 'subtropical tree'.

professional
Professional money-saver almost shows signs of better future – PROMISE
'Professional' is PRO, and 'money-saver almost' is MISE (which is 'almost' MISER). This gives the PROMISE as defined in the rest of the clue.

prohibit
Africans prohibit Trade Union – BANTU
BANTU, says *Chambers*, is the 'official name for African peoples of South Africa'. Here it is made up of BAN ('prohibit') and TU ('Trade Union').

promise to pay
Priest promises to pay, taking the place of the other person – VICARIOUS
So the VICAR has IOUS, and the result, VICARIOUS, means 'taking the place of another'. In fact, a VICAR was originally so called since he held authority as the substitute of another person!

promissory note
Policeman gets promissory notes in plenty – COPIOUS
A COP gets IOUS, making COPIOUS, here defined as 'in plenty'.

pronounced(ly)
Direction is pronouncedly coarse – COURSE
An easy homophone, really. 'Pronouncedly coarse' is COURSE (of course), with the word defined as 'direction'.

propeller
Noisy propeller in enclosure – ROARING
A 'propeller' in the 'enclosure' is an OAR in the RING. This makes ROARING, or 'noisy'.

prophet
Tourists observe the prophets – SIGHTSEERS
A clue that does not immediately yield an obvious defining word – is it 'tourists' or 'prophets'? In the event it is the former, so that the SIGHTSEERS SIGHT the SEERS!

protect
Girl protects duck in prison – GAOL
The 'girl' is the GAL, and the 'duck' is the O. The former 'straddles' the latter to produce the older spelling of 'prison', GAOL (as distinct from JAIL).

provided
Present provided in sports car – GIFT
A 'burial' here, of 'provided' (IF) in 'sports car' (GT). This makes a GIFT, or 'present'. (The GT of the 'sports car' stands for *gran turismo*.)

(to) **provide with weapons**
It's a moral wrong and horrific to provide with weapons – HARM
A bit of pacifist propaganda here. HARM is defined (as in *Chambers*) as 'moral wrong', and is made up of H ('horrific') and ARM ('provide with weapons').

pub(lic) house
Make hostile protest in pub bar – BARRACK
To BARRACK is to 'make hostile protest', and the word is made up of the two elements BAR ('pub') and RACK ('bar')! You doubt that RACK can be defined as 'bar'? The sense is that of the 'rack and pinion' mechanism, where the 'rack' is (quoting *Chambers*) 'a bar with teeth to work into those of a wheel, pinion, or endless screw'.

publicity man
Publicity man gets a penny as supporter – PROP
As you can see, the PRO gets a P as a PROP! For another type of clue, see **enclose**.

publicity, public notice
He stands by public notice, being the director – HEAD
The initial HE thus comprises half the answer, standing by (i.e. coming next to) AD to make the HEAD, or 'director'.

public relations
Gave earnest advice for public relations to every editor – PREACHED
'Gave earnest advice' is the definition of PREACHED, here cryptically analysed as 'public relations' (PR) 'every' (EACH) 'editor' (ED).

public transport
It was hell before public transport! – EREBUS
A satisfying clue with an unexpected answer, perhaps. 'Before' is ERE, and BUS, of course, is 'public transport'. This makes EREBUS, a poetic word of classical origin for 'hell'.

pull(ed) up
Pulled up bottom of ship, the 'Welsh Emblem' – LEEK
The reversal indicated by 'pulled up' here is that of KEEL ('bottom of ship'). This makes LEEK, defined here in the guise of a ship's name as the 'Welsh Emblem'.

pupil
Pupil gets nothing on points, so fails – LOSES
There are more 'points' than other elements in this word, but never mind. 'Pupil' is L, 'nothing' is O, and the 'points' you put on are SES. This makes LOSES, or 'fails'.

purchased
South African purchased French-style shoe – SABOT
The cryptic elements come first: 'South African' (SA) and 'purchased' (BOT). This makes the SABOT, or 'French-style shoe'.

(some) **purpose**
Right purpose of scheme? – RUSE
'Right' is R, 'purpose' is USE. Both these make a RUSE, or 'scheme'.

put in
I'm put in the French trees – LIMES
A 'burial', of course, so that I'M in 'the French' (LES), making the LIMES, 'trees'. For a variation on this clue, see **beset**.

put on
Fruit put on the heap in Ireland – LIMERICK
The 'fruit', thus, is the LIME, which goes on the 'heap' or RICK. This forms LIMERICK, the well-known Irish town that gave its name to the five-line humorous verse so called.

put out
For this reason fresh sauce has to be put out – BECAUSE
'Fresh' SAUCE is an anagram, here working out as ECAUS. 'Straddling' this ('put out') is BE, thus making BECAUSE, defined as 'for this reason'.

put together
Doctors are put together with C.O. and first wife – that's capital! – MOSCOW
That is, the MOS are 'put together' with the CO and 'first *w*ife' (W – the first letter of 'wife'), making MOSCOW – and 'that's capital'!

quarter
Three-quarters seen in outsize try in Shropshire – OSWESTRY
The 'three quarters' (here posing as rugby players) are W, E and S. They are 'seen' or 'buried' between 'outsize try', or OS TRY, making OSWESTRY, the town in Shropshire.

quarterdeck
A chase back up the starboard quarterdeck – PURSUIT
A 'chase' is a PURSUIT, here consisting of

the three elements PU ('back UP'), R ('starboard', or right) and SUIT ('quarterdeck'). See also **US.**

queen (Queen)
The Queen in Ireland – how poetic – ERIN
ER is 'the Queen', and IN is 'in', the two short elements making ERIN, the 'poetic' name of Ireland.

question
Head teacher questions the exercises – TASKS
'Head *t*eacher' is T, 'questions' is ASKS, and that makes the 'exercises', or TASKS.

queue
Leave the queue and you get over it – QUIT
Not such an easy clue! The sole defining word is 'leave'. The rest of the clue contains the cryptic elements: 'queue' (Q) and 'you' (U) 'get over' or join IT.

quick
Quick arrival in this part of London – but surely not in this? – BARROW
'Quick arrival' is ARR, the abbreviation of 'arrival'. This is 'buried' in BOW, a 'part of London', making a BARROW, which although it has London associations (as a street-barrow) is hardly a speedy means of transport!

(a) **quid**
Up-to-the-minute subject provided for a quid – TOPICAL
What initially may look like a difficult clue is in fact a relatively simple 'read-through'. The definition comes first ('up-to-the-minute'), then the three cryptic elements: 'subject' (TOPIC), 'a' (A) and 'quid' (L).

quiet(ly)
Praised and clapped after a very quiet beginning – LAUDED
'Praised' defines LAUDED, which 'after a very quiet beginning', i.e. after APP, would be APPLAUDED, or 'clapped'.

R

rabbit
Want something nice for tea? Pick a rabbit – CREAM BUN
A CREAM BUN is 'something nice for tea', cryptically clued or defined as 'pick' (CREAM) and 'rabbit' (BUN).

raced
Head boy raced for the cereal – BRAN
Not the way for the head boy to behave, of course. But it does give us the elements we need for the 'cereal' or BRAN: 'head *b*oy' (B) and 'raced' (RAN).

race(s)
Old injury in the race results in a fight – BATTLE
Yes, 'race' you can see (TT), and 'fight' (BATTLE), but 'old injury'? By process of deduction, this must be BALE. Let's check this in *Chambers*: 'evil, injury, mischief (*arch.*)'. So there's the confirmation we need, with the '(*arch.*)' indicating an archaic or old meaning (which survives in the word 'baleful'). Such a dictionary check can always be used when an unfamiliar or suspect word or element appears in the answer.

racket
Stanley has a racket and is prepared to play if needed – STAND-IN
As you can see, STAN has a DIN ('racket'), which if differently divided makes a STAND-IN, someone who is 'prepared to play if needed'.

radical
Radical oriental gets in – the grass! – REED
'Radical' is RED, which when an 'oriental' (E) 'gets in' becomes REED, or 'grass'. At its face value in the clue, 'grass' can be taken to be the slang term for an informer (this is in *Chambers*, if needed).

radio-telephone
Palace officer has top use of radio-telephone – COURT
Only the 'palace' is needed for the defining word. The remainder of the clue provides the

cryptic elements: 'officer' (CO), 'top *u*se' (U) and 'radio-telephone' (RT).

RAF information
RAF information has an attempt to name rank – GENTRY
Thus, GEN has a TRY at naming the GENTRY, who are people holding the social 'rank' of gentleman (see *Chambers*).

railway
Wait for sailor by railway – TARRY
TARRY is 'wait', the definition. The word is made up of the 'sailor' (TAR) and the 'railway' (RY).

railways
Railways are all right going east – but don't travel if in this state! – BROKE
The cryptic elements come first: BR ('railways') are OK ('all right') going E ('east'). This is followed by the allusive definition: a traveller will not – or should not – get far if he is BROKE! (If 'in this state' led you to think of an American state, then that's a bonus for the wily compiler!)

raise
In which one drives with raised whip – GOLF
This is a down clue, so anything 'raised' will be a reversal. So sure enough one does 'drive' in GOLF, which as a word is FLOG ('whip') 'raised'.

ramble
Be fond of a ramble after tea – especially if it leads to this! – TREASURE TROVE
To 'be fond of' is to TREASURE. 'Tea' is T, after which is 'ramble' (ROVE). This all leads to TREASURE TROVE, a desirable outcome of a ramble after tea.

range
Examine the range for a trial drive – TEST RUN
Quite simply, TEST the RUN for a TEST RUN!

rate
Girl has the superior rate in the first game, really bounding along! – GALUMPHING
A longish word, with no less than five cryptic elements: GAL ('girl'), U ('superior'), MPH ('rate'), IN ('in') and G ('first *g*ame'). To GALUMPH (the word was coined by Lewis Carroll) is, according to *Chambers*, 'to march along boundingly and exultantly'.

read
Short read before tea – SCANT
SCANT is 'short', SCAN is 'read', T is 'tea'. Short and sweet! (Compare **insect** and **tilt**.)

rear admiral
Fancy headwear – a rear admiral puts it on upside-down! – TIARA
The 'fancy headwear' is the TIARA. And 'a rear admiral' (ARA) puts IT on 'upside down', i.e. is preceded by TI.

rebound
Blunder that can rebound without effect! – BOOB
A simple palindrome, indicated by 'rebound' (in this case 'without effect' as an optional extra). Do you prefer this clue for BOOB, or the one under **love**, for example?

receiver
It would seem to be a very quiet receiver – APPEAR
'A very quiet receiver' is (cryptically) A PP EAR. As a word, APPEAR is defined as 'would seem to be'.

recipe
Curry and fish recipe? – SKATER
That's right: John 'Curry', the SKATER! The word is also cryptically clued as 'fish' (SKATE) 'recipe' (R).

record
A record: the scholar, although confused, has all the letters! – ALPHABET
Not a very easy clue, perhaps. 'A' (A), 'record' (LP), 'the scholar, although confused' (THE BA, anagrammatised as HABET) – those are the cryptic elements. Together, they make the ALPHABET, which 'has all the letters'. Compare **flutter**.

record player
A record player is brought to us on a table. It's easily positioned – ADJUSTABLE
A nice, innocent-looking clue. The first half,

however, bristles with cryptic elements: 'a record-player' (ADJ) is brought to 'us' (US) on a 'table' (TABLE). And that is defined as 'easily positioned'.

recover(y)
Doctor is close to recovery, to all intents and purposes – MORALLY
Thus the MO is close to a RALLY, giving MORALLY, one sense of which (given in *Chambers*) actually is 'to all intents and purposes' – as in 'The attempt is morally bound to fail'.

reduce
Reduce weight by dropping a point if you want to get to holiday isle – WIGHT
Otherwise 'reduce' WEIGHT (by losing the 'point' E) if you want to get the Isle of WIGHT, where many go for their holidays.

reduced
First fireman reduced the stream of water – FLOW
'First *f*ireman' is F, the first letter of 'fireman'. This is followed by 'reduced', which is LOW. F+LOW = FLOW, a 'stream of water'.

referee
Referee has employment but is rejected as worthless – REFUSE
The REF has USE – and this makes REFUSE, which is 'rejected as worthless'. Compare this clue with the one under **again**.

reflect
Stops to reflect: maybe they mean he's caught a disease? – SPOTS
Quite an enjoyable clue. If you 'reflect' or reverse STOPS you get SPOTS, the consequence of which could be as suggested in the rest of the clue!

refusal
Refusal made to Hill with his debts – he's got a bad reputation – NOTORIOUS
'Hill' here, of course, is not the name of a person, but a disguised 'hill' or TOR. The 'refusal' is NO, and his 'debts' are IOUS, giving NO+TOR+IOUS, otherwise NOTORIOUS, defined as having 'a bad reputation'.

refuse
It's commonsense to refuse us – NOUS
NOUS is 'commonsense', saying NO to US!

regiment
I think highly of the announcement that I'm returning to the regiment – ADMIRE
'Think highly of' defines ADMIRE. The rest of the clue provides the cryptic elements: AD ('the announcement, that'), MI (I'M 'returning' or reversing) and RE ('the regiment').

regulation
First fire regulation has an error – FLAW
'First *f*ire' is the first letter of 'fire' (F), and this is followed by 'regulation' (LAW). The result is FLAW, 'an error'.

reject
Girl rejected love on this romantic lake! – LAGOON
'Girl rejected' is a reversal of GAL (LAG). This is followed by 'love on' (O+ON), making the 'romantic lake' or LAGOON. Compare this clue and the one under **old convict**.

relative
Canon is a relative eccentric – BROCARD
Probably the cryptic elements will come more readily than the definition here: 'relative' is BRO, and 'eccentric' is CARD. This makes BROCARD, which, according to *Chambers*, is 'an elementary law or principle: a canon: a gibe'. So there's the 'canon'.

relatives, relations
Relatives in jog? You must be pulling my leg! – JOKING
KIN in JOG? You must be JOKING!

religious
Religious novice is unyielding and he travels to the holy place – PILGRIM
The analysis here is: 'religious' (PI) 'novice' (L) is 'unyielding' (GRIM). This makes a PILGRIM, who 'travels to the holy place'.

religious books
Translate the religious books – using this, no doubt, in America! – TROT
Most British solvers will probably need to check this sense. They should be able to work the cryptic elements, though: TR ('trans-

late') and OT ('religious books'). This gives TROT, one of whose meanings (in *Chambers*) is 'a crib, literal translation (*U.S.*)'.

reluctantly
Reluctantly came to love top secretary – thanks to him? – EROS
'Reluctantly' is ER, 'love' is O, and 'top secretary' is S. EROS, of course, is the god of love, who may have caused this gradual enamourment.

remainder
Forcibly twists the remainder in two directions – WRESTS
WRESTS is defined as 'forcibly twists', and cryptically clued as 'the remainder' (REST) in 'two directions', i.e. 'buried' in W . . . S.

remains
Crushed remains in the Mediterranean – MASHED
The 'burial' in this clue is ASH ('remains') in the MED ('Mediterranean'). This gives MASHED, which is 'crushed'.

remove (from)
Remove her from the boat, it's not in the right direction – WRY
In other words, remove HER from the WHERRY (a type of boat) and you get WRY, which according to *Chambers*'s second definition is 'not in the right direction'.

rent
Rent trouble creates storm – TORNADO
'Rent' is TORN, and 'trouble' is ADO. This creates a TORNADO, or 'storm'. For a variation on this clue, see **bother**.

repeat
Turn repeated by this disco dancer, maybe – GOGO
A 'turn' is a GO, which 'repeated' gives the GOGO dancer – who, 'maybe', is a 'disco dancer'. ('Maybe', since not necessarily.)

representative
Not so wild about rising representative, one who meddles – TAMPERER
'Not so wild' is TAMER, which is 'about', or 'straddles', 'rising representative', i.e. a reversal of REP. This gives TAM-PER-ER which is a TAMPERER, 'one who meddles'.

Republicans
Officer half admits Republicans to be prime lawbreakers – ADMIRAL
An admittedly difficult clue. The definition, at first sight, appears to be 'lawbreakers'. It is in fact 'officer', however, leading to ADMIRAL. The word is cryptically composed as follows: 'half ADMITS' (ADM), 'Republicans' (IRA) and 'prime *l*awbreakers', i.e. the first letter of 'lawbreakers' (L).

resort
Resort has church and plenty of room – SPACE
A much easier clue! 'Resort' (SPA) has 'church' (CE), which gives SPACE, or 'plenty of room'. For quite a different clue for this same word, see **crack pilot**.

resting
Ann resting, being refused permission to take part – BANNED
'Ann resting' is ANN in BED, the two elements combining as BANNED, otherwise 'refused permission to take part'.

rest in peace
Holy man to rest in peace in this long piece of land – STRIP
A gentle 'read-through' here: 'Holy man' (ST) to 'rest in peace' (RIP) gives a 'long piece of land' (STRIP).

restrict
Shame restricts the king, so putting him under stress – STRAIN
The 'shame' is the STAIN, which 'restricts' or 'straddles' the 'king' (R). The result is a STRAIN, or 'stress'.

retire
Star retires and quits for unworthy motives — RATS
A reversal ('retires') of STAR, of course. The definition of RATS is based on that in *Chambers* ('to desert or change sides for unworthy motives'). For another way of using this same reversal, see the clue under **from east to west**.

retreat
Oriental retreat is garden of paradise – EDEN
Just an 'oriental' (E) 'retreat' (DEN) – EDEN, the 'garden of paradise'. Compare the clue under **Eddy**.

(in) **retrospect**
Criminal organisation in America, if a misnomer, in retrospect – MAFIA
The helpful definition and reversed 'burial' indicator ('in retrospect') doubtless soon enabled you to spot MAFIA – backwards, of course – in 'Americ*a, if a m*isnomer'.

return
Went astray but returned to Communist – ERRED
The definition comes first ('went astray'), then the cryptic section, with 'RE-turned' (ER) to 'Communist' (RED). The lost sheep is thus back in the fold.

reveal
Permission to reveal the total advance? – ALLOWING
'Permission' is ALLOWING, and this 'reveals' the two elements ALL and OWING, clued as 'total' and 'advance'.

reverse
Is Mr Rees a man of vision? No, the reverse – SEER
You probably smelt a rat when you saw the unfamiliar 'Mr Rees'. And indeed, simply 'reverse' his name of REES and you get the 'man of vision', or SEER.

revert
Field reverts to soft gold colour – YELLOW
A 'field' that 'reverts' is a LEY that reverses (YEL); 'soft' here is LOW (as in 'soft music'). The combination of the two makes YELLOW, here defined as 'gold colour' (as in *Chambers*'s second definition of the word, 'of the colour of gold').

revolution(ary), revolver
Pain for a revolutionary – ACHE
A 'read-through', with 'pain' meaning ACHE and this word itself consisting of A ('a') and CHE ('revolutionary', i.e. Che Guevara).

revolutionary leader
Revolutionary leader and leaders of Kazakh Army were once the secret police – CHEKA
It's the same 'revolutionary leader' as in the next clue – CHE). He was a real revolutionary leader, but the 'leaders' of the 'Kazakh Army' are simply the first letters of those words – KA. This gives the CHEKA, the former name (or one of them) of the Russian secret police. The word is in *Chambers*, as well as other dictionaries, so can be checked (no pun intended), if required.

revolver
Revolver not affected with recoil – ROTOR
Obviously just a palindrome. It is 'not affected with recoil' since it 'runs' in both directions. (A gun, that has recoil, operates in only one direction.) Compare the clue under **backwards or forwards**.

Rex
A shout of approval for Rex taking a paddle – ROAR
'Rex' is R, and 'taking a paddle' (an OAR) he makes a ROAR!

Rhode Island
Annoyed Edward in Rhode Island – TRIED
Yes, TRIED in the sense of 'annoyed'. 'Edward' here is TED and he 'straddles' 'Rhode Island' (RI) – in other words RI is 'in' TED.

right
Regular journey right out east – ROUTE
Just another 'read-through', with ROUTE ('regular journey') cryptically clued as 'right' (R) 'out' (OUT) 'east' (E).

right hand
Star almost caught in right hand – that's tough! – STARCH
Although all the letters of STAR are in the answer, we only need the first three to begin with, since 'star almost' is STA. Then we have 'caught' (C) 'in' 'right hand' (RH) – and that's where the R comes from. The definition of the completed word, STARCH, is 'tough', since starch is a substance that makes clothes stiff or 'tough'. In other words, 'tough' means 'stiff', and 'stiff' means 'starch'!

right-winger
Gesture by a right-winger indicates he's made his mark – SIGNATORY
As can easily be seen, a SIGN by A TORY makes a SIGNATORY, this being one who has signed or 'made his mark'.

ring
Silver ring gone – AGO
A teasingly brief clue – but actually quite a straightforward one. 'Silver' is AG, 'ring' is O, and 'gone', the definition, is AGO.

rise
Discharge young lady rising – wrong hour for it – BEDTIME
'Rise' indicates a reversal, and here we have two: 'discharge' is EMIT ('rising' as TIME) and 'young lady' is DEB (reversed as BED). And since they are 'rising', we have these elements the other way round in the finished answer – EMITDEB becomes BEDTIME. And that is the 'wrong hour' for 'rising'!

river
River circles Maidenhead – it covers quite an area – ROOM
Possibly 'circles' led you to think of a 'burial'? In fact they are OO, joining 'river' (R) and 'Maidenhead' (M). This gives you the necessary ROOM, which 'covers quite an area'. For the record, the only river that anything like 'circles Maidenhead' is the nearby Thames – but although it passes south of the town in a broad sweep, it does at least 'cover quite an area'.

road
Calls off road works – STOPS
STOPS is defined as 'calls off', and cryptically consists of ST ('road') and OPS ('works'). For a different type of clue that leads to this word, see **amidships**.

rock
Drill through soft rock – BORE
A clue rather like the last, with the definition ('drill through') followed by two cryptic elements of BORE: B ('soft') and ORE ('rock'). For a rather similar clue, see **base metal**.

rodent
Bring rodent to her? Why, of course! – RATHER
'Bring RAT to HER?' RATHER!

Rolls Royce
A Rolls Royce like a tapestry! – ARRAS
Quite an effective advertising slogan, perhaps, suggesting good design, colour and softness! In fact, though, the 'tapestry' is a definition of ARRAS, which is cryptically clued as 'a' (A) 'Rolls Royce' (RR) 'like' (AS).

(of) **Rome, Roman**
Do your best in Rome at forty, say? – EXCEL
The Roman numeral 'forty' is XL. 'Say' this, and you EXCEL, or 'do your best'.

roof
Cosily plain under a tin roof – SNUGLY
In this down clue, 'plain' (UGLY) will come 'under', i.e. after, the 'tin' roof (SN, the symbol for tin). This gives SNUGLY, defined as 'cosily'.

Roosevelt
Cricket stroke of Roosevelt I've followed – OFF-DRIVE
A direct 'read-through' clue, with the definition first ('cricket stroke'), then the cryptic section: OF FDR ('Roosevelt') I'VE. This gives the OFF-DRIVE you need.

(a) **rose-red city**
A poet's composition concerns a rose-red city and a king's honour – PETRARCH
PETRARCH was a famous Italian 'poet', whose 'composition' here is the cryptic one that follows this definition: 'a rose-red city' (PETRA) and a 'king's' (R) 'honour' (CH). The apostrophe S after 'king' is not to be entered in the answer: it simply denotes that the 'honour' belongs to the 'king'.

rotter
Rotter, for example, comes back to beg – CADGE
It's not the 'rotter' or CAD who 'comes back', but 'for example' (EG). We thus have CAD+GE, which is to CADGE or 'beg'.

round
Clear round the swan – OPEN
'Clear' is the definition of OPEN, which consists of the cryptic elements O ('round') and PEN ('swan'). The clue could have been 'clear round the writer', but this is rather unimaginative.

row
Soft row to Duncansby Head for somewhere to stay and eat – BOARD
In this clue the cryptic elements came first: 'Soft' (B) 'row' (OAR) to '*D*uncansby Head', i.e. its first letter (D). This gives BOARD, 'somewhere to stay and eat'.

rowers
French rowers had this on board – FREIGHT
No actual French word is involved here, simply the abbreviation for 'French' (FR). This is followed by 'rowers' (EIGHT) giving FREIGHT, which is normally thought of as goods or cargo 'on board'.

Roy
Roy went first – and we all crowded together – HUDDLED
In other words, HUDD LED, and we all HUDDLED.

Royal Artillery
Gold box for Royal Artillery band – ORCHESTRA
As we can spell it out: 'Gold' (OR) 'box' (CHEST) for 'Royal Artillery' (RA) – 'band', ORCHESTRA.

Royal Engineers
Concern about the Royal Engineers – CARE
CARE is 'concern', here cryptically divided into CA ('about') and RE ('Royal Engineers').

Royal Society
Tea at the Royal Society was a sad display – TEARS
So, TEA at the RS led to TEARS, a 'sad display'!

rubbish
Object to having to step awkwardly round rubbish – PROTEST
We have a 'straddle' and an anagram here. The anagram is STEP 'awkwardly'. This changes to PEST and it 'straddles' ('round') 'rubbish' or ROT. This gives P-ROT-EST or PROTEST, defined as 'object to'.

Rugby (Union)
Rugby Union: Poles v. Scots. But these other players weren't involved! – RUSSIANS
The first half of this clue is purely cryptic: 'Rugby Union' (RU) 'Poles' (SS) v. 'Scots' (IANS). This produces RUSSIANS, who were not involved in this particular match!

ruler
Religious ruler going out to sea – PIER
PI is 'religious', and ER (Queen Elizabeth) is a 'ruler'. The two elements make a PIER, which 'goes out to sea'.

runner
Runner cut off north – SEVERN
But the SEVERN is not a northern river, you say? I fear in a cryptic clue this can be of little consequence. A runner could cut off the north, though, couldn't he? That means that the clue has good and logical face value in itself. In any case, the 'runner' here is a punning definition of a river. In this case we know it is the river SEVERN, since its cryptic elements are SEVER ('cut off') and N ('north').

run over
Run over joke – GAG
A palindrome, indicated by 'run over' and defined by 'joke'. What does the clue mean in itself? Well you could 'run over' a joke from one page to the next, or from one column to the next in a magazine, or you could simply rehearse it, 'run over' it.

Russian
Russian army engineers come to Poles to put things right – REDRESS
Otherwise 'Russian' (RED) 'army engineers' (RE) come to 'Poles' (SS) – to 'put things right', REDRESS.

Russian city
Russian city in the north is very imposing – GRAND
As it stands, the clue appears to refer to

Leningrad, once the imposing St Petersburg. But this being a cryptic clue, we must not take things at their face value! What we have is 'Russian city' (GRAD) with 'north' (N) in, making GRAND, or 'imposing'.

Russian fighter, Russian jet
Russian jet went east. I was inside and got a bad headache! – MIGRAINE
'Russian jet' (MIG) 'went' (RAN) 'east' (E). 'I' was inside, and got a MIGRAINE!

S

's
King Arthur's garden – GARTH
The apostrophe S here indicates a 'burial', that as it were 'belongs to' the previous words. So the GARTH or 'garden' can be found in 'Kin*g Arth*ur'.

Sabbath
Place of retirement for head of cathedral to linger around the Sabbath – CLOISTER
'Head of *c*athedral' is C (its first letter). This is followed by to 'linger' (LOITER) which is 'round', or 'straddles', the 'Sabbath' (S). Thus we can build up C+LOI-S-TER, which gives the CLOISTER, a 'place of retirement'.

(it's) **said**
When everything's said, they're boring instruments – AWLS
That is if ALL'S ('everything's) 'said', you get AWLS, which are 'boring instruments'!

sailor
Sailor to get first taste of pie – TART
A 'sailor' is a TAR. Here he gets 'first *t*aste' (T) to make the TART, or 'pie'.

sailors
Rushed to the sailors – TORN
To 'rush' is to 'tear' (hurry), so here 'rushed' is TORN. The word contains the cryptic elements TO ('to') and RN ('sailors').

saint
Bird fabled to bring babies for saint or king – STORK
Perhaps rather an easy clue, since one hardly needs the cryptic elements! Still, they are there (and with luck may mislead for a while) as 'saint' (ST), 'or' (OR) and 'king' (K).

salesman
Salesman gets a hat – he's inclined to creep! – REPTILE
Which is to say that the REP gets a TILE (a slang word for hat). The resulting REPTILE is 'inclined to creep'. 'Inclined' need not necessarily be understood punningly (in the sense 'leaning downwards', 'bending').

(the) **same** (again)
Deal out the same again to the French – DOLE
To DOLE is to 'deal out', here comprising the cryptic elements DO ('the same again') and LE ('the French').

(the) **same whichever way you look at it**
The affair is the same whichever way you look at it – DEED
DEED is defined as 'affair', and as a word it is a palindrome – 'the same whichever way you look at it'.

sanctimonious
Flier is a sanctimonious character! – PILOT
Thus the PILOT is a PI LOT ('lot' as in a 'bad lot').

sapper(s)
Sapper's previous meal – REPAST
'Sappers' are the RE, 'previous' is PAST. Together they make the REPAST, or 'meal'. Compare the clue under **over**.

Sarah
Almost worship Sarah? This is a real set-back! – REVERSAL
Put another way, 'almost REVERE SAL', with 'almost REVERE' working out at REVER. This gives a REVERSAL, or 'a real set-back'.

sat
Rendered favourable – where wounded pride's sat – PREDISPOSED
A rather enigmatic clue, at first glance, but evolving as a definition ('rendered favourable') and two cryptic elements. The latter

are 'wounded PRIDE'S', or an anagram of PRIDES, and 'sat', POSED. This produces PREDISPOSED, as defined in the first two words of the clue.

Saturday
Fine silk to be worn on Saturday at home? – SATIN
'Fine silk' is SATIN. This is cryptically clued as 'Saturday' (SAT) 'at home' (IN).

say
Czech writer's record, say? – COUNTERFOIL
A punning homophone, indicated by 'say'. So a 'Czech writer's record' can be said as a 'cheque-writer's record', which defines a COUNTERFOIL. Note that the homophone can be either in the answer or, as here, in the clue.

scan
To scan the seat, say, is a rather far-fetched idea – CONCEIT
To 'scan' is to CON, and 'seat, say' (by way of a homophone, as in the last clue above) is CEIT. In combination, the elements make a CONCEIT, which is a 'far-fetched idea'.

scholar
Scholar gets blue in error – it's just childish nonsense! – BAUBLE
The image is that of an Oxford or Cambridge 'scholar' wrongly awarded a 'blue', or sporting honour. Cryptically, the clue tells of a BA with a BLUE that is 'in error', as an anagram. This works out as a BAUBLE, defined as 'childish nonsense'.

schoolwork
Rewarded in advance for schoolwork assistance – PREPAID
PREPAID is 'rewarded in advance'. The word can also be divided as PREP ('schoolwork') and AID ('assistance'), as its two cryptic elements.

science
Science, chemistry and history heads give zero (o) to pupil here – SCHOOL
Did you 'read through' this clue? It tells how '*s*cience, *c*hemistry and *h*istory heads', i.e. the opening letters of 'science', 'chemistry' and 'history' (SCH) give 'zero (o)' (OO) to 'pupil' (L). They do so 'here', referring to the general setting of the clue, which is clearly a SCHOOL (as already cryptically clued). Note the device of 'zero (o)' to produce OO.

scoop out
Slimy creatures have scooped out shell and ears with the top cut off – SLUGS
The 'slimy creatures' are the SLUGS. They consist of a 'scooped out SHELL' (i.e. SL, or SHELL with the middle letters missing) and 'ears with the top cut off' (i.e. LUGS with the L cut off, so – UGS). Thus SL+UGS = SLUGS.

score
Not sure, love, about score – shall we see the copy? – XEROX
A rather devious clue. 'Not sure' is ER and 'love' is O. Together (ERO) these have 'score' (XX) 'about' them, making XEROX, which could be a type of 'copy'. The word is in *Chambers* as a trade name, as well as in most other dictionaries, and doubtless solvers will have heard of it anyway.

(in) **Scotland**
Gloomy lake in Scotland reveals its secret nature – DARKNESS
'Gloomy' is DARK, and the 'lake in Scotland' is (Loch) NESS. This makes DARKNESS, the 'secret nature' of something or someone.

Scot(sman), (the) **'Scotsman'**
Like Scotsmen from the East? – ASIANS
ASIANS are 'from the East'. Cryptically they are 'like Scotsmen', or AS IANS!

Scot's own
First great Scot's own victory – GAIN
'First great' is G, which with 'Scot's own' (AIN) makes GAIN, a 'victory'.

Scottish chimney
Scottish chimney in some quarters was associated with the Gorbals – SLUMS
A 'Scottish chimney' is a LUM. In 'some quarters' (S . . . S) this makes SLUMS, once a feature of the suburbs of Glasgow.

Scottish eye
To an upper-class quiet Scottish eye it's a top cover-up! – TOUPEE
The cryptic elements come first: TO ('to') U ('upper-class') P ('quiet') EE ('Scottish eye'). The punning definition follows, with a 'top cover-up' being a TOUPEE, that is, a wig or hairpiece. Compare the different angle we used for this word under **socially acceptable**.

scoundrel
The scoundrel's on the railway – this'll make it hot for him! – CURRY
The 'scoundrel' is a CUR who is on the 'railway' (RY). The two elements combine as CURRY, which will 'make it hot for him'. We had a similar clue, which compare, under **on**.

script
Lawyer and his script puts an obstacle in the way – DAMS
The 'lawyer' is a DA, who with his 'script', or MS, 'puts an obstacle in the way', or DAMS.

sea
Soldiers by the sea are left behind – REMAIN
A fairly easy clue, in which the 'soldiers' (RE) by the 'sea' (MAIN) 'are left behind', or REMAIN.

sea-monster
'Sea-monster in West: Queen to supply cathedral city!' – WORCESTER
This emergency news headline tells of an ORC in the WEST, with ER ('Queen') supplying the 'cathedral city', or WORCESTER. In fact, 'supply' is really an instruction to the solver, who needs to 'supply' ER to make the complete word.

(a) **second**
Make fun of the second to finish? – SEND UP
To SEND UP is to 'make fun of', with the cryptic constituents of the clue being 'second' (S) and 'finish' (END UP).

second class
Second-class or fifth-class – it's all a wearisome matter – BORE
If 'second-class' is B, then 'fifth-class' is E. The two are linked, as in the clue, by OR. This makes a BORE, a 'wearisome matter'. The word is a versatile one when it comes to a cryptic clue. Compare, for example, our clues for it under **base metal** and **rock**.

secretary
Encourage secretary on the day – SECOND
To SECOND is to 'encourage', and this definition is followed by the three cryptic elements of the answer: SEC ('secretary'), ON ('on') and D ('day').

see
See order appear, but not distinctly – LOOM
A 'read-through' clue: 'see' (LO) 'order' (OM) 'appear, but not distinctly' (LOOM).

seer
Porter half converts seer before the king – CONVEYER
A CONVEYER is a 'porter' (of a kind). This definition is followed by the cryptic elements: 'half CONVERTS' (CONV), 'seer' (EYE) and 'king' (R).

seize
Men seize a middle position – MEAN
There's a 'straddle' here: MEN 'seize' A, giving a MEAN or 'middle position'.

self
Help oneself! – AID
A tricky but actually perfectly fair clue. 'Help' defines AID. 'Oneself' should be regarded as two words to provide the two cryptic elements of the word: 'one' (A) and 'self' (ID).

self-help
Jack's a learner getting involved in self-help slowly! – TARDILY
'Jack' is the usual TAR. He is followed by a 'learner' (L) 'getting involved', i.e. 'buried', in 'self-help' (DIY). The result is defined in the last word of the clue – 'slowly', TARDILY.

semi(-)
Experienced semi-nude up river – UNDERWENT
'Experienced' is the definition of the answer,

UNDERWENT. This is cryptically clued as 'semi-NUDE up', i.e. NU reversed (UN) and 'river' (DERWENT).

send round, send back
It's sent back twice to an Italian artist – TITIAN
As can be seen, IT is 'sent back twice' (TI+TI) to AN, this giving the 'Italian artist', TITIAN.

sergeant-major
Well turned-out sergeant-major has skill – SMART
We can virtually substitute the answer and its elements to restate the clue like this: SMART SM has ART.

servant
Servant thanks Ray – MANTA
MAN ('servant')+TA ('thanks') = MANTA ('Ray'), the manta being a large ray (fish). For a variation on this, see **volunteers**.

service
State service – MASS
An apparently uninformative clue, but one which on consideration reveals two definitions: 'state' (MASS, i.e. the state of Massachusetts) and 'service' (MASS, the church service). Compare the clue for this same word under **church service**.

service charge
Initial calculation of service charge for drink – COFFEE
'Initial *c*alculation' means the first letter of 'calculation' (C), to which are added 'of' (OF) and 'service charge' (FEE) for the answer of COFFEE, defined as 'drink'.

serviceman
Serviceman on foot is present – GIFT
A pun here on the two senses of 'present', so that GIFT is made up of 'serviceman' (GI) and 'foot' (FT). For another way of getting GIFT, see **provided**.

set
Huge soldier set on worker – GIANT
Another GI here ('soldier'), this time 'set' or placed on a 'worker' (ANT). That produces GIANT, defined in the first word of the clue.

setback
Minor setback is a drag – DRAW
A 'minor' here is a WARD, who when 'set back' or reversed turns into DRAW, defined as 'drag'!

settled
Settled on hill next to the Italian coastal district – LITTORAL
A fairly complex clue cryptically, but defined quite clearly. 'Settled' is LIT, which is 'on' or next to 'hill' or TOR, which in turn is 'next' (not 'next to') 'to the Italian' (AL, Italian for 'to the'). These three elements combine to make LITTORAL, otherwise 'coastal district'.

seven (7)
Begs attendance of seven sent hither and thither . . . – INVITES
'Hither and thither' indicates an anagram (not a palindrome, incidentally). The letters involved are VII ('seven') and SENT, which are rearranged as INVITES, defined as 'begs attendance'.

several
Several advertisements for the boys – LADS
'Several' here is L (Roman numeral 50), and it is followed by ADS ('advertisements'). That makes LADS, or 'boys'.

sex appeal
Former lover had sex appeal – that's a departure! – EXIT
The EX ('former lover') had IT – which is an EXIT, or 'departure'!

she
She comes to tea and has a drink – CLARET
'She' here is CLARE, who comes to T ('tea') for a CLARET.

sheep
Man-made port for sheep? Yes, back that! – RAMSEY
The clue opens with a wince-making punning definition, for the 'Man-made port' is the port of RAMSEY on the Isle of Man! This is cryptically made up of RAM ('sheep') and SEY ('YES, back that'). I fear compilers get up to such things at times.

shelter
Shelter for old coppers by northern town – LEEDS
A 'shelter' is a LEE, here with DS ('old coppers') to make the 'northern town' of LEEDS.

(the) **sheriff's men**
Sheriff's men brought ship to Eddie – what got into them? – POSSESSED
So the POSSE ('sheriff's men') brought the SS ('ship') to ED ('Eddie'). What POSSESSED them?

shilling
Cut off with a shilling on the summit? – STOP
To STOP something is (or can be) to 'cut it off'. The word consists of the elements S ('shilling') and TOP ('summit'). For quite a different clue leading to this word, see **good man**.

ship
A ship is the first to come to aid – ASSIST
Four cryptic elements here: 'A' (A) 'ship' (SS) 'is' (IS) '*t*he first', or first letter of 'the' (T). All this 'comes to' ASSIST, or 'aid'.

shivery
Remus's buddy is shivery in the east with this poor player – BRER RABBIT
The definition comes first, with 'Remus's buddy' being BRER RABBIT (the companion of Uncle Remus in the children's stories by the American writer J. C. Harris). He is also clued cryptically, with 'shivery in the east' being E ('east') in BRR ('shivery'), and a RABBIT, being, as *Chambers* nicely defines it, 'a persistent but incomparably inferior player at lawn-tennis or other game'.

short, shorten, shortly
Stop short by first Woolworth's store – STOW
'STOP short' is STO (i.e. 'short' of one letter). This is followed by 'first *W*oolworth's' (W), making STOW, or 'store'.

short week-end
A short week-end for Eddie, the contemptible fellow! – WEED
That is, a WE for ED, who is a WEED.

show
Get at steward going North to show pomp – STATE
This is obviously a down clue, with 'going North' indicating a reversal of the 'burial' that is in turn indicated by 'show'. Reading backwards in 'G*et at s*teward', therefore, we can pick out STATE, defined as 'pomp'. Compare the clues under **dined, gallery, martyr** and **station**.

shut in
Shut in since noon in American armed forces HQ – PENTAGON
The cryptic elements come first: 'Shut in' (PENT) 'since' (AGO) 'noon' (N). This makes the PENTAGON defined in the rest of the clue.

shut up(!)
Twaddle until shut up – TOSH
'Twaddle' is TOSH, divided cryptically as TO ('until') and SH ('shut up').

shy
Creature is shy and backs up – COYPU
'Shy' is COY, 'backs UP' is a reversal of UP, i.e. PU, and the two elements together make the 'creature', a COYPU.

sick(ly)
Puny beginner is sick, so takes one of these – PILL
The '*p*uny beginner' is the first letter of 'puny' (P). This is followed by ILL ('sick') to make the PILL that he takes.

Sid
If Sid turns up with an accusation he'll get this and be out of a job – DISCHARGE
'SID turns up', predictably, is DIS. With an 'accusation' or CHARGE this produces DISCHARGE, which a person gets when he leaves his job.

side
Side is in and French go out – EXIT
Quite a complex little clue. 'Side' is XI, which goes 'in' ET ('and French', or the French for 'and'). This makes EXIT, or 'go out'. A somewhat easier clue for this word was given under **sex appeal**.

side of the stage
Jump from a height on the side of the stage – HOP
The only definition of HOP is 'jump'. The rest of the clue is devoted to the cryptic elements: 'height' gives H (the abbreviation for 'height') and 'side of the stage' gives OP.

Sidney [compare **Sid**]
At home, Sidney has several debts. How underhand! – INSIDIOUS
When IN ('at home'), SID has several IOUS. That is INSIDIOUS, or 'underhand'. (*Chambers*'s fourth definition of the word out of six.)

sign
Sign on the line for a collection of books – LIBRARY
'Sign' is LIBRA here, and it is on the 'line' (RY) to make the LIBRARY as defined.

sign of nerves
The graduate with a sign of nerves concerning a thesis – THEMATIC
'The graduate' is THE MA. He has a 'sign of nerves' or TIC, making THEMATIC, which relates to a theme or 'thesis'.

silence
Silence for the organ – cut! – SHEAR
A frustrated film-maker? Anyway, the clue produces SH ('silence') for the EAR ('organ'), making SHEAR, or 'cut'.

silver
Attacker got silver and gold out of work unit returning to ship – AGGRESSOR
Rather a complex clue. 'Silver' is AG, and 'gold' is OR. These are 'out of', or 'straddle', 'work unit returning', i.e. a reversal of ERG, next to 'ship' (SS). We thus have the four elements arranged as follows: AG+GRE+SS+OR. This makes the AGGRESSOR, defined as 'attacker'.

since
Agreement since despatched – ASSENT
'Agreement' defines ASSENT, cryptically divided into AS ('since') and SENT ('despatched'). Compare the clues at **Anglo-Saxon** and **despatched**.

sing
Sing softly for despondency! – HUMP
HUM is 'sing', P is 'softly', and the resulting HUMP is 'despondency'.

(a) **single**
A hundred singles deserves some ice-creams! – CONES
Whether the 'singles' are runs in cricket or pop records doesn't really matter, so long as we get the 'hundred' (C) 'singles' (ONES) for the 'ice-creams' (CONES)!

(a) **single performance**
Single performance is a real caper – it's great! – GIGANTIC
The 'single performance' is the GIG, and the 'real caper', of course, the ANTIC. This results in GIGANTIC, which is 'great'.

singular(ly)
Scoundrels singularly are poison! – CURARE
'Scoundrels singularly' works out as CUR ('singular CURS'). Together with ARE, given in the clue, this makes the 'poison' known as CURARE.

sit
About to sit and have a rest – REPOSE
'About' is RE, 'sit' is POSE, and in the resulting REPOSE you 'have a rest'!

sited in
Tree sited in Whitechapel mews – ELM
A fairly obvious 'burial', the ELM being 'sited' in 'Whitechap*el m*ews'.

six (6)
Six small stations offer good views – VISTAS
Quite a nice 'read-through' clue, with its 'six' (VI) 'small stations' (STAS) offering 'good views', or VISTAS. ('Small' since an abbreviation is required.)

sleep
Lively bird has sleep in – JAZZY
An unexpected answer? Well, 'lively' is JAZZY, the 'bird' is a JAY, and this has a 'sleep' or ZZ in!

slice (of)
Slice of plum pudding is just a piece of stodge – LUMP

Not so palatable, therefore. 'Slice of' indicates a 'burial', here seen in 'p*lum p*udding'. The resulting LUMP is the 'piece of stodge'.

sloth
Sloth in the navy is regarded as very wet! – RAIN
'Sloth' is AI, here 'buried' in the 'navy' (RN), making RAIN, 'regarded as very wet'. For a clue with a similar tack – but not quite the same – see **first rate**.

small
Small soft cry – WEEP
A nice, neat clue. 'Small' is WEE, 'soft' is P, and the WEEP they make is 'cry'.

small girl
Tunic that small girl has on? – CHITON
Read the clue like this: 'Small girl' (CHIT) has ON – 'tunic, that'. A CHITON can be checked in a dictionary to see if it is the word you want: *Chambers* reassures you that it is 'the ancient Greek tunic'.

smell
Boy goes back to smell – he's such a lout! – YOBBO
'BOY goes back' is a reversal, producing YOB. This links up with BO ('smell') to make the required YOBBO, or 'lout'. (It is thought that the actual word 'yob' or 'yobbo' in fact originated as back slang for 'boy', thus proving that cryptic elements exist outside crosswords in the language as a whole.)

snake
Snake in the arena making a grating sound – RASPING
Otherwise, ASP in the RING is RASPING.

snare
Line nearly snares birds – LINNETS
'LINE nearly' is LIN ('nearly' LINE), and 'snares' is NETS. The two elements produce the 'birds', or LINNETS.

snooker ball
Gets down snooker ball, then miscues – REDUCES
'Gets down' defines REDUCES, which is cryptically clued as 'snooker ball' (RED) and 'misCUES' (UCES, an anagram of CUES).

soar
Pilots are soaring there, nearly, but at a greater distance – FARTHER
The 'soaring pilots' are the reversed RAF (FAR). This, together with 'THERE, nearly' (THER), makes FARTHER, defined in the second half of the clue.

socialist
Socialist newspaper is a cause of infuriation – RED RAG
A self-explanatory clue and answer, really, with the first two words regarded as the cryptic section.

socially acceptable
Socially acceptable in top quarters to wear one of these? – TOUPEE
'Top quarters' clues TOP+EE. In this goes 'socially acceptable' (U), making the TOUPEE that we clued rather differently under **Scottish eye**.

social worker
Petty officer gives mixed gin to social worker – how touching! – POIGNANT
As can be seen in this 'read-through' clue, the 'petty officer' (PO) gives a 'mixed GIN' (IGN) to the 'social worker' (ANT), which is POIGNANT, or 'touching'.

society
Society standards as determined by philosopher – SOCRATES
'Society' (SOC) 'standards' (RATES), the two cryptic elements, are 'determined' or established here by the 'philosopher', SOCRATES.

society-girl
Society-girl, when broadcasting, looks very elegant – DEBONAIR
So the DEB, when ON AIR, looks DEBONAIR!

soft(ly)
One soft drink and one beer? Just one light beer, please – PALE ALE
This bar order breaks down as one 'soft' (P) 'drink' (ALE) and one 'beer' (ALE), making a PALE ALE, or 'light beer'.

so it's said
Nearly a trial, so it's said – ABOUT
'Nearly' is ABOUT, which is 'said' or pronounced as A BOUT, defined as 'a trial' (i.e. a trial of strength or a contest, as a boxing 'bout'). Note that the answer is the original definition ('nearly'), not the one said to be its homophone ('a trial'). Compare the clue at **top grade**.

soldier
Soldier on the road has the French belt – GIRDLE
Three cryptic elements: GI ('soldier') on the RD ('road') has LE ('the French'), making GIRDLE, 'belt'.

(some) **soldiers**
The soldiers have a meal, apparently just a salad – RADISH
The RA have a DISH, a RADISH, eaten as 'a salad'. Compare the clue for this word that we gave under **give**.

some (of), (to) **some extent**
Bought some fine wool (originally from Sydney) – BOTANY
The first two words clue the cryptic elements: 'bought' (BOT) and 'some' (ANY). The rest of the clue defines the answer, apparently punningly, but actually correctly, since BOTANY is a 'fine wool' that originally came from Botany Bay, the settlement at what is now Sydney, Australia.

somersault
Pat somersaults over Edward – she's got him weighed up! – TAPED
PAT 'somersaults', becoming TAP, over ED, making TAPED, or 'weighed up'.

something
Forget to order something – OMIT
'Forget,' or OMIT, can be analysed as 'order' (OM) and 'something' (IT).

something of
Drink is something of a special effect – ALE
An easy 'burial', with the ALE seen in 'spec*ial e*ffect'. Compare the clue under **continental**.

some time
Spasm found some time in toe – THROE
'Some time' (HR) in TOE produces a THROE, or 'spasm'.

song
Write a soft song for the dramatic production – PLAY
A 'soft song' is a P LAY, making the 'dramatic production', or PLAY.

sort of square
Old musical instrument has a back that ends in a sort of square – SPINET
The definition is first, of course, with the word consisting of a 'back' (SPINE) ending in a 'sort of square' (T).

so to speak
You are (so to speak) taken out and enticed – LURED
A homophone and a 'burial' here. 'You are (so to speak)' is UR. This is 'buried' in LED ('taken') which is 'out' or outside it. This produces L – UR – ED, or LURED, which is 'enticed'.

sound (like), **sound as if**
Rent paid sounds as if it should be greater – HIRE
HIRE ('price paid') 'sounds as if' it should be HIGHER, of course, or 'greater'.

sound unit
Sound unit applied to a number of small things in this church building – BELFRY
The 'sound unit' is the BEL, which is 'applied to' or joins the FRY ('number of small things'), making the BELFRY, or 'church building'.

source (of)
Matthew is source of envy of his friend at work – MATE
'Matthew' is MAT, and the 'source of *e*nvy', its first letter, is E. These make his MATE, or 'friend at work'. For a different sort of clue for this word, see **devour**.

south(ern)
Tales of the southern party members – STORIES
Quite a straightforward 'read-through' with

the definition first. Thus the STORIES or 'tales' are of the 'southern' (S) 'party members' (TORIES).

South Africa(n)
Father Christmas is social worker in South Africa! – SANTA
Thus, 'Father Christmas' (SANTA) is a 'social worker' (ANT) in 'South Africa' (SA). Quite an agreeable 'burial'.

South America(n)
The great story of South America and the leaders of the Grand Alliance – SAGA
The 'great story' is the SAGA, consisting of SA ('South America') and the 'leaders', or first letters, of '*G*rand *A*lliance' (GA). The actual Grand Alliance, which led to the War of Spanish Succession, was a European affair and hardly related to South America. But perhaps some enterprising historian has now found a link between the two, and written their 'great story'!

South Dakota
I'd return to South Dakota, and almost die in torment, but I scorned this – DISDAINED
An involved clue, but one that can nevertheless be correctly interpreted if carefully 'read through'. I'D 'return' is DI, followed by 'South Dakota' (SD). Then comes 'AND almost' (AN) with DIE, both 'in torment', i.e. as an anagram. This works out as AINED. Putting all these together, we get DI+SD+AINED, or DISDAINED, defined as 'scorned'. Luckily not all cryptic clues are as tortuous as this.

south-east
Plant in the south-east is identical – SESAME
Not a 'burial' but a 'read-through' clue: 'Plant' (SESAME) is in the 'south-east' (SE) and is 'identical' (SAME). The word could have been clued as a 'burial', like this, say: 'Plant in the south-east is identical, in a way'. This is more involved, of course, as we now have 'in the south-east', i.e. in S . . . E, 'identical, in a way', i.e. an anagram of SAME (working out as ESAM). In other words, we are using different letters of the word for the cryptic elements.

sovereign
Sovereign is in bed having lost blood – BLED
A much easier clue than the last one. 'Sovereign' (L) is in BED, which gives us 'lost blood', or BLED. But perhaps the clue is harder than the one under **at rest**.

Spaniard
Beautiful boy a Spaniard is following – ADONIS
'A Spaniard' is A DON, which with IS following becomes ADONIS. He, of course, was the 'beautiful boy', or one of them, of classical mythology.

Spanish, in Spain
This bend is called the Spanish Bow – ELBOW
An ELBOW is a 'bend', and the word can be cryptically divided as 'the Spanish' (EL) 'bow' (BOW). Rather an obvious clue, but a fair one.

spasm
Article on spasms and grotesque acts – ANTICS
'Grotesque acts' is not an anagram of ACTS! It is in fact the definition of ANTICS, which is cryptically clued as 'article' (AN) on 'spasms' (TICS).

speak
Choose to speak for the voters – ELECTORATE
To 'choose' is to ELECT, and to 'speak' here is to ORATE. Combine the two and you have the ELECTORATE, or 'voters'.

speakeasy
Sight speakeasy at this point – SITE
What we need here is a homophone of 'sight' defined as 'this point'. The answer, of course, is SITE.

spectacles
Thanks to non-drinker, who has spectacles on, we can see the military display – TATTOO
Presumably because he is clear-headed and sharp-sighted enough to reveal it to us! 'Thanks' is TA, 'non-drinker' is TT, and the 'spectacles', therefore, are the OO. This all

links up to give the TATTOO or 'military display'.

speed
Speed round, speed! It's urgent! – DESPERATE
Quite a nice clue, with the first 'speed' involved in an anagram ('SPEED round') and the second simply a cryptic definition ('speed' = RATE). So we finish up with DESPERATE, which is 'urgent'.

sphere
Here's a sphere 'twixt west and east;
Here's misfortune, at the least – WOE
A kind of witch's prophecy of doom, perhaps. The 'sphere' is O, and it is ''twixt west and east' or between W and E. That produces WOE, which is 'misfortune' – 'at the least', since it could be even worse than this.

spirit
Notes officer taking spirit – such propriety! – DECORUM
The 'notes' here, which could be almost anything, are D and E. They are followed by the 'officer' (CO) who 'takes' or adds 'spirit' (RUM). All together that spells out DECORUM, which is 'propriety'.

spiteful woman
Spiteful women holding it back still – STATIC
'Spiteful women' are CATS. If they 'hold' IT they 'straddle' it, producing CITATS. But all this is 'back' or reversed, as STATIC – and that is defined as 'still'!

split
Communion cup chap split with girl – CHALICE
The definition is clearly first, since a 'communion cup' is a CHALICE. The word is then divided into two cryptic elements: CH is 'CHAP split', i.e. half the word CHAP, and ALICE, of course, is the 'girl'.

spoil
Spoil mixed grain after end of voyage, so have this spread instead – MARGARINE
To 'spoil' is to MAR, and 'mixed GRAIN' denotes an anagram, working out here as GARIN. After this comes 'end of voyag*e*', i.e. its last letter, which is E. The result is MARGARINE, which is a 'spread'.

spot (in)
Bird spotted in the wilderness – ERNE
A 'burial' of course, with the 'bird' being the ERNE (or eagle) seen in 'the wild*erne*ss'. Note that if the clue had been 'Bird spotted in Ulster nest', there are *two* possible 'birds' for the four-letter answer! You would have to wait for cross-checking letters to establish which. See **ensconce** for more on this.

spouse
'E's bringing it back to 'is spouse, that's my guess – ESTIMATE
''E's' is ES, bringing IT back (TI) to ''is spouse' (MATE). The result is the ESTIMATE, which is my 'guess'. The ''is' is not significant, but simply matches the initial ''E's'.

spring
Spring line is out of the true for this springer! – SPANIEL
There is no connection between the two 'springs' here, which are simply intended to bemuse the poor solver. The 'spring' is the SPA, and the 'LINE out of the true' is an anagram, working out as NIEL. This makes the 'springer', or SPANIEL. There is in fact such a thing as a 'spring line', *Webster* defining it as 'an imaginary line connecting the two opposite points at which the curve of an arch or vault begins'. Presumably this could be 'out of the true' for some kind of 'springer' (someone who fixes springs?). I mention all this to prove that the clue does have some kind of reasonable face value!

sprite
Sprite is here, and here my endless verse,
So see the time in which I run my course – PERIOD
Another 'magic rhyme'. In this one, 'sprite' translates as PERI, and 'endless verse' as OD ('endless' ODE). The combination is PERIOD, which in *Chambers*'s first definition is 'the time in which anything runs its course'.

spy
Graduate engages spy, reveals reddish purple colour – MAGENTA
MA thus 'engages' or 'straddles' AGENT, getting MAGENTA, the 'reddish purple colour' of the clue.

(kind of) **square**
We came to a kind of square where there was much evidence of the recent rain – WET
A mock Swiftian clue, leading via WE and T ('WE came to a kind of square') to WET, as prosily described in the words that follow. Compare **sort of square** for a completely different type of clue.

staff
Reminder for first member of probationary staff – PROD
A PROD is a 'reminder', here comprising the cryptic clues 'first member of *p*robationary (P) and 'staff' (ROD).

staff officer
The Staff Officer and the German Channel – SOUND
The 'Staff Officer' is the SO of the word, with the UND clued by 'and the German'. This makes the SOUND, or 'Channel'. (There is an English Channel but, as far as I am aware, no strait anywhere known as a German Channel. Perhaps the Staff Officer was proposing one.)

stamped addressed envelope
First form in stamped addressed envelope will be quite secure – SAFE
'First *f*orm' is the first letter of 'form' (F). This in an SAE makes SAFE, or 'quite secure'.

stand
Girl gets dress at right stand – ROBERTA
Why ROBERTA, who is obviously the 'girl'? Well, she gets a 'dress' (ROBE) 'at right' (AT+R) 'stand', i.e. a reversal of ATR, which is RTA. And ROBE+RTA = ROBERTA! This same girl appeared slightly differently under **dress**.

standard
Standard is high in this ecclesiastical district – PARISH
Just a 'read-through' clue: 'standard' (PAR) 'is' (IS) 'high' (H) in this PARISH, or 'ecclesiastical district'.

star
Look towards fellow star – FACE
To FACE is to 'look towards', with the answer clued cryptically as 'fellow' (F) 'star' (ACE).

starboard
Floating mass of logs – starboard, aft – RAFT
The definition comes first, then the two nautical cryptic clues – 'starboard' (R), 'aft' (AFT).

start (of), **starter**
Fascination could start to hurt – CHARM
CHARM is 'fascination', clued cryptically as '*c*ould start', i.e. first letter of 'could' (C), and 'to hurt' (HARM). Compare two other clues for this word under **daily** and **working woman**.

start of an era
Start of an era in strange metal – RADIUM
'Start of an era' is ADI. This goes in 'strange' (RUM) to produce the 'metal', RADIUM.

state
State I've come to is huge – MASSIVE
The 'state' here is Massachusetts or MASS, which with I'VE makes MASSIVE, or 'huge'.

station
Condition of station at Carlisle end – STATE
Just now we used 'state' for our clue, now we are clueing it in turn. Here, defined as 'condition', it is made up of the elements ST ('station'), AT ('at') and E ('Carlisl*e* end', or the last letter of 'Carlisle'). Compare the four other ways we clued this word, under **dined**, **gallery**, **martyr** and **show**.

staunch
Senior youth leaders staunch in their method – SYSTEM
'*S*enior *y*outh leaders' are the first letters of 'senior' and 'youth' (SY). They are followed by 'staunch', understood as STEM, to make the SYSTEM, or 'method'.

steal
Steal the Spanish metal – NICKEL
To 'steal' is to NICK, and 'the Spanish' is EL. This makes NICKEL, which is the 'metal' you need.

steamer, steamship
Headland gives bearings to steamer – NESS
In fact, all four letters of the answer are 'bearings', but here we need only two of them, NE. These go to the 'steamer' (SS) to make the 'headland', or NESS.

stern
Half of MS is written in stern eastern language – TAMIL
'Half of MS' is just M. This is 'written' or 'buried' in 'stern', which is TAIL. The result is TAMIL, an 'eastern language'. Note that 'eastern', for once, does not lead to E but is part of the definition.

stick
Gold stick raised above officer – MAJOR
Read the clue with breaks as follows: 'Gold – stick raised above – officer'. This gives OR with 'stick' (JAM) reversed over it, and the end product is the 'officer', MAJOR.

stitch
Stitch back to start of trimming – in this direction? – WEST
'Stitch back' is a reversal of SEW, i.e. WES. This is joined to the 'start of *t*rimming' (T) to make the 'direction', WEST.

stomach
Put peg to stomach – it goes round and round – TEETOTUM
Put TEE TO TUM for a TEETOTUM, which is a kind of top, so 'goes round and round'. Who knows, this could be an old wives' remedy for indigestion. Compare the clue we had under **hesitation**.

stop
Five stop to offer goods for sale – VEND
'Five' (V) 'stop' (END) – to 'offer goods for sale', VEND.

story
First short story is very unoriginal – STALE
'First *s*hort' is S, and 'story' is TALE. The combination is STALE, which is 'very unoriginal'.

strait
Make sudden move, trapping seaman in strait – START
The definition comes first, in 'make sudden move', then we 'trap' or 'bury' a 'seaman' (TAR) in the 'strait' (ST). And that gives the START.

strange
Strange, disorganised game, a real upheaval – RUMMAGE
'Strange' is RUM, and 'disorganised GAME' is an anagram of it – here MAGE. The result is the 'real upheaval', or RUMMAGE.

street
Style of the street is quite unpretentious – MODEST
'Style' is MODE, and 'street' is ST. Both together, these make MODEST, defined as 'quite unpretentious'.

strike
Scottish strike leads to a fight – SCRAP
You can probably see the elements: SC ('Scottish') RAP ('strike') leads to a 'fight', SCRAP.

string
The string is out – it's quite painful – GOUT
The 'string' is the usual G, which here is OUT. This makes GOUT, which is 'quite painful'.

strong(ly)
Clear, strong air – FAIR
'Clear' is the definition here (*Chambers*'s second for FAIR, out of a total of twenty-seven!), so that the cryptic elements are F ('strong') and AIR ('air').

student
Student points to shelter – LEE
An answer that could have been clued a dozen ways. Here it is simply 'student' (L) 'points' (EE) to 'shelter', the definition of LEE.

study
Study a branch of learning – if you're good, it

will be clear – CONSCIENCE
CON a SCIENCE, therefore, to have a 'clear' CONSCIENCE. Note that 'it' in the clue refers back to 'branch of learning', whereas cryptically it indicates the expected answer.

study hard
First student to study hard? Get away with you! – SCRAM
'First *s*tudent' is S, the first letter of 'student'. After this comes CRAM, 'to study hard'. The two together make SCRAM – otherwise, 'Get away with you'!

stuff
Stuff the weed into the field – PADDOCK
'Stuff the weed' is PAD the DOCK, this making a 'field', or PADDOCK.

stunning blow
Stunning blow in the manner of an Australian bear-like creature – KOALA
A 'stunning blow' is a KO, and 'in the manner of' is ALA. The two elements make a KOALA, who although normally thought of as a 'koala bear' is not properly a bear, and so has to be defined here as 'an Australian bear-like creature'.

subsequently
Great admirer I'd love subsequently – IDOLATER
An IDOLATER is a 'great admirer', and the word is clued cryptically here as 'I'd' (ID) 'love' (O) 'subsequently' (LATER).

such
Such feet are easily cut – SOFT
A fairly easy 'read-through': 'Such' (SO) 'feet' (FT) are 'easily cut', or SOFT.

(to) **suit**
A ceremony to suit a thousand – FORM
One definition of FORM is 'ceremony', and here the word is clued cryptically as 'for a thousand', or FOR M (M being the Roman numeral 1000).

sulphur
Sulphur on metal can cause irritation – SORE
S is the 'sulphur', and ORE the 'metal', both together causing an 'irritation', or SORE. For quite a different clue, see **Cupid**.

summer
Fifty summers for us to go up and down – LADDERS
L is 'fifty', and the 'summers' here are the ADDERS. The resulting LADDERS enable us 'to go up and down'.

sun
The Sun goes to Japan – exclusive! – SOLE
Not a newspaper scoop, but the 'sun' or SOL going to 'Japan', which is the east (E). This is 'exclusive', SOLE!

Sunday
Sunday for a superior meal – SUPPER
'Sunday' is S, and 'superior' is UPPER, the two making the 'meal', SUPPER.

Sunday school
Girl for the French Sunday school – LASS
The 'girl' is the LASS, of course, and she is for 'the French' (LA) 'Sunday school' (SS).

sunk (in)
Tile sunk in North Atlantic – HAT
'Tile' is a slang word for HAT, which here is 'sunk' or 'buried' in the 'Nort*h At*lantic'.

superior (to)
Looks which show that gravity is superior to weapons – GLANCES
So here 'gravity' (G) is 'superior to', i.e. comes before, the 'weapons' (LANCES), as shown in the answer defined by 'looks', GLANCES.

support(er)
It's the right thing to support the Queen – PROPER
A 'support' is a PROP, and 'the Queen' is ER. The resulting word is PROPER, defined in the first half of the clue as 'the right thing'. See **not long** for a different kind of clue.

surgeon
Crowds round physician and surgeon – MOBS
MOBS are 'crowds', with the word here cryptically clued as 'physician' (MO) and 'surgeon' (BS, i.e. Bachelor of Surgery).

surprise
Surprise regarding this timid creature – HARE
'Surprise' is HA, 'regarding' is RE, these combining as 'this timid creature', or HARE.

Surrey
Officer posted to Surrey, where he is very much at home – COSY
'Officer' (CO) 'posted to', i.e. joins 'Surrey' (SY), where he is COSY, as described.

surround
Farm vehicles surround hill crest in cases of fire – CARTRIDGES
With 'surround' indicating a 'straddle', we have the CARTS surrounding the RIDGE, which in the formation CART – RIDGE – S make the CARTRIDGES that are so-called 'cases of fire'.

Susan
Susan's half nude, the undressed kid! – SUEDE
A clue that exploits a happy coincidence to the full, for SUEDE (SUE+DE, i.e. 'Susan's half nu*de*') actually *is* 'undressed kid' as a 'straight', not punning, definition (see *Chambers*).

swallow
Woman turns and swallows one in the gangway – AISLE
No, not an ice-cream, an AISLE, for the 'woman' is ELSA, and she 'turns' (as ASLE) and 'swallows' or 'straddles' 'one' (I). An AISLE, of course, is a 'gangway'.

swear
Mean to swear when coming to mature years – AVERAGE
The defining word is 'mean', which is an AVERAGE. The cryptic components are AVER ('to swear') and AGE ('mature years' – *Chambers*'s fourth sense of the word out of twelve given).

T

(to a) **T**
To seek advice fits a diplomat to a T – CONSULT
The definition comes first ('to seek advice'), and then the two cryptic elements: the 'diplomat' (CONSUL) being 'fitted' to a T. This gives the answer, as defined, of CONSULT.

t'
Stepped on t' pole – TROD
Or, more simply, TROD on T'ROD.

tail
Change head and tail, and this rogue would be a sailor – RASCAL
Something of a cryptic classic, this clue, which appears from time to time. If the 'head and tail' of RASCAL ('rogue') are changed round, you get LASCAR, defined by *Chambers* as 'an Oriental (originally Indian) sailor'.

tailed
Officer tailed by dogs, as it happens – OCCURS
As can be readily seen, the OC is 'tailed' or followed by CURS, making OCCURS, or 'happens'.

tailless
Tailless monkey comes to former point – APEX
'Tailless monkey' is AP ('tailless' APE), who here comes to EX ('former') to make the APEX, or 'point'. For quite a different sort of clue for the word, see **primate**.

take
Wine that she takes king on railway – SHERRY
SHERRY is the 'wine' made by the cryptic elements SHE ('she') R ('king') and RY ('railway').

take aback
Tim taken aback about the bishop's hat – MITRE
Probably all too easy, this clue, since 'bishop's hat', the definition of MITRE, is enough on its own to arrive at the answer. Still, it is also clued cryptically, as TIM 'taken aback', i.e. reversed (MIT), 'about' (RE).

taken
First skier taken to start of Grande Escarpe – on this? – SLEDGE

'First *s*kier' is S. He is 'taken' or LED to the 'start' or first letters of the '*G*rande *E*scarpe'. These elements combine to give the SLEDGE on which, as the final question suggests, he could be taken. The 'Grande Escarpe' is a mock skiing term or location, meaning something like the 'Great Escarpment' or 'Big Slope'.

take in
Bob takes in pupil getting no marks – BLOB
A 'straddle', so that BOB 'takes in' the 'pupil' (L). The result is a BLOB, the slang term for 'zero' – so 'no marks'.

take out
Frenchman taken out of camp shows his hat – CAP
A 'Frenchman' is M (for Monsieur). If this is 'taken out of' or removed from CAMP, we get CAP, here defined as 'hat'. (Say what you like, there are occasions when a 'cap' is actually a 'hat', for example some 'caps' awarded as sports honours are actually 'hats'.)

take to heart
He takes girl to heart – Greek, she is – HELLENE
The 'girl' in this clue is not Helen! She is ELLEN, whom HE 'takes to heart', or 'straddles'. This leads to HELLENE who is a 'Greek'.

take up
Bill takes up rubbish – and makes good show of it! – ACTOR
'Bill' here is 'account', or AC for short. This 'takes up' or adds, reversed 'rubbish' or ROT, thus producing ACTOR, who should make a 'good show of it'.

talented
Quite famous, though not talented – NOTABLE
If 'talented' is ABLE, then 'not talented' is NOT ABLE, which as NOTABLE can be defined as 'quite famous'. Compare the rather easy clue for this word that we gave under **list**.

tavern
Both the tavern (the 'Half Lily') and the town get good media exposure – PUBLICITY
At first sight a somewhat bemusing clue. But re-read it with fresh eyes and you will find a PUB, the 'Half *Li*ly' (LI), and the CITY, which together make PUBLICITY, or 'good media exposure'.

tax
Tax on a container in Roman palace – VATICAN
A fairly easy 'read-through': 'Tax' (VAT) on 'a' (I) 'container' (CAN) in the VATICAN, a 'Roman palace'.

taxi
Southern Taxis – and the blacklegs who drive them? – SCABS
'Southern' (S) 'Taxis' (CABS) make the SCABS, otherwise the strikebreakers or 'black-legs'. Any resemblance to an actual firm of the name is, of course, completely coincidental!

tea
Dread making a mistake after tea? – TERROR
A 'mistake after tea' is an ERROR after T. This produces TERROR, or 'dread'.

tea-break
To begin in it I have a tea-break – INITIATE
A nice 'build-up' clue. To 'begin' is to INITIATE, the word consisting of IN IT I have a 'TEA-break' (or ATE).

team
Like team in German-Italian alliance of 1936, for example – AXIS
Perhaps at first you looked for a 'burial' somewhere? Yet most of the clue is a factual description of an example of AXIS, cryptically defined as 'like' (AS) with 'team' in (XI). So there *is* a 'burial' – but not, perhaps, where you were expecting it!

tea-time
Storm back after tea-time at home for this condiment – VINEGAR
'Storm back' is a reversal of RAGE. This follows 'tea-time' (V) 'at home' (IN), giving VINEGAR, the 'condiment' you need. (A friend I showed this clue to thought the answer was MUSTARD, with 'storm back' a

reversal of DRAT! The trouble was that MUS could not be explained as 'tea-time at home', however ingeniously.)

technique
Conquer by cunning but must change in love technique – OUTSMART
Like most cryptic clues, not what it seems. 'MUST change' is an anagram, working out as UTSM. This is then 'buried' ('in') between 'love' (O) and 'technique' (ART) to produce OUTSMART, as defined in the first three words of the clue.

Ted(dy)
Influence Teddy, he's behaving in such an artificial way – AFFECTED
Or, much more briefly, AFFECT ED, he's so AFFECTED.

tee
Speed off from the tee – there's the line! – TRACE
'Off from' means 'following', so RACE from the T to get the TRACE, or 'line'.

teetotal(ler)
Wait on a teetotaller to complete the course – ATTEND
To ATTEND is to 'wait on', cryptically clued as 'a' (A) 'teetotaller' (TT) 'to complete the course' (END).

telepathy
Telepathy with religious ceremony, almost – there's real comradeship! – ESPRIT
ESP with 'almost' a RITE gives ESPRIT, 'real comradeship'.

ten (10)
Greek orthodox bishop listens, having ten in church – EXARCH
An EAR 'listens', and here it has 'ten' in (X) and is joined by 'church' (CH). This combines as the 'Greek orthodox bishop', or EXARCH.

terminate
Ring road to terminate at this continental port – OSTEND
'Ring' is O, 'road' is ST, and to 'terminate' is to END. The three elements make up the 'continental port' of OSTEND.

terriers (Terriers)
Terriers are first wet, then dry – all rather worthless – TAWDRY
The 'Terriers' are the Territorial Army or TA. They are 'first *w*et' (W), then DRY, so they are TAWDRY, defined by *Chambers* as 'showy without taste or worth'.

Territorials, Territorial Army
Army or Territorial Army, drawing blood? – AORTA
A OR TA? The AORTA, says *Chambers*, is 'the great arterial trunk that carries blood from the heart'.

(voice-)**test**
Pain-relief test making the Scottish retreat – BALMORAL
BALM gives 'pain relief', and a 'test' is an ORAL. The two together make BALMORAL, the famous royal 'Scottish retreat'.

Texas, Texan
Synthetic rubber product sent from Los Angeles to Texas – LATEX
LATEX, the 'synthetic rubber product', joins 'Los Angeles' (LA) and 'Texas' (TEX).

thanks, thank you
Thanks to the horse, Teddy was closely followed – TAGGED
'Thanks' (TA) to the 'horse' (GG) 'Teddy' (ED) was TAGGED, or closely followed.

that is, that's
That's money, that is, 'The Club' – BRASSIE
'Money' is BRASS, 'that is' is IE, and the two combine to make the (golf) 'club', the BRASSIE.

that's right
Points scored without touching the ball banned initially – that's right – BYES
BYES, in cricket, are runs or 'points scored without touching the ball'. Cryptically, these are '*b*anned initially' (B), 'that's right' (YES).

theatre
Actor, say – place for me in right theatre coming up? – PERFORMER
A fairly complex clue. A PERFORMER is an 'actor' ('say' indicating an example of the

sense). The word consists of the cryptic clues FOR ME in 'right' (R) 'theatre' (REP) 'coming up', in other words, reversed. We thus have FORME in PER – R, which gives the PERFORMER.

theatre of war
Commanding Officer and MP arrive at theatre of war, and French retreat to make good the loss – COMPENSATE
This longish word has a longish clue, with four cryptic elements. These are: CO ('Commanding Officer'), MP ('MP'), ENSA ('theatre of war') and TE ('and French retreat', or a reversal of the French for 'and'). This builds up COMPENSATE, defined at the end of the clue as 'make good the loss'.

the end
The end circle has points attached for the belt – ZONE
'The end' (Z) 'circle' (O) has 'points' attached (NE) for the 'belt', or ZONE.

the old
The old northern longing – YEN
'The old' is YE, 'northern' is N, these making a YEN, or 'longing'.

the one here
The one here allowed false Scottish emblem – THISTLE
'The one here' is THIS. 'Allowed false' is what might be called an 'indirect anagram', that is, an anagram of a word that has to be deduced. 'Allowed' is LET, so we need an anagram of that, which here is TLE. THIS+TLE gives the 'Scottish emblem', or THISTLE.

the ones here
Essays – the ones here – student's starting – THESES
THESES are 'essays', cryptically clued as 'the ones here' (THESE) and 'student's starting' (S, the first letter of 'student').

the ones there
Tights are 'dishy' – I get in the ones there – PANTIHOSE
PANTIHOSE are 'tights', cryptically clued as '"dishy"' (PAN) and 'I get in the ones there', i.e. 'I' get in THOSE (as T – I – HOSE). So PAN+TIHOSE makes PANTIHOSE! 'Dishy' is defined by *Chambers* as 'good-looking, attractive'. The slang term is normally used of people, of course, but here we are taking slight liberties and applying it to an 'attractive' garment.

the one there
Straw roofing for the one there, the church – THATCH
Avoiding any political possibilities ('the one there, dear French woman') the compiler decided here in favour of 'the one there' (THAT), 'the church' (CH), to clue the THATCH defined as 'straw roofing'.

there
London, England – made there! – DONE
Quite a nice 'burial', in 'Lon*don, E*ngland', with the result, DONE, being defined as 'made'. ('To do' comes rather low in *Chambers*'s list of definitions for 'make' – thirty-ninth out of forty-two! – but in a general sense I think we can equate the two verbs fairly here.)

therefore
Port of London Authority, therefore, take in garden structure – PERGOLA
The 'Port of London Authority' is the PLA. Here it must 'take in' or 'straddle' ERGO ('therefore') to make the PERGOLA, or 'garden structure'.

Theresa
Doubtful gain for Theresa, she's such a big girl! – GIANTESS
The 'doubtful GAIN' is an anagram, here working out as GIAN. This is joined to TESS ('Theresa') to make the GIANTESS, 'a big girl'.

this
This pet is a darling, Dad! – POP
'This pet' here indicates that the answer is a word which, when joined to PET, will mean 'darling'. The word (and therefore the answer) is POP, additionally defined as 'Dad' – perhaps to reassure solvers who were wondering whether it should be MOP! For a different clue leading to POP, see **piano**.

this month
This month everyone is to get set up and operational – INSTALL
'To get set up' may look like a reversal of SET. In fact it is part of the definition ('to get set up and operational'), which is cryptically clued as 'this month' (INST) and 'everyone' (ALL). The definition is thus of INSTALL.

thoroughfare
Tear round the thoroughfare and you get a delay – RETARD
'TEAR round' is an anagram, making RETA. It is followed by 'the thoroughfare' (RD), producing RETARD, defined as 'delay'.

(a) **thousand (1000)**
Customs have a thousand metal containers – MORES
'A thousand' (M) 'metal containers' (ORES). If doubtful about MORES, and its definition of 'customs', check in *Chambers* or some other dictionary.

(a) **thousand dollars ($1000)**
Put a thousand dollars on this craft and you'll get an illicit profit! – GRAFT
So, put G (a 'grand', or 'a thousand dollars') on the RAFT and you'll get GRAFT, a slang term defined by *Chambers* (among other senses) as 'illicit profit by corrupt means'.

thrice
Thrice run round the balcony – TERRACE
'Round' does not denote an anagram or a reversal, it's part of the cryptic definition of RACE – 'run round'. This follows TER ('thrice') to make the TERRACE, or 'balcony'. For a different kind of clue, see **captive**.

through
Cast through the opening week – THROW
Not a performance schedule for a new play, but 'cast' as the definition of THROW, and the cryptic clues for this word: 'through' (THRO) and 'opening *w*eek' (W – its first letter).

throw
Throw past the passage – LOBBY
'Throw' is LOB, 'past' is BY, and this makes the LOBBY, or 'passage'.

throw back
Catches fish, but throws ten back after start of supper – NETS
'Catches fish' is NETS, which on the other hand ('but') has a cryptic definition: 'throws TEN back' indicates a reversal (NET), and 'after' this comes the 'start of supper' (S).

throw up
Throw up rod with my golf score – DORMY
'Throw up ROD' means reverse it (DOR). Then add MY to make the 'golf score', or DORMY (according to *Chambers*, 'as many holes up or ahead as there are yet to play').

thus
Alternative thus provided in tin for islander – CORSICAN
A 'burial', as you can see. 'Alternative' (OR) 'thus' (SIC) in 'tin' (CAN) for the 'islander' who is a CORSICAN.

tilt
Initially slight tilt, but not really enough – SCANT
'Initially *s*light' is S (the first letter of 'slight'), which with 'tilt' (CANT) makes SCANT, defined as 'not really enough'. For two further clues leading to this word, see **insect** and **read**.

time, The Times
Respect the time in changing the event – VENERATE
An anagrammatic 'burial' here, of 'time' (ERA) in 'changing the EVENT', i.e. in VENTE. This gives VENERATE, or 'respect'.

tin
Tin and silver are quite a catch! – SNAG
'Tin' (SN) and 'silver' (AG) are quite a 'catch', or SNAG! We had a somewhat similar clue under **metal**.

tip (of)
I got on tip of iceberg and nearly reached the sea! – IONIAN
The IONIAN 'sea' here is clued by four cryptic elements I ('I'), ON ('on'), I ('tip of *i*ceberg'), AN ('AND nearly').

to
Pass to our blue or red, for example – COLOUR
'Pass' (COL) to OUR makes a COLOUR, 'blue or red, for example'.

to a certain extent
Nobleman belongs to a social order, to a certain extent – LORD
The 'nobleman' or LORD is thus 'buried' in 'a socia*l ord*er', with the 'burial' indicated by the final phrase of the clue.

to and fro
Canoe goes to and fro – KAYAK
This palindromic 'canoe', that goes 'to and fro', could hardly be other than a KAYAK!

Tom
Tom and family gather this flower – CATKIN
If you 'gather' 'Tom' (CAT) and his 'family' (KIN) you will have a CATKIN, or 'flower'.

top
Tip-top covering for the roof! – THATCH
'Tip-top' means the 'top', or first letter, of '*t*ip' (T). Following this is 'covering' (HATCH) to make THATCH, which is 'for the roof'. Compare this clue with the one under **the one there**.

top grade
Concerning top grade round – ABOUT
ABOUT is 'concerning', cryptically clued as 'top grade' (A) 'round' (BOUT). Compare the clue at **so it's said**.

topless
Topless lass in Mediterranean is ready to attack on a broad front! – MASSED
This Amazonian image in fact involves a 'burial', of 'topless lass' (ASS) in the 'Mediterranean' (MED). This gives MASSED, defined as 'ready to attack on a broad front'.

(Mr) **Torme**
A medley for Mr Torme and the French Angel – MELANGE
'Mr Torme' is MEL, and the 'French Angel' is ANGE (the French for 'angel', of course). The result is a MELANGE, or 'medley'.

torn
Father torn in his role as head of the family – PARENT
An easy cryptic 'split' of PA ('father') and RENT ('torn'), producing the PARENT who is, or could be, the 'head of the family'.

touch (of)
Legal document with humour – and there's a touch of ribaldry in it – WRIT
'Legal document' defines the WRIT, which is made up of WIT ('humour') with a 'touch of *r*ibaldry' (R = its first letter) 'buried' in it.

town
Lack of provisions is a blemish on the town – SCARCITY
To 'read it through': SCARCITY ('lack of provisions') is a SCAR on the CITY.

track
Ancient house on a track – HOARY
HOARY is 'ancient', and the word is cryptically clued as 'house' (HO) on 'a' (A) 'track' (RY).

trade union
Trade union for the navy? That will be a change! – TURN
An easy 'read-through' clue here, with a 'trade union' (TU) for the 'navy' (RN) making a TURN, or 'change'.

trainees
Trainees in New Hampshire are in good nick! – NOTCH
'Trainees', or OTC, when 'buried' in 'New Hampshire' (NH), make a NOTCH, punningly defined as a 'good nick'.

training
House-training gives confidence – HOPE
'House-training' comes down to HO+PE, giving HOPE, or 'confidence'.

train(s)
Transport vehicle by train – CARRY
To CARRY is to 'transport'. That is the definition, cryptically clued as 'vehicle by train', or CAR+RY.

traitor
High-ranking man from car is to punish traitor – ARISTOCRAT

A more complex clue. What does the 'car' have to do with the ARISTOCRAT, or 'high-ranking man'? It is part of an anagram, indicated by 'punish', with the necessary letters to be 'punished' or anagrammatised CAR IS TO. These make a minor change to ARISTOC, with the 'traitor', or RAT, following. After these manoeuvres – one ARISTOCRAT for you!

transgress
Transgress against the king, becoming increasingly degraded as a result – SINKING
SIN against the KING, so SINKING.

translate
Passage from article said to need translation – ADIT
The useful ADIT again (see for example **open**). It's defined as a 'passage', of course, and cryptically devised from 'article' (A) and 'said to need translation' (DIT, the French for 'said').

transport
Transport the French messages – CABLES
The 'transport' here is CAB, which with 'the French' (LES) makes the CABLES, or 'messages'.

trap
Singular clicking instrument will mean you have to throw a trap – CASTANET
To 'throw a trap' is to CAST A NET, the cryptic elements used to make up the CASTANET, or 'singular clicking instrument' ('singular' since the word is normally plural, with an S).

travel
Travel with Reg round to the ravine – GORGE
So, 'travel' or GO with 'REG round' (RGE, as an anagram) to the GORGE, or 'ravine'.

traveller
Traveller comes to Broken Hill, and we have his account – REPORT
The 'traveller' is the REP, and 'Broken Hill' means an anagram of TOR ('hill'), here as ORT. So this gives us his report, or 'account'. Broken Hill, of course, is a mining town in Australia.

tree
Tree in the mixed cover on top – HELMET
A 'burial' here in an anagram – 'tree' (ELM) in 'THE mixed' (HET). This gives HELMET, which is 'cover on top'.

trial
Witness at trial – ATTEST
A good, neat clue. To 'witness' is to ATTEST, and 'at trial', cryptically, is AT TEST.

tribesman
After us returning tribesman comes to African land – SUDAN
Not 'returning tribesman' but 'US returning'. After this (SU) comes the 'tribesman' (DAN) to give the SUDAN, or 'African land'. Compare this clue with the one under **Daniel**.

trim
To tour round trimmed linen is all in the day's work – ROUTINE
To 'TOUR round' is to ROUT, and 'trimmed LINEN' is INE (LINEN 'trimmed' of its first and last letters). The combination of these is ROUTINE, which is 'all in the day's work'.

trouble
After trouble dole out flattery – ADORATION
After 'trouble', or ADO, comes 'dole out', or RATION. This gives ADORATION, or 'flattery'. With this definition, one at first expects to find ADULATION as the answer (the words are similar, and have the same number of letters). The cryptic elements, however, confirm otherwise.

try
Try to do in return that which is worthy – GOOD
'Try' is GO, and 'DO in return' is OD. Together, the two elements make GOOD, 'that which is worthy'. This biblical-style clue is rather harder than the one for the same word under **deity**.

tuck in(to)
Diana tucks into the meat after the end of the

pie – I think I'll have to intervene! – MEDIATE
Things aren't as gross as they seem. DI 'tucks into', or is 'buried' in, the MEAT, after which comes the 'end of the pie' (E). This gives MEDIATE, 'to intervene'. Note that 'I think I'll have' expresses the compiler's wish on behalf of the solver – if he has worked out the cryptic section of the clue correctly!

tune
Rock musical has hard tune – HAIR
A 'hard tune' clues H+AIR. This gives HAIR, the name of the famous rock musical.

turf
Turf over lair is wet through – SODDEN
Otherwise the SOD over the DEN is SODDEN. For a different 'image', see **in this way**.

turncoat
Curse the dead turncoat! – DRAT
DRAT is a type of 'curse', here consisting of the elements 'dead' (D) and 'turncoat' (RAT).

turn (over)**, turn about, turn back**
Turnabout Timothy goes to the East;
Of all the small creatures he's one of the least!
– MITE
A longish rhyme for a short answer. 'Turnabout Timothy' is a reversal of TIM (MIT). This 'goes to' or is joined to the 'east' (E). This makes a MITE, as described in the second line of the couplet.

turn up
Sam turns up on the bed – that'll bring us luck – MASCOT
'SAM turns up', so we have his reversal, which is MAS. He is on the 'bed' or COT, so we finish up with a MASCOT, which should 'bring us luck'. I take 'Sam' of the clue to be a black cat or other pet of good omen.

TV doctor
TV doctor moves half left – that's complete – WHOLE
Thus the 'TV doctor' WHO moves 'half LEFT' (LE), resulting in WHOLE, or 'complete'.

twelve (12)
Having slept, the twelve went to the editor – DOZED
The 'twelve', of course, are the DOZ. They went to the 'editor' (ED), after they had 'slept' or DOZED.

twenty (20)
No more than twenty died, it's emphasised – UNDERSCORED
'No more than' is 'less than', otherwise UNDER. 'Twenty' is a SCORE, and 'died' is D. The three elements combine to make UNDERSCORED, defined as 'emphasised'.

twenty-five pounds (£25)
£25 dog has special hair-do – PONY-TAIL
Would you have found this so easy without the advance knowledge of the PONY? Anyway, £25 is indeed PONY, and 'dog' (think of it as a verb) is TAIL, resulting in the PONY-TAIL, or 'special hair-do'.

twice
Twice cut round a cake – BISCUIT
'Twice' is BIS, and it is followed by CUT 'round', or 'straddling' 'a' (I). This gives a BISCUIT which, like it or not, is actually a form of 'cake'!

twitch
Are you the first sufferer to twitch? Do you live in the country? – RUSTIC
This sounds like the start of a doctor's diagnosis of hay fever. In fact the first question contains the cryptic elements: 'Are you' (RU) 'the first sufferer' (S) to 'twitch' (TIC). The second question suggests the definition – 'in the country', or RUSTIC.

two hundred (200)
Quite an event – 0–200 as I got on – OCCASION
A pseudo-sporting clue! An OCCASION, of course, is an 'event'. Here it is cryptically clued as '0–200' (O–CC) 'as I' (AS-I) got 'on' (ON).

twopence (2p)
I got twopence in the arena – that's excellent! – RIPPING
'I' got PP in the RING – and that's RIPPING!

two pounds (£2, 2lb)
Bachelor gets two pounds for dance – BALL
An easy 'read-through' clue, so that the 'bachelor' (BA) gets 'two pounds' (LL) for the 'dance', or BALL.

two-way
Two-way watcher of the seas and skies – RADAR
Not some classical deity but RADAR, which 'watches the seas and skies' and is 'two-way' as a palindromic word.

(in) **Tyneside, Tyne and Wear**
Hop over to Tyneside – you can make your own arrangements by using this! – PHONE
'HOP over' is an anagram, working out as PHO. This goes to 'Tyneside' (NE), giving the PHONE that enables you to make your visit there, perhaps. There was a time when an indicator might have been needed to show that the answer was an abbreviation, i.e. a short form of 'telephone'. The word PHONE has now become established in its own right, however, to mean 'telephone' (see *Chambers*), so this is not necessary.

type of boat
Type of boat, silent repair vessel – UTENSIL
Did you spot the anagram? It's SILENT, indicated by 'repair'. So 'type of boat' is U, and this is followed by the anagram, as mentioned, which turns out to be TENSIL. Both elements together give UTENSIL, defined as 'vessel'.

type of bomb
Type of bomb on board set all wrong. Whose property is it? – ASSETS
The 'type of bomb' here is A. It is 'on board' (SS) and is SET 'all wrong' (ETS). This produces its ASSETS, or 'property'.

tyro
Stage of course for tyro, for example – LEG
'Tyro' is L, and 'for example' is EG. This gives the LEG, or 'stage of course'.

U

ultimate(ly)
Uncivilised fellow got birch ultimately – GOTH
For once the little linking 'got' is all-important for the answer! So GOT, with 'bir*ch* ultimately' (H, its last letter) makes the GOTH, or 'uncivilised fellow'.

ultimate letter
Ultimate letter comes to an end, a match for ancient sacred writings – ZEND-AVESTA
Z, the 'ultimate letter', comes to an END, with A VESTA ('match') for the resulting ZEND-AVESTA, or 'ancient sacred writings' (of the Parsees, in fact). A 'vesta', *Chambers* reminds us, was both 'a wax-stemmed match' and 'a short match with wooden stem'.

(is) **unable (are unable)**
Virginia is unable to empty this – VACANT
VA (the state of 'Virginia') CANT – and 'this' is to VACANT, 'to empty'.

uncle
Uncle's acting the strong man – SAMSON
SAMSON, of course, is 'the strong man', cryptically represented as 'Uncle's acting', or SAM'S ON. For a rather similar clue, see **acting**.

unconscious
Margaret unconscious? Let's hope she won't do this – PEG OUT.
PEG is a form of 'Margaret', and OUT, of course, is 'unconscious'. To PEG OUT is a slang term for 'to die'. That's the last thing we want Margaret to do!

under
The Editor's under strain – that's emphasised – STRESSED
So, if 'under' denotes a word or element following another, then the ED is 'under' STRESS. And that is STRESSED, or 'emphasised'.

understand
You once understood the splendour of the emperor – POMPEY

'You once' is the cryptic clue for YE (the 'old' form of 'you'). Here it is 'understood', so it follows the rest of the word and is reversed (EY). The 'splendour' is POMP. This gives POMPEY, the 'emperor'. Pedants will point out that Pompey was not actually an emperor, but a triumvir (with Caesar and Crassus).

understudy
Policeman is reliable understudy – CONSTABLE
With 'under' meaning 'following', we thus have the CONSTABLE clued cryptically as STABLE ('reliable') under CON ('understudy'). Compare the clues under **above** and **care of**.

underworld
Change of dress is underworld appearance – DISGUISE
A 'change of dress' is a DISGUISE, clued cryptically as an 'underworld' (DIS) 'appearance' (GUISE).

unfinished
The French song is unfinished, and we can learn from this – LESSON
'The French' here is LES, followed by an 'unfinished' SONG (SON). This gives a LESSON, from which 'we can learn'.

unhesitatingly
Unhesitatingly, the monk provides soup – BROTH
'Unhesitatingly' means 'without hesitation', which in cryptic terms means 'without ER'. So the 'monk' thus will be BROTH (less ER). And of course that makes the 'soup'.

union
First three members of Magicians Union get a large bottle of wine – MAGNUM
A slightly trickier clue than it looks, perhaps. The 'first three members of Magicians' are its first three letters, that is MAG. They are followed by a 'Union', in this case NUM. That makes a MAGNUM, which is a 'large bottle of wine'.

United Nations
Part of speech from 'Disagreement at the United Nations' – NOUN
A NOUN is a (grammatical) 'part of speech'! Here it is derived from 'disagreement' (NO) and 'United Nations' (UN).

United States
In brief, Central and Southern United States will have an official enumeration of their inhabitants – CENSUS
'In brief' denotes some abbreviated forms, so that 'Central' is CEN, 'Southern' is S, and 'United States' is US. A combination of these elements makes the CENSUS as defined in the second half of the clue.

universal
Universal Mixed Ices, an international organisation, initially – UNESCO
Does 'Mixed' indicate an anagram? Yes, but not of ICES! It's the anagram of CONES ('Ices') that is required, and after 'Universal' (U) this works out as NESCO. The answer is thus UNESCO, the 'international organisation'. ('Initially', since we require only the initials of this well-known organisation, not its full title.)

university
University egghead reveals the custom – USAGE
'University' is U, and an 'egghead' (an intellectual) is a SAGE. Together they 'reveal the custom', or USAGE. (A notice over a low stairway in an Oxford bookshop used to read, 'Mind your egghead'.) Compare the clue we used for this word under **aristocratic**.

university man
University man to study the philosopher – BACON
A straightforward 'read-through' clue: 'University man' (BA) 'to study' (CON) 'the philosopher' (BACON). Compare the rather different clue under **battalion**.

unknown (factor)
This tool is an article unknown by the east – AXE
A word with a cryptic clue for each of its three letters: 'an article' (A) 'unknown' (X) 'the east' (E). The resulting AXE is also generally defined, of course, as a 'tool'.

unlimited
Unlimited time, I would say, shows a lack of courage – TIMID
'Unlimited TIME' is TIM (with no 'limit', or final E), 'I would say' is ID (the spelling of 'I'd'), and the combination of these two elements gives TIMID, showing a 'lack of courage'.

unpaid
Graduate gets half-ration (unpaid) for his feat of endurance – MARATHON
There are three cryptic elements here: MA ('graduate'), RAT ('half RATION') and HON ('(unpaid)'). The total is his MARATHON, or 'feat of endurance'.

unpaid debts
Do return unpaid debts, it's offensive as it is – ODIOUS
'Do return' is OD, which with the 'unpaid debts' (IOUS) makes ODIOUS, or 'offensive'.

up(wards), uphill
Woman who gives up her advantage – TESSA
If TESSA 'gives up' she is reversed, and we see her ASSET, or 'advantage'. It is perhaps best to approach a clue like this the other way round, in other words, work out the definition first (ASSET), and then reverse that to get the 'woman' who could be anyone.

up and down
Seed goes up and down over it – what a lark! – PIPIT
The 'seed' is a PIP, which we know is a palindrome as it 'goes up and down'. It is over IT, so making a PIPIT, which is a bird in the 'lark' family.

upbringing
Her upbringing was by ear, on points, and she had to practise – REHEARSE
'Her upbringing' means a reversal of HER (REH). This is followed by EAR and was on 'points' (SE). The outcome is REHEARSE, or 'to practise'.

upper class
Upper-class member shows anger when he's a referee – UMPIRE
'U' MP shows IRE when he's an UMPIRE.

upset
If she's upset, I complain – NAOMI
'I complain' is I MOAN, which 'upset' gives NAOMI. So that's who 'she' is!

Ur
Urgent – in two words – ABRAHAM
It's not the answer that's in two words, but the clue that should be, so that 'Urgent' should be read as 'Ur gent'. This means either 'original man' or 'man from Ur'. 'Original man' cannot be right, as that was Adam. Therefore it must be ABRAHAM, who was the 'man from Ur' in the Old Testament.

uranium
Uranium found in mixed metal by northern town in France – ROUEN
A fairly – but not very – hard clue. 'Uranium' is U. It is 'found' or 'buried' in 'mixed metal'. 'Mixed' indicates an anagram, but not of 'metal' – of its cryptic interpretation, ORE. These two elements combined are followed by 'northern', which is N. And this works out as the 'town in France', which is ROUEN. In other words, U ('uranium') is in ROE ('mixed metal' or ORE) by N ('northern'). As it happens, ROUEN *is* a northern town in France, but that is simply a lucky coincidence!

urge
Urge the director, a real intellectual – EGGHEAD
Otherwise EGG the HEAD, a real EGGHEAD. (Remember the **university** one?) Compare the clue we had for this word under **head**.

US
US quarterdeck can be just the right place – SUITABLE
A 'US' or American 'quarterdeck' is a quarter of a 'deck' or pack of cards, hence a SUIT. 'Can' is ABLE, so the two together are SUITABLE, or 'just the right place'.

us
The responsibility is, quite literally, on us – ONUS
It's not often that you simply have to 'lift' the

answer straight from the clue like this. But this is what you do here, 'literally' – which after all means 'to the letter'! The answer is defined as well ('responsibility') in the usual manner.

utterly
Poet utterly excluded – BARRED
'Utterly' indicates a homophone, so here it is applied to the 'poet' or BARD, who is 'excluded' or BARRED.

value
Note value of packing case – CRATE
The 'note' is C, 'value' is RATE, and the resulting 'packing case' is a CRATE.

vehicle
Vehicle in room on board – CABIN
Put another way, a CAB IN a CABIN, which is 'a room on board'.

veil
Ran veiled by church, getting uplift! – CRANE
'Veiled' indicates a 'straddle', so that here RAN is 'veiled' by CE ('church'). This produces a CRANE, which gives 'uplift'.

versus
The Glen versus The Lane – VALLEY
Not two football teams, but a definition (a 'glen' is a VALLEY) and two cryptic clues: 'versus' (V) 'The Lane' (ALLEY).

very
Book about animals is very good one to have on a train – BESTIARY
'Very good' is BEST, 'one' is I, 'a' is A, and 'train' is RY. These four elements comprise a BESTIARY which is a 'book about animals' ('of a class popular in the Middle Ages', *Chambers* reminds us).

very (good)
Sort of sombrero, very good in Worcestershire – BROMSGROVE
'Sort of' indicates the approaching anagram – of SOMBRERO VG ('very good'). This makes BROMSGROVE, a town 'in Worcestershire' (although since 1974, more precisely, in Hereford and Worcester – but solvers must be prepared for a certain amount of latitude, especially in older clues).

very large, very big
Distorting the very big moral significance – ETHOS
Another anagram – 'distorting THE' (ETH), which with 'very big' (OS) makes the ETHOS, or 'moral significance'.

very little, very small
Beetle is very small and mostly detestable – WEEVIL
Thus the WEEVIL ('beetle') is 'very small' (WEE) and 'mostly detestable' (VIL, i.e. 'mostly VILE').

very loud(ly)
After tea there is a very loud quarrel – TIFF
After T ('tea') there is I ('a') FF ('very loud') – 'quarrel', that is, a TIFF.

very quiet(ly)
Love comes on very quietly, or comes on with a tune;
It comes at a convenient time – quite late or very soon! – OPPORTUNE
To 'read between the lines': 'Love' (O) comes on 'very quietly' (PP), 'or' (OR) comes on with a 'tune' (TUNE). The resulting word is OPPORTUNE, which is 'at a convenient time'!

very soft(ly)
Prescribe a very soft ointment (only half to be used, however) – APPOINT
To 'prescribe' is to APPOINT. The word is made up of the elements A ('a') PP ('very soft') OINT (OINTMENT – but 'only half to be used').

vessel
Headquarters of French vessel – DEPOT
'Headquarters' defines the DEPOT, which consists of DE ('of French') and POT ('vessel').

veto
Legal officer gets veto thanks to railway – NOTARY

A 'read-through' again: the 'legal officer', a NOTARY, gets 'veto' (NO) 'thanks' (TA) to 'railway' (RY).

vice
Vice points to muscular strength! – SINEW
At least, for the purposes of this clue, it does. So 'vice' (SIN) 'points' (EW) to SINEW, or 'muscular strength'.

Vichy water
Soft Vichy water points to a French wine! – BEAUNE
The three cryptic elements here are B ('soft') EAU ('Vichy water') and 'points' (NE). That gives the 'French wine', BEAUNE.

victory
Base victory, I'll say – VILE
'Base' is VILE, divided cryptically into V ('victory') and ILE ('I'll say').

Violet
Violet comes to church and talks wildly, crazily – or is it the other way round? – VICE VERSA
The first word of the answer is fairly easy: VI ('Violet') comes to CE ('church'). The second is a little more complex: 'talks wildly' is RAVES, but you need an anagram of this (indicated by 'crazily'), and that is VERSA. This completes the phrase, which, of course, is defined as 'the other way round'.

violin string
Beginner gets in violin string, too many of them, in fact – GLUT
An easy 'burial', with the 'beginner' (L) 'getting in' the 'violin string' (GUT) to produce the GLUT ('too many of them'). Compare the clue for this word under **g-string**.

Virgil
Virgil's father, also a writer – PATER
'Virgil's father' means you need the Latin for father, which is PATER. This is additionally defined as 'also a writer', referring to the English writer Walter PATER.

Virginia
Virginia points to the weathercock – VANE
'Virginia' (the state, abbreviated as VA) 'points' (NE) to the 'weathercock' or VANE.

virtuous
Virtuous, abstemious, and almost coming to church to get special allowance – PITTANCE
A word of four cryptic elements: PI ('virtuous'), TT ('abstemious'), AN ('AND almost') and CE ('church'). These compose the PITTANCE, or 'special allowance'.

vitamin
Vitamin store will provide hot wine drink – BISHOP
'Vitamin' here is the usual BI, which followed by SHOP ('store') makes a BISHOP, defined appetisingly by *Chambers* as 'a wholesome hot drink compounded of red wine . . . poured warm or cold upon ripe bitter oranges, sugared and spiced to taste'! I hope the answer was not too difficult to arrive at.

volcano
Gold seen on erupting volcano, that's very decorative! – ORNATE
An 'erupting' volcano, of course, is an anagram of one, here of ETNA. So 'gold' (OR) seen on NATE is ORNATE, which is 'very decorative'.

volte-face
Do a volte-face on deal, initially? That's strange! – ODD
A 'volte-face' or reversal of DO is OD, and this is joined by '*d*eal, initially' (D) to make ODD, which is 'strange'.

volume
Point to religious volume as an ideal example – EPITOME
The 'point' here is E, which joins 'religious' (PI) 'volume' (TOME) to result in the 'ideal example', or EPITOME.

volunteers
Ray joins island volunteers – MANTA
The MANTA is a 'ray' (fish), and here it is made up of MAN ('island') and TA ('volunteers'). Compare the clue we had for this under **servant**.

vulgar(ly)
She and I very vulgarly wander about – MEANDER
'She and I very vulgarly' are 'me and 'er' or

MEANDER, which is also defined as 'wander about'.

W

wager
US soldier places second-class wager, but it leads to the gallows! – GIBBET
A straightforward 'read-through': 'US soldier' is GI, 'second-class' is B, and 'wager' is BET. These three elements lead to a GIBBET, or 'gallows'.

want(ing)
Nellie is back, wanting one. She's just the same person! – ELLEN
NELLIE is 'back', so reversed, as EILLEN. But she 'wants one', so is missing 'I'. This makes her ELLEN, which is simply another version of the name NELLIE, with both related to or deriving from 'Helen'. (More precisely, NELLIE is often regarded as a diminutive of ELLEN. But they are still basically the same name, just as 'Tom' and 'Thomas' are.)

War Office
War Office advertisement for plant – WOAD
An easy clue: 'War Office' is WO, 'advertisement' is AD, and the two together make WOAD, the 'plant' that was famous for its blue dye.

was first (to do it)
Loosed a blow for France – was first to do it – UNCOUPLED
The definition of UNCOUPLED is 'loosed', and the word is cryptically clued as 'a blow for France' (UNCOUP, i.e. UN COUP, French for 'a blow') and 'was first to do it' (LED).

was leader (of)
Peter the First was leader of great emperors, initially, and made a solemn promise – PLEDGE
'*P*eter the First' is P (the first letter of 'Peter') and he 'was leader' (LED) of '*g*reat *e*mperors, initially' (GE). All these elements combine to make the 'solemn promise', or PLEDGE.

waste
Note waste in cathedral precinct – CLOSE
The 'note' is C, and 'waste' is LOSE. Both elements make the CLOSE, or 'cathedral precinct'.

was the conductor
Enthusiast was the conductor and produced a trumpet call! – BUGLED
A BUG, here is an 'enthusiast' (as in *Chambers*), and this one 'was the conductor', so LED, which means that he BUGLED, or 'produced a trumpet call'.

water
Soft water is essential for reasoned living – BRAIN
'Soft' (B) 'water' (RAIN) combines as a BRAIN, which is 'essential for reasoned living'. Compare the clues under **Academy** and **bust-up**.

watering place
Watering place has record, even for this boy – SPALPEEN
Thus the 'water place' (SPA) has 'record' (LP) 'even' (EEN) for this 'boy', or SPALPEEN.

water-pipe
Water-pipe is very large at end of drive – maybe we'll need this? – HOSE
'Water-pipe' (H) is 'very large' (OS) at 'end of driv*e*' (E), so maybe we'll need a HOSE.

way
In Tyneside, is waylaid for one's savings – NEST-EGG
'Tyneside' is NE, and 'waylaid' divides into ST ('way') and EGG (that is 'laid'). This results in the NEST-EGG, as defined at the end of the clue.

we
We make light work of it – at least, many of us do – HANDS
The reference, of course, is to the proverb 'Many HANDS make light work.'

weapon
Water-pipe weapon can cause damage – HARM
H ('water-pipe')+ARM ('weapon') =

HARM ('damage'). For another clue for HARM, see **provide with weapons**.

we are
We are Wolverhampton Wanderers – WEREWOLVES
Quite a neat clue, with 'We are' giving WERE and 'Wolverhampton Wanderers' being WOLVES, of course. Notice, however, that there is no actual 'straight' definition in the clue of the answer. Some solvers (or compilers) might feel this to be a failing.

Webster('s)
Unpaid worker gets gold – that's Webster's privilege – HONOR
'Unpaid worker' is HON, and 'gold' is OR. This makes HONOR, or 'privilege', in the American spelling as indicated (and quoted) by 'Webster's'.

we hear
We hear, adds up on board! – POSTERS
What 'we hear' in this clue is 'ads up on board', such 'ads', of course, being POSTERS!

weight
Grace has lost weight – so she should stand a better chance of winning this! – RACE
GRACE has lost 'weight' (G, for 'grams'). This gives the RACE that the slimmer Grace can now perhaps win!

(Mr) **Weller**
Exotic state to be in, like Mr Weller – ASSAM
'Like Mr Weller' is AS SAM, and this makes the 'exotic state' of ASSAM.

well-known lines
Well-known lines of Mr Hardy: 'It keeps the raindrops from my head' – BROLLY
The 'well-known lines' are BR, and 'Mr Hardy' is Oliver or OLLY 'Hardy', the film comedian (with Stan Laurel). His 'quote' defines the umbrella, or BROLLY.

Welsh
Welsh jazzman near Shrewsbury – WELLINGTON
'Welsh' is W, and the 'jazzman' here is Duke ELLINGTON. The two elements combine as WELLINGTON, the town near Shrewsbury. (I can't help feeling that 'Duke' should have been brought into the clue somehow, in view of the word's associations with both ELLINGTON and WELLINGTON.)

went ahead
Mother and I went ahead and sent the letter – MAILED
To 'read through': MA and I LED and MAILED.

we read
Fine French city, we read – NICE
As can be easily seen, NICE meaning 'fine', and NICE the name of the 'French city'. A number of well-known place-names resemble ordinary words, both in Britain (DEAL, HOVE, FIFE, MAN, RYE, WILTS, WICK) and abroad (TOURS, SPLIT, PERM, BUG, INN, LOT, LIEGE). For quite a different sort of clue for NICE, see **Northern Ireland**.

west(ern)
Western snake has a nasty sting – WASP
'Western' (W) 'snake' (ASP) makes a WASP, which, of course, 'has a nasty sting'.

we would
We would embrace closely, probably, if in this state – WEDLOCK
In other words, WE'D LOCK in WEDLOCK! (Notice the cautionary 'probably'.)

what a surprise (!)
Burglar's tool a gem, I hear, what a surprise! – JEMMY
A JEMMY is a 'burglar's short crowbar', says *Chambers*. The word is clued cryptically as 'gem, I hear' (i.e. a homophone of 'gem', which is JEM) and 'what a surprise' (MY).

what your best friend won't talk about
Identify what your best friend won't talk about – it's just a harmless drug – PLACEBO
To 'identify' is to PLACE, and BO is 'what your best friend won't talk about'. These make the 'PLACEBO', or 'harmless drug' (see *Chambers* for the full analysis).

when
When flanked by two escorts initially, relax! – EASE

'When' is AS, which here is 'flanked' or 'straddled' by two '*e*scorts initially', i.e. two Es. This makes EASE, which is 'relax'. Compare the clue for this word under **initially**.

where
Where a big white bird is on the water – SWANSEA
'Where' indicates a place, here punningly devised of the elements SWAN ('big white bird') and SEA ('water').

while
Money caught while hot – CASH
'Money' (CASH) 'caught' (C) 'while' (AS) 'hot' (H). Every word of the clue has a vital role to play here!

whim
Whim of editor lost its originality – FADED
Which is to say that the FAD of the ED has FADED.

whip
Whip a toothed instrument from the ancient burial place – CATACOMB
This 'whip' is a CAT, followed by 'a toothed instrument' (A COMB) to make the CATACOMB, or 'ancient burial place'.

why (apparently)
Why point to model before the affair is finished? – YET
Each of the three letters of the answer has its cryptic clue: Y ('why') E ('point') and T ('model'). The definition of YET is word for word from *Chambers*, where it is the last of seven meanings given.

wicked
Wicked in his generation? That's just playful talk! – BADINAGE
BAD IN his AGE? That's just BADINAGE!

William, Will(ie)
William has mixed gin and it has quite a powerful effect – TELLING
'William' TELL has a 'mixed GIN' (ING), which is TELLING – it 'has quite a powerful effect'.

wine
Kill-joy ruins the wine – SPOILSPORT
Once again, an agreeable 'read-through': the SPOILSPORT SPOILS the PORT.

wise men
Wise men came first – it was like a miracle – MAGIC
The 'wise men' here are the MAGI, who '*c*ame first' (C, the first letter of 'came'). And that was MAGIC, 'like a miracle'. Compare this clue with the quite different one under **American soldier**.

with
Run together with dog – CONCUR
To CONCUR is literally to 'run together' (*Chambers*'s first sense of the word), cryptically divided as CON ('with') and CUR ('dog').

withdraw
Withdraw ace on king and first of two eights in this card game – ECARTE
If the clues have been getting easier and easier, try this! With a careful 'read-through', we get: 'withdraw ACE', or reverse it (ECA) on 'king' (R) and 'first of *t*wo *e*ights' (TE). This gives the 'card game' called ECARTE, which I hope is not as complicated as the clue makes it sound.

within
Point to quarters within the house – SHOW
A 'burial', as 'within' indicates. But what goes 'within' what? The definition is 'point to' (SHOW), which means that the 'house' (HO) is 'within' the 'quarters' (SW).

without
Discussing without using bad language? Hell! – DIS
'Discussing' without CUSSING ('using bad language') is DIS – which in classical mythology was the Underworld, or 'Hell'!

without (the) **extremes**
Dances, tra-la, without the extremes of our forefathers – ANCESTRAL
A fairly complex clue – until you realise that 'without the extremes' means 'minus first and last letters'. So we take DANCES, TRA-LA, knock off its initial D and final A, and so get ANCESTRAL, defined as 'of our forefathers'.

with regard to
Translate: 'with regard to the Italian leader' – REDUCE
'With regard to' is RE, and the 'Italian leader' is the DUCE. The resulting REDUCE can mean, among other things, 'translate'.

(Mr) **Wodehouse**
I'll get in Mr Wodehouse, you greedy thing! – PIG
No idle threat, this! And if 'I' get in PG ('Mr Wodehouse'), we'll have a PIG, or 'greedy thing'.

woman
Small building where woman will need a penny – SHED
A good example of a clue that 'says what it means, but does not mean what it says'. 'Woman' is SHE, and 'penny' is D, this giving the SHED, or 'small building'.

Women's Institute
Women's Institute takes tea before church – but surely *this* woman is not one of their number? – WITCH
True, not quite the 'witch image'. Here the outlawed WITCH is cryptically clued by the 'Women's Institute' (WI) who take 'tea' (T) before 'church' (CH).

work
Chose work with a man – OPTED
'Work' is OP, and the 'man' here is TED. This makes OPTED, or 'chose'.

worker
Worker gets the first supply of sugar – BEET
For once, in this clue the 'worker' is a BEE, not the usual ANT. But where does the T come from? It is '*t*he first' (the first letter of 'the'), with the resulting BEET being the 'supply of sugar'.

workers
Workers get fish as a sign of welcome – HANDSHAKE
That is, the HANDS get HAKE, which is a HANDSHAKE, or 'sign of welcome'.

work hard
Work hard by the nasty smell;
Here's a rhyme for you to tell! – CRAMBO
Perhaps an unexpected 'rhyme to tell'? But that's what CRAMBO is – 'a game in which one gives a word to which another finds a rhyme' (as *Chambers* explains it). The word is cryptically clued here as 'work hard' (CRAM) by the 'nasty smell' (BO).

working woman
Working woman married for her attractions – CHARM
The 'working woman' is the CHAR, who is 'married' (M) for her CHARM, or 'attractions'. Compare the way we clued this word under **daily** and **start**.

works
For a place of entertainment, Di's got the works! – DISCO
An easy clue, with DI'S CO ('works') making the DISCO, or 'place of entertainment'.

world
Take in the sailor's world – ABSORB
To ABSORB is to 'take in', and the word consists of the two elements ABS ('sailor's') and ORB ('world').

world council
In favour of veto on world council, judging by this part of speech – PRONOUN
'In favour of' is PRO, 'veto' is NO, and 'world council' is UN. The three elements combine to make a PRONOUN, or (grammatical) 'part of speech'!

wrinkle
Very fine wrinkle on upper end – TIPTOP
A 'wrinkle' is a TIP. Here it is on the 'upper end', or TOP, which is TIPTOP, or 'very fine'.

writer
Upholder of the law who discovers little licence in writer and artist – POLICE CONSTABLE
The POLICE CONSTABLE is the 'upholder of the law', of course. He is cryptically clued by the 'little licence' (LIC) which is 'buried' in the 'writer' (POE) together with the 'artist' (CONSTABLE).

writing
Public relations is writing 'Spectra' – PRISMS

'Public relations' (PR) 'is' (IS) 'writing' (MS) makes the 'spectra' or PRISMS. 'Spectra' in the clue is meant to sound like some arty commercial or advertising publication.

writing fluid
Doctor has writing fluid that can be taken internally! – DRINK
'Doctor' is DR, and 'writing fluid' INK, making the DRINK that 'can be taken internally'.

wrong
Wrong the king and disappear without trace – SINK
'Wrong' is SIN, and 'king' here K. The combination is SINK, defined as 'disappear without trace'.

(in the) **wrong direction**
Put lever in the wrong direction and have fun! – REVEL
If you put LEVER 'in the wrong direction', you reverse it, which cryptically results in REVEL, 'have fun'.

(the) **wrong way**
Cutting was the wrong way in top of garment – SAWING
'Cutting' is the definition of SAWING, which here is cryptically clued as 'WAS the wrong way' (SAW) 'in' (IN) 'top of garment' (G).

X
'XN' is a real game! – TENNIS
Have you heard of 'XN'? Probably not, but here it clues TENNIS, since 'X' is TEN, 'N' is N (!) and the following word ('is') provides the final two letters of the answer (IS). The definition (a 'real game') also punningly half hints at another sort of TENNIS – 'real tennis'!

yard (Yard)
Ran to the Yard? That's a bit off! – RANCID
RAN to the CID produces RANCID, which is 'a bit off'. This clue is a variation on the one under **police(men)**.

year
Trade year suffers – MARTYR
Not what you were expecting, perhaps. A MART is a place of 'trade', and YR the abbreviation of 'year'. The two elements make a MARTYR, who 'suffers'.

yellow
Soft yellow touch for this picture of someone – PORTRAIT
'Soft' (P) 'yellow' (OR) 'touch' (TRAIT) produces the PORTRAIT, as defined.

yellow pages
Yellow Pages are not worth considering to get this foreign dish – RAGOUT
'Yellow Pages' (RAG) are OUT, or 'not worth considering'. But we need them to combine the two elements and get the RAGOUT, or 'foreign dish'. Compare the clue for this word under **high class**.

you
You get it coming back, this legendary ape – YETI
'You' is YE here, getting 'IT coming back' or reversed. The result is a YETI, the 'legendary ape' (or 'Abominable Snowman', which would have been too obvious a definition).

you and I
You and I 'ave to make cloth – WEAVE
'You and I' is WE, and ''ave' is AVE, so WE 'AVE to WEAVE, or 'make cloth'!

you and me
Object for throwing is a quoit, to you and me – DISCUS
Put another way, a DISCUS is a DISC, to US.

young
Young Diana comes to the Italian detective, confused, and finds it difficult to understand him because of this – DIALECT
Thus, in this saga, 'Young Diana' (DI) comes 'to the Italian' (AL) 'detective, confused' (ECT, an anagram of the 'confused' TEC).

This gives the DIALECT that she found hard to understand.

young hero
Information comes to young hero, but it doesn't relate to anyone in particular – GENERIC
As you can see, the GEN comes to ERIC, but it's GENERIC, so 'doesn't relate to anyone in particular'. Compare the way we clued this word under **news**.

young lady
There's something owing here, and the young lady has it – DEBIT
If the DEB has IT, she has a DEBIT, which is 'something owing'.

young messenger
Bump into young messenger while rushing wildly about – RAMPAGE
Perhaps you could RAM the PAGE while you were on the RAMPAGE, or 'rushing wildly about'.

young thing
Young thing is a beginner, and the result is total confusion – BABEL
The 'young thing' (BABE) is a 'beginner' (L), which creates BABEL, or 'total confusion'!

young whelp
Young whelp has lots of creamy milk – CURD
'Young whelp' is CUR, who has 'lots' (D, literally 500) of CURD, which (in simplified form) is 'creamy milk'. Compare the clue we had for this word under **copper**.

young woman
Young woman has a right to get some money – DOLLAR
So the 'young woman' (DOLL) has 'a right' (A+R) to get a DOLLAR, 'some money'.

you old
You old amateurs! What a joke! – YELL
'You old' is YE, and 'amateurs' are beginners or learners (LL). The result is a YELL, or 'joke'.

your (old)
Your note is just a plant – THYME
'Your' here is THY, and the 'note' is ME (see **note**). The two together make the 'plant' called THYME.

your old
A relative has your old indifference – APATHY
'A relative' is A PA, who has 'your old' (THY) to make 'indifference', or APATHY.

yours truly
Yours truly and Bill returning to great place of pilgrimage – MECCA
'Yours truly' is ME, and 'Bill returning' is a reversal of ACC. Both these give MECCA, the 'great place of pilgrimage'.

Z

zero
Broken bale zero-rated when built up from raw materials – ELABORATED
'Broken BALE' (ELAB) is 'zero-rated' (O-RATED) when ELABORATED, as defined in the clue.

Appendix I

Anagram indicators

The actual number of anagram indicators is virtually unlimited, of course. Any word or phrase that indicates a 'disturbance', rearrangement of letters, or simply that things are not as they should be, can serve as an indicator. The following are a selection of over 500 anagram indicators, with the verbs, as in the main part of the book, capable of use in almost any form or tense. 'Abandon', for example, can also be 'abandons', 'abandoning', 'abandoned' or any compound form such as 'will abandon', 'could abandon', 'had abandoned', etc. Of all verbs, too, the related noun form (in this case, 'abandonment') can also be used. To save space, such related noun forms are not included in this list.

Of all anagram indicators, the most popular appear to be: 'change', 'make', 'order', 'out', 'rough', 'strange', 'unusual' and 'upset'.

abandon
abound
about
absurd(ly)
accidental(ly)
acrobatic(s)
adapt
adrift
affect
afflict
afresh
agitate
ail
all over the place
alter
amend
amok
angry (-ily)
another (sort)
anyway
apart
appear
appropriate(ly)
around
arrange
assemble
assorted
astray
at sea
awful(ly)
awkward(ly)
awry
bad(ly)
bash
batter
beat
become
befuddle
bend
bit off
blast
blow up
blunder
blur
bob about
break
breakdown
broadcast
broken (down)
bruise
buckle
build

bungle
burst
bust
busy (-ily)
by
camouflage
can be
can come
can get
can make
careless(ly)
carve up
casual(ly)
catch up
cavort
change
chaotic(ally)
characters (-istic)
chew up
chop up
clear(ly)
clumsy (-ily)
cocktail
collapse
collect
combine
come a cropper
complicate
compose
concoct
confound
confuse
consider as
construct
contort
contraption
convert
cook
correct
corrupt
could be(come)
could get
could have
could make
crack
crazy(-ily)
crooked(ly)
cross(ly)
crude(ly)
crumble
crush
cryptic(ally)
cure
curious(ly)
custom-built
cut up
damage
dance (about)
decrepit
deform
derelict
derivative
design
destroy
deteriorate
develop
differ
different(ly)
difficult(y)
diffuse
disagree
disarrange
disastrous(ly)
discover
disguise
dishevelled
disintegrate
dismember
disorder
disperse
displace
dispose
dispute
distil
distort
distract
distraught
distribute
disturb
divers(e)
diversify
doctor
drag around
dress
drunk(en) (ly)
duff

eccentric
edit
effect a change
embarrass
emend
enrage
entangle
err
erratic(ally)
erupt
exchange
excite
exercise
exotic(ally)
explode
exposition
extraordinary (-ily)
extravagant(ly)
fabricate
fail
fake
false(ly)
falsify
falter
fancy (-iful)(ly)
faulty
fidget
fillet
fix
flabbergast
flail (about)
flippin'
flop
flow
flutter
fly (around)
foolish(ly)
for
forge
form
fracture
free
free(ly)
frenzied(ly)
fresh(ly)
frolic
from
fuddled

funny
gambol
game
gather
get
ghastly
give
gnarled
go adrift
go haywire
go into
go round
go west
go wrong
graft
grind
grotesque(ly)
haphazard(ly)
harass
hard
hash
haywire
hazy (-ily)
higgledy piggledy
horrible (-y)
hotchpotch
hybrid
illusion
improve
in
in a frenzy
in a muddle
in an accident
in another form
in a stew
in a tizzy
in a way
in a whirl
in chaos
incoherent(ly)
in crumpled condition
in disarray
indiscriminate(ly)
in disorder
in distress
inefficient(ly)
in embarrassment
in error

ingredients
injure
in order
in pieces
in ruins
in smithereens
in strange guise
in the form of
intricate(ly)
in trouble
involve
in wrong directions
irregular(ly)
jerk(y) (-ily)
jittery
jumble
kick around
kind of
knit
knock about
knot
lapse
letters (from)
liberal(ly)
lick into shape
like
loose(ly)
macabre
mad(ly)
make
make a mess of
make into
make up (into)
maltreat
manage
maniac
manipulate
manoeuvre
maybe
melange
members
mend
mess(y) (-ily)
might be(come)
might come (of it)
mince
mischief
mistake
mistaken(ly)
misuse
mix (up)
modify
move (round)
muddle
mysterious(ly)
mystic
nasty (-ily)
naughty (-ily)
need treatment
new
new order
new type
nomadic
not exactly
not good
not properly
not right
not strictly
novel
obscure
odd(ly) (enough)
of
off
order
organise
other
out (of order)
outcome (of)
out of sorts
over
overturn
parts (of)
pass (a)round
peculiar(ly)
perhaps
pervert
place at random
plan
polluted
poor(ly)
possible (-ly)
potential(ly)
prepare
pretend
process
produce

prove to be
pull apart
punish
put in order
put out
rabble
race
rage
ragged(ly)
ramble
ransack
rash(ly)
rave
ready
rearrange
rebuild
recollect
reconstruct
redesign
redispose
reel
refashion
reform
rehash
remake
remarkable
remedy
remodel
remould
reorganise
repair
replace
replan
represent
reproduce
reset
reshape
resolve
restore
restructure
result
revise
revolt
revolution(ary)
rewrite
ridiculous(ly)
riot
rotten(ly)

rough(ly)
round
rude(ly)
ruin
rum
run wild
salvage
scatter (about)
scheme
scramble
serve
set out
shake
shaky (-ily)
shatter
shiver
shoot
should be(come)
shred
shuffle
sick(ly)
silly
6s and 7s
slap-happy
sling
slip
smash (up)
so
somehow
somersault
sort of
sort (out)
spatter
spill
spin
splash
split
spoil
spread (about)
squash
state
stir
storm
straighten
strange(ly)
stray
struggle
stupid(ly)

style
substitute
succumb
suffer
swim
swirl
system
tangle
tear (apart)
tear up
terrible (-ly)
thrash (about)
throb
thus
tipsy (-ily)
to pieces
topple
topsy-turvy
toss (about)
train
transform
translate
transpose
treat
tricky
trip (around)
trouble
try
tumble
tumbledown
turbulent
turn (about)
turner
turn (in)to
turn out
turn over
twinge
twist
twitch
type
uncommon(ly)
uncontrolled(ly)
undo
uneasy (-ily)
unfortunate(ly)
unhappy (-ily)
unorthodox
unruly
unscramble
unstuck
untidy (-ily)
untwist
unusual(ly)
unwind
uproarious(ly)
upset
use
various(ly)
vary
violent(ly)
vulgar(ly)
wag
wander
waver
wayward(ly)
weave
weird(ly)
well designed
well formed
well laid out
well wrapped up
whip
whirl
wicked(ly)
wild(ly)
wind
with
with a difference
with adjustment
with change
with complications
with difficulty
with variations
woolly
work (on)
work out
worried(ly)
would be(come)
would make
wreck
writhe
wrong(ly)

Appendix II

Clues for single letters

Many clues require that a cryptic definition should be given for a single letter of a word, often to add to an element or to link two existing words. A clue leading to CAMERA-SHY, for example, might split the word into CAME, RASH and Y. In such a case, a cryptic definition would be needed for the final Y.

Below is given a selection of such cryptic definitions for the individual letters of the alphabet. The significance of such definitions should be apparent to solvers, who will have seen many of them at work in the main clues quoted earlier in this book.

A a, article, first class, key, note, one, top grade, type of bomb
B bachelor, bee, black, born, bowled, British, key, note, second (class), soft
C about, caught, century, chapter, circuit, cold, Conservative, crowd, great number, head, (a) hundred, key, large number, many, multitude, note, number, sea, see, several
D coin, copper, crowd, day, dead, degree, diamond, died, five hundred, great number, key, large number, late, many, multitude, note, number, old copper, old penny, pence once, penny, several
E bearing, direction, 'e, east(ern), English, Japan (perhaps), key, king, note, orient(al), point, quarter, string
F bad grade, Fascist leader, fellow, feminine, fluorine, follow, key,
G dog-end, force, gee, grand, gravity, key, king, note, string, (a) thousand dollars, weight
H aspiration, hard, height, horrific, hospital, hot, hour, hydrant, hydrogen, type of bomb, water-pipe
I a, I, Italian (leader), myself, one
J jay (Jay), jack (Jack)
K Kay, king, Rex, ruler
L amateur, apprentice, beginner, fifty, great number, lake, large number, learner, left, liberal, many, money, new driver, novice, number, port, pound, pupil, quid, several, sovereign, student, tyro
M crowd, Frenchman, great number, large number, many, married, mass (Mass), mile, Monsieur, motorway, multitude, number, several, thousand

N bearing, direction, (an) indefinite number, name, noon, north(ern), point, pole (Pole), quarter

O address, ball, circle, disc, duck, egg, globe, hole, hug, loop, love, nil, no, nothing, ring, round, sphere, zero

P coin, copper, leaf, page, parking, pence, penny, piano, president, prince, quiet(ly), soft(ly)

Q queue, queen, question

R king, monarch, queen, recipe, revolutionary leader, Rex, right, river, ruler, starboard, take

S bearing, coin, direction, dollar, double bend, martyr, old Bob, point, pole (Pole), quarter, 's, Sabbath, saint, (a) second, shilling, society, south(ern), sulphur, Sunday

T junction, model, sort of square, (kind of) square, (to a) T, t', tea, tee, time, West End

U acceptable, aristocratic, bend, classy, (it's) (what's) done, high class, posh, socially acceptable, type of boat, universal, university, upper class, uranium, you

V against, centre of gravity, (a) few, five, number, tea-time, versus, very, victory

W bearing, direction, point, quarter, Welsh, west(ern)

X cross, (a) few, half a score, half-score, kiss, number, ten, unknown, extra

Y why (apparently), Wye (it appears)

Z last letter, the end, ultimate letter

Appendix III

Cryptic clues for two-letter groups

The lists below give a selection of cryptic clues for all possible two-letter combinations, from AA to ZZ (both of which, admittedly, are highly unlikely to occur in this form, but which could conceivably be required in expanded or separated form, for example with other letters inserted or even in different words).

The aim is to show the sorts of tricks that the cryptic clue compiler gets up to – or indeed *has* to get up to if faced with the necessity to clue a two-letter group. It is suggested that the solver might like to read through the clues and consider, in each case, the method or cryptic 'dodge' used by the compiler to produce the required two letters. No explanation is given for the clues, so that the solver is here on his or her own to deduce that, say, the 'club for drivers' that clues AA is not a reference to a golf-club but to the Automobile Association, and that the 'pepper, say' that leads to KN is not an abbreviation but a way of saying 'Cayenne'.

Clues that obviously need a completing word for their overall sense or grammatical correctness are followed by three dots (. . .), as 'a hard . . .' to clue AH.

AA (the), club for drivers, Mr Milne
AB Jack, mariner, sailor
AC account, bill (Bill), current
AD advertisement, commercial, modern (style), notice, now, year
AE Irish poet, Albert Edward initially
AF Admiral of the Fleet, a loud . . .
AG metal, silver
AH surprise (!), a hard . . .
AI capital, excellent, first class, Great North Road, jolly good, sloth
AJ (Mr) Alan, German approval backed
AK also known, a king
AL Albert, Bert, boy, (Mr) Jolson, to the Italian
AM before noon, early, morning, time
AN article, if (with), one
AO Army Order, a circle, a ring
AP (Mr) Herbert, pressman
AQ achievement quotient, a queen, a queue
AR aright, arrive, a recipe
AS Anglo-Saxon, like, since, when, while

AT	'at, beside
AU	gold, to the French
AV	avenue, average, way, a very
AW	atomic weight, a point, half-awry
AX	American chopper, a ten, a cross
AY	indeed, yes
AZ	first and last, London guide
BA	bachelor, degree, graduate, learned person, scholar
BB	very soft, Miss Bardot
BC	ancient times, British Columbia
BD	church scholar, two notes
BE	become, exist, live
BF	brought forward, blooming fool
BG	big heartless . . ., empty bag
BH	British Honduras, leaders of Royal Academy centre
BI	vitamin, half a bite
BJ	Bachelor of Journalism, first British jumper
BK	book ends, bachelor king
BL	company of cars, legal scholar
BM	London cultural centre, Bachelor of Medicine
BN	Baron, battalion, take notice back
BO	smell, what your best friend won't talk about
BP	Scout leader, fuel company
BQ	black queen, bachelor at head of queue
BR	British, lines, railways
BS	surgeon, British Standard
BT	Baronet, bought, beat
BU	Baptist Union, half a buck
BV	(St) Mary, soft number
BW	black and white briefs, Black Watch
BX	empty box, British Xylonite
BY	in respect of, heartless boy
BZ	British Zone (briefly), bowled at the end
CA	about, accountant, man of account
CB	Citizens Band, soldier punished, radio drivers
CC	measure, two hundred
CD	Civil Defence, diplomatic letters, under the weather, say
CE	church, engineers, (the) establishment
CF	compare, centre forward
CG	centre of gravity, captain-general
CH	award, central heating, chapter, church, companion, medal, title
CI	Channel Isles, leaders of cowboys and Indians
CJ	Chief Justice, sea-jay, by the sound of it
CK	top and bottom of cask, Cape Kennedy letters
CL	chlorine, beginning of centre line
CM	centimetre, small measure, Certificate of Merit

CN canon, cold pole
CO care of, Commanding Officer, company, county, firm, half-cock
CP compare, Carter Paterson, initially
CQ conditionally qualified, in brief, caught at head of queue
CR councillor, credit
CS Civil Service, (irritant) gas
CT caught, Connecticut, cent
CU copper, cubic, Church Union
CV vital statistics, Conservative against . . .
CW clerk of works, hundred Welsh
CX convex edges, 110
CY Cyril, little Cyrus
CZ small Czech, about last letter

DA attorney, district attorney, lawyer
DB sound unit, head of double bed
DC current, American district, Columbia
DD clergyman, divine, doctor, man of the cloth
DE of French, editor returns
DF faithful defender, direction finding
DG by the grace of God, Director General, thank God
DH (Mr) Lawrence, dead heat at first
DI Diana, girl, huntress, 501
DJ record player, dinner jacket
DK deck edges, top and bottom of desk
DL five hundred rounds, legal doctor
DM German money, Daily Mail leaders
DN not across, old copper pole
DO act, as before, celebration, do, note, party, perform, same again
DP refugee, stateless person
DQ first direct question, diamond queen
DR doctor, medical man, physician, (the) wrong way
DS daylight saving to start with, late saint
DT brain disorder, Daily Telegraph leaders
DU of the French, Dutch, duke
DV God willing, 505
DW key point, dead west
DX old copper cross, 510
DY frontiers of Dahomey, first and last delivery
DZ Doctor of Zoology, top of dropping zone

EA each, oriental article
EB Electricity Board, abridged edition of *Encyclopaedia Britannica*
EC city district, Fleet Street area, early closing
ED ’e’d, Edward, editor, journalist, newsman, Ted
EE Scottish eye, Early English, errors excepted

EF extra fine start, expeditionary force leaders
EG for example, for instance
EH what?, he comes back
EI East Indies, heartless old priest
EJ (the) French I back, point to Jack
EK second half of the week, oriental king
EL L(-shaped), overhead railway, the Spanish
EM 'em, measure, baby Emma
EN measure, quarters, in French
EO executive officer briefly, Eastern Orthodox capital
EP disc, electroplated, record
EQ equally short, abbreviated equivalent
ER comparatively, 'er, hesitantly, monarch, (the) Queen, return, ruler
ES 'e's, points
ET and French, half the school
EU Evangelical Union, a third of Europe
EV victory day returns, even half
EW extremes, each way (I'll bet)
EX earlier, former(ly), lover (before), once, out
EY every year to start with, half-year
EZ point to the last letter, Ezra half . . .

FA football body, game body, note
FB fire brigade leaders, full-back briefly
FC Forestry Commission, in short, football clue shortly
FD faithful defender, forward limits, Roosevelt
FE iron, further education, feel half
FF fortissimo, very loud(ly), French fried for starters
FG top of fire guard, limits of fog
FH fire hydrant, short freehold
FI if returning, fellow a . . .
FJ two leave Fiji, entrance to fjord
FK top and bottom of fork, note ruler
FL flourished (briefly), Football League
FM field marshal, (type of) radio transmission
FN brief footnote, heartless fan
FO foreign office, back of . . ., of returning . . .
FP outbreak of fowl pest, start of field punishment
FQ overture to 'Faerie Queene', fellow goes to head of queue
FR churchman, clergyman, father, French, priest
FS top of flying saucer, top and bottom flats
FT foot, Financial Times, fort
FU Farmers Union (briefly), half-full
FV the Noisy Five, fire valve openers
FW introduction of fresh water, Key West
FX sound effects, loud kiss
FY beginning and end of Friday, fly pupil out

FZ start of Free Zone, Fascist leader gets ultimate letter

GA Georgia, General Assembly, half-gaga
GB Britain, (Mr) Shaw
GC award, decoration, Maltese title
GD small grand-daughter, top and bottom ground
GE General Election leaders, for example turning
GF head of Guggenheim Foundation, at first Handel
GG horse, Girl Guide leaders
GH general hospital, bring mercury back
GI American soldier, military man, serviceman
GJ entrance to grand junction, force Jack
GK (little) Greek, (Mr) Chesterton
GL global extremities, half glad
GM medal, guided missile (briefly)
GN guinea, £1.05
GO current fashion, leave, pass, try, turn
GP doctor, medical man, physician
GQ general quarters (shortly), grand queen
GR King George, half a gram
GS the Guineas, grammar school (reduced)
GT great (little), sports car, touring car
GU start of gastric ulcer, note upper class
GV very good turn, first and third members of government
GW Great Western, little George Washington
GX force ten, cross key
GY outskirts of Grimsby, heartless guy
GZ note last letter, grand opening to zoo

HA laugh, surprise
HB hard black, half-back (briefly)
HC hot and cold, House of Commons
HD small hand, had missing article
HE ambassador, (Mr) Bates, explosive, fellow, him, His Excellency
HF high frequency, hard noisy, Holy Father's introduction
HG Home Guard, mercury (Mercury), (Mr) Wells
HH very hard, prince, princess
HI half hide, Hawaiian Isles, hey (!)
HJ run-up to high jump, launch of Honest John
HK Hong Kong shortly, hack top and bottom
HL start of hard labour, top and bottom of the hill
HM headmaster, queen
HN height bearing, horn rims
HO head office, house
HP never-never, (what) sauce, horse power
HQ headquarters, head office
HR hour, (a) period, (some) time

HS	Home Secretary briefly, highest score leaders
HT	height, high tension, heat treated (briefly)
HU	head of Harvard University, bottomless hut
HV	the Hot Five, health visitor briefly
HW	onset of high water, how loveless
HX	first and last hoax, the 'Horrific Ten'
HY	Henry (in short), start and end of highway
HZ	painful-sounding measure, horrific last letter
IA	Iowa, Indiana, one a . . .
IB	a bee, one born
IC	in charge, pronouncedly icy, ninety-nine
ID	fish, I'd, I had, I would, personality
IE	that is, short inside edge
IF	condition, if, provided
IG	industrial group leaders, returning soldier
IH	a hot . . ., one hard . . .
II	eleven, two, parallel bars
IJ	one Jack, a jay
IK	a king, like the French leave
IL	forty-nine, nearly fifty, the Italian
IM	admits, I am, nine-nine-nine
IN	amid, at home, available, batting, fashion(able), not out
IO	ten, Greek goddess, I owe, by the sound of it
IP	one soft, 1p, start of initial phase
IQ	intelligence quotient, degree of cleverness
IR	Irish, half iron, endless anger
IS	is, one shilling, 1/–
IT	child, it, object, sex appeal, something
IU	leaders of International Union, one aristocratic
IV	(a) few, four, tea-time
IW	one western, a bearing
IX	nine, almost ten
IY	international youth leaders, heartless Ivy
IZ	one last letter, topless Liz
JA	German agreement, two thirds of a jar, bottomless jar
JB	John Bull's initiators, joint board leaders
JC	Jockey Club starters, Jack caught
JD	joined the extremities, first juvenile deliquents
JE	French I . . ., beginning and end of June
JF	(Mr) Kennedy, president initially
JG	jog without love, first junior grade
JH	junior high starters, Joseph first and last
JI	Journalists Institute (briefly), Jill half . . .
JJ	Jean-Jacques to begin with, Jack and Jill initially
JK	jerk without hesitation, Jack's extremities
JL	Julia's first and third, junior leader initiates

JM (Mr) Barrie, Jim I leave
JN Littlejohn, join both ends
JO Josephine, (the) little woman
JP magistrate, man of law
JQ Jacques I and IV, joint quiz leaders
JR junior, joint resolution briefly
JS joint service leaders, Jack goes south
JT small joint, beginning and end of jaunt
JU first half of July, half jump
JV introduction to junior varsity, Jack has five
JW leaders of Jehovah's Witnesses, first joint wages
JX Jay has ten, Jenny's first kiss
JY Joy disheartened, first and last members of jury
JZ jay at zoo entrance, final letter after 1st July

KA first of King's Arms, Kay a . . .
KB Knight Bachelor, kitchen and bathroom initially
KC Kennel Club leaders, King's Counsel
KD first knocked down, killed in extremis
KE King Edward, half bake
KF King Ferdinand the First, Kenya Farmers leaders
KG top and bottom of keg, King George
KH kilohertz, bow and stern of ketch
KI King's Square, half kill
KJ initial knee jerk, King John first
KK two little kings, king and knight
KL Kuala Lumpur popularly, kilolitre
KM Knight of Malta, kilometre
KN half a knot, pepper, say
KO floored, kick off, knockout
KP king's pawn initially, introduction to King's Parade
KQ king and queen initially, first king and queen
KR krypton, King Richard I
KS beginning and end of Knossos, king's
KT knight, Catherine, I hear
KU keep up at first, Kuwait without delay
KV kilovolt, schoolboys' warning sound
KW electric power, King William the First
KX ruler unknown, Kay has ten
KY Kentucky, lucky at last
KZ king's last letter, king of Zion at first

LA Los Angeles, note, the French
LB leg before, pound, weight
LC brief letter of credit, left centre (in short)
LD lord, limited extremes
LE the French, left eye opens
LF low frequency, top and bottom of loaf

LG log with centre missing, introduction to Lloyd George
LH left hand, start of licensing hours
LI Long Island, half a lira
LJ Lord Justice, opening of life jacket
LK front and rear of lock, left king
LL two pounds, London Library initially
LM loveless Herbert, Lord Mayor's introduction
LN London West End and East End, Mr Chaney disheartened
LO behold, look, little Lolita
LP disc, record, leading members of Labour Party
LQ left queen, beginner has question
LR left and right, beginning and end of labour
LS Law Society initiates, pounds
LT lieutenant, first and last light
LU half a lump, Lake Superior
LV meal ticket, 55
LW heartless law, long wave (initially)
LX sixty, love begins with a kiss
LY lay disheartened, second half of July
LZ fifty at zoo opening, Liz I leave

MA art master, degree, mother, one of the family, scholar
MB doctor, medical man, musical bachelor, physician
MC compare, master of ceremonies, military award
MD doctor, Maryland, medical man
ME me, Middle East, note, yours truly
MF medium frequency, Miners Federation leaders
MG sports car, small measure, magnesium
MH a thousand hard . . ., military hospital initially
MI Mississippi, motorway, note, I'm coming back
MJ introduction to management job, 1st March to 1st June
MK mask as taken out, top of the milk – and the bottom
ML small amount of liquid, first motor launch
MM milligram, small measure
MN Scotsman lacking love, man has missing article
MO medical man, Missouri, moment
MP legislator, Military Police, Parliamentarian
MQ Frenchman at head of queue, married queen
MR Mister, municipal reform leaders
MS draft, manuscript, writing, Miss or Mrs
MT eminence, mount(ain)
MU Mothers' Union, Greek letter
MV motor vessel, 1005
MW short medium wave, a thousand point (to) . . .
MX Middlesex, missile, 1010
MY my, semi-myth, what a surprise (!)
MZ a thousand have initial zeal, mile to start of zone

NA North America, not applicable, sodium
NB note well, take notice, New Brunswick
NC North Carolina, northern command leaders
ND no date (in short), North Dakota, nothing doing, for a start
NE corner, district, New England, Tyne and Wear
NF entrance to New Forest, National Federation leaders
NG no good (in short), nag a departing . . .
NH National Health, New Hampshire, born hard
NI back in, Northern Ireland, nickel
NJ New Jersey, quarterjack
NK half the Russian secret police, not known (in short)
NL nothing I take away, national frontiers
NM New Mexico, nautical mile, in short
NN name and number, sister without you (apparently)
NO disagreement, no, number, refusal
NP new paragraph (in short), Nationalist Party leaders
NQ abbreviated edition of Notes & Queries, northern queen
NR near, nor love departs
NS extremes, poles apart, Nova Scotia
NT book(s), do(es)n't, New Testament
NU National Union leaders, name unknown for a start
NV point five, short New Version
NW corner, district, London area
NX born ten, northern cross
NY American city, New York, state
NZ New Zealand, start of neutrality zone

OA love a . . ., first over all
OB died, old boy, outside broadcast
OC officer commanding, Oxford and Cambridge firsts
OD do put back, old pupil leaves
OE Old English, one Pole leaves
OF of, start of old-fashioned . . .
OG go back, Olympic Games starters
OH address, ouch, love hard
OI love one, 0–1, officer-in-charge leaves
OJ orange juice starters, from beginning of October to beginning of June
OK acceptable, all right, approve, fine
OL look back, oil I left
OM award, honour, man, little old man
ON acting, concerning, in advance, no returns, on
OO glasses, two eggs, a couple of rounds, loves
OP operation, side of the stage, work
OQ round start of quarter, address head of queue
OR alternative, gold, if not, or, yellow
OS extra large, huge, very big
OT book(s), Holy Writ, Old Testament, to return, return to . . .

OU	Oxford University leaders, introduction to Open University
OV	half over, 0–5
OW	little old woman, Old Welsh
OX	bull's mate, round ten, love and kiss
OY	hey (!), oh why sound
OZ	ounce, wizard place
PA	pressmen, Daddy, father, Pennsylvania
PB	lead, push button starters
PC	copper, small postcard, percent(age)
PD	frontiers of Poland, paid (in short)
PE	exercise(s), physical education
PF	soft and loud, first and last proof
PG	lodger, Prosecutor-General (briefly)
PH	first push hard, beginnings of past history
PI	page one, half a pint
PJ	(Mr) Proby, brief physical jerks
PK	small pack, pork alternative out
PL	introduction to 'Paradise Lost', patrol leader
PM	afternoon, leader, time, post mortem
PN	short promissory note, pin I left
PO	Italian flower, pilot officer, post office
PP	twopence, very quiet(ly), very soft(ly)
PQ	penny to queen, personality quotient briefly
PR	pair, public relations
PS	afterthought, footnote
PT	exercise(s), small part, training
PU	back up, paid up (in short)
PV	page five, soft number
PW	penny point, Penny West
PX	page 10, soft kiss, limits of peace in Rome
PY	pay a departure, Penny points out
PZ	first parking zone, page zoo first
QA	Queen Anne the First, Queen Alexandra briefly
QB	Queen's Bench, quarterback
QC	lawman, head of Queen's College
QD	limits of quad, Queen Edith the Second
QE	Queen Elizabeth's leaders, liner
QF	start of quick fire, quite funny initially
QG	query (the) gravity, first quarter to note
QH	introduction to Queen's Hall, queue at hospital
QI	Queen Diana the Second, Queen's Institute leaders
QJ	question first judge, queen and jack
QK	quick short, query the king
QL	first quarter pound, quite lively introduction
QM	quartermaster, supply officer
QN	short question, limits of quotation

QO queue to get duck, Queen's Own Leaders
QP Queen's Park (in short), queen's pawn
QQ two queens, questions (in short)
QR short quarter, Queen's Royal Introduction
QS quarter sessions (briefly), queues, apparently
QT softly on this, small-size quart
QU question, query
QV which see, question five
QW Queen Winifred the First, question the direction
QX queen has ten, head of queue unknown
QY first and last query, west and east end of quay
QZ limits of quartz, queen gets ultimate letter

RA Academy, artillery, gunners, man of art, rear admiral, soldiers
RB Rifle Brigade leaders, Rex Black
RC church, Roman Catholic, Red Cross initiates
RD highway, road, thoroughfare, refer to drawer, in short
RE about, again, concerning, engineers, regiment, sappers, with regard to
RF radio frequency, right key
RG heartless Roy, first of reserve guard
RH right hand (first), Royal Highness
RI Rhode Island, religious instruction
RJ frontiers of the raj, king jay
RK top and bottom of rick, CO abandons Rock
RL first reading list, Rugby League
RM Marines, ram article out
RN navy, sailors, service
RO or return, semi-roan, radio operator (briefly)
RP hit one out, Received Pronunciation, in short
RQ our queue pronouncedly . . ., king and queen
RR bishop, Rolls Royce
RS Royal Society, kings, Royal Scots leaders
RT radio-telephone, right
RU Rugby (Union), are you sounding
RV Revised Version, king versus . . .
RW top and bottom of row, raw one leaves
RX starboard 10, take ten
RY line(s), railway, train(s)
RZ king comes to the end, take first zone

SA South Africa(n), South America(n), sex appeal, in short
SB savings bank initially, sob having no love
SC learning, namely, science
SD South Dakota, limits of sound
SE corner, district, Kent, London area, south-east
SF science fiction, San Francisco (in short)
SG Sunday gravity, beginning and end of string

SH	be quiet, hush, mute, half-shut
SI	is returning, half-size
SJ	Jesuit, St John initiates
SK	short slip knot, half skip
SL	squadron leader, half slip
SM	sergeant major, quarter mile
SN	extremes, metal, poles apart, tin
SO	in this way, note, staff officer, thus
SP	betting, odds
SQ	small square, introduction to sick quarters
SR	senior (briefly), Southern Region (in short)
SS	Nazi troops, ship, steamer, Sunday school, saints
ST	good fellow, highway, martyr, road, saint, station
SU	us back, back America, Scottish Union leaders
SV	southern victory, quarter to five
SW	corner, district, London area, Devon and Cornwall
SX	Southern Cross, Essex, I hear
SY	sly pupil leaves, spy softly departs
SZ	sez 'e goes out, Sunday at the end
TA	gratitude, soldiers, terriers, thanks, volunteers
TB	lung disease, small torpedo boat
TC	start of twentieth century, small traveller's cheque
TD	Territorial Decoration, Teaching Diploma
TE	(Mr) Lawrence, half-term, and French backing
TF	tax free, in short, Territorial Force leaders
TG	entrance to Tate Gallery, 1st and 4th target
TH	half of this, the endless . . .
TI	it's back, half-time
TJ	start of triple jump, beginning of 'Tom and Jerry'
TK	top and bottom of trunk, limits of tank
TL	start of threshold limit, tell the Spanish to leave
TM	short trademark, disheartened Tim
TN	little town, front and rear of train
TO	at, small turnover, tailless tom
TP	tip one out, top with nothing missing
TQ	tea queue, by the sound of it, start of 'The Quest'
TR	translate, half trim, small trace
TS	(Mr) Eliot, (the) wrong way
TT	abstainer, man of no spirit, Manx race, teetotal(ler)
TU	Trade Union, half turn
TV	television, small test vehicle
TW	twit losing it, model bearing
TX	square cross, Junction 10
TY	end of party, limits of territory
TZ	t' last letter, time the end
UA	under age, in short, United Artists leaders

UB topless tub, roofless pub
UC you see (say), urban council leaders
UD middle of Bude, aristocratic crowd
UE posh English, classy note
UF upper-class fellow, you loud . . .
UG ugly – not half, universal gravity
UH socially acceptable hour, university hospital (in short)
UI you and I, apparently, classy one
UJ small-size Union Jack, high class start to jump
UK United Kingdom, Britain
UL aristocratic pupil, United Labour leaders
UM hesitant(ly), (I'm) not sure
UN international organisation, United Nations
UO universal love, you owe, say
UP out of bed, not down
UQ you start queue, two types of boat
UR ancient city, biblical town, patriarch's birthplace
US America(n), country, United States, you and me
UT Utah, first and last unit
UU Ulster Unionist (briefly), you and you
UV (short) ultra-violet
UW upper class quarter, aristocratic bearing
UX University Cross, bend ten
UY Universal Youth leaders, headless guy
UZ classy final letter, done at entrance to zoo

VA Virginia, five first class
VB volunteer battalion leaders, very black (in short)
VC award, decoration, heartless Vic
VD briefly void, victory day (shortly)
VE day of victory, against the east
VF five loud . . ., voice frequency briefly
VG very good, against gravity, in short
VH very hot (in short), five hard . . .
VI early evening, half a dozen, six, Violet
VJ day of victory, a five and a jack
VK very first king, victory comes to ruler
VL five-and-fifty, heartless Val
VM Votre Majesté, *tout court*, vim I left
VN five northern . . ., empty van
VO 5–0, short voice-over
VP vice-president (briefly), 5p
VQ five at head of queue, very quick leaders
VR Queen Victoria, against monarch
VS fives, 5/–
VT short videotape, five to tea
VU very posh (in short), five classy . . .
VV two fives, very very little

VW Volkswagen, heartless vow
VX five unknown, Victory 10
VY very unhesitatingly, Vyvyan the Third, half the navy
VZ very last letter, in short, 'Five go to Zoo Opening'

WA West Africa, half warm
WB world boxing leaders, web with middle missing
WC (at your) convenience, London district
WD War Department, short word
WE extremes, first half of the week, you and I
WF small wing forward, World Federation leaders
WG (Mr) Grace, wig I left
WH who is loveless, White House leaders
WI Women's Institute, London district
WJ point to first jump, quarter-jack
WK point to king, wink in leaving
WL top and bottom of wall, short waiting list
WM (little) William, introduction to William and Mary
WN west and east of Washington, worn gold out
WO alas, I hear, War Office
WP short form of worship, whip top and bottom
WQ point to head of queue, western queen
WR Western Region, war article missing
WS point-to-point, short whisky and soda
WT short weight, wet oriental left
WU Western Union (in short), World Union leaders
WV point five, West Virginia openers
WW world war (in short), first 'Who's Who'
WX western cross, direction unknown
WY way article goes, first and last whisky
WZ wildlife zoo opening, Western Zimbabwe leaders

XA cross one, kiss a . . .
XB Cross Class 2, kiss bachelor
XC ninety, cross about
XD tenpence once, cross by dead . . .
XE former lover returns, unknown quarter
XF extra loud, ten strong
XG ten thousand dollars, unknown string
XH extra hot, ten hard . . .
XI eleven, side, team
XJ the ten and the jack, cross to Jesuit leader
XK a ten and a king, kiss the king
XL kiss at love's beginning, excel, I hear, forty
XM cross over motorway, from ten to a thousand
XN cross point, the unknown north
XO a kiss and a hug, 10-nil
XP 10p, extra soft

XQ ten at head of queue, kiss the queen
XR cross to starboard, unknown ruler
XS sounds too much, ten shillings
XT extra ten, cross at junction
XU ten aristocratic . . ., frontiers of Xanadu
XV fifteen, rugby team
XW extra point, ten Welsh . . .
XX score, twenty
XY artist abandons x-ray, unknown youth leader
XZ ten at start of zone, cross at the end

YA half a yard, yak loses tail
YB backward loveless boy, why be sound
YC Young Conservative leaders, why, see, hearing
YD yard, first and last of yield
YE the old, you old . . .
YF start of Youth Festival, fly back without pupil
YG Your Grace initially, first and last young
YH youth hostel, turn hay and article disappears
YI why apparently one . . ., first Young Independent
YJ Jay returns with missing article, Joy comes back with lost love
YK from one end of York to the other, Yank loses a point
YL lay back without a . . ., start of young love
YM half the YMCA, may come back without a . . .
YN yawn loses a point, start and finish of yarn
YO you lose the end, half your . . .
YP young people initially, Young Pioneer leaders
YQ why queue, I hear, turn quay losing to the French
YR year, your first and last . . .
YS yes, 'e's gone, first young soldier
YT toy returned with ring gone, yet 'e went
YU a quarter Yugoslav, Yale University initiates
YV Young Volunteers leaders, little Yvonne
YW way back without one, Your Worship briefly
YX why (apparently) ten, x-ray turned up with half area missing
YY too wise, I hear, yesterday first and last
YZ last two letters, Zachary's back from first to last

ZA half zany, the end and the beginning
ZB last letter (second class), Zen Buddhist initiates
ZC beginning and end of zodiac, top and bottom of zinc
ZD zero defect initially, last letter of five hundred
ZE second half of maze, half zeal
ZF Zoology Fellow (in brief), start of Zone F
ZG Albanian king lost nothing, Zoological Gardens initially
ZH start of zero hour, beginning and end of Zachariah
ZI the last letter I . . ., half-zinc
ZJ 'First and Last of Jazz' is back, the last letter to Jay

ZK	last letter to king, Zack loses account
ZL	the end for the pupil, Liz comes back without one
ZM	openers of zoo museum, first and last zoom
ZN	zinc, ultimate letter goes to Pole
ZO	inverted weight, semi-zone
ZP	zip loses centre, Zanzibar and Pemba initially
ZQ	first Zulu comes to queen, last letter of first quarter
ZR	start of zone redevelopment, final letter to king
ZS	Zeus first and last, Zoological Society briefly
ZT	start of zone time, zest losing points
ZU	half Zulu, last letter to you
ZV	zoo vets initially, the end for Victoria I
ZW	ultimate letter goes west, zero weight, to begin with
ZX	last letter with a kiss, the end of the unknown
ZY	zany losing article, the last letter – and the last but one
ZZ	sleep, two ultimate letters

Appendix IV

Select list of -ER nouns

A special feature of the cryptic clue is the noun ending in -ER that seems to mean one thing but actually (of course) is used to mean another. The noun ADDER, for example, instantly conjures up the snake. As a cryptic word, however, it is used to mean someone or something that *adds*, such as an accountant or a calculator. Perhaps the classic cryptic -ER noun of this type is the FLOWER, which is nothing to do with the petalled plant of field or garden, but changes both its sense and its pronunciation to become something that *flows*, and specifically a river.

The cryptic -ER noun is thus always a 'doer' of some kind, with the part of the noun preceding the -ER being the verb that provides the agent. Obviously, the most rewarding standard -ER nouns used in this way are ones (like the ADDER and FLOWER just mentioned) that do not suggest any verbal action at all.

Below is a short list of some of the most useful standard -ER nouns, together with their interpretations for cryptic purposes. Some, like the FLOWER, have become well established in cryptic crossword vocabulary. Others are less often used, but perhaps none the less effective in their different ways.

ADDER	someone or something that *adds*, as a clerk, accountant or calculator
BETTER	someone who *bets*, as a gambler, card-player or racegoer
BUTTER	someone or something that *butts*, as a goat or ram
FLOWER	something that *flows*, especially a river or stream
HANGER	something that *hangs*, as a picture
HOWLER	someone or something that *howls*, as a dog, wolf or baby
JUMPER	someone or something that *jumps*, as a horse, athlete or cat
KIPPER	someone or something that *kips* (i.e. sleeps), as a dormouse
LAYER	something that *lays*, especially a hen or bird of some kind
LETTER	someone who *lets*, such as a landlord
LOCKER	something that *locks*, especially a key
LOWER	something that *lows*, especially a cow

NUMBER	something that *numbs*, as ice, the cold, an injection or a shock
SEWER	someone or something that *sews*, as a seamstress or a needle
SHOWER	someone or something that *shows*, as an exhibitor or a shop window
SPANNER	something that *spans*, especially a bridge
SUMMER	someone or something that *sums* or adds, as an accountant (see ADDER)
TOWER	someone or something that *tows*, as a car, engine, horse or husky

Appendix V

Famous people known by their initials

A number of famous people, especially writers, have come to be known by their initials and surname, rather than a forename and surname. These initials can prove convenient for clueing particular letters in an answer, so that 'Mr Eliot' provides TS, 'Lawrence' offers either DH or TE, and 'Grace' (which can pose as a girl's name) gives WG.

A selection of forty such names follows.

A. J. Alan
W. H. Auden
J. M. Barrie
H. M. Bateman
H. E. Bates
A. C. Benson
E. C. Bentley
R. D. Blackmore
G. K. Chesterton
A. E. Coppard
A. J. Cronin
E. E. Cummings
J. P. Donleavy
T. S. Eliot
W. C. Fields
C. S. Forester
E. M. Forster
W. S. Gilbert
W. E. Gladstone
W. G. Grace
L. P. Hartley
A. P. Herbert
W. W. Jacobs
M. R. James
J. F. Kennedy
B. B. King
D. H. Lawrence
T. E. Lawrence
A. A. Milne
J. B. Priestley
P. J. Proby
J. D. Rockefeller
G. B. Shaw
C. P. Snow
R. L. Stevenson
A. G. Street
W. M. Thackeray
H. G. Wells
T. H. White
P. G. Wodehouse

Bibliography

This select bibliography is divided into two sections. The first section comprises books that deal with crosswords, their history, compilation and solution, in some detail. These will be found absorbing reading, either individually or collectively, for anyone, solver or compiler, who wishes to know more about crosswords. The second section gives particulars of the five books recommended in the Introduction as helpful to solvers.

I General books on crosswords

Abbott, May, *How to do Crosswords Better*, Collins, Glasgow and London, 1982.

Arnot, Michelle, *A History of the Crossword Puzzle*, Macmillan Papermac, London, 1982.

Crowther, Jonathan (ed.), *The AZED Book of Crosswords*, Pan Books, London, 1977.

Higgs, Barry O., *Guide to Solving Crosswords: Cryptics and Anagrams,* Orbis Publishing, London, 1978.

Kurzban, Stan, and Rosen, Mel, *The Compleat Cruciverbalist*, Van Nostrand Reinhold, New York, 1981.

Macnutt, D. S., *Ximenes on the Art of the Crossword*, Methuen, London, 1966.

Millington, Roger, *The Strange World of the Crossword*, M. & J. Hobbs, Walton-on-Thames, 1974.

Robins, Alec, *The ABC of Crosswords*, Corgi Books, London, 1981 (originally published as *Teach Yourself Crosswords*, Hodder & Stoughton, London, 1975).

II Aids for the solver

Chambers Twentieth Century Dictionary with Supplement, edited by A. M. Macdonald, Chambers, Edinburgh, 1977.

Everyman's Dictionary of Abbreviations, ed. John Paxton, Dent, London, 1981.

The Hamlyn Crossword Dictionary, general editor J. M. Bailie, Hamlyn, London, 1978.

Lehnert, Martin, *Reverse Dictionary of Present-Day English*, VEB Verlag Enzyklopädie, Leipzig, 1973.

Roget's Thesaurus of English Words and Phrases, new edition prepared by Susan M. Lloyd, Longman, Harlow, 1982.